Major League
Baseball Players of 1916

Major League Baseball Players of 1916

A Biographical Dictionary

Paul Batesel

McFarland & Company, Inc., Publishers
Jefferson, North Carolina, and London

LIBRARY OF CONGRESS CATALOGUING-IN-PUBLICATION DATA

Batesel, Paul, 1938–
Major league baseball players of 1916 : a biographical dictionary / Paul Batesel.
p.   cm.
Includes bibliographical references and index.

ISBN 13: 978-0-7864-2782-6
softcover : 50# alkaline paper ∞

1. Baseball players—United States—Biography—Dictionaries.
2. Baseball players—United States—Statistics.   I. Title.
GV865.A1B386   2007   796.3570922—dc22 [B]   2006027114

British Library cataloguing data are available

©2007 Paul Batesel. All rights reserved

*No part of this book may be reproduced or transmitted in any form
or by any means, electronic or mechanical, including photocopying
or recording, or by any information storage and retrieval system,
without permission in writing from the publisher.*

*On the cover (left to right): (top row) Jack Bentley, Luke Boone;
(middle row) Eddie Collins, Hank Gowdy, Dutch Leonard, Eddie Murphy;
(bottom row) Sam Rice, Amos Strunk, Hippo Vaughn, Rollie Zeider
(all photographs from the Library of Congress)*

Manufactured in the United States of America

*McFarland & Company, Inc., Publishers
Box 611, Jefferson, North Carolina 28640
www.mcfarlandpub.com*

Acknowledgments

The book one writes may not be the book one intended to write. Such is the case with this one. A tribute to the major league players of 1952 — the first group of players I knew — somehow became a study of the players of 1916. I suspect that the 1982 publication of Richard Marazzi and Len Fiorito's *Aaron to Zuverink: A Nostalgic Look at the Baseball Players of the Fifties* may have helped in that decision. Thanks to Cy Turkin's monumental *Official Encyclopedia of Baseball*, now largely succeeded by *Total Baseball*, *Baseball Encyclopedia* and the online *Baseball-Reference.com*, the statistical information required for this study has long been available.

But the life of a major league baseball player is like that of the Venerable Bede's sparrow. After a short and graceful public flight that dazzles the senses, he "immediately vanishes out of your sight, into the dark winter from which he had emerged." What happens in that "dark winter" of emergence and vanishing is the information I found most interesting and most difficult to acquire.

I want to acknowledge the help of numerous persons and agencies in securing this information: My alma mater, the University of Missouri, made available the microfilm of *Sporting News*, which became the basis of the biographical dictionary section. The Hall of Fame Library in Cooperstown, New York, allowed me to access the files of individual players. The Society for American Baseball Research has provided research tools and resources that I could only dream of when I began this work.

I also want to thank librarians and archivists around the country for looking up obituaries and information about players. Many of these went beyond normal duties to put me in touch with people who held additional information.

I especially want to thank the relatives of players who graciously shared information about them. The most uplifting part of this undertaking was listening to their stories.

My biggest thanks go to two groups at Mayville State University in North Dakota: first, the interlibrary loan librarians at Byrnes-Quanbeck Library, who took an interest in this venture and helped track down elusive obituaries; second, the computer help desk staff for solving technical problems with maps and photos. I could not have completed this study without the help of Margit Eastman, Mary Chilvers, Shannon Hofer, Lukas Dziengel and Dean Kostuck.

And to Sarah, who endured this undertaking.

Contents

Acknowledgments v

Preface 1

Introduction 3

The Players 5

Appendix A. The 1916 Season 167

Appendix B. What Manner of Men Were These? 170

Appendix C. Career Baseball Statistics 175

Appendix D. Occupational and Mortality Data 188

Selected Bibliography 191

Index 193

Preface

Since the founding of the National League in 1876, more than 15,000 men have worn a major league uniform. As fans we revel in statistics about their performance and in anecdotes about their lives. We may view the players as role models whose habits are to be emulated, or as living lessons of what is to be avoided. In either case we want to read more about those whose deeds we follow.

The importance we attach to the exploits of major league players and the fascination we have with the details of their lives provide the impetus for the biographical dictionaries available. Given the pool of potential candidates, biographical dictionaries tend to be selective in the players they include. Even those that focus on a team or an era generally cover only selected players. As early as October 1883 the *Boston Daily Globe* featured a section titled "Our Boys," brief biographies of the Boston players who had just won the National League championship. Even so, the *Globe* covered only one "substitute" from the team. SABR's *Deadball Stars of the National League* and its companion *Deadball Stars of the American League* contain in-depth biographies of players, covering not only their playing careers but also their lives outside of baseball. But between them, the two volumes offer only 300 biographies from all the deadball-era players. Biographical dictionaries that cover the entire history of baseball are even more selective. For example, *Biographical Dictionary of American Sports: Baseball* features 1450 players, all of whom made significant contributions to the game. Even so mammoth a work as *The Ballplayers*, subtitled "Baseball's Ultimate Biographical Reference," contains only 6000 of the 15,000 players.

Richard Marazzi and Len Fiorito, in their book *Aaron to Zuverink*, limit their study to a particular time period, but they include every player who appeared in a major league game in the decade of the 1950s. They provide career statistics and post-baseball information — a difficult undertaking when dealing with living persons. In the same way, Bill Lee's monumental *The Baseball Necrology* includes every player — more than 7,600 — for whom a death record was available.

I began this study because I wanted to know the answers to two questions: First, what, on average, can a player talented enough to reach the major leagues expect by way of a career? How many lines might he receive in *Total Baseball* or *Baseball Encyclopedia*? And more importantly, what is the meaning of a major league career in terms of life after baseball? Do the skills and so-called "intangibles" necessary for success in baseball transfer to other areas of life?

I chose the players of 1916—a convenient midpoint year between the inaugural 1876 group and 1976 when I first considered this project—to provide answers to these questions. *Major League Baseball Players of 1916* is a biographical dictionary of the men who played major league baseball during that season. Included is every one of the 527 men who appeared in a major league game in 1916—including those whose entire major league career consisted of a single pinch-running experience or an inning in the field.

I began creating the player biographies by using the "Necrology" columns in *The Sporting News*, long the chronicle of baseball events. But these columns were inconsistent. At times they would include full obituaries; other times they offered only brief accounts limited to the player's baseball career. Files of individual players at the Baseball Hall of Fame Library in Cooperstown, New York, filled in gaps. State newspaper archives also turned out to be good sources for obituaries. In some cases I was able to speak with the family members of players; naturally these were invaluable sources of information. An important source of corroborating information was Historical ProQuest, made available to members of the Society for American Baseball Research. Providing access to the *New York Times, Chicago Daily Tribune, Washington Post, Los Angeles Times, Atlanta Constitution* and *Boston Daily Globe,* Historical ProQuest enabled me to follow the careers of individual players through contemporary newspaper accounts. After the model of *Biographical Dictionary of American Sport: Baseball,* I include the sources consulted with each entry.

In addition to the biographical dictionary, *Major League Baseball Players of 1916* contains four short appendices of conclusions drawn from these lives. Appendix A, "The 1916 Season," summarizes the events of that year's play. Appendix B, "What Manner of Men Were These?" gives general information on the ethnic and geographical origin of the players as well as distributions of their ages, heights and weights. Appendix C, "Career Baseball Statistics," charts player performance in games, hits, runs, home runs, runs batted in and batting averages for field players and wins, games, innings, saves, strikeouts and earned run averages for pitchers. These charts show the percentage of players who actually achieved a "solid" major league career. Appendix D, "Occupational and Mortality Data," summarizes post-playing careers and gives mortality statistics. Considering both playing and post-playing careers, it divides players into four groups: those who were very successful in both baseball and post-baseball; those who were only relatively successful in both areas; those who were far more successful after leaving baseball; and those who were far more successful as players.

In describing the limitations of *Major League Baseball Players of 1916,* I will paraphrase Bill Lee. This is not a baseball book so much as a book about men who played major league baseball. I would add that it is a book about people who realized a dream beyond the reach of most of us and what they did with the dream.

Baseball is truly a game of statistics, and this book contains a great many, used both to develop baseball lives and to measure those lives against norms of success. However, it is not a substitute for a book of baseball statistics; in other words, it is not a substitute for the "Big Mac." Finally, it is not intended as a baseball hagiography. In researching the lives of 527 people, one is likely to uncover information one would rather not know. While it is not my place to sanitize the lives of these men, I hope I have not exploited their weaknesses or tragedies.

As I was finishing this manuscript, the Library of Congress made available the George G. Bain collection of photographs. The collection contains some very fine portraits of the 1916 players—both the famous and not-so-famous. For an old baseball card collector, seeing those pictures was like being 12 years old again. For all who treasured their cards—whether of Tom Qualters or Warren Spahn—I hope you will enjoy seeing the photos of those who realized at least a piece of the American Dream.

Introduction

F. Scott Fitzgerald's observation about rich people, that they are "different from you and me," also holds true of major league baseball players—at least in the way that we perceive them. For the most part, we become acquainted with them when we are very young. People of my generation knew them first as names—names often as strange as, but learned more quickly than, those in *The Iliad* or *Ivanhoe*, names we often had to rescue from the vagaries of the box score (e.g. Sch'nd'st, 2b) or the tongues of announcers such as Dizzy Dean. Later we came to know them as pictures on baseball cards, the uniform cap giving a heroic cast to the face, hiding more human flaws. Still later we knew them as television performers, the snowy black and white images giving at best only a general notion of forms, stances and deliveries. Above all we knew them as statistics, as homers and wins, as batting averages and earned run averages, figures which we committed to memory and compared endlessly.

My father owned a small sawmill by which he fed and clothed his family through the Depression, but to me that was, in John Steinbeck's terms, "just stuff people do." Major league players, on the other hand, performed epic feats in the Polo Grounds and Yankee Stadium, arenas as distant and exotic as the Plains of Troy. And their actions profoundly affected our lives. Few things I have ever experienced disappointed me so much as the collapse of the Indians in the 1954 World Series; few things have given the satisfaction that I received from Bill Mazeroski's homer in 1960.

The aura of Mt. Olympus never quite fades from those who have worn a major league uniform. Mickey Owen, former Dodgers catcher, was running for sheriff of Greene County, Missouri, in 1964. For him, I'm sure, a pass through the stands at the Missouri state softball tournament was shrewd political strategy; for those of us in the stands it was an opportunity to share in the world of an ex–big leaguer. All of us somehow felt a need to be recognized by him in some special way, to receive his smile, his banter, and even his card. Many tried, at least figuratively, to reach out and touch him by reminding him of that moment—almost a quarter of a century earlier—when his dropped third strike with two outs in the ninth had cost the Dodgers a World Series game. Probably for the millionth time he laughingly agreed that this was probably how he would perform as sheriff, and so he collected our votes; we went away feeling that we had been in the presence of greatness.

This aura works against our seeing a major leaguer as a person who, like us, cleans out his garage occasionally and probably worries about mortgage payments. Evidence to the contrary, most of us believe that major leaguers have long, productive baseball careers, and if they work at all after baseball, they work for ESPN as color commentators.

My own experience with major leaguers and former major leaguers is limited. I would like to say that I know seven. But that is a gross exaggeration. A local hero, Bill Virdon, became the Cardinals centerfielder during my senior year in high school. During the off season he was a top-flight basketball referee in the West Plains area, and he also became part owner of a large sporting goods store in Springfield. When I entered the high school coaching ranks, I had dealings with him in both of those roles. That he might have actually needed the $10 for refereeing a basketball game never occurred to me. Another local hero, Preacher Roe, retired from the Dodgers and bought a grocery store in West Plains when I was a junior in high school. Even at that age it was a thrill for me to go into the store and see the Preacher behind the meat counter or working a cash register. My first reaction was always, "Hey, there he is—in person." I once had the honor of having him yell at me a few years later when I was umpiring an informal little league game which encroached on the practice time of his American Legion team. At Southwest Missouri State I shared an education class with Yankee pitcher Ralph Terry. He was kind enough to give me tips on the final that he had taken early because of spring training. Even today I suspect that the help actually received made less of an impression than the fact that it came from someone who had faced American League batters.

My other major league "acquaintances" are even more slight. Virdon's partner in the sporting goods store was Kansas City shortstop Jerry Lumpe, later a banker in Warsaw, Missouri. He once said "Hi" to me at a farm sale near Edwards, Missouri. Fortunately I had no dealings with Mickey Owens in his role as sheriff, so the incident above is the sum of my relationship with him. Former Cub Bob Speake played in that state softball tournament as a first baseman for Springfield Foremost. I never quite got used to seeing a former major leaguer in the close quarters of a softball park, but I was just part of the cheers behind him. Finally, former Browns outfielder Ted Gullic operated an insurance agency in West Plains, one which did not insure me. I do remember seeing him at Hardee's shortly before his death in 1999.

These encounters, limited though they were, have significance for me. Why else would I remember that I saw Jerry Lumpe at a farm sale almost forty years ago and that he actually spoke to me? In some scale of values I possess, these people were special. They all achieved some measure of success in baseball, and so far as I know are — or were — successful and productive members of society. However, since none of these seven seems to fit the stereotype, I wondered to what extent they are typical of the men who have played major league baseball.

I began the present study wanting to answer two questions. First, what constitutes a major league career? Do the realities of performance and tenure often fall short of the high dreams one carries on entering the majors? The second question is, what is the meaning of a major league experience? What happens to men once they have removed the uniform? Does reaching an elite level of athletic performance translate into a comparable quality of life? In general are these men freed from the financial, social and physical anxieties to which the rest of us are subject?

To answer these questions I selected a year—1916—and tried to reconstruct the lives of the 527 men who played in the majors that year to see how they performed and what they were able to make of their experience.

The Players

Merito Acosta, a Cuban outfielder who weighed only 140 pounds, was with the Senators for parts of five seasons and with the A's in 1918. He hit .298 for 52 games in 1918, his career totals showing a .255 average for 180 games. He was 16 years old and had been playing baseball for only two years when he first came to the Senators camp in 1913. Playing in the American Association for Louisville after 1919, Acosta was beaned in 1927, suffering a skull fracture. In later years he was involved in Cuban politics as a congress-

Merito Acosta

man and as consul in Chicago. He also became president of the Havana club in the Florida-International League. Acosta is a member of the Cuban Sports Hall of Fame. He died in Miami on November 17, 1963, at age 67. (*Sporting News; Washington Post; New York Times; Baseball-Reference.com*)

Charles (Babe) Adams walked only 18 batters in more than 260 innings in 1920; for his career he issued only 1.29 walks per nine innings, fewest of any 20th century pitcher.

Babe Adams

Sam Agnew

He had 194 career wins—all with the Pirates. This total includes two 20-win seasons and three others with more than 15 wins. He twice led the NL in shutouts on the way to a career 2.76 ERA. The hero of the 1909 World Series (3 wins, a 1.33 ERA), he also pitched in the 1925 World Series and was still a major league pitcher at age 44. He pitched in one game for the Cardinals in 1906 and two games for the Pirates in 1907 before going 12–3 for the Pirates in 1909. Adams operated a farm at Mt. Moriah, MO, while serving as a sports writer and a war correspondent during World War II. He later became a farmer in Silver Spring, MD, where he died on July 27, 1968, at age 86. (*Sporting News; Deadball Stars of the National League; Baseball-Reference.com; New York Times*)

John (Bert) Adams began his major league career as a 19 year old, catching 43-year-old Cy Young. In eight seasons of catching for the Indians and Phillies, he hit .202 in 267 games. Joining the Indians in August 1910 from Memphis, Adams played briefly also in 1911 and 1912. He played in the minors in 1913 and 1914 before coming to the Phillies in 1914. In 1918, his busiest season, he played in 84 games. Sold to Seattle of the PCL in 1920, Adams played in the minors until 1928. The Texas native then became a stagehand in the Paramount movie organization, a position he held at the time of his death. He died in Los Angeles on June 24, 1940, at age 49. (*Sporting News; Total Baseball; Los Angeles Times; Washington Post*)

Sam Agnew broke into the majors in 1913 as the regular catcher for the Browns, coming from Vernon of the PCL. In seven major league seasons, three as a regular, he hit .204 and twice led the AL in errors. In 1914 he jumped to Kansas City of the Federal League, but reneged when the promised money was not forthcoming. In the high point of his career, he caught Babe Ruth's two victories in the 1918 World Series. Sold by the Senators to San Francisco after the 1919 season, Agnew played eight seasons with the Seals before retiring from baseball to open a service station in Boyes Springs, CA. Having an acute coronary condition, he died at Sonoma, CA, on July 19, 1951. He was 63 years old. (*Sporting News; Los Angeles Times; Chicago Daily Tribune; Baseball Encyclopedia*)

Eddie Ainsmith caught 994 games in 15 major league seasons, working more than 75 games behind the plate on six occasions. He

Eddie Ainsmith

was Walter Johnson's regular catcher in 1917–18, leading the AL in total chances per game both years. In 1922 he hit .293 in 119 games for the Cardinals, setting a club record for catchers with 13 homers. Ainsmith came to the Senators in mid 1912 from Lawrence of the New England League. After leaving the majors in 1924, he remained in baseball as a player in the high minors, as an umpire in the Southern Association, as a scout for the Giants, as an instructor at the New England School of Baseball and as director of the New York School of Baseball. A native of Massachusetts, Ainsmith moved to Fort Lauderdale, FL, where he died on September 6, 1981, at age 91. (*Hall of Fame file; Total Baseball; Washington Post; Sporting News*)

Grover Cleveland (Pete) Alexander

threw 90 shutouts among his 373 victories before finishing a 20-year major league career in 1930 at age 43. The Nebraskan joined the Phillies in 1911 after going 29–11 at Syracuse, and immediately posted 28 victories as a rookie. He had three straight 30-win seasons before World War I but is best remembered as the hero of the 1926 World Series, when he posted two victories and a save for the Cardinals. In a seven-year period 1911–17 he led the NL in innings six times, in wins, shutouts, complete games and strikeouts five times. Suffering from epilepsy, bouts of alcoholism, growing deafness, and an ear infection — the result of a World War I shrapnel wound — he drifted from job to job after leaving the majors. He played with the House of David team, worked in a penny arcade and a flea circus, and served as a guard at a defense plant. After several years of declining health, he died of a heart attack at St. Paul, NE, on November 4, 1950. He was 63 years old. Alexander was in the third group of players elected to the Hall of Fame in 1938. (*Sporting News; Baseball Encyclopedia; Deadball Stars of the National League; New York Times*) **Photograph on page 138**

Walt Alexander

played five seasons in the majors as a back-up catcher for the Browns and Yankees, hitting .188 in 162 games. In 1913, his busiest year, he caught in 43 games for the Browns. In all, Alexander spent 20 years in professional baseball as a player, and in addition, managed teams in the Texas and East Texas leagues. He was a native of Georgia, but lived in the Dallas–Fort Worth area for more than 60 years, working in construction after he retired from baseball. He died at Fort Worth on December 29, 1978, at age 87. (*Fort Worth Star-Telegram; Total Baseball; Hall of Fame file*)

Artemis Ward (Nick) Allen

was named for a humorist, but nicknamed for the devil because of his playing style. In six major league trials in three leagues, he hit .232 in 216 games. Originally the property of the White Sox, he jumped from Fargo to the Buffalo Federals in 1914. With the Cubs briefly in 1916, he then played with the Reds 1918–20, with time out for service in World War I. In his busiest season, he caught 84 games for Buffalo in 1915. After being released by the Reds in 1921, Allen played and managed in the minors through 1936, when ill health forced him to retire. His St. Paul team won the American Association in 1924, and his Tulsa team won the Western Association in 1929. Allen died on October 16, 1939, at the Veterans Administration Hospital at Hines, IL. He was 51 years old. (*Sporting News; Chicago Daily Tribune; Baseball Encyclopedia; Atlanta Constitution; Encyclopedia of Minor League Baseball*)

Frank Allen

, a left-hander from Newbern, AL, won 23 games for the Pittsburgh Federals in 1915. In six major league seasons — spent mostly with mediocre Brooklyn and Boston clubs — he posted a 50–66 record, with a respectable 2.93 ERA. After playing four years at Southwestern University, he entered professional baseball. He pitched for Memphis and Mobile of the Southern Association, being named to the Southern Association all star team, before coming to the Dodgers in 1912. In 1918 he retired from baseball to take up farming at his home in

Alabama. He died of a heart attack at Gainesville, AL, on July 30, 1933. He was 43 years old. (*Total Baseball; Boston Daily Globe; Atlanta Constitution; New York Times;* information supplied by Mrs. Ann Jay; SABR Collegiate Database; *Encyclopedia of Minor League Baseball*)

Milo (Pete) Allison, a left-handed hitting outfielder, had four major league trials with the Cubs and Indians, totaling 49 games, in which he hit .217. Unable to find roster space for Allison, the Cubs sent him to Memphis in 1915; Cleveland later purchased him from New Orleans in 1916. After leaving the majors in 1917, he played at Beloit, WI, until 1919 and later went into business there. Allison died of a stroke at Kenosha, WI, on June 18, 1957, at age 66. His death certificate says that he had been a watchman at American Brass Company. On a Hall of Fame questionnaire, his wife listed his occupation as "farmer." (*Hall of Fame file; Wisconsin Certificate of Death; Chicago Daily Tribune; Baseball Encyclopedia*)

Jesse Altenburg, a left-handed hitting outfielder, had two trials with the Pirates in 1916 and 1917, batting .290 in 19 games. The Pirates called him up from Wheeling in September 1916. During World War I he served as an infantry officer and as a naval officer during World War II. Altenburg remained in baseball as a minor league manager until 1940. Having attended the University of Michigan, he then opened his own advertising service and publicity bureau in Lansing, MI. His fiancée dying on the eve of their wedding, Altenburg remained a lifelong bachelor. He died at Lansing on March 12, 1973, at age 80 (*Hall of Fame file; Baseball Encyclopedia; Encyclopedia of Minor League Baseball; New York Times*)

Leon (Red) Ames won 22 games for the 1905 NL champion Giants, but pitching behind Christy Mathewson and Iron Man McGinnity, he managed only one inning of relief in the World Series that year. Overall he pitched in the majors for 17 seasons, ten with the Giants. He won 10 or more games 12 times, finishing with 183 wins and a 2.63 ERA. He also holds the NL record with 30 wild pitches. After missing most of 1908 because of a kidney ailment, he won 7 games late in the season to help the Giants tie the Cubs for the NL championship. Going to the Reds in 1913, he led the NL with 23 losses in 1914, before moving on to the Cardinals in 1915. Ames finished with the Phillies in 1919 and retired from baseball in 1924. Returning to his hometown of Warren, OH, he "accepted a position at the Peerless Electric Co., and managed Warren semi-pro teams." Ames died suddenly on October 8, 1936, "following an attack of asthma." He was 54 years old. (*Warren Daily Tribune; Deadball Stars of the National League; baseball-reference.com; New York Times*)

Fred (Spitball) Anderson won 53 games—32 for Buffalo of the Federal League—in seven major league seasons. He won 19 games for Buffalo in 1915 and posted a 1.44 ERA in 162 innings for the Giants in 1917. A graduate of Davidson College and the University of Maryland Dental School (1909), he gave professional baseball a trial before entering dental practice. In that same year he was signed by the Red Sox from Wilson of the Eastern Carolina League and pitched in one game. Anderson was called into the army as a dentist in 1918 and retired from baseball. Entering private dental practice, he served in Winston-Salem, NC, from 1920 until his retirement. In ill health, he killed himself with a shotgun on November 8, 1957. He was 71 years old. (*Sporting News; Winston-Salem Register; Washington Post; Total Baseball*)

Ed Appleton turned in a 5–12 record for the Dodgers in 1915–16, working 185.1 innings. Brooklyn had purchased him from Newark for 1915, and he pitched 138 innings that season. After serving in France during World War I, he was sent to Beaumont and ultimately played for a number of Texas

Ed Appleton

teams before retiring from baseball. Appleton then became a special agent for the Missouri-Kansas-Texas Railway and trained bird dogs as a hobby. He died of apoplexy on January 27, 1932, at age 39. (*Sporting News; Fort Worth Star; Fort Worth Press; Total Baseball*)

Angel Aragon, a tiny utility infielder/outfielder, hit .118 in 32 games during three trials with the Yankees. Born in Havana, Cuba, Aragon came to the United States to play for the Long Branch (NJ) Cubans of the Atlantic League, from whom he was signed by the Yankees in 1914. Sold to Toledo in 1917, he subsequently played for Memphis and Richmond. Aragon made his home in New York City and scouted for the Giants. He died at his home on January 24, 1952, at age 58. A son, Jack, played in one game for the Giants in 1941. (*Sporting News; Total Baseball; Cubans in the Major League; New York Times*)

Jimmy Archer, an Irish-born catcher, entered professional baseball after graduating from St. Michael's College in Montreal. He spent 12 years in the majors, nine with the Cubs, hitting .249. His initial trial came with the Pirates in 1904. Sent to Atlanta, he was drafted by the Tigers for a brief trial in 1907. The Cubs purchased him from Buffalo, and he went on to become their regular catcher through 1916. Archer developed the squat stance, which made him particularly adept at throwing out base runners. He led NL catchers in assists in 1912, when he also hit .280 in 120 games. After leaving baseball because of brittle hands, he became a resident of Chicago, working as a hog buyer for Armor & Company. Following surgery, Archer died of a heart ailment at Milwaukee on March 29, 1958, at age 74. (*Hall of Fame file; Atlanta Constitution; Baseball Encyclopedia; Chicago Daily Tribune; Deadball Stars of the National League*)

Jimmy Austin, a Welch-born third baseman, spent more than 28 years in the American League. He joined the Yankees in 1909 from Omaha and came to the Browns in 1911, staying with them as player, coach and "Sunday Manager" until 1933, when he shifted to the White Sox. A career .256 hitter in 1580 games, he hit as high as .266 in both 1913 and

Angel Aragon

Jimmy Archer

1915 and .271 as a part-timer in 1920. A good fielder, he led AL third basemen in total chances 6 times, in double plays 4 times, and in fielding in 1913. Even after his retirement in 1937, Austin still served as a spring training coach with the White Sox until after World War II. In his retirement years, he became a city councilman in Laguna Beach, CA. He died there of a heart seizure on April 6, 1965, at age 85. (*Register[Laguna Beach]; Baseball Encyclopedia; Chicago Daily Tribune*)

Yancy (Doc) Ayers learned to pitch by reading a book entitled *How to Become a Pitcher*. He came to the Senators at the end of 1913 after completing a 29–8, 390 strikeout season in the Virginia League. At that time he was identified as a senior at the Medical College of Virginia, hence his nickname. He went on to win 66 games in seven full seasons and parts of two others with the Senators and Tigers. One of the better spitball pitchers—an underhander—he had 10 or more victories four times, topped by a 14–9, 2.21 ERA season in 1915. Returning to Virginia, Ayers became a farmer outside of Draper and managed local Pulaski baseball teams. He died of a heart attack at Pulaski on May 26, 1968, at age 78. (*Hall of Fame file; Southwest Times [Pulaski, VA]; Sporting News; Virginia Certificate of Death; Washington Post*)

Jim (Sarge) Bagby won 31 games for Cleveland's 1920 World Champions, almost a quarter of his major league total of 127 wins. Backed by Elmer Smith's grand slam homer and Bill Wambsganss's unassisted triple play, he defeated the Dodgers 8–1 in

Game 5 of the World Series despite giving up 13 hits. After a 1912 trial with the Reds, he came to the Indians from New Orleans. From 1916 through 1921 his win totals read 16, 23, 17, 17, 31, and 14. In 1920 he led the AL in wins, percentage, games, complete games, and innings. After closing his major league career with the Pirates in 1923, he pitched in the minors for seven more seasons. The native of Marietta, GA, operated a gasoline station and a dry cleaning establishment in Atlanta before returning to baseball as an umpire in 1941. In 1942 Bagby suffered a stroke which left him partially paralyzed. He died on July 28, 1954, at age 64. A son, Jim, Jr. pitched for the Red Sox, Indians and Pirates. (*Sporting News; New York Times; Washington Post; Baseball-Reference.com*)

Fred Bailey played three seasons for the Braves while attending Washington and Lee University, hitting .185 in 60 games. He joined the Braves in August 1916, getting into 6 games. When he entered military service in 1918, his major league career ended. The left-handed hitting outfielder played at Columbus in 1919 and at Hartford in 1920. After graduating from college in 1920, he returned to his native West Virginia, where he worked as a real estate broker. Bailey died of coronary artery disease at the Veterans Administration Hospital in Huntington, WV, on August 16, 1972. He was 77 years old. (*Hall of Fame file/Washington Post; SABR Collegiate Database; Total Baseball*)

Doug Baird played with five NL clubs (the Cardinals twice) in six seasons. Despite an anemic .234 career batting average, he was a regular third baseman for five of those seasons. Entering the majors from Sioux City in 1915, Baird established himself as a regular with the Pirates. In 1918 he left the Cardinals to do essential war work. By 1920 he appeared in only 13 games between the Dodgers and Giants. Returning to the minors, he hit over .300 four times in the American Association and Southern Association, setting an American Association record with 72 stolen bases while playing at Indianapolis. A native of St. Charles, MO, he became a resident of Thomasville, GA, where he died on June 15, 1967, at age 75. The cause of death is listed as "possible CV accident." The "usual occupation" line on his death certificate is blank. (*Sporting News; Georgia Certificate of Death; New York Times; Atlanta Constitution*)

Del Baker was a back-up catcher for the Tigers for three years (1914–16), appearing in 172 games and hitting .209. Overall, he spent 50 years in baseball. After leaving the Tigers he played at San Francisco, Portland, Mobile and Oakland — with time out for military service in World War I. He managed in the minors (Beaumont, Sacramento and San Diego), and coached for the Tigers, Indians and Red Sox (twice). As a coach he was particularly adept at stealing signs. In the majors he managed the Tigers (1933 and 1937–1942) and the Red Sox (1960). His 1940 Detroit team won an AL championship. Baker was a native of Sherwood, OR, but made his home in San Antonio, TX, where he died on September 11, 1973, following a lengthy illness. He was 81 years old. (*Sporting News; Los Angeles Times; Atlanta Constitution; Total Baseball; New York Times*)

Frank (Home Run) Baker led the AL in homers four times, hence his nickname. The career .307 hitter actually had more career triples (103) than homers (96), a feat almost unheard of today. In a monster 1912 season he had 200 hits, including 40 doubles, 21 triples, and a league-leading 10 homers with 130 runs batted in. The third baseman on Connie Mack's "$100,000 infield" in Philadelphia, he led the AL in putouts seven times, placing him seventh on the career list. In 25 World Series games he hit .363, his seven doubles placing him 8th on the all-time list. Angry at being sold to the Yankees, Baker sat out the entire 1915 season before joining the Yankees in 1916. After the pennant-winning years of 1921 and 1922, he

Home Run Baker

left baseball. A Trappe, MD, farm boy, he bought up land there so that he could farm and raise hunting dogs when he retired. He was also director of a Trappe bank. Baker was elected to the Hall of Fame in 1955 and died at his home in Trappe on June 28, 1963. He was 77 years old and had suffered two strokes. (*Sporting News; Baseball Encyclopedia; New York Times*)

Dave Bancroft played 1873 games as a NL shortstop. In his 16-year career, he led the league in total chances/game five times and is among career leaders in both putouts (1st) and assists (5th). In addition, he hit over .300 five times, finishing with a .279 average. Bancroft also helped four teams—the 1915 Phillies and the 1921, 1922 and 1923 Giants—win league championships. He reached the majors in 1915 after hitting .271 at Portland. Because of Bancroft's reputation as a very smart, heads-up player, John McGraw brought him to the Giants in 1920 and made him the team captain. After serving as playing manager of the Braves and playing coach of the Giants, he left the majors in 1930. At various times afterwards he managed in the minors at Minneapolis, Sioux City (his hometown) and St. Cloud and managed "Max Terry's traveling all-girls team." Then he "became a warehouse supervisor for Interprovincial Pipeline Company." Bancroft was elected to the Hall of Fame in 1971, and died the following year at Superior, WI, on Oct. 9, 1972. He was 81 years old. (*Baseball's Best; Cooperstown; Deadball Stars of the National League; Total Baseball; New York Times*)

Walter Barbare played all infield positions during an eight-year major league career with the Indians, Red Sox, Pirates and Braves. A career .260 hitter, he hit .302 as the regular shortstop for the Braves in 1921. He broke into the majors with Cleveland in September 1914. After getting into 77 games in 1915, he spent most of the next three seasons in the minors and in military service. The Pirates drafted him from New Orleans in 1919 and traded him to the Braves in 1921. He played at Toledo and Memphis after leaving the majors, and he managed briefly in the Cotton States League before returning to his native Greenville, SC, where he was involved in local sports. Barbare was a high school coach and a coach in the Southern Textile Basketball league, which he helped organize. Following a five-month illness, he died from cerebral thrombosis at Greenville on October 28, 1965, at age 74. His death certificate lists his occupation as "steamfitter." (*Greenville News; South Carolina Certificate of Death; Sporting News; Total Baseball*)

Turner Barber was a good-hitting outfielder/first baseman with the Senators, Cubs and Dodgers. A career .289 hitter, he hit .310, 313 and .314 with the Cubs but, except for 1921, could not find a regular position. A dedicated family man, he would often leave the club to care for his ailing wife back home. After a career at Union University, he joined the Senators at the end of 1915, "corralled from the wilds of Tennessee," and hit .302 in 20 games. Hitting only .212 in 1916, he was sold to Baltimore, to be rescued by the Cubs at the end of 1917. In all, he spent 22 years in professional baseball, playing in the Southern Association with Atlanta and Memphis after leaving the Dodgers in 1923. Following a breakdown in 1932, Barber was committed to the Tennessee State Mental Hospital. In 1948 he returned to his home at Milan, TN, where he died of a heart attack on October 20, 1968. He was 75 years old. (*Milan Mirror Exchange; Baseball Encyclopedia; Washington Post; Chicago Daily Tribune; Atlanta Constitution; information supplied by Mrs. Virginia Sohns; SABR Collegiate Database*)

Jesse Barnes was the hero of the 1921 World Series when he pitched 16.1 innings of relief for the Giants, winning twice. In a 13-season career the Oklahoma left-hander won 152 games. Twice leading the NL in losses while pitching for the Braves, he twice won 20 for the Giants, including a league-leading 25 in 1919. Barnes joined the Braves from Davenport in June 1915. Traded to the Giants in 1918, he spent most of that season in military service. He was traded back to the Braves in 1923, finishing with Brooklyn in 1927. After leaving baseball, Barnes moved to El Dorado, KS, where he became a captain in the police department, a position he held until the first of a series of heart attacks forced him to retire. While on a trip, he died at Santa Rosa, NM, on September 9, 1961, at age 69. A younger brother Virgil was a right-handed pitcher, also with the Giants and Braves. (*Sporting News; Total Baseball; New York Times; Boston Daily Globe*)

Ed Barney played two seasons in the outfield with the Yankees and Pirates, hitting .224 in 88 games. He came to the Yankees from Jersey City in July 1915; in August he was waived to the Pirates. A native of Amery, WI, he served in the U.S. Navy during World War I. After leaving baseball, Barney owned and operated a tavern in Rice Lake, WI, where he died of cancer on October 4, 1967, at age 77. (*New York Times; Baseball Encyclopedia; Wisconsin Certificate of Death*)

Jack Barry was signed by Connie Mack directly from Holy Cross in 1908, and by 1909 he had become the shortstop on the

Jack Barry

famous "$100,000 infield" in Philadelphia. In 11 seasons he hit only .243 but was regarded as an exceptionally fine fielder and played on four winning World Series teams. In Series play he hit .368 in 1911 and .300 in 1913. Traded to Boston in 1915, Barry led AL second-basemen in fielding in 1917 while serving as manager. He was in the U.S. Navy during World War I, retiring from baseball in June 1919. After leaving baseball, he operated a successful automobile agency. In 1920 he became baseball coach at his alma mater, where his 1952 team won the NCAA championship, and he was voted national Coach of the Year. Barry died of lung cancer at Shrewsbury, MA, on April 23, 1961, at age 74. (*Sporting News; Baseball Encyclopedia; SABR Collegiate Database; New York Times*)

Bill Batsch drew a base on balls as a pinch hitter in his only major league game with the Pirates on September 9, 1916, before serving in World War I. Born in Mingo Junction, OH, he played at Bethany (WV) College prior to entering professional baseball. He was a 40-year resident of Canton, OH, where he worked as a salesman for Ewing Chevrolet agency. He died at Canton on December 31, 1963, at age 71. (*Canton Repository; SABR Collegiate Database; Baseball Encyclopedia*)

Charles (Paddy) Baumann played in only 295 games with the Tigers and Yankees in seven big league seasons despite being a career .274 hitter and putting .292 and .287 seasons back to back in 1915–16. He was used primarily at second base but also played third and the outfield. After leaving the majors in 1917, he played, managed and umpired in the minors for several years. A bachelor and life-long resident of Indianapolis, he then became a maintenance worker for J.I. Holcomb Company. Following a stroke, he died on November 20, 1969, at age 83. (*Hall of Fame file; Baseball-Reference.com; New York Times*)

George Baumgardner

George Baumgardner won 37 games and averaged 218 innings in his first three seasons after joining the Browns in 1912. Early on the lefthander developed a reputation for eccentric behavior: "It is easy come,

Paddy Baumann

easy go with him." In 1915 he arrived at spring training out of condition and was suspended. He spent the summer pitching semi-pro baseball around West Virginia, refusing to communicate with the Browns. When Baumgardner left the majors in 1916, his five-year totals showed 38 wins and a 3.22 ERA. After serving in World War I, he returned to his hometown of Barboursville, WV, and retired. His death certificate lists no post-baseball occupation, a fact confirmed by a relative. He died of a heart attack on December 13, 1970, at age 79. (*Atlanta Constitution; Total Baseball; West Virginia Certificate of Death;* information supplied by Mrs. Edmund Baumgardner)

Stan Baumgartner had five trials with the Phillies before leaving the club in 1922 to work for Bethlehem Steel Company. An outstanding three-sport star at the University of Chicago, he signed with the Phillies in 1914 before his senior year. He returned to baseball in 1924, winning 13 games with the A's. In eight major league seasons, the Texas-born lefty compiled a 27–21 record. He coached three sports at the University of Delaware, and after finishing his college degree, he joined the staff of the *Philadelphia Inquirer* in 1926. As a sports writer for the *Inquirer* and correspondent for *The Sporting News*, he became one of the foremost baseball authorities of the time. After a three-year illness, he died in Philadelphia on October 4, 1955, at age 60. (*Sporting News; Total Baseball; Washington Post and Times Herald; New York Times; SABR Collegiate Database*)

Johnny Beall had trials as an outfielder with the Indians, White Sox, Reds, and Cardinals. In four seasons he appeared in 58 games, batting .231. The Indians drafted Beall from Denver in 1913 and waived him to the White Sox after six games. A month later the White Sox traded him to Milwaukee. The Reds brought him up in 1915 but returned him to Milwaukee in 1916. In 1918 Beall had a 19-game trial with the Cardinals. After leaving baseball, he became a building contractor in his hometown of Beltsville, MD. He died there of "acute myocarditis" on June 13, 1926. He was 44 years old. (*Maryland Certificate of Death; Total Baseball; Chicago Daily Tribune; Los Angeles Times*)

Zinn Beck, a light-hitting third baseman, played five seasons in the majors, one as a Cardinal regular, hitting .232 in 1914. When he came to the Cardinals from Waco in 1910, he was described as having "one of the best throwing arms ever seen in the big show." Only a .226 hitter in 290 major league games, Beck became a strong minor league hitter, reaching .380 in the SALLY League in 1920. In that same year he became manager of Columbus of the SALLY League, developing talent to sell to major league teams. He later managed at Greenville in the same league. Then in 1931 he became an employee of the Griffith family, first in Washington and then in Minnesota. Beck was still serving as a full-time scout for the Twins at age 93. He died at West Palm Beach, FL, on March 19, 1981, at age 95. (*Hall of Fame File; Total Baseball; Washington Post; New York Times; Encyclopedia of Minor League Baseball*)

Fred Beebe led the National League in strikeouts in his rookie season of 1906 and in games started in 1909. Born in Lincoln, NE, Beebe grew up in Chicago, where he was a schoolboy great at Hyde Park High School. A star football and baseball player at the University of Illinois, he was signed by the Cubs, but toiled most of his professional career with the lowly Cardinals, winning 63 games in seven seasons. In 1916, while still pitching professionally, he became baseball and track coach at Indiana University, a position he held for two years. After leaving baseball, he "became associated with" the Peoples Gas Company in Chicago, where he retired in 1937 due to ill health. He died at LaGrange Park, IL, on October 30, 1957, at age 76. (*Citizen Newspapers [LaGrange Park, IL]; Chicago Daily Tribune; SABR Collegiate Database; Sporting News*)

Chief Bender

Albert (Chief) Bender, whose mother was a full-blooded Chippewa from Minnesota, won 210 games while helping the A's win five AL championships. A great clutch pitcher, he completed nine of 10 World Series starts, winning 6 with a 2.44 ERA. The Dickinson College product led the AL three times in winning percentage: 23–5 in 1910, 17–5 in 1911, and 17–3 in 1914. Connie Mack said of him, "If everything depended on one game … I just gave the ball to Albert." After his productive years as a major league pitcher ended in 1917, he pitched and managed in the minors, coached the Yankees and White Sox (for whom he pitched one inning in 1925), and coached at the U.S. Naval Academy (1923–28). But from 1939 on, he coached the A's, serving as their battery coach from 1950 until the time of his death. Bender was elected to the Hall of Fame in 1953. After a long illness, he died in Philadelphia on May 22, 1954, at age 71. (*Sporting News; Total Baseball; SABR Collegiate Database; New York Times*)

Jack Bentley had two major league careers. Joining the Senators in 1913 — directly from amateur ranks — the 18-year-old Bentley pitched well, but an arm injury led to his release to Baltimore in 1917. During World I he became a first lieutenant in the U.S. Army, serving on the front line, where he was gassed. After the War, he became a heavy-hitting first baseman, and he regained his pitching form. Enjoying a major league renaissance, Bentley won 40 games for the Giants in 1923–25, while setting a major league record in 1923 with a .427 average in 89 at bats. In World Series play in 1923–24, he hit .417 with a homer and outdueled Walter Johnson in Game 5 in 1924. Released by the Giants in 1927, he pitched, played first base and managed in the minors through 1932. After leaving baseball, Bentley worked as a salesman for a paint company and also coached at the U.S. Naval Academy. Troubled by arthritis, he retired to the family farm at Sandy Springs, MD, where he died following a heart attack on October 24, 1969, at age 74. (*Hall of Fame file; Total Baseball; Sporting News; Washington Post*)

John (Rube) Benton won 156 games in 15 seasons with the Reds and Giants, winning at least 11 games seven times. Purchased

Jack Bentley

by the Reds from Macon in mid–1910, Benton spent most of 1911 at Chattanooga before being recalled. In 1912 the lefty from North Carolina led the NL in starts while throwing 302 innings. In the 1917 World Series he didn't give up an earned run in two starts, shutting out the White Sox in Game 3. Testifying before a grand jury, Benton stated that he had had knowledge of the 1919 World Series fix and that he had profited from that knowledge. First suspended, he was reinstated and pitched in the majors through 1925. He then pitched for Minneapolis until the end of 1934, when he retired and moved to Cincinnati. The 50-year-old Benton died at Dothan, AL, on December 12, 1937, of injuries received in a car wreck while visiting his brother. (*Cincinnati Enquirer; Eight Men Out; Bill James Historical Baseball Abstract; Deadball Stars of the National League; Total Baseball; Dothan Times*)

Joe Benz, a right-handed knuckleball pitcher from Indiana, won 76 games and had a 2.42 ERA in 9 seasons with the White Sox. Acquired from Des Moines in August of 1911, he debuted on the day he signed. Having 15 wins in 1915, 14 in 1914 and 13 in 1912, he also led the AL with 19 losses in 1914 despite a 2.26 ERA. After leaving the majors in 1919, he pitched independent ball in the Midwest Baseball League. Chicago newspapers generally referred to him as the "Butcher Boy" because he worked in a slaughterhouse in his youth and continued to work in one after leaving baseball. Later in life Benz "became a custodian at St. Killion's Church in Chicago and also worked at O'Hare Field." On April 23, 1957, the 71-year-old Benz died in Chicago, following a stroke. (*Sporting News; Baseball-Reference.com; Chicago Daily Tribune*)

Al (Dutch) Bergman earned 11 letters in football, basketball, baseball and track at Notre Dame, where he played with Knute Rockne and Gus Dorais. Following his graduation in 1916, he joined the Indians, hitting .214 in eight games as a second baseman. During World War I Bergman was a captain in the field artillery, and after the war he left baseball to become plant manager at American Stationery Company of Peru, IN. For the last 18 years of his life he was a patient in a tuberculosis hospital at Fort Wayne, where he died on June 20, 1961, at age 71. His younger brother Arthur — also nicknamed Dutch — also played at Notre Dame — with George Gipp — and later coached football at Catholic University. (*Fort Wayne Journal-Gazette; Washington Post; Sporting News; SABR Collegiate Database; Total Baseball*)

Bob Bescher, a 200-pound speedster, led the NL in stolen bases four times. Despite a career .258 batting average, he stole 81 bases in 1911, scored 120 runs in 1912, and held regular outfield status for eight of his 11 big league seasons. After prepping at Notre Dame, Bescher became an outstanding football and baseball player at Wittenberg College. He came to the Reds from Dayton in September 1908 and played with them through 1913. He also played with the Giants (1914) and the Cardinals (1915–17) before finishing with the Indians in 1918. He continued to play in the minors through 1925 and then became an oil inspector for the state of Ohio and also managed the Eagles Lodge. Bescher was killed in a car-train crash near his home in London, OH, on November 29, 1942, at age 58. (*Sporting News; SABR Collegiate Database; Enquirer Library; Deadball Stars of the National League*)

Christian Frederick Albert John Henry David (Bruno) Betzel joined the Cardinals in September 1914 from Columbia, SC, going hitless in seven games. But he was a regular at third base in 1915 and at second in 1916, while also seeing action at shortstop and in the outfield. A career .231 hitter, Betzel reached .251 in 1915. Sent down to Louisville in 1919, he played in the minors until he became manager at Indianapolis in 1927. He also managed at Louisville and Montreal, finishing at Toronto in 1956. Betzel later served as a scout for the A's, Yankees,

Indians and Dodgers. Born at Chattanooga, OH, he died at West Hollywood, FL, on February 7, 1965, at age 70. (*Sporting News; Total Baseball; Chicago Daily Tribune; Washington Post; Encyclopedia of Minor League Baseball*)

Carson Bigbee joined the Pirate outfield from Tacoma in 1916 and stayed for 11 years, seven as a regular. A career .287 hitter, he hit as high as .350 in 1922. In the seventh game of the 1925 World Series, he drove in the go-ahead run, allowing the Pirates to defeat Walter Johnson. By 1925 injuries and failing eyesight had reduced Bigbee to reserve duty. In 1926 he was let go by the Pirates because of his role in attempting to have club vice-president Fred Clarke removed from the bench. After played two seasons in the PCL, Bigbee retired. He had attended the University of Oregon before entering professional baseball and made his home in Portland, where he entered "the automotive business." After a lingering illness he died at Portland on October 17, 1964, at age 67. His brother Lyle pitched for the A's in 1920–21. (*Oregonian [Portland]; Sporting News; New York Times; Total Baseball*)

John (Josh) Billings hit .217 in 240 major league games during an 11-year career (1913–23) with the Indians and Browns. In 1917 and again in 1920 he played in 66 games — mostly as a catcher. Sent down in 1924, Billings played at Los Angeles, Kansas City and Dallas. In 1930 he began a managerial career, at one time being both manager and club president of Baton Rouge/Clarksville in the Dixie League. He was also an instructor for the All-Star Baseball School in Hot Springs, AR. Born in Grantsville, KS, he played at Oklahoma A&M before entering professional baseball. Billings died on December 30, 1981, in Santa Monica, CA, at age 89. (*Sporting News; Hall of Fame file; Total Baseball; SABR Collegiate Database*)

Earl Blackburn played professionally in both baseball and football. An outstanding three-sport start at Massillon (OH) High School, he played with four major league teams in five seasons, appearing in 71 total games — 61 as a catcher — hitting .262. The Pirates purchased him from Springfield (IL) in 1912 and after one game sold him to the Reds. After playing for the Reds in 1913 and Indianapolis in 1914, he returned to the majors with the Braves, for whom he hit .273 in 47 games in 1916 and with the Cubs, for whom he played two games in 1917. In 1918 he shifted to professional football, playing with the Massillon Tigers. Following his professional sports career, Blackburn moved to Mansfield, OH, and became an employee of the Mansfield Tire and Rubber Co. He died at Mansfield on August 4, 1966, at age 74. (*Mansfield News; Journal; Sporting News; Baseball-Reference.com*)

Jim Bluejacket (James Smith), a Cherokee Indian from Adair, OK, was given his name because of the naval uniform — his only clothing — he wore when he entered

Jim Bluejacket

professional baseball. In three major league seasons he won 13 games, all with the Brooklyn Federals. The Giants signed Bluejacket from Bloomington in July 1914, but he jumped to the Brook-Feds or Tip-Tops less than a month later. Released by the Reds to Dallas in 1916, he pitched in the minors until 1921. A "Down Memory Lane" entry in *The Sporting News* states that Bluejacket was "in charge of a large oil corporation's interests on the Isle of Aruba." Bill Lee found that "he was a welder foreman for Standard Oil of New Jersey." Bluejacket died in Pekin, IL, on March 26, 1947 "after an extended illness." He was 59 years old. (*Baseball Encyclopedia; Sporting News; Baseball Necrology; Washington Post; New York Times*)

George Boehler pitched in parts of nine major league seasons between 1912 and 1926 with the Tigers, Browns, Pirates and Dodgers. Overall, the right-hander appeared in 60 games, winning six. Over the same period, he was an outstanding pitcher in the minors, leading the Western League (1920, 1922) and the PCL (1924–26) in strikeouts. With Tulsa in 1922 he pitched 441 innings, winning 38 games. On the other hand, his busiest major league season was 63 innings with Detroit in 1914, a season in which he won two games. A native of Lawrenceburg, IN, Boehler became a member of the Greendale Fire Department there. He died on June 23, 1958, at age 65. (*Dearborn County Record [Lawrenceville, IN]; Washington Post; Los Angeles Times; Total Baseball; Encyclopedia of Minor League Baseball*)

Joe Boehling, a left-hander from Richmond, VA, won 54 of his career 55 games in a four-year period. The Senators signed him in 1912 from the amateur champion Richmond Battleaxes. Fast but wild, he reached the Senators at the end of his first professional season. In his first full year with the Senators in 1913, he compiled a 17–7, 2.14 ERA record, following that with 13, 14 and 11-win seasons. Traded to Cleveland in 1916, he served in the military in 1918. A 1920 comeback attempt was not successful. Released to Oakland, he subsequently played with Toronto, Bridgeport and New Haven before retiring for good at the end of 1921. Boehling was "engaged in the feed and seed business" in Richmond and pitched semipro baseball until his death. On September 8, 1941, he died from injuries received in a fall from a second-story porch of his home. He was 50 years old. (*Sporting News; Total Baseball; Washington Post; New York Times*)

Sammy Bohne (Samuel Cohen) had a 14-game trial with the Cardinals in 1916, coming from San Francisco of the PCL. After playing with Oakland and Seattle, he returned to the majors as the regular second baseman for the Reds (1921–24). The Jewish Bohne joining the Portuguese Lou Fonseca, the Irish Jimmy Caveney and the Italian Babe Pinelli in an international infield, all four members of which were natives of San Francisco. In 1921 he hit .285 and led the NL in fielding. Leaving the majors in 1926, Bohne remained in baseball into the 1930s. After a stint as a stage magician, he returned to San Francisco and worked his way up into "a successful business career," first in the garment industry and later in real estate. He died at Menlo Park, CA, on May 23, 1977, at age 80. (*Sporting News/Hall of Fame file; Total Baseball; Los Angeles Times*)

Bernie Boland posted a 13–7 record for the Tigers as a 23-year-old rookie in 1915. Coming from Nashville, he held the White Sox to one run in his first start. A small right-hander with a big curve, he had a 67–47 record after five seasons, topped by a 16–11, 2.65 ERA record in 1916. Early in 1920 he broke his arm and was out of baseball before he was thirty. Remaining in Detroit, Boland opened Tiger Construction Co., a cement firm. Still later he became a construction foreman with the Detroit Department of Public Works, a position he held until he retired in 1957. He died at Detroit on September 12, 1973, at age 81. (*Detroit Free Press; Chicago Daily Tribune; Total Baseball*)

Luke Boone

Lutie (Luke) Boone was the Yankees regular second baseman in 1914–15, leading the AL in total chances per game in 1915. During a five-year major league career, he played in 314 games, hitting .209. Beginning in 1912, Boone spent 24 seasons in baseball, mostly as a player in the American Association. At Crookston (MN) he played all positions on the team — in addition to being club owner, president, and manager. At the same time he was also president of the Northern League. A native of Pittsburgh, he died there on July 29, 1982, at age 92. (*Sporting News; Total Baseball; Washington Post; Encyclopedia of Minor League Baseball*)

William (Babe) Borton was a star first baseman with the St. Louis Terriers of the Federal League in 1915, hitting .286 and leading the FL in runs scored, putouts and double plays. When he arrived with the White Sox in 1912, he was described as a "fielding 'find,'" an ideal first baseman. But after two years of utility work, he was sold to Venice of the PCL. After hitting .307 there, Borton jumped to the Terriers. A utility player with the Browns in 1916, he finished a four-year big league career with an average of .270 in 317 games. After serving in World War I, he returned to the PCL with Vernon, where he admitted to bribing players from Portland and Seattle to enable Vernon to win the 1919 PCL Championship. While charges against Borton were dropped, Dennis Snelling asserts that "he was effectively suspended for life as a result of his involvement." In 1927 Borton became a resident of Berkeley, CA, where he worked as a Process Operator for Standard Oil Company. Developing lung cancer and a brain tumor, he died at Berkeley on July 29, 1954, at age 65. (*Hall of Fame file; The Pacific Coast League 1903–1958; Chicago Daily Tribune; Los Angeles Times; Baseball Encyclopedia*)

Jack Bradley, a 23-year-old catcher, played in two games for the Indians in 1916, going hitless in 3 times at bat. The Denver

Babe Borton

native had played three years at the University of Illinois and was captain his senior year. He and Illini battery mate Red Gunkel joined the Indians on the same day. In August Bradley was sent down to Columbus. After leaving baseball, he became an independent oil operator in Oklahoma. He died of cardiac arrest at Tulsa on March 18, 1969, at age 75. (*Hall of Fame file; Baseball Encyclopedia; SABR Collegiate Database; Tulsa Daily News; Chicago Daily Tribune; New York Times*)

Fred Brainerd played every infield and one outfield position for the Giants in 1915, hitting .201 in 91 games. He also had 2-game trials in 1914 and 1916 before serving as a second lieutenant in the Field Artillery during World War I. The University of Illinois product came to the Giants from Austin of the Texas League in October 1914. After playing and managing in the minors, Brainerd retired to his ranch in 1927, coming back to manage Dallas of the Texas League in 1933 and 1934. He died of a heart attack at Galveston, TX, on April 17, 1959, at age 67. (*Sporting News; Encyclopedia of Minor League Baseball; Baseball-Reference.com*)

Raymond (Rube) Bressler began his major league career as a left-handed pitcher. The AL champion A's acquired him from Harrisburg in 1914, and he posted a 10–4, 1.77 ERA mark. Sent to the minors in 1916, he compiled a 25–15 record at Atlanta and returned to the majors in 1917 as a pitcher/outfielder with the Reds. By 1921, after service in World War I, he had completed the conversion to an outfielder/first baseman. A mediocre hitter as a pitcher, he became a career .301 hitter, putting together consecutive .347, .348 and .357 seasons in 1924–26. Traded to the Dodgers in 1928, he led NL outfielders in fielding that year. When his playing career ended with the Cardinals in 1932, Bressler opened Rube Bressler's Tavern near Cincinnati, later managing other taverns in addition to doing radio broadcasting. He died of cancer at Cincinnati on November 7, 1966, at age 72. (*Cincinnati*

Yankee outfielders in spring training 1916. Don Brown (left) and Gene Layden (center) failed to make the team. Brown played with the A's in 1916 before disappearing. Layden played at Toronto. Tim Hendryx (second from left), Elmer Miller (second from right) and Hugh High (far right) made the team.

Post-Times; Sporting News; Total Baseball; New York Times)

Tony Brottem had trials with the Cardinals, Senators and Pirates in 1916, 1918 and 1921. Used primarily as a catcher, he appeared in 62 games, hitting .215. After leaving the Pirates, he played at Birmingham and Louisville. The native of Halstad, MN, spent 16 years as a player in organized baseball before he was released by Dayton of the Central League on July 29, 1929. This release "brought on despondency," and he took his own life in Chicago on August 5, 1929. He was 37 years old. (*Sporting News; Baseball Encyclopedia; Washington Post; Atlanta Constitution*)

James Donaldson (Moose) Brown is on the SABR Biography Committee list of most wanted players. He played in one game as a Cardinal outfielder in 1915, picked up from Topeka and returned within a week. Drafted by the Yankees, he was sent to Columbus the following spring. He played in 14 games with the A's later in that season before being sent down again. In all, he hit .250 in 44 at bats. Brown presents a daunting research problem. His hometown, formerly listed as Laurel, IN, is now listed as Laurel, MD. His name appears as DON Brown in *Baseball Encyclopedia* and as JIM Brown in *Total Baseball*. *Sport Americana Baseball Address List* gives his name as Donald G. Brown with a 1917 address in Beatrice, NE, the same hometown listed on the 1916 Yankee roster. In 1995 his file in the Baseball Hall of Fame Library contained only one item: a hometown card. (*New York Times; Washington Post*) **Photograph above**

Mordecai (Three Finger) Brown achieved success in spite of—or because of—a maimed pitching hand, the result of

Three Finger Brown

two farm accidents. It was said that his maimed hand "could knock a fly off a toothpick with a curve ball." In the first decade of the century, he compiled six straight 20-win seasons and six sub-2.0 ERA seasons in a seven-year period. During the Cubs 116-win season of 1906, he had 26 wins, 10 by shutouts, and a microscopic 1.04 ERA. In all, he won five World Series games, three by shutouts. Brown began his major league career with the Cardinals in 1903, promoted from Omaha, and went to the Cubs in 1904. Finishing a 14-year career with the Cubs in 1916, he had 239 wins and a 2.06 ERA, third lowest in history. He pitched and managed in the minors through 1920. After leaving organized baseball, Brown opened a gas station in Terre Haute, IN, which he operated until 1946, while managing a semi-pro team. He died at Terre Haute on February 14, 1948, at age 71 and was posthumously named to the Hall of Fame the following year. (*Baseball's Best; Deadball Stars of the National League; Total Baseball; New York Times; Chicago Daily Tribune*)

Jesse Buckles, a big, 26-year-old lefty from California, made two relief appearances for the Yankees in 1916. In a major league career of four innings, he gave up one earned run. Like Fred Snodgrass, he played at St. Vincent's (Loyola-Marymount) before entering professional baseball. The Cubs claimed him from Medicine Hat in 1915, where he had led the Western Canadian League with 25 wins and 196 strikeouts, but he did not make the team. He also had a 1917 trial with the Phillies. After leaving baseball, he returned to California and became a law enforcement officer. He was city marshal of Placentia, a captain of police in Santa Ana, and a deputy sheriff in Orange County. Buckles died in the Los Angeles suburb of Westminster on August 2, 1975, at age 86. (*Baseball Encyclopedia; SABR Collegiate Database; Chicago Daily Tribune; information supplied by Mrs. Jess Buckles*)

Ed Burns, a graduate of St. Mary's College of Engineering, spent seven seasons in the majors, primarily as a backup catcher for the Phillies. He played in one game for the Cardinals in 1912, coming from Tacoma. Released to Montreal, he was acquired by the Phillies in 1913. Despite a light bat (.230 career average in 321 games), he caught all five games in the 1915 World Series, hitting .188. In 1916 he played in 78 games, hitting .233. Retiring after the 1918 season, Burns returned to the Bay Area to become a clothing merchant in Monterey. He died of a heart attack on June 1, 1942, at age 53. (*Sporting News; SABR CollegiateDatabase; Total Baseball; Boston Daily Globe*)

George Burns, called "Tioga George" to distinguish him from the Giants outfielder of the same name, spent 16 seasons as an American League first baseman. The Tigers acquired him in 1914 from Sioux City, and he immediately became a regular, maintaining that status with the A's, Indians and Red Sox. A career .307 hitter, he twice led the AL in hits. In 1926 he had a record 64 doubles among his 216 hits, giving him a .358 average and the AL's Most Valuable Player award. After leaving the majors in 1929, Burns played and managed in the Pacific Coast League until 1935. While he grew up in Tioga, PA, he settled in Seattle to manage apartments. In 1947 he became a deputy sheriff for King County, WA, and held that position until he retired. Burns died at Kirkland, WA, on January 7, 1978, at age 84. (*Biographical Dictionary of American Sports: Baseball; Total Baseball; New York Times; Washington Post*)

George Burns, a smallish (5'7", 160 pounds) NL outfielder, produced numbers similar to those of the AL George Burns. The NL version had 59 more career hits (2077 to 2018) in 13 fewer games, but hit 20 points less (.287 to .307). He led the NL in runs and walks five times and in stolen bases twice. After joining the Giants from Utica in October 1911, Burns became a regular in 1913. In his 11 seasons with the Giants, he played in three World Series, banging out 11 hits in 1921. Traded to the Reds in 1922, he finished his major league career, hitting .292 for the

George Burns

Phillies in 1925. After playing and managing in the minors (1926–30), he coached the Giants (1931). Returning to Gloversville, NY, he operated a pool hall and worked as a payroll clerk. Burns died at Gloversville on August 15, 1966, at age 76. (*Biographical Dictionary of American Sports: Baseball; Deadball Stars of the National League; Total Baseball; New York Times*)

Leslie (Bullet Joe) Bush was, according to Connie Mack, one of the three fastest pitchers he had ever seen, the others being Walter Johnson and Amos Rusie. Bush also is credited with inventing the forkball or splitter, a pitch that helped him win 196 major league games. When the Yankees won the 1922 AL championship, Bush contributed 26 wins, but he was even more impressive in 1916 when he won 15 games for the A's, a team that won only 36. Pitching in five World Series, he had two wins and 5 complete games. When Bush defeated the Giants 8–2 in 1913, he became, at age 20, the youngest man to start and win a World Series game.

Bullet Joe Bush

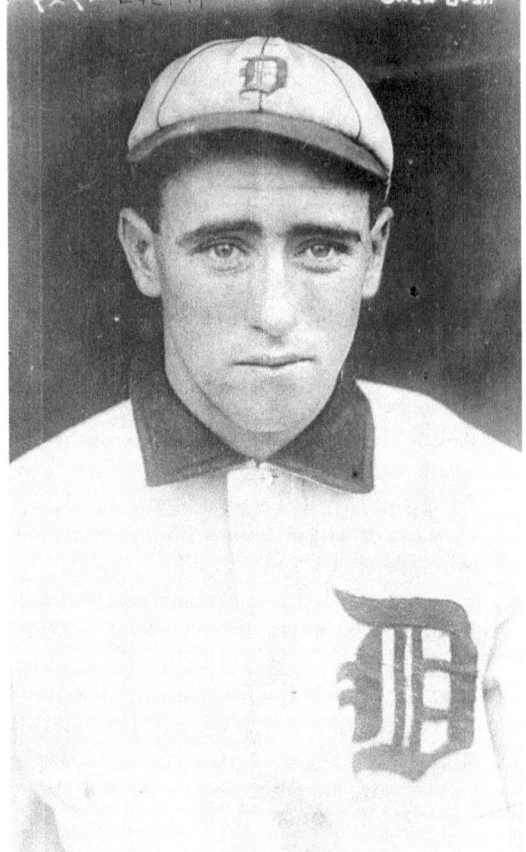

Donie Bush

At that time he was only a year from Class D Missoula, where he won 29 games in 1912. After leaving the majors in 1928, Bush continued to pitch and manage in the minors before becoming a pari-mutuel clerk at racetracks in New Jersey and Florida. Born at Brainerd, MN, he died at Ft. Lauderdale, FL, on November 1, 1974, at age 81. (*Sporting News; Total Baseball; New York Times*)

Owen (Donie) Bush spent 13 of his 17 major league seasons as the regular shortstop for the Tigers. One of the smallest players in the AL (5'6", 140 pounds), he led the league in walks five times and in runs once, while holding a .250 career batting average and being an AL leader in sacrifices. Bush also led AL shortstops in assists five times and in putouts and total chances three times. The 20-year-old joined the Tigers in August 1908, called up from Indianapolis in time to play 20 games. The following season he helped the Tigers win an AL championship, hitting .261 in the World Series. In all, he spent 65 years in baseball, managing the Senators (1923), the Pirates (1927–29), the White Sox (1930–31) and the Reds (1933). In addition, he managed at Minneapolis and Louisville — where he was also club president. A life-long resident of Indianapolis, he was part owner of that club. He also scouted for the Red Sox and was scouting for the White Sox at the time of his death. After a short illness, he died at Indianapolis on March 28, 1972, at age 84. (*Sporting News; Baseball Encyclopedia; Washington Post; New York Times*)

Art Butler (Arthur Bouthillier) played six seasons in the majors, two as the regular shortstop for the Cardinals. A career .241 hitter, he batted .280 for the Pirates in 1913; in 1916 he led the NL with 13 pinch hits. Having ruined his arm (by "showing off," he said), he was sent down in 1917 and played in the minors for 12 years, including stops at

Bobby Byrne

Los Angeles, Kansas City, Hartford, and Providence. Then he "worked in a gas station for six years, drove buses for five, assembled washing machines, worked in a submarine equipment company, sold coal and oil, and patrolled a supermarket as a security guard." Butler was a life-long resident of Fall River, MA, where he died on October 7, 1984, following hernia surgery. He was 96 years old. (*Hall of Fame file; Total Baseball; Los Angeles Times; New York Times; Sporting News*)

Bobby Byrne, a 145-pound third baseman, spent 11 seasons in the majors, 9 as a regular. He led the NL twice in fielding, twice in assists and three times in errors. Only a .254 career hitter, he led the NL in hits and doubles while batting .296 in 1910. He played all seven games for the Pirates in the 1909 World Series and pinch-hit once for the Phillies in the 1915 World Series. Bryne began his major league career in 1907 with the Cardinals, coming from Shreveport. After leaving the playing ranks with the White Sox in 1917, he managed minor league clubs for two years, but in 1923 he returned to his home in St. Louis. There he pursued soccer, bowling and golf while being employed by the City of St. Louis, by the U.S. Government at Lambert Field and by Scullin Steel Company. He died at Wayne, PA, on December 31, 1964, his 80th birthday. (*Hall of Fame file; Sporting News; New York Times; Total Baseball*)

Leon Cadore won 68 games for the Dodgers but is best remembered for the 26-inning 1–1 tie he pitched against the Braves in 1920. He felt that he never had the "same stuff" after that, and by 1924, he was out of baseball. Cadore first came to the Dodgers in 1915 from Wilkes-Barre. After a 25-win season at Montreal in 1916, he was up to stay; 55 of his victories came between 1917 and 1921. A college graduate (Gonzaga) and war hero (battlefield promotion to captain after the Argonne campaign), he married Maie Ebbets, the owner's daughter, and formed connections with a Wall Street brokerage firm, selling stocks and bonds. After the crash of 1929, Cadore returned to Hope, ID, to operate the family copper mines. He died of cancer at the Veterans Administration Hospital in Spokane, WA, on March 16, 1958, at age 67. (*Sporting News; Baseball-Reference.com; SABR Collegiate Database; New York Times*)

Forest (Hick) Cady was from the tiny village of Bishop Hill, IL, hence his nickname. He entered the majors in 1912 from Newark. As a back-up catcher, he played on three AL championship teams in Boston — 1912, 1915 and 1916. In 1915, his best year, he hit .278 in 78 games and .333 in four World Series games. After finishing an eight-year major league career with the Phillies in 1919, Cady played in the minors until 1927, when he became an umpire. He worked as a minor league umpire until 1942, when the Three-I League disbanded due to World War II. On March 3, 1946, he died in his hotel room in Cedar Rapids, IA, "smothered by smoke from a fire in his bed," caused by a faulty heat pad. He was 57 years old. (*Sporting News; Baseball Encyclopedia; Boston Daily Globe*)

Ray Caldwell occasionally played outfield or first base and pinch-hit on days when he wasn't pitching. He won 134 games in twelve seasons in the American League, including 20 for the champion Indians in 1920 and back-to-back 18- and 19-win seasons for the Yankees. He joined the Yankees from McKeesport in September 1910. Over the next 11 seasons he averaged more than 200 innings. In the 1920 World Series he started Game 3 but lasted only ⅓ of an inning. Returned to the minors in 1922, he played until 1932 — when he was 45 years old — primarily with Birmingham. Having worked as a railroad telegrapher before entering baseball, Caldwell returned to that occupation after leaving baseball. He also operated a tavern and worked as a steward at a rod and gun club. A native of Corydon, PA, he lived at Salamanca, NY, where he died on August 17, 1967, at age 79. (*Hall of Fame file; New York Times; Atlanta Constitution; Washington Post; Total Baseball*)

Mike Cantwell, a left-hander from Washington, DC, pitched two innings of relief for the Yankees in 1916, following his college career at Rock Hill College and Georgetown University. Subsequent trials with the Phillies in 1919–1920 resulted in a career 1–6 record for 54.2 innings. Cantwell served in the U.S. Marine Corps in World War I; he also served in World War II. His death certificate lists his home as Silver Spring, MD, and his occupation as "salesman." Caldwell died of "coronary insufficiency" at the Veterans Hospital at Oteen, NC, on January 5, 1953. He was 58 years old. His older brother Tom pitched for the Reds in 1909–10. (*Hall of Fame file; Washington Post; SABR Collegiate Database; Total Baseball*)

Max Carey (Maximilian Carnarius) led the NL ten times in stolen bases in his 20-year career as a Pirate and Dodger outfielder, ending with 738 steals, fourth on the all-time list. In 1913 and 1916 he exceeded 60 steals. A career .285 hitter, he had six .300 seasons, topped by a .343 mark in 1925. In the World Series that year he had 11 hits. As an outfielder he stands third in career putouts and double plays, and seventh in career assists. Born in Terre Haute, IN, Carey attended Concordia College to prepare to become a minister before entering baseball. He came to the Pirates from South Bend at the end of 1910 and was traded to Brooklyn in mid-1926. After finishing as a player in 1929, he remained active in baseball, coaching the Pirates, managing the Dodgers, managing in the minors and organizing the All-American Girls Professional Baseball League during World War II. He also worked as a racetrack official. Elected to the Hall of Fame in 1961, Carey died at Miami, FL, on May 30, 1976, at age 86. (*Baseball's Best; Deadball Stars of the National League; Total Baseball; New York Times*)

Paul Carpenter, a right-handed pitcher, had a 1.17 ERA in five relief appearances for the Pirates in 1916. The Pirates acquired him from Chillicothe when the Ohio State League folded in July. Carpenter was leading the league in strikeouts at the time. In August,

Bill Carrigan

the Pirates released him to Charlotte. After serving with the U.S. Army in France during World War I, he had a trial with the Yankees, but was assigned to Toledo. Carpenter later pitched in the independent Midwest Baseball League. A resident of Newark, OH, Carpenter became an employee of the Street Department of that city (1928–44) and later worked for the Ohio State Department of Highways until his retirement in 1954. He died at Newark on March 14, 1968 at age 73. (*Hall of Fame file; Baseball-Reference.com; New York Times; Chicago Daily Tribune*)

Bill (Rough) Carrigan, a native of New England, spent his entire major league career with the Red Sox — six years as a player, three as a player-manager and three as a manager. He caught 110 games in 1910 and hit as high as .296 in 1909. Overall, he hit .257 in 706 games, participated in three World Series, and managed the Red Sox to two straight World Championships in 1915–16. Carrigan joined the Red Sox in 1906 from Holy Cross but hit only .211. He spent 1907 at Toronto and missed part of 1908 with appendicitis before starting a six-year string as a regular, leading AL catchers in fielding in 1912 and 1914. Carrigan left baseball in 1917 to operate a chain of movie houses around New England but returned to the Sox in 1927, managing them to three straight last-place finishes. He then became a banker in his hometown of Lewiston, ME, where he died on July 8, 1969, at age 85. (*Hall of Fame file; Total Baseball; SABR Collegiate Database; New York Times*)

Ralph (Doc) Carroll caught in 10 games for the A's in 1916, hitting .091. The Worcester, MA, native was a graduate of College of the Holy Cross, Tufts University Dental School and Washington University. He played baseball at both Holy Cross and Tufts, where he was a teammate of future major leaguers Heinie Stafford, Doc Whittacker, and Hod Ford. Later Carroll was on the staff of St. Vincent Hospital and the Forsythe Dental Infirmary for Children in Boston, while also serving as Athletic Director at Worcester Tech and coaching football and baseball at Worcester area high schools. He died in Worcester on June 29, 1983, at age 91. (*Worcester Telegram; Baseball-Reference.com; SABR Collegiate Database*)

Paul (Nick) Carter, a tall right-hander, posted a 21–25, 3.32 ERA record in seven seasons with the Indians and Cubs. According to Bill James, he is alleged to have tried to fix Cubs games and was "*persona non grata* after 1920." Certainly the Cubs traded him to Kansas City before 1921, and he pitched for the Blues until 1923. Carter attended Rhodes College in Memphis, where he played for two seasons before signing with the Indians in 1914. Sent down to Indianapolis, he was purchased by the Cubs in 1916. After leaving baseball, Carter became a farmer in his native Lowndas County, GA, where he also operated the Lake Park Peat Moss Co. He died at Lake Park, GA, on September 11, 1984, at age 90. (*Valdosta [GA] Daily Times; Bill James Historical Baseball Abstract; SABR Collegiate Database; Baseball-Reference.com; Chicago Daily Tribune*)

George Chalmers, a Scottish-born right-hander, spent seven seasons (1910–16) with the Phillies. Originally considered a better prospect than Pete Alexander, Chalmers ended his major league career with 29 wins. He was a product of Manhattan College and joined the Phillies in August 1910 from Scranton, where he had compiled a league-leading 25–6 record. In 1911, his best season,

George Chalmers

he had 13 wins and four saves. Released in 1914, Chalmers was re-signed in 1915, when he had a 2.48 ERA in 170 innings to help the Phillies win the NL championship, losing a 2–1 duel to Ernie Shore and the Red Sox in Game 4 of the World Series that year. He was released again at the end of 1916. A 1950's note in *The Sporting News* described him as being "in the insurance game in New York City." After suffering a second stroke, Chalmers died in the Bronx on August 5, 1960, at age 72. (*Sporting News; Total Baseball; Chicago Daily Tribune; Atlanta Constitution; Encyclopedia of Minor League Baseball*)

Harry Chapman had trials with the Cubs (1 game in 1912), the Reds (2 games in 1913) and the Browns (18 games in 1916). He had more success with the St. Louis Federals, catching about one-third of their games in both 1914 and 1915. His five-year major league totals show a .199 average in 147 games. A native of Severance, KS, Chapman was purchased by the Cubs from Topeka in 1912. The Reds acquired him in 1913 and sold him to Atlanta. Sent down by the Browns, Chapman played for Little Rock in 1916 and 1917 before retiring to a farm near Springfield, MO. On October 21, 1918, he died of "pneumonia following influenza" at a sanitarium at Nevada, MO. He was 31 years old.

Harry Chapman

(*Sporting News; Total Baseball; Chicago Daily Tribune*)

Ray Chapman, the only player ever killed in a major league game, was an 8-year regular at shortstop for the Cleveland Indians. He joined the Indians from Toledo in August of 1912, hitting .312 in 31 games. A career .278 hitter, he had hit .302 in 1917, .300 in 1919, and was hitting .303 at the time of his death in 1920. Three times he led the AL in sacrifices and once in runs. In the field, he led AL shortstops four times in total chances per games and three times in putouts. Hit in the head by a pitch thrown by submariner Carl Mays of the Yankees, Chapman died of a fractured skull in New York on August 17, 1920. The Kentucky native was 29 years old. (*Sporting News; Baseball Encyclopedia; New York Times; Boston Daily Globe*)

Larry Chappell became famous overnight in 1913 when the White Sox purchased his contract from Milwaukee for $18,000, the largest amount paid to that time. Failing to live up to expectations, he hit only .231 in 60 games as an outfielder. In a five-year career with the White Sox, Indians and Braves, Chappell hit .226 in 109 games. The White Sox returned him to Milwaukee in 1915; the Indians acquired him for 1916; he finished his major league career with the Braves in 1917. After entering military service, the McClusky, IL, product died of influenza in an Army hospital in San Francisco on October 8, 1918. He was 28 years old. (*Sporting News; Total Baseball; Chicago Daily Tribune; Atlanta Constitution*)

Hal Chase is generally regarded as "the game's greatest defensive first baseman." His range is indicated by his career ranking in putouts per game (15th) and total chances per game (10th). He also developed into a very solid hitter, leading the FL in homers (17) in 1915 and the NL in hits (184) and average (.339) in 1916. Chase also is generally regarded as the epitome of the dishonest ballplayer. In 1910, 1913 and 1918 he was

Hal Chase

charged with fixing games. Finally he "disappeared from the Giants' September lineup" in 1919 and was not offered a contract for 1920. He played at Santa Clara University and the Los Angeles Angels before joining the Yankees in 1905. After being barred from the Pacific Coast League in 1920 for attempted bribery, he spent the rest of his life playing and managing outlaw league teams in mining towns in Mexico, Arizona and California. He died at Colusa, CA, on May 18, 1947, of "complication of liver and kidney ailments." He was 64 years old. (*Bibliographical Dictionary of American Sport: Baseball; Sporting News; Total Baseball; New York Times; Bill James Historical Baseball Abstract*)

Larry Cheney worked 919 innings for the Cubs in three seasons (1912–14), winning 67 games. He was the NL leader in wins (26) and complete games (28) in 1912 and in saves (11) in 1913. For the NL champion Dodgers of 1916 he won 18 with a 1.92 ERA, trailing only Pete Alexander in strikeouts; despite this record, he was given only 3 innings of mop-up work in the World Series that year. The career totals for the Belleville, KS, native show 116 wins in nine seasons. He had spent seven seasons in the minors mastering a spitball before he reached the majors in September 1911 from Louisville. Traded to the Dodgers in 1915, he finished with the Phillies in 1919. Cheney returned to the minors and pitched until 1923, when he began to operate an orange grove near Hines City, FL. He died at Daytona Beach on January 6, 1969, at age 82 (*Hall of Fame file; Total Baseball; Deadball Stars of the National League*)

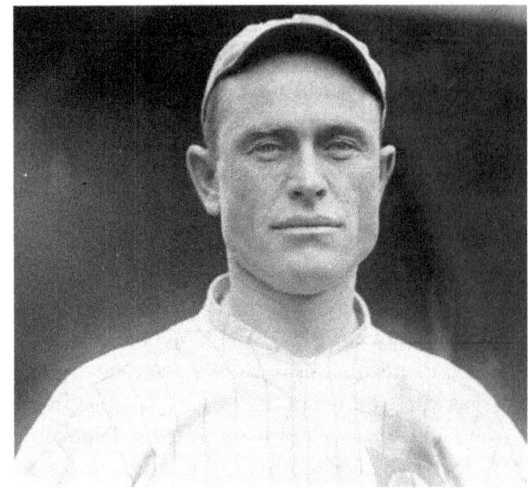

Larry Cheney

Eddie Cicotte won at least 10 games for 12 consecutive seasons, and his production was increasing, as he won 20 games in three of his last four seasons. AL-leading 28- and 29-win seasons in 1917 and 1919 pushed his career total to 208. Five times his ERA dipped below 2.00, helping him to a career 2.37 mark. Despite these performances, his salary never exceeded $6,000 in a season. Owner Charles Comiskey promised him a $10,000 bonus if he ever won 30 games, then ordered him benched when his 1919 total reached 29. He also had two World Series wins, both over Slim Sallee — a 2–1 Game 1 win in 1917 and a 4–1 win in Game 6 of 1919. After a 1905 trial with the Tigers, Cicotte developed a knuckle curve at Indianapolis and Lincoln, which earned him a trip back to the majors with the Red Sox. The most contrite of the "Eight Men Out," Cicotte confessed and was banned from baseball after 1920. The Detroit native continued to live there, using a pseudonym to protect his family. Cicotte worked for Ford Motor Company and raised prize strawberries. He died at Detroit on May 5, 1969, at age 82. In a poignant note, his death certificate lists his occupation as "baseball player — Chicago White Sox." (*Hall of Fame file; Biographical Dictionary of American Sport: Baseball; Total Baseball; New York Times; Eight Men Out*)

Tommy Clarke, a regular catcher in 1913–14, spent nine years with the Reds, hitting .265 in 670 games. He joined the Reds in August 1909 from Montreal, and ended his major league career after catching one game for the Cubs in August 1918. From 1919 through 1935 he served as a minor league player, coach and manager and as a coach for the Giants. Clarke then opened a cafe in Corona, Queens, NY, and began scouting for the Giants. He died of hardening of the arteries, "tending bar at his cafe" on August 15, 1945. He was 57 years old. (*Sporting News; Total Baseball; Atlanta Constitution; New York Times*)

Clem Clemens (Clement Ulatowski) joined the Chicago Federals after graduating from Notre Dame in 1914. The *Chicago Daily Tribune* in both 1914 and 1917 credits him with service with the White Sox and Browns before jumping to the Federal League, but these claims are not reflected in baseball statistics. In three trials as a catcher with the Chi-Feds, Whales and NL Cubs, he hit .109 in 34 games. Retiring from baseball in 1916 to practice law, Clemens was one of the founders of the short-lived Fraternity of Professional Base Ball Players. After serving as a laundry officer in World War I, Clemens became an attorney in his hometown Chicago. In 1957 he retired to St. Petersburg, FL, where he died on November 2, 1967, at age 80. (*St. Petersburg Times; Total Baseball; SABR Collegiate Database; Chicago Daily Tribune*)

Verne (Tubby) Clemons caught 117 games for the Cardinals in 1921, hitting .320, the high point of his seven-year major league career. But weight problems began to cut into his workload, so that by 1924, he caught in only 24 games despite hitting .321. His career totals show a .286 average for 474 games over 7 seasons. In 1916 Branch Rickey brought Clemons from Louisville to the Browns, with whom he found little playing time. After World War I, Rickey brought Clemons to the Cardinals, where he played out the rest of his career. When Clemons retired from baseball in 1925, he became the owner of a farm and orange groves near Orlando, FL. He died from "a complication of diseases" at Bay Pines Veterans Hospital on April 2, 1959, at age 66. (*Sporting News; Total Baseball; New York Times*)

Ty Cobb retired from baseball in 1928, ranked in the top five in almost every offensive category except home runs and slugging percentage. While his 4189 hits and 892 stolen bases have been surpassed, it is doubtful that his career .367 average or his 12 AL batting championships ever will be. Joining the Tigers in 1905 from Augusta, he hit .316 as a 19-year-old regular in 1906 and closed by hitting .323 as a 41-year-old regular with the A's in 1928. He hit over .400 three times, topped by a .420 in 1911. During World War I, he served overseas as a captain in the Chemical Warfare Division. From 1921 through 1926 he served as a playing manager for the Tigers. As a result of his offensive output, he was among the five original inductees into baseball's Hall of Fame in 1936. Cobb was paid well for his services, reaching $50,000, and he invested well — especially in Coca-Cola stocks — so that he was able to retire to Georgia as a gentleman of leisure. In 1953 he donated a reported $100,000 to the Cobb Educational Foundation to assist young Georgians in attending college. Suffering from diabetes and prostate cancer, he died at Atlanta on July 17, 1961, at age 74. (*Baseball-Reference.com; Total Baseball; New York Times; Atlanta Constitution*) **Photograph on page 34**

Ty Cobb (left) with his friend and batting rival Shoeless Joe Jackson in 1914.

Bob Coleman, a slow-footed, strong-armed catcher, played in 116 games in three trials with the Pirates and Indians. He first came up with the Pirates in 1913, and in 1914 played in 73 games, hitting .267. He played briefly with the Indians in 1916 and worked in a defense plant during World War I. In all he wore a baseball uniform for 47 seasons as player, coach and manager, spending 24 years managing in the Three-I League. Coleman managed the Braves in 1944–45 and spent four seasons as a coach for the Red Sox, Tigers and Braves. At the time of his death he was a full-time scout for the Braves. Born in Huntington, IN, Coleman died of cancer in Boston on July 16, 1959, at age 68. (*Sporting News; New York Times; Baseball Encyclopedia*)

Eddie Collins, the second-baseman on Connie Mack's famous "$100,000 infield," played 25 seasons in the American League, appearing in six World Series for the A's (1910, 1911, 1913, 1914) and White Sox (1917, 1919). He joined the A's in September 1906 (under the name Eddie Sullivan); 1908 was the first of 20 seasons as a regular. His career totals show 3315 hits (eighth on the all-time list), good for a .333 average. He also hit .328 in 34 World Series games, stealing a record 14 bases. Returning to the A's in 1927, he became a coach and finished his playing career with them in 1930. A Columbia University graduate, Collins became vice-president, treasurer and business manager for the Boston Red Sox in 1933, holding these positions until the time of his death. He was among the fourth group of players elected to the Hall of Fame in 1939. Collins died in Boston of a heart condition on March 25, 1951. He was 63 years old. (*Baseball's Best; Baseball-Reference.com; SABR Collegiate Database; New York Times*)

John (Shano) Collins spent 16 seasons with the White Sox and Red Sox, 12 as a regular outfielder/first baseman. Coming to the White Sox from Springfield in 1910, he became the regular right fielder despite a .197 batting average. He later platooned in right field with left-handed hitting Nemo Leibold for the 1917 and 1919 AL champion White Sox. A career .264 hitter, he hit .303 in 1920 and .290 in 1912. In 10 World Series games he hit .270. Released by the Red Sox in August 1925 to manage at Pittsfield, Collins then continued to manage in the minors through 1930. After managing the Red Sox in 1931–32, he left organized baseball and became a painter for the Hotel Kenmore, retiring in 1951. A lifelong resident of the Boston area, he died suddenly at his home in Newton on September 10, 1955, at age 69. (*Sporting News; Hall of Fame file; Baseball Encyclopedia; Chicago Daily Tribune*)

John (Zip) Collins, whose nickname came from the strength of his throwing arm, hit .292 between the Pirates and Braves in 1915. A left-handed hitting outfielder, he played in 286 major league games, hitting .253. The 22-year-old began with the Pirates in 1914. After finishing with the A's in 1921, Collins played minor league ball until 1925 and then managed in the minors before becoming a salesman for Consolidated Edison. During World War II he worked in a defense plant. Later he became a leader in efforts to construct a retirement home for former major league baseball players. The Brooklyn native died of a heart ailment at Manassas, VA, on December 19, 1983. He was 91 years old. (*Sporting News; Washington Post; Baseball Necrology; Total Baseball*)

Anna (Pete) Compton hit .280 as the Browns regular right fielder in 1912, but in a major league career covering parts of six seasons, he hit only .241 in 286 games. He joined the Browns at the end of 1911 from Battle

Eddie Collins

Doc Cook

Creek, and later he played for the St. Louis Federals, the Braves, the Pirates and the Giants. After leaving the Giants in 1918, he played at San Francisco, Houston, Wichita and Denver. He managed in the Texas League in 1925 and in the Arizona State League in 1928. Compton was a native of San Marcos, TX, but resided in Kansas City, MO, where he was an American Association star in 1914–15. There he managed and coached amateur baseball teams in the Ban Johnson and Three and Two leagues. He died in Kansas City on February 3, 1978, at age 88. (*Kansas City Star; Hall of Fame file; Sporting News; Total Baseball; New York Times; Los Angeles Times*)

Joe Connolly hit .306 as a regular outfielder for the "Miracle Braves" of 1914. A three-year regular with the Braves, he hit a career .288. The Braves had acquired him from Montreal via inter-league waivers in 1913. Released to Indianapolis in 1917, he played semi-pro ball in Providence instead. Thereafter he served as baseball coach at Providence College and Sacred Heart Academy. From Woonsocket, RI, the city that produced Henri Rondeau and Larry Lajoie, Connolly was elected to the Rhode Island General Assembly, serving two years each in the House and Senate. He also acquired a farm and worked for nine years as an investigator for the State Board of Milk Control. Connolly died of heart disease at his home in North Smithfield, RI, on September 1, 1943, at age 57. (*Providence Journal; Sporting News; Total Baseball; Boston Daily Globe*)

Luther (Doc) Cook was the regular right fielder for the Yankees in 1914 and 1915, hitting .283 in 1914 and .271 in 1915. He attended Vanderbilt University before entering professional baseball and came to the Yankees from Austin of the Texas League in August 1913. Early in 1916 he was assigned to Oakland and in 1917 was sold to Memphis. Born in Witt, TX, Cook was a long-time resident of Lawrenceburg, TN, where he died on June 30, 1973, at age 87. Neither his obituary nor his death certificate lists an occupation other than professional baseball player. (*Hall of Fame file; Lawrenceburg Times; Tennessee Certificate of Death; Los Angeles Times; SABR Collegiate Database*)

Jack Coombs won 70 games in three years (1910–12) for the A's. In 1910 he won 31 games, 13 by shutouts and had a 1.30 ERA. After typhoid fever settled in his spine in 1912, he missed two seasons and was never so effective again, finishing a 14-year career with 159 victories. Playing in three World Series, he won 5 games without a loss. Coombs joined the A's in July 1906 directly from Colby College and turned in a 10–10 record for the remainder of the season. Released by the Dodgers in 1918, he had one unsuccessful managerial stint with the Phillies and one year of coaching with the Tigers in 1920. Thereafter Coombs became a very successful college coach, spending 26 years at Duke and writing a textbook on baseball strategy. He died of a heart attack at his home in Palestine, TX, on April 15, 1957. He was 74 years old. (*Sporting News; Total Baseball; SABR Collegiate Database; New York Times*)

Claude Cooper joined the Giants in 1913 from Fort Worth of the Texas League. Previously he had enjoyed a standout career at

Jack Coombs

Claude Cooper

Texas Christian University. As a rookie he hit .300 in 27 games and played in two World Series games. Jumping to the Federal League in 1914, he was a two-year regular with Brooklyn, hitting .294 in 1915. Subsequent trials with the Phillies in 1916 and 1917 were not successful. After serving in World War I, he had a solid career with Oakland of the PCL, retiring in 1930. Returning to Plainview, TX, Cooper operated a tobacco store and worked at odd jobs. He died of pneumonia on January 21, 1974, at age 81. (*Hall of Fame file; information supplied by Sid Cooper, Jr.; New York Times; SABR Collegiate Database; Los Angeles Times*)

Wilbur Cooper, a left-handed sinker specialist, won 216 major league games, 202 with the Pirates, a club record. In a remarkable record of consistency, he averaged more than 270 innings, 22 complete games, and 17 victories for 12 consecutive seasons. In 1920, his best season, he had 24 wins and a 2.39 ERA. A control pitcher, Cooper averaged only 2.2 walks per nine innings over his career. He came to the Pirates from Columbus in August 1912, throwing two shutouts in his six-game trial. Traded to the Cubs in 1924, Cooper saw his career decline. Sent down in mid-1926, he pitched in the minors through

Wilbur Cooper

1930 and later managed (1935–37) in the Pennsylvania State Association before leaving baseball. The native of Bearsville, WV, made his home in Pittsburgh, where he became a successful real estate salesman. In 1969 he was voted the left-handed pitcher on the all-time Pittsburgh team. Cooper died at Encino, CA, on August 7, 1973, at age 81. (*Sporting News; Baseball-Reference.com; New York Times; Deadball Stars of the National League*)

Roy Corhan was the regular shortstop for the Cardinals in 1916, hitting .210 in 92 games. An earlier 43-game trial with the White Sox in 1911 had yielded a .214 average. He had joined the White Sox from St. Joseph. Beaned by the Yankee's Russ Ford, Corhan was sent down to San Francisco, where he was considered the best fielding shortstop in the PCL. In 1917 the Cardinals returned him to the Seals. Corhan refused a 1921 trade to Vernon because of the business interests he had developed in San Francisco, where he ultimately spent 30 years as an insurance broker with Mutual Life Insurance Company. He died there of a heart attack on November 24, 1958, at age 71. (*California Certificate of Death; Sporting News; Chicago Daily Tribune; Los Angeles Times*)

Dan Costello, a much sought after basketball and baseball star at Mount St. Mary's College, played two games with the Yankees in 1913 before graduating from college. Beginning in 1914 he played three seasons as a Pirate outfielder, hitting .297 in 21 games in 1914. His career totals show a .243 average for 154 games. Released to Toronto in 1916, he retired to enter Harvard Law School. Costello played briefly for Toronto in 1917 and for Vancouver in 1921 before retiring to St. Mary's, PA. He died there of pneumonia on March 26, 1936. He was 43 years old. (*Pennsylvania Certificate of Death; Washington Post; Baseball Encyclopedia; Hall of Fame File; SABR Collegiate Database*)

Frederick (Fritz) Coumbe had a 2.79 ERA and 38 wins in an 8-year major league career with Boston, Cleveland and Cincinnati. The Red Sox drafted him from Utica for the 1914 season, trading him to the Indians in mid-season. In his best season Coumbe worked 150 innings while winning 13 games for the 1918 Indians. Sent down in 1919, he won 19 games at St. Paul to earn a final trial with the Reds. After leaving the majors in 1921, he played and managed in the minors through 1931. Coumbe was a resident of South Corning, NY, and following his baseball career, he became a carpenter, working in construction for Corning Glass Works. Suffering from bronchial pneumonia, the 88-year-old Coumbe died at Paradise, CA, on March 21, 1978. (*Hall of Fame file; California Certificate of Death; Sporting News; Total Baseball; Boston Daily Globe*)

Harry Coveleski (Kowalewski) earned the nickname "The Giant Killer" when he defeated the Giants three times in the last five days of the 1908 season, depriving them of the NL championship. He had only four wins that season. He had first joined the Phillies at the end of 1907, coming from Wildwood, NJ. Born of Polish parents in Shamokin, PA, Coveleski won 81 games with a 2.39 ERA in nine seasons before leaving the majors in 1918 with a sore arm. But in a three-year

Harry Coveleski

period (1914–16) the left-hander turned in 22–12, 22–13 and 21–11 records for the Tigers. He always refused to pitch against his brother Stan when the Tigers played Cleveland. After two comeback trials in the minors, Coveleski left baseball, working as a plainclothesman at a Ford plant, as a policeman, as a bartender, as a cafe operator, and as a watchman at a silk plant. In 1937 he opened his own cafe, "The Giant Killer," in Shamokin, PA. He died at Shamokin on August 4, 1950, at age 64. (*Sporting News; New York Times; Total Baseball; Chicago Daily Tribune*)

Stan Coveleski (Kowalewski), the younger, right-handed half of the pitching Kowalewski brothers, threw eleven straight 225-inning seasons for the Indians and Senators, winning 20 games five times. Among his 215 career victories were four consecutive seasons of 22, 24, 24, and 23 wins. Along the way he led the AL twice in shutouts and twice in ERA. In the 1920 World Series he had three complete game victories, downing the Dodgers 3–1, 5–1 and 3–0. These achievements earned him a place in the Hall of Fame in 1969. He pitched briefly for the A's at the end of 1912, and came up to stay with the Indians in 1916, coming from Portland. After finishing his major league career with the Yankees in 1928, Coveleski moved to South Bend, IN, and operated a service station. He died at South Bend on March 20, 1984, at age 94. (*Hall of Fame file; Washington Post; New York Times; Total Baseball*)

Maurice (Molly) Craft joined the Senators one year out of high school. As a 20 year old, he was promoted from Norfolk of the Virginia League. His four trials with the Senators as a pitcher (1916–19) resulted in a 0–4, 3.57 ERA record for 80.1 innings. In 1919 the Senators sent him down to Minneapolis, ending his major league career. Craft continued to pitch and play outfield in the minors into his forties. According to his daughter-in-law, he became a police officer after leaving baseball. Craft was a native of Portsmouth, VA, but died in Los Angeles on October 25, 1978, at age 82. (*Sporting News/information supplied by Mrs. M. M. Craft, II; Total Baseball; Washington Post*)

Otis (Doc) Crandall was a doctor of sick ballgames, making 168 relief appearances in 10 seasons. Thirty-seven of his 102 wins were in relief, and he had an additional 21 career saves. As a 20-year-old rookie he started 24 games, winning 12, for the 1908 Giants and compiled a 17–4 mark in 1910. In the 1911 World Series he threw four scoreless innings in relief and was the winning pitcher in Game Five. In 1915 Crandall had 21 wins for the St. Louis Federals. A career .285 hitter, he also played 85 games in field positions. Released by the Browns to Oakland in 1916, Crandall spent the remainder of his playing career — except for five games with the Braves in 1918 — in the PCL, where he won 224 more games before retiring in 1929. He continued in baseball as a coach for the Pirates and later as a coach and manager in the minors before leaving baseball in 1938. After a long illness, Crandall died at Bell, CA, on August 17, 1951. He was 63 years old. (*Sporting News; Deadball Stars of the National League; Baseball Encyclopedia; Los Angeles Times*)

Doc Crandall

Sam (Red) Crane played in 174 games in a seven-year major league career with four clubs. The A's promoted the 19-year-old from Greensboro of the North Carolina League at the end of 1914. Considered a "flashy fielder and not so hot with the bat," Crane played briefly with the A's (1914–16) and the Senators (1917), but spent more time in the minors. In 1921, his best year, he played in 73 games as a Reds shortstop, hitting .233. After leaving the Dodgers early in 1922, he played in the Pacific Coast and International Leagues through 1927. In 1929 he was convicted of the second-degree murder of a former girlfriend Della Lyter and her escort Jack Oren, a crime for which he spent 15 years in Graterford Prison in Eastern Pennsylvania. Connie Mack helped secure Crane's release from prison in 1944 and found him a job as a checker for U.S. Lines. He died of cancer in Philadelphia on November 12, 1955, at age 61. (*Hall of Fame file; Pennsylvania Certificate of Death; Baseball Encyclopedia; Sporting News*)

Clifford (Gavvy) Cravath had unimpressive trials with the Red Sox, White Sox and Senators before becoming, at age 31, one of the best power hitters in the National League. During an eight-year period (1912–19) he led the NL in homers six times. In 1915 he hit a then major league record 24 homers, helping the Phillies become NL champions. The Red Sox had bought the 27 year old from Los Angeles in 1907. After he hit .363 with 29 homers at Minneapolis, the Reds acquired him in 1912. Released as player/manager by the Phillies in 1920, Cravath spent two seasons in the minors and then used his baseball savings to invest in Laguna Beach, CA, real estate. As the town grew and prospered, his investments paid off. For 36 years he also served as a justice of the peace for Laguna Beach. Cravath died there on May 23, 1963, at age 82. (*Sporting News; Total Baseball; Deadball Stars of the National League; New York Times*)

Sam Crawford hit 309 career triples, making him the most prolific of all time. A 17-year regular for the Reds and Tigers, he banged out 2961 hits for a .309 average, along the way leading the leagues in triples (6 times), homers (twice), RBI's (3 times) and runs (once). These numbers led to his election to the Hall of Fame in 1957. He entered the Reds lineup in September 1899 with less than a season of minor league ball behind him, hitting .307 in 31 games. In the NL/AL war, he was awarded to the Tigers in 1903 and began batting behind Ty Cobb. He played on three pennant-winning teams in 1907–1909, but hit only .243 in 17 World Series games. After leaving the Tigers, he moved to California in 1918 to play for the Los Angeles Angels and, at age 39, led the PCL with 239 hits. In 1921 he retired to his home in Burbank, CA, where he raised roses and lived a quiet, Spartan lifestyle. He died at Hollywood, CA, on June 15, 1968, at age 88. (*Baseball's Best; Total Baseball; New York Times; The Glory of Their Time; Los Angeles Times*)

Minot (Cap) Crowell joined the A's directly from Brown University in 1915. *The Washington Post* noted that he "seemed to have good control, plenty of smoke, a good curve, and great change of pace." In parts of two seasons the right-hander compiled a 2–11 record with a 5.17 ERA before being sent down to Baltimore. The Massachusetts native served with the 26th Engineers Division in Europe during World War I. He then moved to Central Falls, RI, where he became a vice-president and secretary of a printing firm. He died there on September 30, 1962, at age 70. (*Sporting News; SABR Collegiate Database; Total Baseball; Washington Post*)

Walt Cruise, a left-handed hitting outfielder, spent 10 years in the majors, half as a regular with the Cardinals and Braves. He came to St. Louis in 1914 from Jacksonville and was traded to the Braves in 1919. He hit .346 in 1921 and finished with a career average of .277. Twice in his career he hit 500-foot homers into the right field stands at Braves Field, a feat no other player was able to do even once. After leaving the majors in 1924, Cruise operated a hardware store in his hometown of Sylacauga, AL, and then became supervisor of the city water filtration plant, using his spare time to manage semipro teams and scout for the Cardinals. He died at Sylacauga on January 9, 1975, at age 84. (*Sporting News; Total Baseball; Atlanta Constitution*)

Norman (Nick) Cullop, a "fast" left-hander "with a good assortment of curves," spent more than 20 seasons in organized baseball. In six major league seasons he won 57 games—36 for Kansas City of the Federal League—with a 2.73 ERA. He came to the Indians in 1913 from New Orleans. In 1916, following his FL sojourn, he turned in a

Nick Cullop

13–6, 2.05 ERA season with the Yankees. Following military service in World War I, Cullop played, managed or coached in the minors until 1932 — except for four games with the Browns in 1921. Then he moved to Bishop, VA, and became manager of a mine team from the Pocahontas Fuel Company in the 6-team industrial league. By rule he had to be on the mine payroll, so he operated a machine inside the mine and stayed with the company after the baseball league folded. Following a stroke, Cullop died at Tazewell, VA, on April 15, 1961, at age 73. (*Hall of Fame file; Virginia Certificate of Death; Baseball-Reference.com*)

George Cunningham posted a 2.75 ERA in 150 plus innings of work as a Tiger rookie in 1916. He came to the Tigers after leading the Southern Association with 24 wins and 167 strikeouts while pitching for Chattanooga. When his arm began to go bad in 1918, he played 20 games in the outfield, but hit only .233. Returned to Chattanooga in 1919, he pitched and played outfield for the Lookouts, earning another brief trial with the Tigers in 1921. He left the Tigers with 16 major league wins and a .224 batting average. The Minnesota-born right-hander returned to Chattanooga (where he continued to play) and married a former Miss Chattanooga. He later retired there. Cunningham died at Chattanooga on March 10, 1972, at age 77. (*Hall of Fame file; Chattanooga News-Free Press; Encyclopedia of Minor League Baseball; Atlanta Constitution; information supplied by Mrs. Ruby Gay*)

Murphy Currie, a right-hander from Fayetteville, NC, had a scintillating 1.88 ERA in 14.1 innings of relief for the 1916 Cardinals. In December 1917 he joined the navy for service in World War I. Currie was "found dead in bed" in a residence hotel in Asheboro, NC, on June 18, 1939. The listed cause of death was "probable heart attack." His death certificate listed him as divorced and unemployed for the past year. Currie had last worked as an insurance agent for Connecticut Mutual. He was 45 years old at the time of death. (*North Carolina Certificate of Death; Baseball Encyclopedia; Washington Post*)

George Cutshaw played second base for the NL champion Dodgers in 1916, hitting .260 and leading the NL in putouts and assists. His career offensive statistics show a .260 average and 271 stolen bases. A regular for 11 of his 12 major league seasons, he led NL second-basemen in putouts 5 times, in assists and total chances four times and in fielding three times. Born in Illinois, Cutshaw played at Notre Dame in 1908 before entering baseball. The Dodgers drafted him from Oakland in 1912. In addition he played at Pittsburgh and Detroit, where he also coached. Before leaving baseball, he had purchased a ranch near Brawley, CA, which he later converted into a grapefruit orchard. He died at San Diego on August 22, 1973, at age 85. (*Sporting News; Baseball Encyclopedia; Los Angeles Times; SABR Collegiate Database*)
Photograph on page 45

Gene (Jean) Dale worked 296 innings for the Reds in 1915, his record being 18–17 with a 2.46 ERA. In four seasons he compiled a 21–28 record. The Cardinals had acquired him from Dallas in 1911 and sent him to Montreal in 1912 with a 0–7 major league record. The Reds picked him up from Montreal for 1915. Dropped by the Reds in mid–1916 for "indifferent work," he never again pitched in the majors. In 1919, pitching for the Salt Lake City Bees in the PCL, Dale allegedly collected bonus money from gamblers who had fixed the PCL championship in favor of the Vernon Tigers. While he was not one of the players officially banned from the PCL, his *Hall of Fame file* suggests that his career ended there. He pitched for Dallas in 1920, but in 1921 he was expelled by the National Association of Minor Leagues. Dale returned to his native St. Louis, where he worked as a plater for Steel Products Co. He died of hypertension at St. Louis on March 20, 1958. He was 68 years old. (*Hall of Fame file/Missouri Certifi-*

cate of Death; Total Baseball; St. Louis Post-Dispatch; Sporting News; Washington Post; Los Angeles Times)

Talbot (Jack) Dalton is one of baseball's great disappearance acts. The University of Virginia product made his major league debut with Brooklyn in 1910, coming from Des Moines. Hitting only .227, he was optioned to Newark in 1911. He helped Toronto and Newark win IL championships in 1912 and 1913 respectively. Recalled, he hit .319 for the Dodgers in 1914 and jumped to the Buffalo Federals in 1915 after a salary dispute. After hitting .293 there, Dalton was ultimately signed by the Tigers for 1916, but after 8 games was sold to San Francisco. In 1917 he was released as player/manager by Joplin. Attempts by baseball researchers to trace his career after that have proved fruitless. One report had him serving as a high-ranking official in the Veterans Administration, but this rumor could be neither proved nor disproved by employment records. (*Hall of Fame file; New York Times; SABR Collegiate Database; Los Angeles Times*)

Tom Daly, a Canadian-born catcher/outfielder/infielder, appeared on major league rosters for eight seasons—seven in Chicago. He came from Lowell to the White Sox at the end of 1913, appearing in one game but qualifying for the "Round the World" tour organized by the Giants and White Sox. Daly hit .233 in 61 games for the White Sox in 1914 and .238 in 51 games for the Cubs in 1921. Between Chicago engagements he played for the Indians in 1916. Dropped by the Cubs to Los Angeles in 1922, he played in the minors through 1931. After managing Toronto in 1933, Daly served as a Red Sox coach until 1944, when he became their chief scout. After a year's illness, he died at his home in Bedford, MA, on November 7, 1946, at age 54. (*Sporting News; Total Baseball; Chicago Daily Tribune; Los Angeles Times*) **Photograph on page 44**

Dave Danforth joined the A's from Baylor University in August 1911 and went on to receive his DDS from the University of Maryland in 1915, pitching for that college team after his professional debut. A left-hander with a sailing fastball, he spent 10 seasons in the majors, winning 71 games, 28 in relief. The strong hands, which allowed him to succeed as a dentist, also allowed him to get such movement on his pitches—"described as a combination of the fast ball, the spit ball and the emery ball"—that he was often accused of tampering with the ball. He pitched in 50 games, winning 11 and saving 9 for the champion White Sox in 1917, and he won 31 games as a Browns starter in 1923–24. Leaving the majors after 1925, Danforth then devoted full time to his dental practice. He died at Baltimore on September 19, 1970, at age 80. (*Hall of Fame file; SABR Collegiate Database; Atlanta Constitution; Washington Post; Total Baseball*)

Jake Daubert came from Shamokin in the anthracite region of Pennsylvania, the same town that sent the Coveleski brothers and Steve O'Neill to the majors. Purchased by the Dodgers from Memphis in the fall of 1909, Daubert spent 15 years as a regular first baseman—for the Dodgers (1910–18) and then for the Reds (1919–24). A solid fielder, he twice led the NL in fielding and double plays. He also won two NL batting championships in 1913 and 1914 and hit over .300 ten times, for a career average of .303. He won the Chalmers Award in 1913 as the NL's Most Valuable Player and captained two NL champion teams—the 1916 Dodgers and the 1919 Reds. Daubert became ill late in the 1924 season and died in Cincinnati on October 9, 1924, "from complications following an appendectomy." He was 40 years of age. (*Biographical Dictionary of American Sport: Baseball; Deadball Stars of the National League; Sporting News; Total Baseball; New York Times*) **Photograph on page 45**

George (Hooks) Dauss was a small right-hander with a big curve—hence the nickname. He won 221 games for the Tigers between 1912 and 1926—still a Detroit record.

White Sox rookies, catcher Tom Daly (left) and pitcher Red Faber, during the 1914 Round the World Tour.

In 14 full seasons Dauss never won fewer than 10 games and had only three losing years. In 1915 he reached 24 victories and won 21 games during two other seasons. He worked more than 200 innings 12 times in a 13-year period and closed with a 3.30 ERA. The Indianapolis native joined the Tigers in September 1912 from St. Paul and completed both his starts that fall. Because of a heart ailment, Dauss retired after the 1926 season and operated a farm near St. Louis. After a long illness he died at St. Louis on July 27, 1963, at age 73. (*Sporting News; New York Times; Total Baseball; Washington Post*)

1916 Dodger infield. From the left: First baseman Jake Daubert, second basemen George Cutshaw, shortstop Ivy Olson and third baseman Mike Mowrey.

Dave Davenport led the FL in games, starts, complete games, innings, strikeouts and shutouts in 1915 while compiling a 22–18 record for the St. Louis Terriers. In six seasons with the Reds, Terriers, and Browns, the 6'6" right-hander from DeRidder, LA, won 73 games with a 2.93 ERA. He pitched in an AL-leading 59 games in 1916, and his 17 wins in 1917 placed him 5th. Davenport entered the majors in 1914 when the Reds purchased him from San Antonio. After leaving the Browns in 1919, he pitched semi-pro ball in Idaho and Colorado until 1925, when he returned to organized baseball. Until his death from prostate cancer on October 12, 1954, Davenport worked in a factory and later drove a taxi in El Dorado, AR. He was 64 years old. (*Evening Times[El Dorado]; Baseball Reference.com; Sporting News*)

Harry Davis joined the Giants in 1895 from Pawtucket and went on to become a 13-season regular at first base. He played with the Giants, Pirates, Louisville and Washington—all NL clubs—into 1899 before being returned to the minors. Shifting to the A's in 1901, he led the AL in homers four times and in triples three times while playing on three World Championship teams, also serving as the A's captain. A career .277 hitter, Davis hit over .300 four times and hit .353 in the 1910 World Series. After managing Cleveland for part of 1912, he returned to the A's as a coach, playing a few games each season through 1917. A graduate of Girard College, Davis worked for the A's as both an accountant and a scout from 1919 to 1927, while also serving on the Philadelphia City Council. After losing most of his baseball earnings

Harry Davis

during the depression, he became a private detective. Following a stroke, Davis died in Philadelphia on August 11, 1947. He was 74 years old. (*Sporting News; Total Baseball; New York Times*)

Charlie Deal was the third baseman on the 1914 "Miracle Braves," hitting .210 in 79 games. Refused a $500 bonus, he signed with the St. Louis Federals in 1915. However, his best years were with the Cubs (1917–21) when he twice hit .289 (more than 30 points over his career average), led the NL in fielding three times, and helped win a NL championship in 1918. Deal first came to the majors with Detroit from Jackson of the Southern Michigan League in 1912. He later played in the PCL (1922–25) and in the Southern Association, finishing with New Orleans in 1927. Deal was a native of Wilkinsburg, PA, but lived most of his life in Pasadena, CA. He died at Covina, CA, on September 6, 1979, at age 87. His obituary mentions no post-baseball occupation, but Bill Lee asserts that Deal "was a special agent for Southern California Gas Company." (*Hall of Fame file; San Gabriel Valley Tribune[Covina, CA]; Total Baseball; Baseball Necrology*)

John (Hank) DeBerry played one year at the University of Tennessee before entering professional baseball in 1914. After brief trials with the Indians in 1916 and 1917, he served in the U.S. Navy during World War I. From 1922 through 1930 he was the regular catcher for Hall of Fame pitcher Dazzy Vance in Brooklyn. In his best season he hit .301 in 85 games for the Dodgers in 1922. Overall he hit .267 for 11 seasons. Sent down in 1931, DeBerry had three stints as a minor league manager, one as an umpire and one as an executive, but spent most of the rest of his life as a scout for the Giants. He also had "considerable property interests" in Savannah, TN, where he made his home. He died unexpectedly there on September 10, 1951, at age 56. (*Sporting News; Baseball Encyclopedia; New York Times*)

Art Dede was hitless in his only time at bat in the majors while catching for the Dodgers on October 4, 1916, and then served as a bullpen catcher during the 1916 World Series. The *New York Times* describes him as a "semi-professional." A native of Brooklyn, he played for and managed semi-pro clubs in the New York City area following his experience with the Dodgers. Dede later scouted for the Dodgers, but was scouting for the Yankees at the time of his death. He died of prostate cancer at Keene, NH, on September

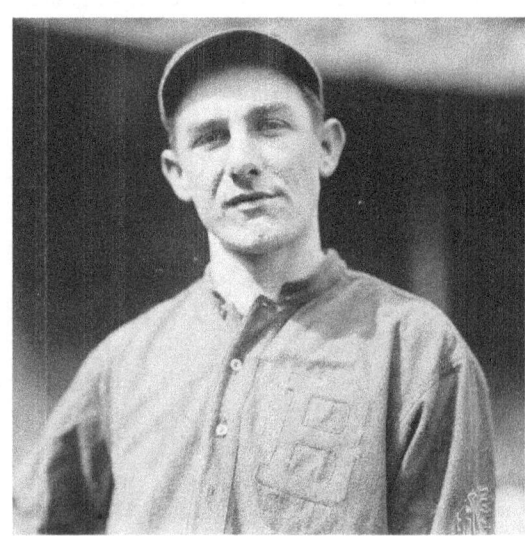

Charlie Deal

6, 1971, at age 76. (*Sporting News; New Hampshire Certificate of Death; New York Times; Baseball Encyclopedia*)

William (Wheezer) Dell was the only Nevada-born player among the Men of '16. The big (6'4") right-hander posted a 2.55 ERA for more than 430 major league innings. He had 11–10 and 8–9 records for the Dodgers in 1915–16, his only full seasons in the majors, and pitched one inning in the 1916 World Series. Dell pitched in three games in 1912 after the Cardinals signed him from the independent ranks. The Dodgers acquired him in 1915 after he had led the Northwestern League with 21 wins for Seattle. Sent down in 1917, Dell pitched in the minors until 1926, finishing with Beaumont. After leaving baseball, he moved to California, where he worked as a lineman in heavy construction. He died of bronchopneumonia at Independence, CA, on August 24, 1966, at age 79. (*California Certificate of Death; Sporting News; Total Baseball; Encyclopedia of Minor League Baseball*)

Al Demaree pitched eight seasons in the majors, winning 80 games with a 2.77 ERA. In a four-year stretch (1913–16) he won 56 games, including 13 for the NL champion Giants in 1913 and 14 for the NL champion Phillies in 1915. Demaree was the starter and loser in Game 4 of the 1913 World Series. He joined the Giants in September 1912 after winning 18 games at Mobile. In his most

Al Demaree

productive major league season, he went 19–14 for the 1916 Phillies. Having attended the Chicago Art Institute, Demaree began selling cartoons while still an active player. After leaving baseball, he became a nationally syndicated sports cartoonist, whose work appeared in more than 200 newspapers. *The Sporting News* used his cartoons regularly for more than 30 years. Demaree died at Los Angeles on April 15, 1962, at age 77. (*The Ballplayers; Chicago Daily Tribune; Total Baseball; Atlanta Constitution; New York Times*)

Wheezer Dell

Paul (Shorty) Des Jardien, from the small Kansas town of Coffeyville, was a two-time football all–American at the University of Chicago. There he won twelve letters in football, basketball, baseball and track. Upon graduation the 6'5" right hander signed with Cleveland and pitched one inning in relief on May 20, 1916, giving up two earned runs before being sent to Marshaltown. He coached football at Oberlin and then began to pitch in the independent Midwest League. Commissioned a second lieutenant of artillery, Des Jardien served in World War I. After the War he also played professional football in the Chicago area. Later Des Jardien became president of a sheet metal company in Los Angeles. At age 62, he died of a heart attack on March 7, 1956, at his home in Monrovia, CA. (*Sporting News; Hall of Fame File; Baseball Encyclopedia; SABR Collegiate Database; Chicago Daily Tribune*)

Edward (Moxie) Divis, a star with the amateur Cleveland Tellings, was given a tryout by Connie Mack in 1916. Appearing in 3 games, one as an outfielder, the 22-year-old Divis collected a single in six at bats. After playing for Oklahoma City in 1917, he returned to the Tellings, for whom he played until 1931. For the last 33 years of his life Divis served as a district circulation manager for the *Cleveland Plain Dealer*. He died in the Cleveland suburb of Lakewood on December 19, 1955, at age 61. (*Cleveland Plain Dealer; Baseball-Reference.com*)

Bill Doak won 19 games with a NL leading 1.72 ERA as a 23 year old in 1914. In a 16-year career — primarily with the Cardinals — he won 169 games, including a 20-win season and another ERA crown. A native of Pittsburgh, Doak pitched in one game for the Reds in 1912 and then joined the Cardinals from Akron in 1913. Remaining with the Cardinals through 1923, Doak was traded to the Dodgers in 1924. Out of baseball in 1925–26 to sell real estate, he returned to win 11 games in 1927. Out two more seasons, he

Bill Doak

finished with the Cardinals in 1929. Moving to Bradenton, FL, Doak operated a confectionery store, served as golf professional at the country club, and coached and sponsored youth baseball clubs. He also collected "handsome royalties" from Rawlings Sporting Goods for his signature glove model. Doak was found dead in his bathtub, an apparent heart attack victim, on November 16, 1954, at age 63. (*Sporting News; Baseball-Reference.com; Deadball Stars of the National League; New York Times*)

William (Wild Bill) Donovan led the NL in walks in 1901 to gain his nickname; however, for his career he walked only 3.2 men per nine innings, an average figure. In the 1901–10 decade he won 171 of his 186 career victories. He went 25–15 for the Dodgers in 1901 and 25–4 for the AL champion Tigers in 1907. Despite a 1.29 ERA for 21 innings, he had only a loss and a tie in two World Series starts that year. Donovan first pitched in the majors with the Washington Nationals in 1898, coming from Waterbury. He managed Providence in 1913–14 and became playing manager of the Yankees (1915–17). After service in the Naval Reserves in World War I, he managed Jersey City (1919–20). Donovan later managed the Phillies and at the time of his death, he was manager of New Haven of the Eastern League. Donovan was killed in a train wreck near Forsyth, NY, on December 9, 1923, at age 47. (*Sporting News; Total Baseball; New York Times; Los Angeles Times; Atlanta Constitution*)

Charles (Red) Dooin spent four years trying to catch on in organized baseball before being signed by the Phillies in 1902. Despite weighing less than 150 pounds, he spent eight seasons as their regular catcher, but played every field position except shortstop in his 15 years in the majors. He claimed to be the first catcher to wear shin guards, using rattan and paper-mache pads under his stockings. A career .240 hitter, he hit .328 as a part-time catcher in 1911. Dooin was a player-manager for the Phillies (1910–14) and player-coach for the Giants in 1916, before being sent down to Rochester. He also managed and caught for Reading in 1919. Having considerable savings and real estate holdings, Dooin retired to Atlantic City, but the Depression wiped out his savings and most of his real estate. At this point he went back to performing in vaudeville and singing on the radio. Dooin died of a heart attack at his home in Rochester, NY, on May 14, 1952, at age 72 (*Sporting News; Deadball Stars of the National League; Total Baseball; New York Times*)

Michael (Mickey) Doolan (Doolittle) was a regular shortstop for the Phillies (1905–13) and for the Baltimore Federals (1914–15), despite a career .230 batting average. He led NL or FL shortstops in games at the position, assists and double plays six times and in putouts 5 times. At the end of the 1913 season, Doolan was selected to the touring team organized by John McGraw and Charles Comiskey which played in 14 foreign countries. Before entering professional baseball, he had played collegiate ball at both Bucknell and Villanova. After closing his playing career with Brooklyn in 1918, he coached the Cubs (1926–28) and the Reds (1930–32). Having studied dentistry at Vil-

Wild Bill Donovan

lanova, Doolan then entered that profession. The Orlando, FL, resident suffered a stroke in 1949. On November 1, 1951, he died of peritonitis from a ruptured appendix. He was 71 years old. (*Sporting News; Hall of Fame file; New York Times; SABR Collegiate Database; Baseball Encyclopedia*)

Larry Doyle, the Giants captain, won the Chalmers Award in 1912 as the most valuable player of the NL, when he hit .330. A career .290 hitter, he had four other seasons over .300, including a league-leading .320 in 1915. He led the NL twice in hits and once each in doubles and triples. Called "Laughing Larry" because of his sense of humor, Doyle played on three consecutive NL championship teams in 1911–13. The coal miner's son joined the Giants in 1907 from Springfield, IL, and immediately became the regular second baseman though he fielded only .917. After retiring as a player at the end of the 1920 season, he remained in the Giants organization in various capacities until he was diagnosed with tuberculosis in 1942. Doyle lived in the Trudeau sanatorium at Saranac Lake, NY, until 1954 and then retired in the town. He died there on March 1, 1974, at age 87. (*New York Times; Baseball Encyclopedia; Deadball Stars of the National League*)

Mike Driscoll, a right-hander from Rockland, MA, joined the A's following graduation from the University of Maine. He pitched in one game on July 6, 1916. Tagged for 6 hits and 3 earned runs in five innings, he took the loss. After serving in World War I, he became a resident of Brockton, MA, where he worked as an industrial machinist. Driscoll died of bronchopneumonia at Foxborough State Hospital, MA, on March 22, 1953, at age 60. (*SABR Collegiate Database; Baseball-Reference.com; Massachusetts Certificate of Death*)

Jean Dubuc entered organized baseball after graduating from Notre Dame and studying for the priesthood. In nine major league seasons, he had 85 wins with a 3.04

Jean Dubuc

ERA. With the Tigers he had records of 17–10 in 1912 and 17–12 in 1915. Bill James asserts that while pitching for the Giants in 1919, Dubuc was involved with Hal Chase and Heinie Zimmerman in trying to fix games, that he had advance knowledge of the 1919 World Series fix, and that he was banned from baseball for life. But Dubuc later played at Syracuse and Toledo and coached and scouted for the Tigers. He also coached baseball at Brown University and served as general manager for the Providence hockey team. After 1936 he spent 20 years as a printer's ink salesman. After a long illness, he died at Fort Myers, FL, on August 29, 1958, at age 70. (*Sporting News; Cappy Cagnon; Bill James' Historical Baseball Abstract; Baseball-Reference.com; SABR Collegiate Database*)

Oscar Dugey was a utility player on two consecutive World Champion teams—the 1914 "Miracle Braves" and the 1915 Phillies. The Braves brought him up from Waco in September 1913. In six seasons Dugey played in 195 games, primarily at second base, hitting .195. Sent down to St. Paul in 1918, he returned for five games with the Braves in 1920. An accomplished sign stealer, Dugey coached for the Cubs from 1921 through 1924. He was a native of Palestine, TX, but lived his last 40 years in Dallas, where he worked as a painter. Dugey died of pneumonia on January 1, 1966, at age 78. (*Total Baseball; Sporting News; Dallas Morning News; Texas Certificate of Death*)

George Dumont, a right hander of French descent, enjoyed his best season in 1917, when he compiled a 2.55 ERA in more than 200 innings for the Senators. He joined Washington in September 1915 from Fargo of the Northern League. His first four starts resulted in three complete games—two shutouts and a 10-inning loss; however, his career totals show a 10–23 record in five seasons. Sold by the Red Sox to Atlanta in 1918, Dumont pitched for the Crackers through 1924, when he was sold to Minneapolis. After retiring from baseball, the Minneapolis native operated a tavern there and later worked as a foreman at Durkee Atwood Corp. Dumont died of coronary thrombosis at Minneapolis on October 13, 1956. He was 61 years old. (*Hall of Fame file; Baseball-Reference.com; Washington Post; Atlanta Constitution*)

Ben Dyer played 105 games in six seasons as a utility infielder for the Giants and Tigers. In 1919, his final season, the Chicago native played in 44 games, hitting .247. He had joined the Giants as a 21-year-old in 1914, playing 14 games over the next two years. The Tigers acquired him from Denver in 1916. After leaving organized baseball, he went to Kenosha, WI, to work for Simmons Mattress Co. and play for the Bed-Makers in the independent Midwest League. Dyer also organized and managed the first Kenosha Junior League baseball team. After a long illness he died at Kenosha Hospital on August 7, 1959, at age 66. (*Kenosha News; New York Times; Chicago Tribune; Baseball-Reference.com*)

Dick Egan became the regular second baseman for the Reds in 1909, hitting .275 and leading the NL in total chances per game. After four years at second, he became a regular at shortstop for the Dodgers in 1914, the year he was selected as a member of John McGraw's all-star team that toured around the world. He finished a nine-year major league career in 1916 with a .249 batting average. Born in Portland, OR, Egan attended Fordham University before entering professional baseball. The Reds drafted him from Harrisburg in September, 1908. Egan managed Aberdeen in 1918, and letters to the Reds in his *Hall of Fame file* suggest that he continued his involvement in baseball as an agent or scout on the Pacific Coast. Egan died of cirrhosis of the liver at Oakland, CA, on July 7, 1947. He was 63 years old. (*Baseball-Reference.com; SABR Collegiate Database; California Certificate of Death; Hall of Fame file*)

Howard Ehmke won 166 games in a 15-year major league career. He pitched briefly for Buffalo of the FL and then joined the Tigers in 1916 after posting a 31–7 record at Syracuse. He worked 185 or more innings for 10 consecutive years—with a year out for the U.S. Navy—and won at least 10 games nine times. In 1923 Ehmke had 20 wins and 28 complete games for the Red Sox. He led the AL with 315 innings in 1924 and in complete games (22) in 1925. Despite pitching only 54 innings for the A's in 1929, Ehmke was a sur-

George Dumont

prise starter in Game 1 of the World Series, striking out a then record 13 Cubs in a 3–1 victory. Retiring early in 1930, he opened a canvas fabricating company near Shibe Park, where he was able to sell infield covers to both the A's and Phillies. Ehmke died in Philadelphia on March 17, 1959, at age 64. (*Sporting News; Total Baseball; New York Times; Encyclopedia of Minor League Baseball*)

Harold (Rowdy) Elliott caught almost half of the Cubs games in 1917, hitting .251 in 85 games. But trials with the Braves in 1910, the Cubs in 1916 and 1918, and the Dodgers in 1920 totaled only 72 additional games. The Braves drafted him from Birmingham in September 1910 and released him to the same club in 1911. Player-manager at Oakland, he was purchased by the Cubs in 1916. After service in World War I, he was released back to Oakland in 1919, from where he was sold to Brooklyn. Released by the Dodgers in 1921, Elliott played with eight different minor league teams. For a while thereafter he worked as an oiler on a Pacific Coast cargo steamer. When Elliott died in San Francisco on February 12, 1934, "from injuries received in a fall from an apartment house window," he was 43 years old and destitute. (*Sporting News; Total Baseball; Los Angeles Times; Chicago Daily Tribune*)

Bert Ellison played five seasons as a utility infielder for the Tigers, hitting .216 in 135 games. He joined the Tigers at the end of 1916 appearing in two games. Over the next four years — with time out for military service — he had four additional trials, the best being 61 games and a .219 average in 1920. But he rocked PCL pitching for 307 hits, 188 RBI's and 496 total bases while playing for San Francisco in 1924. Ellison also managed the Seals from mid–1923 to mid–1926. The University of Arkansas graduate later became an appraiser for the U.S. Customs Service in San Francisco. On August 11, 1955, he died following unsuccessful surgery to remove a cancerous obstruction in the throat. He was 58 years old. (*Hall of Fame file; Sporting News; Baseball Encyclopedia; Encyclopedia of Minor League Baseball*)

Frank Emmer had two trials with the Reds, more than ten years apart. He hit .146 in 42 games as a utility player in 1916. In 1926 he returned to play 79 games at shortstop, hitting .196. He earned his return trip to the majors with his play at Seattle. Overall, Emmer played professional baseball for 18 years, primarily in the Pacific Coast league. In 1927 he set an American Association record for a shortstop by handling 140 chances between errors. After leaving baseball, he was employed as a police chief by Westinghouse Corporation. A native of Crestline, OH, he retired to Homestead, FL, where he died on October 18, 1963, at age 67. (*News Leader [Homestead, FL]; Total Baseball; Los Angeles Times; Boston Daily Globe*)

Clyde Engle was a regular at first base, third base or the outfield during five of his eight major league seasons with the Yankees, Red Sox, Buffalo Federals and Indians. The Dayton, OH, native reached the majors with the Yankees in 1909, coming from Newark. A career .265 hitter, he batted .289 with the Red Sox in 1913 but was released the following season and went to the Federal League. After a brief trial with the Indians in 1916, and a year spent as player/manager at Topeka/Joplin, Engel became baseball coach at the University of Vermont and was later freshman baseball coach at Yale. He also scouted for Toronto of the IL. Engle died of a heart attack at his winter hotel quarters at Boston on December 26, 1939. He was 55 years old. (*Sporting News; Baseball Encyclopedia; New York Times; Boston Daily Globe*)

Eric Erickson, a Swedish-born right-hander, was signed from the Jamestown, NY, sandlots. He had a trial with the Giants at the end of 1914, was dealt to the Tigers, and sent to the PCL. After winning 31 games (with 307 strikeouts and a 1.93 ERA) for San Francisco in 1917, he came to the majors to

Baseball; Baseball-Reference.com; Los Angeles Times)

Bill Evans, a right-hander from Reidsville, NC, posted a 2–13 record for the Pirates in three seasons. He played college ball at both Elon College (1914) and North Carolina State (1915). In 1916, his rookie season, he had a 3.00 ERA in 63 innings after joining the Pirates from the North Carolina League. Evans served in World War I, and pitched for the Pirates in 1919 until he was sent down to Kansas City in June. Later he returned to North Carolina and became a traveling salesman. Following a heart attack, he died at Graham, NC, on December 21, 1946. He was 53 years old. (*North Carolina Certificate of Death; Baseball Encyclopedia; SABR Collegiate Database; Boston Daily Globe; Atlanta Constitution; Washington Post*)

Joe Evans, a graduate of the University of Mississippi, played 11 seasons in the majors with the Indians, Senators and Browns while pursuing a medical degree from Washington University in St. Louis. His career totals show a .259 average for 732 games. He joined the Indians in July 1915 directly from college. After part of a season at Portland in 1916, he became the Indians regular third baseman in 1917. Being in the medical reserves, he played part time in 1918 and 1919 while continuing medical studies. He hit .349 as a part time player in 1920 and .308 in four World Series games that year. Traded to Washington, he was an outfield regular in 1923 and for the next two years he was a part-timer with the Browns. Finishing his internship, Evans became a physician in Gulfport, MS. He took time out to manage the local Cotton States League team in 1927, then spent the remainder of his life practicing medicine. He died at Gulfport on August 9, 1953, at age 58. (*Sporting News; Total Baseball; SABR Collegiate Database; Washington Post*)

Johnny Evers won the Chalmers Award as the NL's most valuable player in 1914, when he helped the "Miracle Braves" win the

Eric Erickson

stay in 1918. With time out for military service, Erickson spent five years with the Tigers and Senators. His career totals show 34 wins with a 3.85 ERA, 12 of those wins coming for the Senators in 1920. When he left professional baseball late in 1922, Erickson returned to Jamestown and worked in the shipping department of Art Medal, Inc., while operating a berry and garden produce farm. In 1930, at age 38, he shut out the Boston Braves while pitching for a Jamestown semi-pro club. Erickson died at Jamestown on May 19, 1965, at age 70. (*Jamestown Post-Journal; Encyclopedia of Minor League*

Johnny Evers

World Championship. He is best remembered, however, as the man between Tinker and Chance on the great Cubs teams of the first decade of the century. A career .270 hitter, he hit as high as .341 in 1912 and .316 in 20 World Series games. The 20-year-old Evers came to the Cubs in 1902 from Troy of the New York State League, weighing just 115 pounds. He was a regular for 11 of the next 12 seasons. After leaving the active playing ranks in 1917, Evers managed the Cubs (1921) and White Sox (1924), coached the White Sox and Braves, scouted for the Giants, was assistant manager for the Braves and general manager for Albany. After 1936 he was appointed stadium superintendent and overseer of sandlot baseball in Albany, NY. Evers suffered a paralytic stroke in 1942 and died following a second stroke on March 28, 1947, a year after being inducted into the Hall of Fame. He was 65 years old. (*Sporting News; Baseball's Best; Deadball Stars of the National League; Total Baseball; New York Times*)

Urban (Red) Faber, the last legal spitball pitcher in the American League, won 254 games in 20 seasons—all with the White Sox. In 16 of those seasons he worked more than 154 innings. He had four 20-win seasons, leading the AL twice in ERA and twice in complete games. In the 1917 World Series he had complete game victories in Game 2 and Game 6 and won Game 5 in relief. In June 1918 he enlisted in the Navy, missing most of the season; in 1919 he developed a sore arm, missing the World Series. Faber came to the White Sox in 1914 after striking out 265 batters at Des Moines. Earlier he had pitched at Loras College. Before he had pitched in an AL game, he made the round-the-world tour as a member of the White Sox. After leaving the White Sox in 1933, Faber operated a bowling alley until 1946, coached the White Sox for three years, and then became a surveyor for the Chicago Highway Department. He was elected to the Hall of Fame in 1964. Faber died at Chicago on September 25, 1976, at age 88. (*Baseball's Best; Total Baseball; Chicago Daily Tribune; New York Times*)
Photograph on page 44

Albert (Bunny) Fabrique, a tiny shortstop, had two trials with the Dodgers in 1916–17, totaling 27 games in which he hit .200. When he came up in 1916 from Providence, he was considered to be "the best shortstop the minors has turned out in years." But in 1917 he was released to Toledo. After serving with the U.S. Navy in World War I, he was sent to Seattle and ultimately to Los Angeles. Fabrique later returned to his hometown of Clinton, MI, where he was employed by Ford Motor Company and later by Clinton Machine Company. Fabrique died at the Veterans Administration Hospital in Ann Arbor, MI, on January 10, 1960. He was 72 years old. (*Ann Arbor News; New York Times; Washington Post; Total Baseball; Los Angeles Times*)

Floyd (Jack) Farmer made some impact when he broke in with Pittsburgh in 1916. Coming from Nashville, the Cumberland College product appeared in 55 games, primarily as a second baseman, hitting .271. After playing with Portland in the PCL, he earned a 1918 trial with the Indians, hitting .222 in seven games as a third baseman. Before finishing as a player, Farmer returned to Portland and also to Nashville. He later managed in the lower minors for the Cardinal organization before World War II and for the Yankee organization until 1950. Farmer made his home at Girard, LA, and died of lung cancer at Columbia, LA, on May 21, 1970, at age 77. (*Hall of Fame file, Richland [LA] Beacon-News; Baseball Encyclopedia; Sporting News; Encyclopedia of Minor League Baseball; Atlanta Constitution; Los Angeles Times*)

Joe Fautsch had one turn at bat in the majors, an unsuccessful pinch hit attempt for the White Sox on April 24, 1916. In early May the 29-year-old infielder was released to Richmond. A bachelor of German descent, he lived with his brother in Minneapolis and worked as a utility meter reader. He was "not interested in … Hall of Fame" attempts to locate former major leaguers. Fautsch died of cancer of the esophagus at New Hope, MN, on March 19, 1971, at age 84. (*Hall of Fame file; Total Baseball; Chicago Daily Tribune*)

Oscar (Happy) Felsch patrolled the White Sox outfield for six seasons (1915–20) before he was banned from professional baseball as a result of his involvement in the "Black Sox" scandal of 1919. A product of the Milwaukee sandlots, Felsch hit .314 for the Milwaukee Brewers in 1914, leading the AA in homers, to gain a trial with the White Sox. After a .248 rookie season, he became a career .293 hitter, reaching .338 in 1920. He hit .273 in the 1917 World Series but only .192 in the 1919 World Series. A tremendous outfielder, he led the AL twice in fielding, once in putouts and once in assists. Felsch returned to the Milwaukee sandlots, playing semi-pro ball until he was past forty. He built a grocery store, operated a number of taverns, and finally worked as a crane operator. Felsch died at Milwaukee on August 17, 1964, at age 73. (*Milwaukee Journal; Baseball-Reference.com; Eight Men Out; New York Times; Sporting News*)

Bill Fincher had a 2.14 ERA in 21 innings for the Browns in 1916 before being released to Portland. The Atlanta native began his professional career with Little Rock in 1915 and was sold to the Browns at the end of that season. He served in World War I, and after his playing career was over, he became a general salesman for Standard Oil Co. Having been in ill health for some time, he took his own life on May 7, 1946, at his home in Shreveport, LA. He was 51 years old. (*Hall of Fame file; Baseball-Reference.com; Louisiana Certificate of Death; Atlanta Constitution*)

Bill Fischer was a regular catcher for the Chicago Federals in 1915, for the Cubs and Pirates in 1916 and for the Pirates in 1917. He hit .329 for the Chi-Feds and .286 for the Pirates, settling for a five-year average of .274 in 412 games. He began his career with the Dodgers in 1913, recalled from Wilkes-Barre. Released to Binghamton in 1918, he played and managed in the minors until 1928. Upon retiring from baseball, the New York City native became an employee of the Endicott-Johnson Corporation. But as early as 1919 the *Washington Post* noted that Fischer "is now a shoe drummer, and a successful one, too." He died at Richmond, VA, on September 4, 1945, at age 54. (*Sporting News; Total Baseball; Atlanta Constitution; Washington Post*)

Bob Fisher was the regular shortstop for the Dodgers in 1913 and the Cubs in 1915, when he hit .287. In seven major league seasons he hit .276 in 503 games. He came up with the Dodgers in 1912 and later played with the Reds and Cardinals, as well as the Cubs. Sent down by the Cardinals in 1919, he continued to play in the minors until 1925. After retiring as a player, he became business manager for his home town Jacksonville club and was employed by the city of Jacksonville in its recreation department. After a long illness he died at Jacksonville on August 4, 1963, at age 76. (*Sporting News; Total Baseball; New York Times*)

Ray Fisher won 100 games in 10 years with the Yankees and Reds, posting an 18–11, 2.11 ERA season for the Yankees in 1915 and a

Ray Fisher

14–5, 2.17 ERA season for the Reds in 1919. The Middlebury, VT, product played at Middlebury College (1907–08) prior to turning professional and joined the Yankees in 1910. He was in military service during World War I, and joined the Reds in 1919, losing a 3–0 duel with Dickie Kerr in Game 3 of the World Series that year. In 1921 he left the Reds over a contract dispute and accepted the coaching position at the University of Michigan, a position he held for 38 years. Reds owner August Herrmann placed his name on the ineligible list, so Fisher was banned from professional baseball for life. In 1960 Fisher was declared to be a "retired player in good standing." He died at Ann Arbor, MI, November 3, 1982, at age 95. (*Sporting News; SABR Collegiate Data Base; Total Baseball; New York Times*)

Wilbur Fisher made one unsuccessful pinch-hitting appearance for the Pirates on June 13, 1916. Two weeks after his debut, the Pirates released him. Before entering professional baseball, Fisher had attended Marshall University. After leaving baseball, he returned to his native West Virginia, becoming a general mine foreman. A resident of Pageton, WV, he died of a heart attack at Welch, WV, on October 24, 1960, at age 66. (*West Virginia Certificate of Death; Total Baseball; Washington Post; SABR Collegiate Database*)

Ed Fitzpatrick spent three years (1915–17) with the Braves as a utility infielder/outfielder, appearing in 251 games and hitting .227. The Braves purchased him from Toronto in 1915, and he appeared in 105 games that season. Owning a "good-sized farm" near Phillipsburg, NJ, he left the Braves in 1918 because he felt that he "could make more money there than he could in baseball." Fitzpatrick's death certificate lists his occupation as "foreman — retired." Bill Lee identifies his position as being with Baker Chemical Company. Fitzpatrick died of generalized arteriosclerosis at Bethlehem, PA, on October 23, 1965, at age 75. (*Boston Daily Globe; Hall of Fame file; Total Baseball; Baseball Necrology*)

Max Flack, a left-handed hitting leadoff batter, began his major league career with the Chicago Federals. He joined the Chi-Feds from Peoria and hit .314 in 1915. Awarded to the Cubs in 1916, he had back-to-back .300 seasons in 1920–21 and finished his 12-year major league career with a .278 average. In both 1916 and 1921 he led NL outfielders in fielding. In 1922 Flack had the distinction of being traded from the Cubs to the Cardinals between games of a doubleheader. Released to Oakland in 1924, he refused to report and was reinstated in 1925. After finishing with the Cardinals, he served as chief custodian at East St. Louis High School. Flack died at his home in Belleville, IL, on July 31, 1975, at age 85. (*Hall of Fame file; Total Baseball; Chicago Daily Tribune*)

Art Fletcher played 13 seasons at shortstop for the Giants and Phillies, hitting .277, with a high of .319 in 1911. Along the way he played in 25 World Series games for four NL champions in New York and led NL shortstops in assists four times. In 1923 he retired as an active player to manage the Phillies, a position he held for four years. In 1927 he began a 19-year stint as a Yankee coach, collecting 10 World Series checks during this period before a heart attack ended his association with baseball in 1945. In 1930 he had rejected an offer to succeed Miller Huggins as manager of the Yankees. The graduate of Draughton's Business College then became a director of the First National Bank of Collinsville, IL, his hometown. On February 6, 1950, at age 65, he died of a heart attack while driving in Los Angeles. (*Sporting News; New York Times; Baseball Encyclopedia*)

Gary Fortune had trials with the Phillies in 1916 and 1918 and the Red Sox in 1920, resulting in a 0–5 career pitching record. He pitched for Asheville in 1915 before joining the Phillies and was recalled in 1918 from New London. In 1919 Fortune won 24 games to help Pittsfield win the Eastern League and earn himself a trial with the Red Sox. Back in the minors he led the Eastern League again with 23 victories in 1924. A 1926 note in *The Sporting News* states that Fortune "had been in the Eastern League for virtually ten years." Having attended Weaver College, he ultimately became a marketing specialist with the United States Department of Agriculture. A resident of Arlington, VA, he died at the Georgetown University Hospital on September 23, 1955, at age 60. (*Washington Star; baseball-reference.com; Encyclopedia of Minor League Baseball; Washington Post*)

Eddie Foster, a 5'6" third baseman, was a regular with the Senators and Red Sox for 10 of his 13 major league seasons. He joined the Yankees in 1910 from Jersey City, getting into 30 games. Released to Rochester for 1911, Foster returned to the majors with the Senators in 1912, hitting .285 in his first full sea-

Eddie Foster

son, 21 points over his career average. Released by the Browns at the end of the 1923 season, the Chicago native became a welder. On January 15, 1937, he died in Washington, DC, as a result of injuries suffered when his car "crashed through a signboard." He was 49 years old. (*Hall of Fame file; Sporting News; Washington Post; Atlanta Constitution*)

George (Rube) Foster looks small standing beside Babe Ruth and Ernie Shore in the picture of the Red Sox starting pictures, but he turned in three heavyweight seasons, going 14–8, 1.65 ERA in 1914, 19–8, 2.11 ERA in 1915, and 14–7, 3.06 ERA in 1916. In addition, he had two complete game victories over the Phillies in the 1915 World Series. The Red Sox had purchased him from Houston after a 24–7 record in 1912. Foster began to have a problem with his deltoid in 1916, causing him to retire after the 1917 season. His five-year major league totals show a 58–33 record. From the small town of Bokoshe, OK, he returned there after leaving baseball and operated a farm. He died at Bokoshe on March 1, 1976, at age 88. (*Hall of Fame file; Poteau[OK] News; Total Baseball; Encyclopedia of Minor League Baseball*; information supplied by Mrs. Beverly Teague) **Photograph on page 58**

From the left: Rube Foster (14–7), Carl Mays (18–13), Ernie Shore (16–10), Babe Ruth (23–12) and Dutch Leonard (18–12) formed a formidable starting rotation for the 1916 World Champion Red Sox.

Jacque (Jack) Fournier was the regular first baseman for the White Sox (1914–16), Cardinals (1920–22), Dodgers (1922–25) and Braves (1927). In 15 seasons he hit .313 and led the AL with a .491 slugging percentage (1915) and the NL with 27 homers (1924). His most productive offensive years were those in Brooklyn when he hit .351, .334, and .350. Fournier joined the White Sox as a 21 year old in 1912, coming from Moose Jaw. When his hitting fell off in 1916, he was sent to the PCL, where he played through 1919 — except for a wartime 27 games for the Yankees. Purchases by the Cardinals in 1920, he began his greatest years. Following his playing career, he remained in baseball coaching at UCLA, managing in the minors, and scouting for the Browns, Cubs, Tigers, and Reds. Born in Michigan of a French-Canadian logging family, he grew up in and lived most of his life in Washington state. He died at Tacoma on September 5, 1973, at age 80. (*Biographical Dictionary of American Sport: Baseball; Total Baseball; New York Times; Chicago Daily Tribune; Los Angeles Times*)

Frank Fuller, the son of Ignatz Baranowski, was born in Detroit. He played in 34 games at second base and shortstop for his hometown Tigers in 1915–16, hitting .143. A veteran of World War I, he returned to the majors from San Antonio in 1923, playing in six games for the Red Sox. He continued to play in the minors until 1928. After leaving professional baseball, Fuller worked for Ford Motor Company until he retired. He died of a heart attack at Warren, MI, on October 29, 1965, at age 72. (*Hall of Fame file; Michigan Certificate of Death; Total Baseball; Sporting News*)

Del Gainer, a career .272 hitter, had averages of .308, .302, and .295 at different points

Del Gainer

in his career, but was a regular in only one of his ten major league seasons—1913, when he led AL first basemen in total chances per game while playing for the Tigers. Because of the number of serious injuries in his career, he was described as "one of the most unfortunate players in major league baseball." The Montrose, WV, product broke in with the Tigers from Grafton in October 1909. Sold to the Red Sox in 1914, he remained with that club through 1919, with a year out for military service. After finishing his major league career with the Cardinals in 1922, he played in the minors through 1929 and managed for one year. Gainer then became a deputy U.S. Marshal for northern West Virginia. The 50 year old died of a sudden heart seizure at his home in Elkins, WV, on January 29, 1947. (*Sporting News; Total Baseball; Washington Post; Baseball-Reference.com*)

Melvin (Bert) Gallia was, for two years, the number-two man on the Senators pitching staff behind Walter Johnson. He had back-to-back 17-win seasons in 1915–16 and four 200-inning seasons. His career totals show 66 wins and a 3.14 ERA in nine seasons, all spent with second division teams. The native of Beeville, TX, attended St. Mary's (TX) Institute in 1910 and came to the Senators in 1912 from Kansas City. Because of control problems he was returned to Kansas City for 1914. Traded to the Browns in 1918, he finished with the Phillies in 1920. Gallia then became a resident of Natalia, TX, where he worked as a self-employed electrician. He died at a nursing home in Devine, TX, on March 19, 1976, at age 84. (*Hall of Fame file; Devine News; Total Baseball; SABR Collegiate Database; Washington Post*)

Arnold (Chick) Gandil was once described as "the only first baseman around who didn't need a glove." In nine major league seasons he led the AL in fielding four times and in assists three times. In addition, he carried a career batting average of .277. A "roughhouse" character from St. Paul, MN, he had run away from home at age 17, playing outlaw ball in Mexico, working as a boilermaker in a copper mine and boxing for

Chick Gandil

high as .318 in 1914. One of the ringleaders of the Black Sox scandal, he was banned for life after 1920 but was already under suspension for sitting out the 1920 season. He moved to California and became a plumber, retiring to Calistoga, CA. He died there on December 12, 1970, at age 83. (*New York Times; Eight Men Out; Total Baseball; New York Times*)

Bob Gandy had a one-game trial with the Phillies as a first baseman on October 5, 1916, going hitless in two times at bat. The Phillies had purchased him from Portsmouth of the Virginia League, where he played in the outfield. Gandy returned to his hometown of Jacksonville, FL, becoming a clerk for a coal company. On June 19, 1945, he died of a self-inflicted pistol shot while sitting in his car in front of his home. He was 51 years old. (*Florida Times-Union[Jacksonville]; Baseball Encyclopedia; New York Times*)

$150 a fight. In a 1910 trial with the White Sox, he hit only .193 in 77 games and was sent down. However, from 1912 through 1919 he was a regular first baseman with Washington, Cleveland and the White Sox, hitting as

Larry Gardner led AL third-basemen in assists 5 times and in double plays three times in 13 seasons as a regular with the Red

Larry Gardner

George Gibson

Sox, A's, and Indians. A career .289 hitter, he had eight .300 seasons, hitting .319 in 1921. Playing for four World Championship teams, Gardner appeared in 25 World Series games. He joined the Red Sox in June 1908 upon graduation from the University of Vermont. He became the club's regular second baseman in 1910 and was shifted to third the following season. Traded to the A's in 1918, he became the property of Cleveland in 1919, helping them win a World Championship in 1920. After finishing his playing career, he became athletic director and baseball coach at his alma mater. Gardner died at St. George, VT, on March 11, 1976, at age 89. (*Sporting News; Total Baseball; SABR Collegiate Database; Washington Post; Atlanta Constitution; New York Times*)

Joe Gedeon was the regular second baseman for the Yankees in 1916 and for the Browns in 1918–20. A light hitter for most of his career (.244 lifetime), he raised his average to .292 in 1920. He also led the AL in fielding twice. Washington had acquired him from San Francisco in 1913 and sent him to Los Angeles for much of 1914 and to Salt Lake City for 1915. Because of his friendship with two members of the White Sox, he was tipped off about the fix on the 1919 World Series and used the information to make money betting on Cincinnati. Because of this he was banned for life after 1920. The Sacramento native twice owned his own speakeasy or bar, but was unsuccessful as a businessman. Ultimately he tended bar for others in San Francisco, claiming that each day he was paid $5, stole $5, and drank $5. He died in San Francisco of liver disease on May 19, 1941, at age 47. (*Hall of Fame file; Washington Post; Total Baseball; Los Angeles Times; Bill James Historical Baseball Abstract*)

Gus Getz hit .258 as the Dodgers third baseman in 1915, leading the NL in total chances per game. But he never exceeded 55 games in any other of his seven major league seasons, hitting only .219 in 339 games. After trials with the Braves in 1909–10, he spent three years in the minors at Newark before returning with the Dodgers in 1914. He had one pinch hitting appearance in the 1916

World Series. After finishing with the Indians and Pirates in 1918, he played in the high minors, managed at Scranton and umpired in the Middle Atlantic League until 1933. His death certificate lists his occupation as "construction worker" in "heavy construction." Born in Pittsburgh, he was a resident of Keansburg, NJ, where he died on May 28, 1969, at age 74. (*Sporting News; Hall of Fame file; Baseball Encyclopedia; New York Times*)

Edward (Patsy) Gharrity was supposed to catch for the Senators at the end of 1915 when the Minneapolis season was over, but since he was not told this, he went home. Thus, he first played for the Senators in 1916 and after working in the shipyard in 1918, became the regular catcher 1919–23. A career .262 hitter, he hit .310 in 1921 when he caught 115 games. A family illness caused him to leave the professional ranks in 1923 and play independent ball with the Fairbanks-Morse Fairies in Beloit, WI, his hometown. Returning to Washington as a coach, Gharrity played briefly in both 1929 and 1930 and coached until 1935. Remaining in baseball, he umpired until 1937, managed until 1939 and scouted in 1949–50. Following his baseball career, he was sales supervisor for Wright & Wagner Dairy. Gharrity was found dead on a sidewalk in Beloit on October 10, 1966, at age 74. (*Beloit Daily News; Total Baseball; Washington Post*)

George Gibson was the regular catcher for the Pirates from 1906 through 1915, catching more than 100 games six times. In a three-year period 1908–10 he caught 433 games. Gibson hit .265 to help the Pirates win the 1909 World Championship and caught all 7 games of the World Series. Only a .236 career hitter, he did a solid job as a catcher, leading the NL three times in fielding and twice in double plays and putouts. After finishing his playing career with the Giants in 1918, Gibson coached at Toronto and managed the Pirates twice (1920–22 and 1932–34) and the Cubs once (1925). A native of New London, Ontario, he retired to a farm at Mt. Bridges Ont. For one year Gibson served as president of the PONY League team at New London. He died on January 25, 1967 at age 86. (*Hall of Fame file; Baseball Encyclopedia; Sporting News; New York Times*)

Frank (Flash) Gilhooley hit .276 in 112 games for the 1918 Yankees, the only season in nine trials that he held regular status. A very quick outfielder — hence his nickname — he first came to the Cardinals from Adrian at the end of 1911. The Yankees acquired him from Montreal in 1913 and traded him to the Red Sox in 1919. Let go by the Red Sox at the end of the season, he became an outfield star in the International League, playing ten seasons there and managing Jersey City in 1929. He had attended St. John's University, so after leaving baseball, he returned to Toledo, his native city, and became a deputy county treasurer, also serving as a deputy sheriff and helping form the adult probation department. He died at Toledo on July 11, 1959, at age 66. (*Sporting News; Toledo News; Total Baseball; Encyclopedia of Minor League Baseball; SABR Collegiate Database*)

Billy Gleason had three trials totaling 40 games as a second baseman with the Pirates and Browns, hitting .246. A product of the Lynn, MA, sandlots, he came to Pittsburgh from Chattanooga in 1916. An injured ankle limited his play to one game in 1916 and 13 games in 1917. After serving in the Navy, he returned to Chattanooga and earned a trial with the Browns in 1921. Gleason continued to play and manage in the minors through 1936. Born in Chicago, he moved to Holyoke, MA, where he served as a juvenile probation officer. After a short illness, he died at Holyoke on January 9, 1957, at age 63. (*Sporting News; Atlanta Constitution; Baseball-Reference.com*)

Mike Gonzales, the most successful of the six Cubans playing in 1916, spent 17 seasons in the majors — primarily as a catcher — and

14 more as a Cardinals coach. In 1924, his best season, he caught 117 games for the Cardinals, hitting .296 — more than 40 points over his career average. He entered the majors at the end of the 1912 season from the Cuban Stars, playing one game for the Braves. The Reds acquired him from Havana in 1914, and he achieved regular status, catching 83 games. He went on to play for the Cardinals (1915–18, 1924–25, and 1931–32), the Giants (1919–21), and the Cubs (1925–29). He led NL catchers in fielding in 1926 and played in two games in the 1929 World Series. Gonzales managed Havana in the Cuban winter league and was associated with Havana clubs until Fidel Castro banned professional sports. Having invested well, Gonzales lived the life of a national sports hero in Cuba. He died in Havana of a heart attack on February 19, 1977, at age 86. (*Sporting News; Total Baseball; New York Times; Chicago Daily Tribune*)

Wilbur Good broke into professional baseball as a pitcher, making it to the Yankees in 1905, his second year. After hitting .370 at Akron in 1908, he came back to the majors as an outfielder with the Indians and lasted ten more seasons, a career .258 hitter. He was a regular outfielder for the Cubs in 1914 and 1915, hitting .272 and .253. After finishing with the White Sox in 1918, he played for and managed Kansas City, winning an AA pennant in 1923. Good led the Southern Association in hitting in 1925 as a 40-year-old. He continued to play until 1931 — when he was 46 years old — and to manage until 1942. The native of Punxsutawney, PA, died at Brooksville, FL, on December 30, 1963, at age 78. (*Sporting News; Total Baseball; Encyclopedia of Minor League Baseball; Chicago Daily Tribune*)

Marv Goodwin won 11 games with a 2.51 ERA for the Cardinals in 1919. For parts of seven major league seasons, the right-hander from Gordonsville, VA, posted a 21–25 record. After Washington signed him from the semi-pro ranks in 1916, Goodwin led the Blue Ridge League with 19 wins before joining the Senators in September. The Cardinals purchased him from Milwaukee in July 1917 and he spent 1918 as a military aviator in World War I, reaching the rank of Lieutenant. The Cardinals sold him to Houston in 1922 where he pitched and managed. After a 21–4 record in 1924 he came back to the Reds, but was returned to Houston. On October 22, 1925, Goodwin died of injuries suffered in an airplane crash. He was 32 years old. (*Sporting News; Total Baseball; Washington Post; Chicago Daily Tribune; New York Times*)

Al Gould, a 5'6" right-hander from Muscatine, IA, pitched in 57 games for the Indians in 1916–17, posting a 9–11, 3.05 ERA record. He came to the Indians after leading the Three-I League in wins and strikeouts in 1915. In Gould's first season the *New York Times* referred to him as a "kindergarten pitcher" and as being "half as big as an ordinary pitcher." He remained in baseball into the 1930s, pitching in the PCL. After leaving baseball, he spent 35 years as the owner/operator of a Texaco Station in Los Gatos, CA. Gould died at Los Gatos on August 8, 1982, at age 89. (*Sporting News; Baseball-Reference.com; New York Times; Encyclopedia of Minor League Baseball*)

Hank Gowdy was the first major leaguer to enlist in the armed forces in World War I, seeing action as a sergeant at Chateau Thierry and the Argonne Forest. In World War II he again volunteered and served as a Special Services officer at Ft. Benning, GA. A good-hitting catcher (a career .270 average), he lasted 17 seasons in the majors, being a regular for the 1914 "Miracle Braves" (hitting .545 in the World Series) and for the 1923 Giants (hitting .325 for the season). The 6'2" Gowdy came to the majors as a first baseman with the Giants in September 1910. Sent down to the minors in 1925 — despite a .325 average — he returned in 1929 with the Braves, for whom he coached until 1937. He also coached for the Reds (1938–42 and

Hank Gowdy

1945–46) and the Giants (1947–48). He died at Columbus, OH, his hometown, on August 1, 1966, at age 76. (*Sporting News; Total Baseball; New York Times; Boston Globe*)

Jack Graney pitched 3.1 innings for the Indians in 1908 and came back from Portland in 1910 to play 13 seasons for them as an outfielder. Despite an anemic bat (.250 career average), he led the AL twice in bases on ball, once in doubles and once in pinch hits. In 1916 he stole 72 bases on a .241 average. Graney was a utility player for the 1920 World Champions, going 6 for 12 as a pinch hitter. After leaving baseball in 1922, the Canadian became a prosperous automobile dealer in Cleveland, but was wiped out in the Depression. He then became the play-by-play radio announcer for the Indians, a position he held until he retired in the fall of 1953. He died at Bowling Green, MO, on April 20, 1978, at age 91. (*St. Louis Post-Dispatch; Total Baseball; Los Angeles Times*)

Vean Gregg won 32 games and struck out 376 batters at Portland in 1910 before reaching the majors. He then won 63 games in his first three seasons with the Indians, compiling a 1.80 ERA as a rookie. A lefthander with a "particularly sinuous curve ball," Gregg compiled a 91–63 major league record. Before beginning his professional career with Spokane in 1909, he pitched at South Dakota State, so he was 26 years old when he entered the majors. After he was traded to the Red Sox in 1914, his production tailed off, and he was sold to Providence in 1916. He returned to the majors with the A's in 1918 before another PCL stint with Seattle. Gregg had a final trial with the Senators when he was 40 years old. His baseball career over, he became a farmer in Canada and later operated the Home Plate Cigar Store in Holquaim, WA, where he resided for 38 years. He died at Aberdeen, WA, on July 29, 1964, at age 79. His brother Dave pitched briefly with the Indians in 1913. (*Aberdeen Daily World; Total Baseball; Los Angeles Times; SABR Collegiate Database*)

Tommy Griffith, who performed vaudeville while still playing major league baseball, was a ten-year regular in the outfield for the Reds and Dodgers during his 13-year big league career. He hit .307 during his first full season for the Reds and later put together back-to-back .312 and 316 seasons for the Dodgers. But in the 1920 World Series he hit only .190. The Braves had brought him into the majors from New Bedford in 1913. Griffith went to the Reds in 1915, the Dodger in 1920, and finished with the Cubs in 1925. Following his baseball career, he was in the radio and sporting goods business; then he became a deputy clerk in the Hamilton County Common Pleas and Domestic Relations courts. Finally he entered insurance, opening his own business. He died at Cincinnati on April 13, 1967, at age 77. (*Cincinnati Post; Cincinnati Enquirer; Total Baseball; Chicago Daily Tribune; Atlanta Constitution*)

Burleigh Grimes was called "Ol' Stubblebeard" because the slippery elm bark he chewed to help his spitter irritated his skin, so he didn't shave on days he pitched. He won 270 games (18th on the career list) in 19 seasons, including five 20-win seasons. He also had seven complete games in 9 starts in

World Series play. In the 1931 World Series, he beat both of Connie Mack's aces Lefty Grove and George Earnshaw as the Cardinals prevailed. The Wisconsin native joined the Pirates in September 1916 from Birmingham. Traded to the Dodgers, he won 23 games for the 1920 NL champions. During his career he pitched for every National League team except the Phillies, finishing with the Yankees in 1934. Grimes stayed in baseball, managing the Dodgers (1937–38), and later coaching for the Dodgers, managing in the minors, and scouting for the Yankees and Orioles. Elected to the Hall of Fame in 1964, he died of cancer at his home in Clear Lake, WI, on December 6, 1985, at age 92. (*Sporting News; Total Baseball; New York Times; Atlanta Constitution*)

Dan Griner

Charlie Grimm, a 17-year-old outfielder, signed from the St. Louis sandlots, hit .091 in twelve games for the A's in 1916, beginning a 20-year playing career. After seasoning at Little Rock, he became a regular at first for the Pirates and Cubs from 1920 through 1934, leading the NL in fielding 7 times. A career .290 hitter, he hit .345 in 1923 and .331 in 1931. In World Series play, Grimm hit .389 in 1929 and .333 in 1932, in two losing efforts. Grimm had three stints at managing the Cubs 1932–38, 1944–49 and 1960, and he also managed the Braves 1952–56. Despite a reputation of being too easy going, he had four NL championship teams in Chicago. Between times he served as a minor league manager, as an announcer, and finally as a Cubs executive. On November 15, 1983, Grimm died at Scottsdale, AZ, while being treated for Hodgkin's disease. He was 85 years old. (*Sporting News; Total Baseball; New York Times; Atlanta Constitution; Chicago Daily Tribune*)

Dan Griner, called "Big Dan" because of his 200-pound frame, turned in a 28–55 record in 6 seasons with the Cardinals and Dodgers. The Cardinals purchased him from Cleveland, TN, of the Appalachian League in 1912. With the last place Cardinals in 1913, he had a league leading 22 losses, but the following year he compiled a 2.51 ERA while winning 9. Sold to St. Paul after the 1918 season, he won three games for the Saints in the 1919 Class AA Series against Vernon of the PCL. Griner's Hall of Fame informant states that he attended Southerland Methodist College in Florida. His South Carolina death certificate lists his occupation as medicine salesman. On June 3, 1950, Griner died of a heart attack at Bishopville, SC, at age 62. (*Hall of Fame file; South Carolina Certificate of Death; Total Baseball*)

Henry (Heinie) Groh, a third baseman/leadoff hitter for the Giants and Reds, is most remembered for his bottle bat and squared stance. These allowed him to hit over .300 four times and carry a career .292 average with 308 doubles. The Giants purchased him from Buffalo in 1912, and he became a regular with the Reds in 1913 before returning to the Giants in 1922. In 1917 he led the NL with 182 hits; in 1918 he led in runs while hitting .320. Groh played on five NL champions, going 9 for 19 in the 1922 World Series. As a fielder he led the NL in double plays 8 times, in fielding 7 times and in putouts 3 times. A knee injury ended his effectiveness after

1924, though he played in the majors through 1927. After serving as a playing manager in the minors for five years, he then scouted for the Giants and Dodgers. Returning to Cincinnati, he became "a cashier at River Downs Race Track." He died in Cincinnati on August 22, 1968, at age 78. (*Sporting News; Total Baseball; Deadball Stars of the National League; New York Times*)

Bob Groom began his major league career with a 7–26 record for the 1909 Senators, leading the AL in walks. The 24-year-old right-hander had come to the Senators from Portland. Despite a respectable 3.10 career ERA, he had only 2 winning seasons in 10 years, leading his league in losses three times. In his best year, 1912, he had a 24–13 record. Asked to take a pay cut following a 16-win season in 1913, he jumped to the St. Louis Federals for the next two seasons and was then awarded to the Browns. When he retired from the majors in 1919, he became a successful "president and operator" of two coal companies in Belleville, IL, and director of a bank. In addition, he promoted and coached boys teams in his home town. After a three-year illness, he died at Belleville on February 19, 1948, at age 63. (*Sporting News; Baseball Encyclopedia; Washington Post*)

Roy Grover played second base on some very bad A's teams, joining them in 1916 when they won 36 games and being a regular on the 1917 team that won 55. In 1919 he was traded from a team that won 56 to a Washington team that won 57. His three-year totals show a .226 average for 207 games. The Snohomish, WA, native joined the A's from Butte of the Northwestern League. In 1919 the Senators returned him to Oakland. He later scouted for the Yankees and became Personnel Director for Bremerton Navy Yards in Seattle. After his retirement there, Grover lectured on baseball at San Jose State and published a book of poems about baseball. He died at Milwaukie, OR, on February 7, 1978, at age 86. (*information supplied by Mrs. Carol Mehrtens; San Jose News; Oregonian[Portland]; Total Baseball; Washington Post*)

Lou Guisto was a football and baseball star at St. Mary's College in California before entering professional baseball. The "big Italian first sacker" joined the Indians from Portland in September 1916. He played through 1923 with time out for World War I, when he was gassed in Belgium. His career totals show a .196 average for 156 games. Guisto played for Oakland in the PCL until 1929, and, after two minor league managing trials, became baseball coach at St. Mary's, a post he held from 1931 until the mid-fifties. He also worked in the student store there. In 1947 he was named to the all-time St. Mary's football team. On October 15, 1989, Guisto died of throat cancer at Napa, CA, at age 94. (*Sporting News; Total Baseball; SABR Collegiate Database; New York Times; Chicago Daily Tribune*)

Woodward (Red) Gunkel pitched one scoreless inning of relief for Cleveland on June 18, 1916, following his graduation from the University of Illinois. After entering military service in 1917, he retired from organized baseball. Gunkel later pitched for Fairbanks-Morse and Logan Squares in the independent Midwest Baseball League. A Business Administration graduate of the University of Illinois, he entered the insurance business as a salesman. On April 17, 1954, the Sheffield, IL, native died of heart failure at the Veterans Administration Hospital in Downey, IL. He was 60 years old. (*Hall of Fame file; Chicago Daily Tribune; Total Baseball; SABR Collegiate Database*)

Zerah Zequel (Rip) Hagerman had a successful trial with the Cubs in 1909 (a 1.82 ERA for 79 innings) coming from Topeka, but was returned to the minors. Cleveland acquired him from Portland in 1914, and he posted a 15–29 record over the next two seasons, making 46 starts, and working 349 innings. Early in 1916 the Kansas native was returned to Portland. By 1921 he was pitching in the Chicago-based independent Midwest Baseball League. After contacting tuberculosis in 1927, he moved to Albuquerque, NM, where he died on January 30, 1930. He was 41 years old. (*Hall of Fame file; New Mexico Certificate of Death; Total Baseball; Chicago Daily Tribune*)

George Hale had four trials as a catcher with the Browns, totaling 60 games. He played six games for the Browns in 1914, coming from Burlington, and finished with 12 games in 1918. In 1917, his best year, he played in 38 games, hitting .197. After finishing his playing career in 1926, the native of Dexter, KS, moved to Wichita and opened Hale's Cafe, which he operated for 18 years. He also operated the Sports Bowl and for a time served as sheriff of Sedgwick County. He died in Wichita on November 1, 1945, at age 51. (*Hall of Fame file; Wichita Eagle; baseball-reference.com; Kansas Certificate of Death*)

Richard (Pat) Haley caught three seasons (1915–17) for the Red Sox and A's, hitting .248 in 81 games. Born in Iowa of Irish parents, he attended Western Illinois University before entering professional baseball. Haley was reportedly signed by the Federal League before joining the Red Sox. Sent down to Providence, he returned to the A's, with whom he closed his major league career. Haley served in the U.S. Army in World War I and then became a farmer in Bloomington, IL. He died at Bradenton, FL, on October 8, 1973, at age 82. (*Hall of Fame file; Total Baseball; Chicago Daily Tribune; New York Times; SABR Collegiate Database*)

Charley (Sea Lion) Hall was born Carlos Clolo of Mexican parents in Ventura, CA. He made 85 relief appearances for the Red Sox over the four-year period 1910–13, twice leading the AL in relief wins. He had a 15–8 record for the 1912 World Champions and relieved twice in the World Series. Hall first entered the majors in 1905, coming from Seattle to the Reds. Released to Columbus in 1908, he was resurrected by the Red Sox in 1909. He also pitched for the Cardinals (1916) and the Tigers (1918), finishing with a 54–47, 3.09 ERA record. Hall played in the minors through 1926 and also coached at Minneapolis in 1928. After his retirement as a player, he operated a restaurant in his hometown and became a policeman there and later served as a jailer and a sheriff. Hall died at Ventura on December 6, 1943, after a long illness. He was 58 years old. (*Sporting News; Total Baseball; Los Angeles Times; Boston Globe; Washington Post*)

Newt Halliday, a 20-year-old first baseman, played in one game for the Pirates on August 19, 1916, striking out in his only plate appearance. He had been promoted from Owensboro of the Kitty League. The Chicago native died of pneumonia at Great Lakes Naval Training station on April 6, 1918, being the first of the Men of '16 to die. He was 21 years old. (*Chicago Daily Tribune; Washington Post; Baseball Encyclopedia*)

Earl Hamilton, an undersized lefty, was a workhorse for the Browns prior to World War I and turned in strong years for the Pirates after the War. In 12 plus seasons, he pitched over 2300 innings, winning 116 games. In 1914, his best year, he pitched over 300 innings in compiling a 17–18, 2.50 ERA record. The Browns drafted him from Springfield, IL, in 1911, and the 19-year-old posted a 5–12 record. Sent down to Columbus in 1917, he was rescued in 1918 by the Pirates, for whom he won 55 games through 1923. After finishing with the Phillies in 1924, he pitched for the Los Angeles Angels into 1927. For a number of years he was involved in baseball as a minor league manager, as a scout and as a club owner. Later in life he opened a retail lumber business in Anaheim, CA. He died at Anaheim on November 17, 1968, at age 77. (*Hall of Fame file; Total Baseball; New York Times; Los Angeles Times*)

Bob Harmon, a big right-hander from Liberal, MO, pitched 348 innings for the

Cardinals in 1911, winning 23 games and leading the NL in games started. He had only one winning season in 9 with perennial second division Cardinal and Pirate teams, but won 107 total games and won at least 13 games five times. He joined the Cardinals from Shreveport in June 1909, posting a 6–11 record that year. In 1911 the *Atlanta Constitution* carried an article suggestion that he might replace Mathewson as the premier pitcher in the National League. After closing with Pittsburgh in 1918, Harmon became "a prominent planter and dairy farmer in Ouchita Parish" in Louisiana. He died at Monroe, LA, on November 27, 1961, at age 74. (*Sporting News; Chicago Daily Tribune; Total Baseball; Atlanta Constitution*)

George Harper hit .331, .340 and .349 in three of his six seasons as a regular outfielder and finished with a career .303 average in 11 major league seasons. Joining the Tigers in 1916, he beat out Sam Crawford for a starting position, but injuries limited him to 44 games. He ultimately reached the $10,500 salary mark in 1928 when the NL champion Cardinals acquired him from the Giants. Harper played professional baseball until 1936 when he was 44 years old. A carpenter by trade, he worked in a defense plant during World War II and then retired to Magnolia, AR. He died at Magnolia on August 18, 1978, at age 86. (*Sporting News; Magnolia Banner-News; information supplied by Clarence Harper; Baseball Encyclopedia*)

Harry Harper came from the Hackensack, NJ, sandlots to win 57 games for the Senators, Red Sox, Yankees and Dodgers. When he signed with the Senators in 1912, his contract stipulated that he would not have to pitch on Sundays. In 1916, his best season, the left-hander won 14 games with a 2.45 ERA, but he also led the AL with 21 losses in 1919. Harper pitched in one game for the Dodgers in 1923 and left the club to manage his business interests in Hackensack. He used his first paycheck to buy a truck, with which he opened a junk business, and this later became a trucking company. He also opened a highway construction firm, owned a supermarket, and operated a fuel and beverage concern. These activities made him the largest taxpayer in Hackensack. Harper died at Layton, NJ, on April 23, 1963, at age 68. (*Sporting News; Total Baseball; Washington Post*)

Grover Hartley became a catcher after reading an article by Charles Comiskey advising young players to try out for that position. He first came to the Giants in 1911 from Toledo, appearing in 11 games. The Indiana native went on to play in 14 major league seasons, twice as a regular with the St. Louis Federals in 1915 and the Red Sox in

Grover Hartley

1927. In the middle of his career he spent a seven-year period (1917–24) in the American Association with Columbus. He also played with the Browns (1916–17, 1934), and the Indians (1929–30). In 569 career games he hit .268. He then made the transition to coach with the Indians (1928), the Pirates (1931–33) and the Browns (1933–36). Still later he became a minor league manager, becoming a resident of Daytona Beach, FL, when he managed there in 1947. He died at Daytona Beach on October 26, 1964, at age 76. (*Sporting News; New York Times; Los Angeles Times; Total Baseball*)

Roy Hartzell was a regular outfielder, a regular third baseman, and a regular second baseman at different times in his 11-year career with the Browns and Yankees. He also played 155 games—more than 10 percent of his career games—at shortstop. A career .252 hitter, he reached .296 for the Yankees in 1916. Hartzell joined the Browns from Peoria in 1906, hitting .213 in 113 games. The Yankees sent him down to Baltimore in July, 1916, and he became manager of Denver in 1917. Hartzell, a graduate of Colorado School of Mines, became an employee of Standard Oil Company in 1921, reaching the position of Assistant Safety Director. He retired in 1946 after 25 years with the company. On November 5, 1961, he died of a heart attack at his home in Golden, CO, at age 80. (*Sporting News; Hall of Fame file; Baseball Encyclopedia; New York Times*)

Roy Hartzell

Robert (Ziggy) Hasbrook (Hasbrouck) had two trials with the White Sox, seven games at first base in 1916 and 2 games at second in 1917, hitting .111. He came to the White Sox from Muscatine of the Central Association in 1916. Sent down to Columbus in 1917, he was recalled in time to be World Series eligible. In 1918 the White Sox sold him to Mobile. He later played for Des Moines and San Francisco. Following his baseball career, the native of Grundy Center, IA, became a sales engineer for A. Y. McDonald Manufacturing Co. He died at Garland, TX, on February 9, 1976, at age 82. (*Hall of Fame file; Chicago Daily Tribune; Atlanta Constitution; Los Angeles Times; Baseball-Reference.com*)

Tom Healy attended the University of Pittsburgh, going to dental school by day and playing football, basketball and baseball after classes. He was signed by Connie Mack as a third baseman and played in 29 games for the A's in 1915–16, hitting .230. Healy passed the state board dental exams, was in the Army in France during World War I, and quit professional baseball. After playing professional football for Cleveland in 1919, he went on to serve 41 years as head of oral surgery at St. John's Hospital in Cleveland while also serving as supervisor of oral hygiene for the Cleveland Board of Education. He died at Cleveland on January 15, 1979, at age 81. (*Hall of Fame file; Cleveland Plain Dealer; Baseball-Reference.com; SABR Collegiate Database; Washington Post*)

Harry Heilmann, a lifetime .342 hitter, won four AL batting titles for the Tigers. In the odd-numbered years of 1921, 1923, 1925, and 1927, he hit .394, .403, .393, and .398. An outfielder/first baseman, he began his professional career at Portland of the Northwest League after attending St. Mary's College. Purchased from San Francisco, he entered the majors in 1914 with Detroit. In 1919 he began a string of 12 consecutive .300 plus seasons. His 17-year career ended in 1930 because of arthritis, although he played briefly in 1932 before becoming a Reds coach. His insurance business having failed in the Depression, he then accepted an offer to become a radio announcer for the Tigers, holding that position from 1933 until his death. Heilmann died in Detroit of lung cancer on July 9, 1951, at age 56. He was named to the Hall of Fame posthumously in 1952. (*Cooperstown; New York Times; Baseball-Reference.com; Los Angeles Times*)

Claude Hendrix turned in a monster season with the Chicago Federals in 1914. With

Olaf Henriksen

Tim Hendryx came to the majors as a third baseman in 1911 when the Indians acquired him from Yazoo City. Sent down to New Orleans, he led the Southern Association in hitting in 1915 and was sold to the Yankees. After shifting to the outfield, he became a regular with the Yankees (1917) and hit .279 for the Browns in 1918. After leading the American Association in hitting in 1919, he hit .328 for the Red Sox in 1920. His career totals show a .276 average for eight seasons. Hendryx finished with St. Paul, San Francisco and Mobile. The native of LeRoy, IL, moved to Corpus Christi, TX, where he drove a taxi for the Checker Cab Company. He died of a heart attack at Corpus Christi on August 14, 1957, at age 66. (*Hall of Fame file; Total Baseball; Sporting News*) **Photograph on page 23**

Olaf Henriksen, a Danish-born outfielder, played with three AL champions during his seven seasons with the Red Sox. Caddying behind the Speaker-Hooper-Lewis trio, he saw limited service, hitting .269 in 311 games. He is remembered for driving in the tying run in the seventh game of the 1912 World Series. Joining the Red Sox in 1911, Henriksen hit .366, .321 and .375 in his first three seasons. Released in 1917, he became baseball coach at Boston College in 1922. His death certificate lists his occupation as "painter." He died at Norwood, MA, on October 17, 1962, at age 74. (*Sporting News; Massachusetts Certificate of Death; Baseball-Reference.com; Washington Post*)

John Henry caught 9 years in the majors, four as a regular for the Senators. The Senators signed him directly from Amherst College in 1910. A career .207 hitter, he hit as low as .169 as a regular, but reached .249 in 1916. Henry led AL catchers in fielding in 1913 and in total chances per game in 1914. Sold to Minneapolis in 1919, he later played with Shreveport, San Antonio and Mobile

34 complete games in 37 starts, he worked 362 innings, winning 29 games with a 1.62 ERA. Earlier with the 1912 Pirates he had gone 24–9. Later in 1918 he won 20 games for the NL champion Cubs. His major league record shows 143 wins in ten seasons. The Pirates acquired Hendrix in 1911 from the Cheyenne Indians, an independent team. He jumped to the Federal League in 1914 and was awarded to the Cubs for 1916. The Cubs unconditionally released the Kansas native before the 1921 season for allegedly agreeing to "throw" a game he was to pitch. Although misconduct was never proved, Hendrix was "eased" out of baseball at age 31 and never rehired by another team. Having attended Fairmount College, predecessor of Wichita State, he worked as a bank clerk throughout his career, but after leaving baseball, he moved to Allentown, PA, and opened a café. On March 22, 1944, he died of tuberculosis there at age 54. (*Hall of Fame file; Sporting News; Deadball Stars of the National League;*

Buck Herzog

before retiring in 1924. The native of Amherst, MA, opened a box factory, which was destroyed by fire. He then umpired in the Arizona-Texas League in 1937–38 before becoming a civilian employee on the military base at Fort Huachuca, AZ. He died there of a heart attack on November 24, 1941, at age 51. (*Bisbee Daily Review; Sporting News; Baseball Encyclopedia; SABR Collegiate Database; Washington Post*)

Charles (Buck) Herzog led NL third basemen in putouts, assists and total chances in 1912. He led NL shortstops in putouts and double plays in 1916, and he led NL second basemen in total chances in 1918. In 13 seasons, 11 as a regular, he hit .259 and played on four NL champion Giants teams—1911–13 and 1917. He hit .400 in the 1912 World Series. Unconditionally released by the Cubs after the 1920 season, Herzog signed with Louisville for an American Association record salary. Before entering the majors, Herzog played at the University of Maryland, and joined the Giants in 1908 from Reading, hitting .300 in 64 games; after leaving baseball, he worked as a passenger representative for the Baltimore and Ohio Railroad and in the pari-mutuels department of Maryland racetracks. Sixty-eight years old and broke, he collapsed in a hotel lobby and later died of pneumonia in Baltimore City Hospital on September 4, 1953. (*Sporting News; Baltimore Sun; Baseball-Reference.com; Deadball Stars of the National League; New York Times*)

George Hesselbacher joined the A's in June 1916 directly from Penn State University, where he had played both baseball and soccer. Starting four games, he posted a 0–4 record. After serving in World War I, he left baseball to become a civil engineer at Rydal Park, PA. He died there of a heart attack on February 18, 1980 at age 85. (*Hall of Fame file; SABR Collegiate Database; Baseball Encyclopedia; information supplied by George Hesselbacher, Jr.*)

Jim Hickman began his major league career with Baltimore of the Federal League in 1915. He then played four seasons with the Dodgers, being the regular centerfielder in 1917. In 1920 Hickman was released to Toledo, "his batting not being heavy enough." In a career of 253 games, he hit only .217. In 1921 he began to play independent baseball but was reinstated in 1924 and assigned to the Eastern League. At the close of his professional baseball career, he joined the NCR Corporation. The native of Johnson City, TN, served as NCR sales agent in Watertown and Utica, NY. He died in Brooklyn on December 30, 1965, at age 71. (*Hall of Fame file; Total Baseball; New York Times; Washington Post*)

Hugh High was the oldest of three brothers who played in the majors. He advanced from the St. Louis sandlots to become an outfield regular for the Yankees. In six seasons, three as a regular, he hit .250 in 516 games. In 1916, his best year, he hit .263. High came to the Tigers in 1913 after leading the Connecticut League in hitting at Hartford. After two years with the Tigers, he was claimed on waivers by the Yankees. Released in 1919, he played several years in the Pacific Coast League before returning to his hometown, where he became a plumber. His younger brother Andy spent 13 seasons as a National League third baseman. His youngest brother Charlie had two trials with the A's. Hugh High died in St. Louis on November 16, 1962, at age 75. (*Sporting News; Washington Post; Total Baseball; Los Angeles Times; Dictionary of Minor League Baseball*) **Another photograph on page 23**

Hugh High

Carmen Hill had a 1.15 ERA in 47 innings for the 1915 Pirates as a 19-year-old in his first season of organized baseball. For the next twelve years he bounced among the Pirates and Giants and minor league clubs. Assigned to Birmingham in 1917, the bespectacled Hill led the Southern League with 27 victories. He served in World War I, pitched outlaw ball, and returned to the minors with Indianapolis. Through 1926, at age 31, he had a major league record of 9–8. In 1926, after a 21–7 record at Indianapolis, Hill rejoined the Pirates. There he suddenly emerged as the ace of the staff, winning 22 games for the NL champions. After another solid 16–10 season, he finished his major league career in 1930 with 47 career wins and a 3.44 ERA. Retiring from baseball, he moved to Indianapolis and worked for General Motors as a safety inspector. He died at Indianapolis on New Year's Day, 1990, at age 94. (*Sporting News; Total Baseball; Dictionary of Minor League Baseball; Atlanta Constitution; Los Angeles Times*)

Bill Hinchman had two major league careers. After two trials with the Reds, he became an outfield regular with the Indians in 1907–09, hitting .258 in 1909. The Indians returned him to Columbus, where he spent the next five seasons as player and manager. After leading the American Association with a .366 average in 1914, he was purchased by the Pirates. Over the next two seasons he hit .307 and .315, leading the NL in triples in 1916. When his playing career ended in 1920, he became a Pirate scout (1921–59) and coach (1923). In 1907 he and his brother Harry, a second baseman, played together in Cleveland. Bill Hinchman died at Columbus, OH, on February 21, 1963 at age 79. (*Sporting News; Total Baseball; Washington Post; Dictionary of Minor League Baseball*)

Bill Hobbs had two trials as an infielder with the Reds—four games in 1913 and six games in 1916. In the ten games he hit .133. The Kentucky native entered the majors from Hamilton, OH, in August 1913. Sent down to Dayton, he returned to the Reds in 1916. In 1918 he entered military service and retired from baseball to become a beer distributor in Hamilton, OH. The 52-year-old Hobbs was killed in a hunting accident near his home on January 5, 1945. (*Sporting News; Baseball-Reference.com*)

Dick Hoblitzell was a regular first baseman for the Reds and Red Sox from 1909 through 1917, hitting .278 in eleven seasons. He attended the University of Pittsburgh on a football scholarship and later attended

Dick Hoblitzell

dental school while playing with the Reds. Entering the majors in September 1908 from Wheeling, Hoblitzell was immediately installed at first base. Sold to the Red Sox in 1914, he helped them win two World Championships, hitting .273 in 10 World Series games. In 1918 he entered the U.S. Army Dental Corps, marking the end of his major league career. After World War I, he managed and umpired in the minors, with time out to operate a real estate business. In 1932 he left baseball to manage the family cattle farm at Wood County, WV. Entering Republican politics, he served as county commissioner and county sheriff. Hoblitzell died at Parkersburg, WV, on November 14, 1962, at age 74. (*Parkersburg News; Deadball Stars of the National League; Baseball Encyclopedia*)

Arthur (Solly) Hofman played every infield and outfield position in a 14-year career—spent primarily with the Cubs. A product of the St. Louis Trolley League, Hofman entered the majors with Pittsburgh in 1903 and joined the Cubs in late 1904. He had difficulty breaking into the Cubs veteran lineup, but became a regular outfielder from 1907 through 1911, and a regular second baseman for the Brooklyn Federals in 1914. A .269 career hitter, he reached .325 in 1910 and hit .298 in 16 World Series games. After finishing his career with the Yankees and Cubs in 1916, Hofman operated a baseball school and a haberdashery in Chicago before returning home to St. Louis to join the family business, but later returned to Chicago as a high school baseball coach. He died at St. Louis on March 10, 1956, at age 72. (*Sporting News; Deadball Stars of the National League; Total Baseball*)

Walter Holke, a switch-hitting first baseman, was a regular for nine of his 11 major league seasons after joining the Giants on Labor Day 1916. He led NL first basemen three times in double plays and set a then NL record for fielding .997 in 1921. A career .287 hitter, he had back-to-back .311 and .300 seasons for the Phillies in 1923 and 1924. In the 1917 World Series he hit .286. Sent down to Indianapolis in 1926, he went on to manage in the minors from 1929 until 1942, with one year out to coach the Browns. During World War II he worked as an inspector at a glass plant at Crystal City, MO, and conducted a company-sponsored baseball program. He also owned and operated a farm at DeSoto, MO. After a long illness, he died at Crystal City, MO, on October 12, 1954. He was 62 years old. (*Sporting News; Baseball Encyclopedia; New York Times*)

Harry Hooper, a civil engineering graduate from St. Mary's College, signed with the Red Sox in 1909 only with the promise that he could help with the engineering problems associated with the building of Fenway Park. He went on to play 17 seasons, 12 with the Red Sox, hitting .281 and serving as the Red Sox captain. He formed with Tris Speaker

Harry Hooper

and Duffy Lewis, one of the greatest outfields of all time, helping the Red Sox to four World Championships. Hooper hit .293 in 24 World Series games and saved the final game of 1912 with a barehanded, fall-into-the-stands catch of Larry Doyle's certain homer. He left baseball after the 1925 season, when his $13,250 salary was cut to $7,000. Hooper dabbled in California real estate, coached Princeton for two years, and then took a temporary job as postmaster of Capitola, CA. This turned out to be a 25-year job. He was elected to the Hall of Fame in 1971 and died at Santa Cruz, CA, on December 18, 1974, at age 87. (*Baseball's Best; Baseball-Reference.com; SABR Collegiate Database; New York Times*)

Rogers Hornsby was arguably the greatest right-handed hitter of all times. A career .358 hitter, he won seven NL batting championships — six consecutively — hitting over .400 three times. Also hitting with power, he won triple crowns in 1922 and 1925 and led the NL nine times in slugging percentage. For these achievements, he was elected to the Hall of fame in 1942. He hit only .246 in an 18-game tryout at the end of 1915, coming from Denison, but was a regular the following season and by 1920 had won his first batting crown. The NL leader in batting, homers, RBI's and slugging in 1925, Hornsby was awarded the MVP award. The following season he led St. Louis to a World Series victory over the Yankees. He spent his entire life in baseball: as a player/manager of the Cardinals, Cubs and Browns, as a minor league manager for a number of years, as a manager of the Browns, and as a coach of the Reds and Cubs. He died of a heart attack while undergoing cataract surgery on January 5, 1963, at age 66. (*Baseball's Best; Total Baseball; Deadball Stars of the National League; New York Times*)

Ivan Howard followed his brother Del to the majors in 1914. Already 31 years old when he reached the majors, Ivan had been a utility player with the Los Angeles Angels for a number of years. He spent four years with the Browns and Indians, hitting only .233 but filling all infield and outfield positions, before being returned to the PCL. In 1925 Howard was appointed manager of Oakland and held that position until the club was sold in 1930. His 1927 team won the PCL by 15 games. The native of Kenny, IL, lived at Hornbrook, CA, after his retirement but died of a cardiac arrest at Medford, OR, on March 30, 1967, at age 84. His death certificate lists no occupation other than "baseball player." Bill Lee asserts that Howard and his brother "operated Camp Lowe near Hornbrook, CA, for a number of years." (*Oregon Certificate of Death, Total Baseball; Los Angeles Times; Baseball Necrology*)

Miller Huggins, called "The Mighty Mite" because of his 5'6", 140 pound frame, joined his hometown Reds in 1904, after playing at the University of Cincinnati and at St. Paul. Huggins lasted 13 years as a player in the majors, 11 as a regular second baseman. A career .265 hitter, he reached .304 in 1912, and he twice led NL second basemen in assists, double plays and errors. However, he made his Hall of Fame reputation as a manager. After serving as player-manager of the Cardinals (1914–16) and manager (1917), Huggins shifting over to the Yankees. In twelve years (1918–29) his teams earned six AL championships and three World Championships. Late in the 1929 season a protracted cold developed into influenza. At the time he also suffered from an infection on the face that developed into erysipelas. This combination of ailments brought about his death on September 25, 1929. He was 50 years old. (*Sporting News; New York Times; Total Baseball; SABR Collegiate Database*)

Tom Hughes, at age 31, became a prominent relief pitcher for the Braves, appearing

Miller Huggins

in 50 games in 1915 and 40 in 1916, leading the NL in relief wins both years. His 16–3 record led the NL in winning percentage in 1916. Hughes joined the Yankees in 1906 after leading the Southern Association with a 25–5 mark at Atlanta. Sent down to Montreal in 1907, he was recalled in August. Sold to Rochester in 1911, he returned in 1914 in time to help the Braves close out their pennant drive. When Hughes left the majors in 1918, he had compiled 55 wins and a 2.56 ERA in nine years. The Colorado native then moved to Los Angeles, where he became a shipping clerk in a retail-clothing establishment. He died at Los Angeles on November 1, 1961, at age 77. (*California Certificate of Death; Boston Daily Globe; Atlanta Constitution; New York Times; Total Baseball*)

Emil Huhn began his major league career in 1915 in the Federal League as the regular first baseman for Newark. Newark had purchased him from Seattle of the Northwest League, where he had hit .295. Subsequent trials with the Reds in 1916–17 gave him a career major league total of 184 games, in which he hit .229. Remaining in baseball, Huhn managed Augusta (1921) and Mobile (1923 and was appointed player-manager of Augusta in the Sally league early in 1925. He was killed in an automobile accident on September 5, 1925, near Camden, SC, as the team was en route to Spartanburg. He was 33 years old. (*Camden Chronicle; Chicago Daily Tribune; Boston Daily Globe; Total Baseball; Encyclopedia of Minor League Baseball*)

Herb Hunter had four major league trials with the Giants, Cubs, Red Sox and Cardinals. Playing in 39 games at third, first, second and the outfield, he hit .163. Hunter was involved in minor league baseball for a number of years as a player, umpire and club owner, but he is most remembered for his association with Japanese baseball. Beginning in 1921, he took all-star teams to Japan and coached baseball at six different universities there, thus helping baseball catch on as a popular sport. A native of Boston, Hunter died at Orlando, FL, on July 25, 1970, at age 73. Bill Lee identifies him as a "retired hotel manager" who later "engaged in real estate sales" in Florida. (*Sporting News; Total Baseball; New York Times; Los Angeles Times; Baseball Necrology*)

Joseph (Shoeless Joe) Jackson was only 31 years old when he was banned from organized baseball for his part in the fix of the 1919 World Series. In just over nine full seasons he had already amassed 1774 hits, good for a .356 average, reaching .408 in 1911. Ty Cobb asserted that Jackson was "the finest natural hitter in the game." Despite his accomplishments, Jackson's salary never exceeded $6,000. He joined the A's from Greenville at the end of 1908 and became a regular at Cleveland in 1911 after hitting .354 with New Orleans. The illiterate son of textile workers, Jackson opened a cleaning and pressing business in Savannah, GA, after being banned, supplementing his income by playing semi-pro ball. In 1929 he moved back to Greenville, SC, his hometown, and opened another cleaning and pressing business, continuing in semi-pro ball until he was 46 years old. In his later years he operated a package liquor store. Jackson died at Greenville on December 5, 1951, at age 62. (*Sporting News; Eight Men Out; New York Times; Total Baseball; Bill James Historical Baseball Abstract*) **Photograph on page 34**

Elmer Jacobs, a right-hander with a sharp-breaking curve, won 50 games in nine major league seasons. With the last-place Pirates in 1917, he had a 2.81 ERA in 227 innings. He pitched in 14 games for the Phillies in 1914 after a 20-win season at Burlington, IA. Among the Pirates, Phillies and Cardinals, Jacobs won 30 games in the 1916–20 period. Three 20-win seasons in the PCL with Seattle led to a recall by the Cubs, for whom he had his best major league season (11–12) in 1924. Another 20-win season with Los Angeles led to his final major league trial. After finishing with the White Sox in

1927, Jacobs pitched for the San Francisco Seals until 1932, leading the PCL in strikeouts and ERA in 1928. He coached at a baseball camp for several years and then became a full-time custodian at the First Baptist Church in his home town of Salem, MO. Jacobs died there of a heart attack on February 10, 1958. He was 65 years old. (*Salem News; Sporting News; Encyclopedia of Minor League Baseball; Baseball-Reference.com*)

Merwin Jacobson had trials totaling 12 games with the Giants and Cubs before World War I. After the War he starred with the Baltimore Orioles of the IL, leading the league in hits in 1919 and hitting .404 in 1920. He had two more trials with the Dodgers in 1926–27, giving him a .230 average for 133 major league games. Returning to the International League, he played until 1932, leading IL outfielders in fielding in 1928. In 1932 he became an employee of Rustless Iron and Steel Corporation of Baltimore. After World War II Rustless appointed him "veterans' coordinator" to supervise the re-employment of returning service men. He died of cancer at Baltimore on January 13, 1978, at age 83. (*Baltimore Sun; Hall of Fame file; Baseball Encyclopedia; Encyclopedia of Minor League Baseball; information supplied by John A. Newton*)

Bill James, a 6'4" right-hander, was referred to as "Big Bill" to distinguish him from another Bill James, a Braves pitcher who stood only 6'3". "Big Bill" had 15 wins for the 1914 Browns, 14 wins for the Browns/Tigers in 1915, and 13 wins for the 1917 Tigers, giving him 65 wins in eight seasons. James had pitched briefly for the Indians in 1911 and 1912, and after a 24-win season at Portland in 1913, he came to the Browns. He relieved Lefty Williams in the final game of the 1919 World Series in his last major league appearance before being released to Minneapolis. He won 21 games for the Millers in 1920 and 21 for the Vernon Tigers in 1922 before retiring in 1923. The Detroit native then moved to Venice, CA, where he found employment as a foreman in the WPA. He died of a heart attack on May 25, 1942, at age 55. (*Hall of Fame file; Sporting News; Total Baseball*)

Charlie Jamieson hit .303 over an 18-year major league career with the Senators, A's, and Indians. In 13 years as a regular outfielder, he hit over .300 eight times, reaching .359 in 1924. He also led the AL with 222 hits in 1923, when he hit .345. In the 1920 World Series he hit .333. Such numbers ultimately raised his salary to $12,500. After hitting .323 at Buffalo he joined the Senators in 1915. Hitting only .171 in 1917 he was traded to the A's, who passed him along to Cleveland in 1919. There, at age 26, he became a major league hitter. After leaving the majors in 1932, he played briefly for Jersey City in 1933 and then became an automobile salesman. Shifting to law enforcement, he spent 19 years as a security Guard for Wright Aeronautical before becoming a special officer in the Paterson, NJ, borough of Hawthorne. He died at Paterson on October 27, 1969, at age 76. (*Hall of Fame file; Baseball Encyclopedia; Washington Post; New York Times*)

Hal Janvrin, regarded at one time as Boston's greatest schoolboy athlete, played ten seasons in the major leagues with the Red Sox, Senators, Cardinals and Dodgers. The 18-year-old joined the Red Sox in 1911 directly from high school. Sent out to Jersey City in 1912, he returned to the Sox in 1913. He split time at all infield positions, so he held regular status with the Red Sox of 1914–16 without holding a regular position. Only a .232 career hitter, Janvrin hit .269 for the 1915 World Champions. He served as a lieutenant in the Army during World War I before finishing his major league career in 1922. After retiring from baseball, he became an Internal Revenue Service agent. A lifetime resident of the Boston area, he died at Boston on March 2, 1962, at age 67. (*Boston Globe; Washington Post; Total Baseball*) **Photograph on page 78**

Henry (Hi) Jasper pitched 107 innings for his hometown St. Louis Cardinals in 1916,

Hal Janvrin

Johnson served in the U.S. Navy during World War I. After the war, he moved to Los Angeles and worked as a laborer with a motion picture studio. At age 58 he died of a heart attack in Los Angeles on November 5, 1950. (*Hall of Fame file; Total Baseball*).

Ernie Johnson was the regular shortstop for the White Sox in 1921–22, ten years after he first broke in with the club. A product of the Chicago amateur and semi-pro leagues, Johnson joined the White Sox in late 1912, hitting .262 in 21 games. In a ten-year major league career he hit .265, but reached .295 in 1921. After finishing his major league career with the Yankees at the end of the 1925 season, he remained in baseball, serving as player-manager for Portland and Seattle (1926–32) and as a scout for the Boston Red Sox (1933–52). A native of Chicago, Johnson died of bronchial asthma in a Monrovia, CA, sanatorium on May 1, 1952. He was 64 years old. His son Don was an infielder for the Chicago Cubs in the 1940's. (*Sporting News; Baseball-Reference.com; Chicago Daily Tribune*)

posting a 5–6 record. He had trials with the White Sox in 1914–15, coming from Dubuque. He also started ten games for the Indians in 1919, compiling a 4–5 record. Overall he won 10 games in the majors with a 3.48 ERA. Released by the Indians in 1920, he signed with Beaumont, but jumped from that club to play Trolley League in St. Louis. In 1925 Jasper was sold to Des Moines but didn't report. After leaving organized baseball, he was employed by a St. Louis man who operated a tavern and a hauling service. Jasper died on May 22, 1937, from head injuries received when he was jolted from the back of a truck. He was 56 years old. (*St. Louis Post-Dispatch; Total Baseball; Chicago Daily Tribune*)

Bill Johnson joined the A's as an outfielder in late September 1916, hitting .267 in four games. The Chicago product played 48 games the following season, leaving the majors with a .185 average for 52 games.

Russell (Jing) Johnson joined the A's directly from Ursinus College in 1916. In 1917 he went 9–12 with a 2.78 ERA and 13 complete games (for a team that was 55–98) before serving in the U.S. Navy during World War I. Because of a leaking valve in his heart, he retired from active play in 1929, leaving the majors with 24 victories. While serving as baseball coach and athletic director at Ursinus College, from 1930 through 1943, he also worked as a research chemist at Bethlehem Steel. During World War II Johnson worked as a training officer in the U.S. Marine Corp and as rehabilitation and recreation director for the Veterans Administration. After the war he became the manager of an electrical appliance store in Pottstown, PA. Johnson was killed in a car wreck on December 6, 1950, at age 56. (*Hall of Fame file; Pottstown Mercury; Baseball Encyclopedia*)

Walter Johnson (right) with young catcher Muddy Ruel (who did not play in 1916).

Walter Johnson is simply the greatest American League pitcher of all time. His 417 career victories include a record 110 shutouts. Ten seasons of sub-2.0 ERA led to a career 2.17. He finished third in career innings pitched (5923) and fifth in complete games (531). In a single season (1913) he led AL pitchers in seven categories — wins (36), percentage (.837), ERA (1.09), complete games (29), innings (346), strikeouts (243) and shutouts (11). He led AL pitchers in strikeouts 12 times, in wins six times and in ERA five times. Johnson was signed from the Idaho State League, "the Woolly West," in June 1907. By 1910 he was a 25-game winner. Thirty-seven years old when Washington finally won a pennant in 1924, Johnson made six World Series starts, with five complete games and three wins. When he retired as a player in 1927, Johnson raised purebred cattle on a farm in Maryland and entered Maryland politics. Returning to baseball, he managed the Senators 1929–33 and the Indians 1933–35 and later served as a radio announcer for the Senators. Johnson died of a brain tumor on December 10, 1946, at age 59. He was in the first group of players inducted into the Hall of Fame in 1936. (*Sporting News; Baseball's Best; Total Baseball; Washington Post; New York Times*)

Jimmy Johnston stole 124 bases in 1913 while playing in the PCL. The right-handed half of the Johnston brothers from Cleveland, TN, became a regular with the Dodgers in 1916 after two previous trials with the White Sox and Cubs. In ten full seasons and parts of three others, he hit .294, with consecutive seasons of .325, .319 and .325 in 1921–23. The White Sox had acquired him from Ottumwa in 1911 and sent him to Birmingham after one game. The Cubs bought him from San Francisco in 1914, and the Dodgers picked up his contract from the Federal League in 1915. After leaving the majors in 1926, he played and managed in the minors—primarily with his hometown Chattanooga Lookouts—and coached the Dodgers until 1932. Johnston finally became maintenance supervisor at Engel Stadium in Chattanooga. He died at Chattanooga on February 14, 1967, at age 77. (*Sporting News; Total Baseball; Encyclopedia of Minor League Baseball; Atlanta Constitution; Los Angeles Times*)

Wheeler (Doc) Johnston played first base for the Indians in the 1920 World Series when his younger brother Jimmy played third for the Dodgers. Doc Johnston spent 11 seasons in the majors, 8 as a regular for the Indians and Pirates. He moved from the Chattanooga Lookouts to Cincinnati in 1909. After leading the Southern Association in total bases in 1912, he returned to the majors with Cleveland and Pittsburgh. Sent down again in 1916, he returned to Cleveland in 1918. A career .263 hitter, he put together .305, .292 and .297 seasons for the Indians in 1919–21. After leaving the majors in 1922, he spent seven seasons playing or managing in the minors before retiring in 1929. A product of the Chattanooga sandlots, Johnston returned to Chattanooga and entered the fuel oil business. After a long illness he died at Chattanooga on February 17, 1961, at age 73. (*Sporting News; Atlanta Constitution; Baseball Encyclopedia*)

Carroll (Deacon) Jones had three trials with the Tigers totaling 151 innings and 7 wins. Brought up from Topeka in September 1916, he posted a 4–4 record the following season. Released by the Tigers to Portland in 1919, the right-hander ended his playing career with Sacramento in 1920. He was a native of rural southeastern Kansas, and after leaving baseball, he worked as a coal miner, as a brakeman for Kansas City Southern Railroad and as a coal company employee. Jones died at Pittsburg, KS, on December 28, 1952, at age 60. (*Pittsburg Headlight; Sporting News; Total Baseball; Los Angeles Times*)

Samuel (Sad Sam) Jones amassed 229 career wins in a 22-year career with six different AL clubs—this despite having only four wins before his 25th birthday. Trials with the Indians (1914–15) and Red Sox (1916–17) resulted in a 4–11 career record. His breakout year was 1918 when he went 16–5 with the Red Sox. Before retiring in 1935, at age 43, he had 10 or more wins 11 times and 20 wins twice. While playing with four pennant winners—the 1918 Red Sox and the 1922, 1923, and 1926 Yankees—he led the AL in winning percentage in 1918 and in shutouts in 1921. He also led in losses in 1925. In 22 innings of World Series play, he had a 2.05 ERA and a save. Jones was a lifelong resident of Woodsfield, OH, where he served as president of the Woodsfield Savings and Loan Association after his retirement from baseball. He died at Barnesville, OH, on July 6, 1966, at age 73. (*Sporting News; Baseball-Reference.com; New York Times*)

Ted Jourdan played in 75 games for the White Sox between 1916 and 1920. He joined the Sox in September 1916 from St. Joseph. After 7 games in 1918, he entered the U.S. Army, and spent 1919 at Minneapolis. In 1920 the first baseman played in 48 games, hitting .240 before being dealt to Salt Lake City. He continued to play in the minors until 1931, leading the International League in fielding with Jersey City in 1929. A lifelong resident of New Orleans, Jourdan became a bookkeeper there. He died of bronchopneumonia at the Veterans Administration Hospital in New Orleans on September 23, 1961, at age 66. (*Sporting News; Louisiana Certificate of Death; Chicago Daily Tribune; New York Times; Total Baseball*)

Joe Judge was the Senators' first baseman from 1916 through 1930, hitting over .300 nine times. In 20 seasons he hit .298 and played in two World Series, getting 10 hits in 1924. He hit .326 in 1930 and .324 in 1924. Despite his relatively small size (5'8"), he led AL first basemen in fielding 5 times and in double plays three times. A native of Brook-

Benny Kauff

lyn, Judge learned baseball "on the cobblestones of Yorkville." He came to the Senators at the end of 1915 after hitting .320 at Buffalo and leading International League first basemen in fielding. He later became a transplanted resident of D.C., where he operated "a flourishing restaurant business." Judge coached baseball at Georgetown University (1937–58) and coached the Senators (1945–46). He died at Washington, DC, on March 11, 1963, at age 68. (*Biographical Dictionary of American Sport: Baseball; New York Times; Baseball Encyclopedia; Total Baseball; Washington Post*)

Erving Kantlehner attended Santa Clara University on a rugby scholarship but left to play professional baseball. In 1913 he won 23 games and struck out 253 batters at Victoria. Joining the Pirates in 1914, he posted a 13–29, 2.84 ERA record in three seasons before developing arm trouble. Released to the Phillies in 1916, Kantlehner was sent down to Indianapolis in 1917. After two more trials with the San Francisco Seals, he left baseball to go into farming. Returning to college, he obtained a teaching degree and went on to coach all sports at Esparto (CA) High School for 30 years. He died at Santa Barbara, CA, on February 4, 1990, at age 97, the last known survivor of the Men of '16. (*Hall of Fame file; Santa Barbara News Press; Total Baseball; Los Angeles Times; Encyclopedia of Minor League Baseball*)

Benny Kauff, "The Ty Cobb of the Federal League," led the FL in hitting and stolen bases in both 1914 and 1915. But when he joined the Giants in 1916, he became very good rather than great, hitting over .300 twice in five NL seasons. Originally Yankee property, Kauff played in only five games in 1912 before being sent down. Farmed out again in 1914, he saw the Federal League as a vehicle for showing what he could do. A mineworker as a youth, he adopted a flashy lifestyle as a major leaguer. There were rumors that he was implicated in the Black Sox scandal, and he was arrested on charges of automobile theft and receiving stolen

Ray Keating

property. Acquitted in court, Kauff was still banned for life in 1921 for consorting with thieves. Losing his suit to be reinstated, he then became a clothing salesman for John R. Lyman, Co. in Columbus, OH. The 74 year old died of cerebral thrombosis at Columbus on November 17, 1961. (*Hall of Fame File; Sporting News; Deadball Stars of the National League; Baseball Encyclopedia*)

Marty Kavanaugh was the Tigers' second baseman as a rookie in 1914; in 1915 he led the AL in pinch hits while splitting time between first and second base; in 1916 he hit the first pinch grand slam homer in AL history. After three seasons as a utility player with the Tigers, Indians and Cardinals, Kavanaugh left the majors with a .249 batting average for 369 games. He played in the minors until 1922, when he moved to the Detroit suburb of Taylor. There he coached sandlot baseball and drove a truck for one of the automotive companies. Kavanaugh died of a heart attack at Eloise, MI, on July 28, 1960. He was 69 years old. (*Sporting News;*

Baseball Encyclopedia; Michigan Certificate of Death)

Ray Keating, a right-handed spitball pitcher from Bridgeport, CT, won 30 games in seven seasons with the Yankees and Braves. He joined the Yankees in 1912 after compiling a 26–11 record for Lawrence, MA. In his best season, 1914, he had 14 complete games and a 2.96 ERA for 210 innings. Leaving the Braves after the 1919 season, he went on to star in the PCL, pitching one season for Los Angeles and six for Sacramento. For the Solons in 1928 he won 27 games. After retiring from baseball in 1932, Keating spent 25 years as a bartender at the Klaven Club in Sacramento. He died of acute renal failure at Sacramento on December 28, 1963, at age 72 (*Hall of Fame file; Sacramento Union; Sporting News; New York Times; Chicago Tribune; Los Angeles Times*)

Albert (Duke) Kelleher caught in one game for the Giants on August 18, 1916, leaving the majors without a turn at bat. He had played four years at Princeton, finishing in 1916. A veteran of World War I and a resident of New York City, Kelleher died in the Veterans Hospital on Staten Island, NY, on September 28, 1947, two days before his 54th birthday. His death certificate, filled out by the hospital personnel, states that he was a bachelor and that his death was due to natural causes. It lists no occupation. (*New York Certificate of Death; SABR Collegiate Database; Baseball Encyclopedia*)

Jack Kelleher, a utility infielder, hit a solid .293 in 235 major league games—primarily with the Cubs. In 1921, his best year, he hit .309 in 95 games. Kelleher signed with the Cardinals in 1912 out of Brookline (MA) High School, where he was a football and baseball star. The 19-year-old hit .333 in 8 games that year. Returned to the minors, he was acquired by the Dodgers from Denver in 1916 and got into two Dodger games that season. After serving in World War I, he played three seasons in Chicago before finishing with the Braves in 1924. From 1929 until 1941 he served as baseball coach at Brown University. After leaving Brown, Kelleher became a foreman in the Brookline Highway Department. He died at Boston on August 21, 1960, at age 66. (*Boston Herald; Boston Daily Globe; Total Baseball; New York Times*)

George Kelly became a major league hitter in his fourth trial in 1919. In ten seasons as a regular, he hit over .300 seven times, finishing with a .297 average. Kelly also led the NL in RBI's twice and in homers in 1921. He led NL first-basemen in putouts and assists in 1920 and 1921 and stands fourth in career chances per game. Along the way he led the Giants to four straight NL championships (1921–24). He first came to the Giants in 1915 from Spokane, but before becoming a major league regular, he served in France during World War I. Traded to the Reds in 1926, he also played for the Cubs and Dodgers. When his playing days had ended in 1932, he coached for the Reds (1935–37 and 1947–48) and Braves (1938–43) before becoming a dispatcher at the San Francisco Airport. Elected to the Hall of Fame in 1973, Kelly died following a stroke on October 13, 1984, at age 88. A brother Ren pitched for the A's in 1923. (*Sporting News; Baseball Encyclopedia; New York Times*)

Joe Kelly was an outfield regular for the Pirates in 1914 and the Braves in 1917, but a light bat (.224 career average) limited his major league career to five seasons. After hitting only .222 as a rookie in 1914, Kelly was sold to Indianapolis. But after leading the American Association in stolen bases, he was acquired by the Cubs in 1916 and traded to the Braves at the end of the season. After three seasons the Braves sold him to Toledo in 1919, ending his major league connections. Overall he spent 25 years in baseball, including a managerial stint at St. Joseph, MO, where he made his home. After leaving baseball, Kelly was employed by the Sheridan-Clayton Paper Company of St. Joseph. He died on August 17, 1977, at age 90. (*St. Joseph News-Press; Total Baseball; Chicago Daily Tribune; New York Times*)

Ray Kennedy lined out as a pinch hitter for the Browns on September 8, 1916. This was his only major league appearance. But the Pittsburgh native entered organized baseball in 1912 and was still active at the time of his death in 1969. During World War I, he served in the U.S. Army in France, seeing action in the Argonne and St. Mihiel. Later he held such positions as Director of Player Personnel for Pittsburgh, Detroit and Kansas City and General Manager for the Pirates, Newark, and Binghamton. At different times in the minors he served as club president, coach, scout, business manager, and field manager. He died at Casselberry, FL, on January 18, 1969, at age 73. (*Sporting News; Total Baseball*)

Bill Killefer caught more than a thousand major league games in 13 seasons, leading the NL in fielding four times. A career .238 hitter, he reached .286 in 1919. He was Grover Cleveland Alexander's battery mate at both Philadelphia and Chicago, helping both teams win NL championships. Like his brother Red, he was a college man (St. Edward's) and also like his brother, he chose to remain in baseball, spending almost fifty years as player, manager, coach and scout. Killefer reached the St. Louis Browns in September 1909 from Houston. He came up to stay with the Phillies in 1912, becoming their regular catcher that season. Named playing manager of the Cubs in 1921, he retired as a player in order to give his attention to managing. His managerial stints also include the Browns (1930–33). He was a coach for the pennant-winning Cardinals of 1926. Killefer died at the Veterans Administration hospital at Elsmere, DE, on July 3, 1960, at age 72. (*Sporting News; Deadball Stars of the National League; Total Baseball; SABR Collegiate Database; New York Times*)

Wade (Red) Killefer hit .248 in seven seasons—mostly as a utility infielder/outfielder—but hit .272 as the regular centerfielder for the Reds in 1915. Detroit brought him up from Kalamazoo in September 1907 and traded him to Washington in 1909. Cincinnati acquired him from Minneapolis in 1914 and sent him to the Giants in 1916. After leaving the majors in 1916, Killefer began a managerial career in the minors that lasted until 1941, splitting time between the Pacific Coast League and the American Association. He and his brother Bill were both natives of Bloomingdale, MI, and Red attended Purdue and Michigan before entering professional baseball. He died of cancer at Palos Verdes Estates, CA, on September 4, 1958, at age 74. (*Sporting News; Total Baseball; Baseball-Reference.com; Los Angeles Times; Encyclopedia of Minor League Baseball*)

Lee King, an outfielder from Hundred, WV, was a regular with the Pirates in 1917 and with the Giants and Phillies in 1920–21. He hit .276 in 93 games for the 1920 Giants, but in seven seasons he hit only .247. King came to the Pirates from Wheeling at the end of 1916, was sold to the Giants in 1919, and was traded to the Phillies in 1921. The Giants rescued him from Toledo in time for the 1922 World Series, in which he got into two games. King later played for Portland of the PCL and in the Middle Atlantic League. A veteran of World War I, he returned to West Virginia, where he became a 30-year employee of Matthiesson-Hegeler Zinc Co. of Spelter. He died at Shinnston, WV, on September 16, 1967, at age 74. (*Shinnston News; New York Times; Los Angeles Times; Sporting News; Baseball Encyclopedia*)

Lee King, an outfielder from Waltham, MA, played in 42 games with the A's in 1916. He was a graduate of the University of Massachusetts, where he played four years. After serving in World War I, King finished his major league career by played in two games with the Braves in 1919, his career average .186 in 44 games. King died in Soldiers Home Hospital at Chelsea, MA, on September 7, 1938. His death certificate lists his occupation as auditor and his causes of death as nephritis, uremia and hypertensive heart disease. He was 44 years old. (*Massachusetts Certificate of Death; SABR Collegiate Database; Baseball-Reference.com*)

Ed Klepfer turned in a 14–4, 2.37 ERA record for the Indians in 1917. He had pitched for the Yankees briefly in 1911 and 1913, coming directly from Penn State, where he played 1909–11. In 1914 he led the PCL with 212 strikeouts before being sold to the White Sox, who shipped him to Cleveland as part of the deal to acquire Joe Jackson. As an infantry lieutenant, Klepfer was gassed during World War I, shortening his baseball career. He pitched only seven innings in the majors after the war, leaving with a career record of 22–17. Klepfer then became "an independent oil operator and broker." After a long illness he died at Tulsa, OK, on August 10, 1950, at age 62. (*Sporting News; Los Angeles Times; SABR Collegiate Database; Baseball Encyclopedia*)

Otto Knabe was the regular second baseman for the Phillies (1907–13) and the Baltimore Federals (1914–15), when he also served as manager. He was a career .247 hitter for 11 seasons—with a high of .282 in 1912—but as a fielder he twice led the NL in assists and led the FL in fielding in 1915. He played briefly with the Pirates in 1905 and, following a season at Toledo, became a regular with the Phillies in 1907. After finishing with the Cubs in 1916, Knabe coached the Cubs 1917–20 and managed Kansas City (1921–22). He later operated a cafe and tavern in Philadelphia. He died in Philadelphia on May 17, 1961, at age 77. (*Sporting News; Baseball Encyclopedia; Washington Post; Encyclopedia of Minor League Baseball*)

Elmer Knetzer won 38 games in two seasons with the Pittsburgh Federals, his eight-year major league record showing a 69–69 record. He first entered the majors with Brooklyn in 1909, coming from Lawrence of

First baseman Ed Konetchy (left) and catcher Ivy Wingo of the St. Louis Cardinals.

the New England League. He left organized baseball in 1913 to pitch independent ball in Pittsburgh and continued in the Federal League. After he left Cincinnati in 1917, the right-hander pitched in the minors until he was almost 50 years old. After finishing his 26th season as a player in 1934, Knetzer became a watchman for the Joseph Horne Co., where he retired in 1954. He died at Pittsburgh on October 3, 1975, at age 90. (*Sporting News; Hall of Fame file; Pittsburgh Post-Gazette; Total Baseball; Baseball Necrology*)

Brad Kocher played in 62 major league games with the Tiger (1912) and the Giants (1915–16). He caught 56 games, hitting .180 in 139 at bats. When Kocher came to the Tigers from Toronto, Ty Cobb reported that he had been "head and shoulders above any catcher in the International League." But at the end of the season, he was sent down to Providence. The Giants brought him back from Toronto in September 1915 but released him before the 1917 season. A lifelong resident of White Haven, PA, Kocher became a funeral director there following his playing career. He died of a heart attack on February 13, 1965, at age 77. (*Baltimore City Certificate of Death; Atlanta Constitution; Total Baseball*)

Ed Konetchy was one of the great fielding first basemen of all time. A 15-year regular, he led the NL or FL in fielding 8 times, in putouts and assists five times each and in total chances per game four times. On the career list he stands second in putouts and total chances and 11th in assists. He was also a career .281 hitter, with four seasons over .300. Konetchy joined the Cardinals from La Crosse in June 1907 and became a regular from the start. After tours with the Cardinals (1907–13), the Pirates (1914), the Pittsburgh Federals (1915), and the Braves (1916–18), he landed with a pennant winner. Konetchy hit .308 for the 1920 Dodgers. After finishing his major league career with the Phillies in 1921, Konetchy played and managed in the minors, finishing with Ft. Worth in 1927. He operated a restaurant and chicken farm near Ft. Worth, but managed his hometown La-Crosse, WI, team in 1940–42. During World War II he served as a foreman in a Corvair plant. Konetchy died in his sleep at Fort Worth on May 27, 1947, at age 61. (*Sporting News; Baseball Encyclopedia; New York Times; Dictionary of American Sport: Baseball*)

Ernie Koob, a lefthander from Keeler, MI, pitched four seasons for the Browns, his best year being 1916 when he posted an 11–8 mark. While attending Kalamazoo Normal (Western Michigan), he pitched for Kalamazoo and Battle Creek before joining the Browns in 1915. One of his six victories in 1917 was a 5–0 no-hitter against the White Sox. After serving in World War I, he finished with the Browns in 1919, leaving the majors with a 23–31 record. Traded to Louisville in 1920, he pitched in the minors until 1930. Koob then became "a foreman for a St. Louis manufacturing concern." He died of a lung ailment in a St. Louis sanatorium on November 12, 1941. He was 48 years old. (*Sporting News; Total Baseball; New York Times; SABR Collegiate Database*)

Larry Kopf played shortstop for the World Champion 1919 Reds, hitting .270, his key triple responsible for a win in Game 2. He spent 10 seasons in the majors, six as a regular for the A's, Reds and Braves. Until 1914 Kopf played professionally under the name "Fred Brady" because he was still participating at Fordham University under his real name. He had a six-game trial with the Indians in 1913. Sent to Toledo, he became the property of the A's in 1914. Sent down to Baltimore in 1916, he returned with the Reds. Closing his career with the Braves in 1923, he finished up with a .249 average. Twice Kopf had left baseball to pursue business interests before entering the real estate business in Cincinnati in 1923. He died in Cincinnati on October 15, 1986, at age 95. (*Sporting News; Baseball-Reference.com; Total Baseball; Washington Post; Chicago Daily Tribune*)

Kowalewski *see* **Coveleski**

Larry Lajoie

Napoleon (Larry) Lajoie led the AL in batting three times on the way to a 3242-hit, .338-batting average career. In the field he led the NL or AL six times in double plays, in total chances per game and fielding. He ranks fifth among second basemen in career putouts and seventh in career assists. In 1937 Lajoie became the sixth man elected to the Hall of Fame. He joined the Philadelphia Phillies from amateur ranks in 1896, hitting .326 in 39 games. In 1901 he jumped to the American League Philadelphia A's and immediately led the league in runs, hits, doubles, average, homers, RBI's, and slugging. To defeat an injunction preventing him from playing for the A's, Lajoie was dealt to

Larry Kopf

Jack Lapp

Cleveland in 1902. He was player/manager for Cleveland 1905–09. After leaving the majors in 1916, he played for and managed two minor league teams and briefly served as a league commissioner. A resident of Cleveland, Lajoie became a salesman for a rubber company before retiring to Daytona, FL. He died there of pneumonia on February 7, 1959, at age 83. (*Baseball Encyclopedia; New York Times; Sporting News; Cooperstown*)

Otis Lambeth recorded an 11–9, 3.18 ERA mark in three seasons with the Indians. He came to Cleveland in July 1916 from Topeka. Called into the U.S. Army in 1918, he was the first American League player to be decorated for bravery. After the War he pitched for Kansas City until his release in 1921. Following his baseball career, Lambeth entered the U.S. Postal Service, working first as postmaster and later as a rural carrier at Moran, KS, in his native Allen County. He died at Moran on June 5, 1976, at age 86. (*Hall of Fame file; Total Baseball; Chicago Daily Tribune; Washington Post; Iola[KS]Register*)

Les (Red) Lanning appeared in 19 games for the 1916 A's. Tried as an outfielder, he hit .182 in nine games. Tried as a pitcher, he posted a 0–3, 8.14 ERA for 6 games. Elected baseball captain at Wesleyan University, he signed with the A's in January 1916, before his senior year, and joined them in June. After leaving baseball, he became an executive with the New Departure Division of General Motors in Bristol, CN. Lanning died at Bristol on June 13, 1962, at age 67. (*Sporting News; Baseball Encyclopedia; SABR Collegiate Database; New York Times*)

Jack Lapp shared catching duties on Connie Mack's great 1910–14 teams. He hit .292 in 90 games in 1912 and .272 in 112 games in 1915. The Athletics acquired him from Syracuse in 1908. Sent down to Newark, he was recalled in 1909 and was released to the White Sox in 1916. Lapp played in only 40 games before "being dropped on account of ill health." Described as "a good hitter," he hit .263 over 9 seasons and .235 in 5 World Series games. After played independent baseball in the Philadelphia area, he died on February 7, 1920 "of pneumonia, aggravated by an injury to the throat received while playing baseball." He was 35 years old. (*Sporting News; Baseball Encyclopedia; New York Times*)

John (Doc) Lavan, a graduate of the University of Michigan, attended medical school while playing baseball, completing his medical degree with the help of his 1913 World Series share. A career .245 hitter over 12 seasons, he was the regular shortstop for the Browns (1914–17), the Senators (1918) and the Cardinals (1919–22). In 1918 he and teammate Del Pratt were awarded damages in a suit against Phil Ball, Browns President, who had publicly accused them of "laying down." The Cardinals released him to Kansas City in 1924, and he finished his baseball career managing Lincoln in 1927. After three years of private practice, he headed public health programs in Toledo, Kalamazoo, Grand Rapids, Kansas City, and St.

Jim Lavender

Louis. At the time of his death Lavan was director of social hygiene in Wayne County, MI. During World War I he served in the Navy Medical Corps and was commander of the Naval Hospital in Brooklyn during World War II. At one time he was director of research for the National Infantile Paralysis Foundation. Following a brief illness, Lavan died in Detroit on May 30, 1952, at age 61. (*Sporting News; Baseball Encyclopedia; SABR Collegiate Database; Washington Post*)

Jim Lavender made at least 20 starts and won at least 10 games in each of his five seasons with the Cubs, his best season being 1912, his rookie year, when he pitched more than 250 innings and won 16 games. His career totals were 63 wins and a 3.09 ERA. As an engineering student, Lavender had attended Georgia Tech but did not make the varsity team. The Cubs drafted him from Providence at the end of 1911. There he gained the nickname "Iron Man," appearing in 49 games and winning 19. At the end of 1916 he was traded to the Phillies and left the majors in 1917. When he left professional baseball in 1922, he went to work for the Georgia Highway Department. A resident of Cartersville, GA, Lavender died there of coronary thrombosis on January 12, 1960, at age 74. (*Georgia Certificate of Death; Total Baseball; Chicago Daily Tribune*)

Otis Lawry, a 130-pound second baseman/outfielder joined the Philadelphia A's after graduating from the University of Maine in 1916. Playing in two seasons, Lawry hit .191 in seventy-one games. After serving in the Chemical Corps in World War I, he also played for Baltimore and Jersey City of the International League, leading the IL in hits in 1918 and in batting average in 1919. He later became an employee of the Bureau of Taxation for the State of Maine and, following his retirement, was on the assessing board for his native town of Fairfield, ME. Lawrey died at Waterville, ME, on October 23, 1965, at age 71. (*Morning Sentinel [Waterville,ME]; Baseball Encyclopedia; SABR Collegiate Database; Encyclopedia of Minor League Baseball; Washington Post*)

Billy Lee had two trials with the Browns as an outfielder/second baseman in 1915–16, hitting .186 in 25 games. The Senators originally signed him from the Bayonne, NJ, sandlots, and the Browns acquired him from Atlanta. In 1916 Lee was turned over to Nashville, ending his major league career. After leaving baseball, he became football, basketball and baseball coach at Bayonne High School, serving for almost 30 years. He died at West Hazleton, PA, on January 6, 1984, at age 92. (*Jersey Journal[Bayonne, NJ]; Washington Post; Total Baseball*)

Harry (Nemo) Leibold, a 5'6" left-handed hitter, platooned with Shano Collins in right field for the White Sox when they won AL championships in 1917 and 1919. A roommate of Buck Weaver, he nonetheless remained ignorant of the 1919 fix, and later played in the 1924 and 1925 World Series for the Senators. He came to the Indians in 1913 from Milwaukee and finished with the Senators in 1925, holding regular status in nine of his 13 seasons. Batting leadoff, Leibold hit .302 in 1919 and .306 for the Red Sox in 1921, finishing his career with a .266 average. He played in the minors through 1931 and managed through 1949. After a bit a scouting, he retired to his Detroit home to spend time with his family. Leibold died at Detroit on February 4, 1977, at age 84. (*Hall of Fame file; Total Baseball; Washington Post; Chicago Daily Tribune*)

Hubert (Dutch) Leonard set a major league record in 1914 when he recorded a microscopic 1.01 ERA over 212.1 innings with the Red Sox. He pitched for St. Mary's College in California in 1912; a year later the 21-year-old posted a 14–16 record for the Red Sox. Among his 139 career wins were 9 seasons of at least 10 wins and a 19–5 record in 1914. In two World Series starts the lefthander out-dueled Pete Alexander 2–1 in 1915 and Rube Marquard 6–2 in 1916. Sent down by the Tigers in 1925 (following an 11–4 season), Leonard refused to report and retired "to enter the California fruit and wine business." A year later he sold letters to AL President Ban Johnson implicating Ty Cobb, Tris Speaker and Joe Wood for fixing a late-season game in 1919. But when Leonard refused to testify against the three, the charges were dropped. Leonard became the owner of the "largest grape growing, packing, shipping and storage business" in Fresno County, CA, and he was the founder of the California Growers Winery of Calgro. In poor health from a stroke suffered in 1944, Leonard died at age 60 on July 11, 1952, at Fresno. (*Sporting News; SABR Collegiate Database; Total Baseball*) **Another photograph on page 58**

Joe Leonard, a West Chicago native, played in five seasons as a utility infielder with the Pirates, Indians and Senators, hitting .226. He came to the Pirates in 1914 from Des Moines and played in 53 games. After playing at Columbus and Kansas City in 1915, he returned to the majors with Cleveland in 1916. Traded to Washington after three games, he finished his career with the Senators. Leonard served in the U.S. Navy during World War I, missing the entire 1918 season. After one game in 1920 he became ill, dying at Washington, DC, on May 4, 1920, of a "gangrenous condition" that "extended to the lungs," the result of a ruptured appendix. He was 25 years old. (*Sporting News; Washington Post; Washington Star; Total Baseball*)

George (Duffy) Lewis was a member — along with Tris Speaker and Harry Hooper — of the Red Sox outfield that many regard as the finest of all time. Lewis, a career .284 hitter, played left field and was particularly adept at playing the incline, which came to be known as "Duffy's cliff." After eight seasons, including three AL championships, with the Red Sox and a year in World War I,

Dutch Leonard

he finished his 11-year career with the Yankees and Senators. In 18 World Series games Lewis hit .299. He had played at St. Mary's College, where his career intersected Hooper's, and starred at Oakland before being called up to the Red Sox in 1910. In 1931 Lewis became traveling secretary with the Braves and remained with the Braves in Milwaukee until his retirement in 1961. At age 91 he died at Salem, NH, on June 17, 1979. (*Boston Globe; Los Angeles Times; SABR Collegiate Database; Total Baseball*)

Axel Lindstrom, a Swedish-born right-hander, recorded a save in his only major league appearance with the A's on October 3, 1916. He was 20 years old at the time. After leaving the majors, he served in World War I and then played in the minors until 1932, notably with Nashville. Lindstrom also umpired in the Northern and Piedmont leagues in 1933. A resident of Manchester, NH, he died as the result of a fall on the streets of Asheville, NC, on June 24, 1940. The death certificate of the 44-year-old Lindstrom lists his occupation as "Base Ball Umpire." (*Hall of Fame file; Baseball Encyclopedia; North Carolina Certificate of Death; Atlanta Constitution; Boston Daily Globe*)

John (Hans) Lobert was a regular at shortstop or third base for 8 of his 14 big league seasons, twice leading the NL in putouts and fielding. A career .274 hitter with the Pirates, Cubs, Reds, Phillies and Giants, he had four seasons over .300. His speed was so great that in 1910, wearing his uniform, he circled the bases in 13.8 seconds and once beat a race horse over 200 yards in Havana. Torn knee ligaments in 1915 ended his regular status, but he played through 1917. He first came to the Pirates in 1903 from Carnegie Tech and the semi-pro ranks and came up to stay with the Reds at the end of 1905 from an outlaw league. His is essentially a life in baseball: he coached at West Point; coached for the Giants, Phillies and Reds; managed at Bridgeport, Jersey City and the Phillies; and scouted for the Giants from

Hans Lobert

1945 until his death. Lobert was a native of Wilmington, DE, but died in Philadelphia on September 14, 1968, at age 87. A younger brother Frank played in the Federal League. (*Sporting News; Baseball Encyclopedia; New York Times; SABR Collegiate Database; Deadball Stars of the National League*)

Howie Lohr played a total of 21 games as an outfielder for the Reds in 1914 and the Indians in 1916, hitting .204. Sold to Memphis in 1914, Lohr played independent ball instead until he was acquired by the Indians. He left organized ball entirely in 1918 to play independent ball where salaries were potentially higher, playing in his native Philadelphia and New York City until he was past 40. While playing baseball, he began a 40-year career with the Pennsylvania Railroad, retiring as an accountant in 1957. Lohr was also a director of Provident Savings Association of Philadelphia. He died on June 9, 1977, as age 85. (*Philadelphia Enquirer; Baseball-Reference.com; Atlanta Constitution; Washington Post*

Tommy Long led the NL with 25 triples in 1915. He earned a trial with the Senators in 1911 after leading the Southeastern League in batting, hits, runs, and homers. The *Washington Post* noted that his shoes were too heavy to show off his speed. Returned to Atlanta in 1912, he led the Southern Association in hits in 1913. Beginning in 1915, he became a three-year regular in the Cardinals outfield, hitting .294 and .293 in 1915–16, before falling to .232 in 1917. He later played for Birmingham. A native of rural Clarke County, Alabama, he returned to that area, probably as a farmer, according to Clarke County baseball historian Larson Edge. Long died at Jackson, AL, on June 15, 1972, at age 82. (*Baseball Encyclopedia; Washington Post; Encyclopedia of Minor League Baseball;* information supplied by Larson Edge)

Joe Lotz pitched in twelve games for the Cardinals in 1916, going 0–3 with a 4.38 ERA. Born in Iowa of German descent, he attended Creighton University. "Smokey Joe" was drafted by the Cardinals from Oshkosh at the end of 1915 but did not debut until July 1916. Following his baseball career, he moved to Hayward, CA, and became a salesman for Insurance Security Trust Fund. On New Years Day, 1971, he died of a heart attack at Castro Valley, CA. He was 79 years old. (*Hall of Fame file; California Certificate of Death; Total Baseball; New York Times; Washington Post*)

William (Baldy) Louden hit .313 as the regular shortstop for the Buffalo Federals in 1914. He was also the regular second baseman for the Tigers in 1912, for Buffalo in 1915 and for the Reds in 1916. In a six-year career, Louden hit .261. After a four-game trial with the Yankees in 1907, he was drafted by the Tigers from Newark for 1912. Sent down in 1913, he jumped to the Federal League and, after it closed, signed with Cincinnati. Retiring as an active player in 1917, he managed in the minors for one season. Louden then returned to his home in Piedmont, WV, and "entered the garage business, which he conducted until the time of his death." He died at Piedmont on December 8, 1935, at age 50. (*Sporting News; Baseball-Reference.com; Atlanta Constitution*)

Baldy Louden

Edward (Slim) Love, a 6'7" lefthander from Love, MS, led the AL in walks in 1918 while pitching for the Yankees. In six seasons with the Senators, Yankees and Tigers, he won 28 games—13 coming in 1918—with a 3.04 ERA. The Senators acquired him from Atlanta at the end of 1913 and used him in 5 games before sending him to Los Angeles. Sold to the Yankees in 1916, he spent three years in New York before being traded to the Tigers in 1919. Released by the Tigers in 1920, he pitched for various minor league clubs—including Mobile, Memphis, and Kansas City—until he ended his career with Baton Rouge in 1930. At the time of his death Love was employed as a steamfitter at the Millington, TN, Naval Base. On November 30, 1942, he was struck by an automobile and died as a result of the injuries. He was 49 years old. (*Sporting News; Total Baseball; Los Angeles Times; Washington Post*)

Grover Lowdermilk had the reputation of being "the wildest hurler in organized, unorganized and disorganized baseball," walking 5.74 men per nine innings. The tall right-hander pitched for seven clubs during his nine big league seasons, posting a 23–39

Grover Lowdermilk

record. Thirteen of his wins came in the 1915 season, when he worked 250 innings for the Browns and Tigers. Sold to the White Sox in 1919, Lowdermilk pitched one inning in relief in the World Series, finishing his major league career in 1920. After leaving baseball, he became a coal miner in Odin, IL. Lowdermilk died at Odin on March 31, 1968, at age 83. He pitched beside his brother Lou on the 1911 Cardinals, the two combining for a 3–5 record. (*Salem [IL] Times-Commoner; Washington Post; Chicago Daily Tribune; Total Baseball*)

Fred Luderus was the regular first baseman of the Phillies for nine seasons (1911–19), leading the NL in assists five times, but also leading in errors 4 times. A career .277 hitter for 12 seasons, he hit as high as .315 for the 1915 NL champions (and .437 in the World Series), when he also served as the Phillies captain. Over a four-year period (1911–14), he hit 66 homers. The Milwaukee sandlot product joined the Cubs at the end of 1909 after leading the Wisconsin-Illinois League in hitting. Traded to the Phillies in 1910, he remained with them until 1920. Luderus then played and managed in the minors until 1928, when he worked as a handyman at the Milwaukee Yacht Club. He later built his own home at Three Lakes, WI, and started his own toy company. Luderus died of a heart attack at his home on January 4, 1961, at age 75. (*Milwaukee Journal; Deadball Stars of the National League; Ency-*

Fred Luderus

clopedia of Minor League Baseball; New York Times)

Byrd Lynn spent five years with the White Sox as a backup to Hall of Fame catcher Ray Schalk. Since Schalk seldom took a day off, Lynn played in only 116 games, hitting .237. He joined the White Sox in 1915 from Salt Lake City. Being a member of two AL championship teams, he played in both the 1917 and 1919 World Series. Lynn's obituary describes him as a "former major league baseball player, umpire and sports figure." His death certificate lists his occupation as "attendant" at Napa State Hospital. He died at Napa, CA, on February 5, 1940, following an operation to correct a perforated duodenal ulcer. He was 50 years old. (*Hall of Fame file; California Certificate of Death; Total Baseball; Napa Daily Journal*)

Gene Madden made one pinch hitting appearance for the Pirates on April 20, 1916. He had been drafted from Galveston, where he hit .312. The Pirates optioned the outfielder to Syracuse in May 1916. Recalled in August, he did not play and was returned to Syracuse for 1917. Madden was a native of West Virginia, but after leaving baseball, he began a successful business, manufacturing automobile springs in Utica, NY. Madden died of coronary thrombosis at Utica on April 6, 1949. He was 58 years old. (*Hall of Fame file; information supplied by Eugene Madden, Jr.; Total Baseball; Boston Daily Globe*)

Lee Magee (Leopold Hoernschmeyer) played with seven big league clubs in 9 seasons. He joined the Cardinals as a second baseman in 1911. After three seasons as a regular outfielder, he jumped to Brooklyn of the FL as a player/manager in 1915, hitting .323. Awarded to the Yankees in 1916, he also played with the Browns, Reds, Dodgers and Cubs. Magee hit .290 with the Reds and .292 with the Cubs, giving him a career .276 average. Able to play both outfield and second base, he held regular sta-

Lee Magee

tus for seven seasons. Dropped by the Cubs after 1919 and unable to sign with another club, he sued the NL for blacklisting him. He lost that case after allegations were brought that he had bet against his own team in 1919. Magee then returned to Ohio where he became owner of a coal company. He died in Columbus of arteriosclerotic heart disease on March 14, 1966. He was 76 years old. (*Sporting News; Ohio Certificate of Death; New York Times; Total Baseball; Chicago Tribune*)

Sherry Magee was the NL batting champion in 1910, hitting .331. In a 16-year career with the Phillies, Braves and Reds, he hit .291. He hit over .300 four times and led the NL four times in RBI's and twice in slugging. In 1904 the 19-year-old joined the Phillies fresh from semi-pro ball. That season he hit .277 in 95 games. Traded to the Braves in 1914, he was passed on to the Reds in 1917. Magee finished his major league career with the World Champion Reds in 1919, pinch hitting twice in the World Series. After playing with Milwaukee, Minneapolis and Baltimore, he became an umpire in the New

Sherry Magee

York–Pennsylvania League in 1927, returning to the National League as an umpire in 1928. After developing pneumonia, he died at his home in Philadelphia on March 12, 1929. He was 44 years old. (*Sporting News; Deadball Stars of the National League; Baseball Encyclopedia; New York Times*)

Billy Maharg, a Philadelphia sandlot player, appeared in one game as a replacement for striking Tiger players in 1912 and one game with the Phillies in 1916, going hitless in both games. In the latter case he is described as "a friend of Alexander's," who "posed" in right field. Only 5'4" tall, he boxed professionally, owned a string of pacer and trotter horses, and taught at a dance academy. Maharg later testified that he had acted as a go-between in the 1919 Black Sox scandal, but he was never officially banned. He finally worked as a plant guard for the Lincoln division of Ford Motor Company in Philadelphia. He died of a heart attack in Philadelphia on November 20, 1953, at age 72. (*Hall of Fame file; Eight Men Out; New York Times; Pennsylvania Certificate of Death*)

John Walter (Duster) Mails was the toast of Cleveland in 1920. Called up in late season from Sacramento, the colorful lefthander from St. Mary's College went 7–0 with a 1.85 ERA; then in the World Series he pitched 15.2 innings of scoreless ball against the Dodgers. Only 18 years old when he first came to the Dodgers in 1915 after a 24–18 record in the PCL, he was described by Wilbert Robertson as the "freshest kid I ever saw." Advertising himself as "The Great Mails," he compiled a 32–25 record in seven major league seasons before a shoulder injury send him back to the minors, 14 of his victories coming in 1921. After 11 more seasons in the minors, he then became a public relations agent for the San Francisco Seals, and later headed the Speakers' Bureau for the Giants. Suffering from Parkinson's Disease, he died at San Francisco on July 5, 1974, at age 78. (*Sporting News; Hall of Fame file; SABR Collegiate Database; New York Times; Total Baseball*)
Photograph on page 95

Frederick (Fritz) Maisel led the AL with 74 stolen bases in 1914 despite a .239 average. A career .242 hitter, he was an infield regular four times in his six seasons with the Yankees and Browns. He joined the Yankees in August 1913, purchased from Baltimore for the unheard of price of $12,000 and two players. Traded to the Browns in 1918, Maisel returned to Baltimore a year later. Except for those six seasons, he maintained a lifetime association with the Baltimore Orioles. He was a player and team captain (1919–30) manager (1931–34) and scout (until his death). Off the diamond, Maisel was chief of the Baltimore County Fire Department from 1938 until 1951. Earlier he had been a county records clerk and cashier. A native of Catonsville, MD, he died at Baltimore on April 22, 1967, at age 77. (*Maryland Historical Society files; New York Times; Total Baseball*)

George Maisel, the younger brother of Fritz Maisel, had one outstanding season as a centerfield for the Cubs in 1921, hitting .310. But his major league career was cut short after he was hit in the head by a thrown ball. Signed by Baltimore in 1912, he had a trial with the Browns in 1913. The Tigers purchased him from Scranton in 1915 but shipped him to Montreal after eight games. With time out for military service, he played

Duster Mails

in the PCL with San Francisco and Portland until the Cubs brought him back in 1921. Returned to the minors in 1922, he played at Toronto, Reading and Wilkes-Barre until 1927. After leaving baseball, Maisel worked as a supervisor with Consolidated Engineering Company and later as an official with the Baltimore County Sanitation Bureau. He died in Baltimore on November 20, 1968, at age 77. (*Maryland Historical Society files; Total Baseball; Los Angeles Times; Chicago Daily Tribune; Washington Post*)

Lew Malone played in 133 games during four trials with the A's and Dodgers. As an 18-year-old rookie in 1915 (playing under the name Lew Ryan) he hit .204 in 76 games. Sent down to St. Paul in 1916, he returned to Brooklyn. After service in the Signal Corps in 1918, Malone closed his major league career, hitting .204 in 51 games in 1919. He

Fritz Maisel

then played a number of years in the International League, leading the IL second basemen in fielding in 1928. In 1948 he was appointed baseball coach at St. Francis College in Brooklyn. The Baltimore native died in Brooklyn on February 17, 1972, at age 74. (*Hall of Fame file; Baseball-Reference.com; New York Times; Atlanta Constitution*)

Al Mamaux won 76 games during a 12-year major league career, 42 of those coming in back-to-back 21-win seasons for his hometown Pirates in 1915–16. The right-hander also had twelve wins and three World Series relief appearances for the 1920 Brooklyn NL champions. Mamaux came to the Pirates in 1913 after playing at Duquesne University and Huntington of the Ohio State League. Suspended twice for training rules violations, Mamaux was traded to Brooklyn in 1918, a season spent "in khaki." He was waived by the Dodgers in 1923 because he didn't "take baseball more seriously." Leaving the majors in 1924, he pitched and managed in the minors through 1936, leading the International League in wins in 1927 and leading Newark to IL pennants in 1930–31. Throughout his baseball career he starred as a singer on the vaudeville circuits. After leaving baseball, Mamaux sold insurance, worked for the railroad, and worked as a guard at an amusement park. For a time he held an appointment as Recreation Director at Newark, NJ. He died at Santa Monica, CA, on January 2, 1963, at age 68. (*Sporting News; Washington Post; Atlanta Constitution; Total Baseball*)

Les Mann joined the Braves as a 20-year-old outfielder in 1913 and remained in the majors for 16 years, the first 8 as a regular, helping the 1914 Braves and the 1918 Cubs win NL championships. His career .282 average was enhanced by part-time service in which he hit over .300 five times. Mann earned his shot with the Braves by leading the Northwestern League in homers in 1912 while hitting .300. When his playing career had ended, he held a number of administrative positions involving athletics. He was the founder of the National Amateur Baseball Association; he was instrumental in helping get baseball made into an Olympic sport; in 1933 he helped found a baseball school. Mann also served as director of Physical Education at Rice Institute and later as head baseball and basketball coach at Indiana University. He was Director of Athletics for the USO in Hawaii during World War II. A native of Lincoln, NE, Mann died at Pasadena, CA, on January 14, 1962, at age 68. (*Sporting News; California Certificate of Death; Total Baseball; Washington Post; Encyclopedia of Minor League Baseball*)

Walter (Rabbit) Maranville played 23 seasons in the majors, 17 as a regular shortstop or second baseman. He led the NL in putouts seven times, in double plays and fielding five times each and in assists four times. A .295 hitter for the 1922 Pirates, he settled for .258 over his career. However, he hit .308 in World Series play for both the 1914 Braves and the 1928 Cardinals. Maranville entered the majors with the Braves at the end of 1912, coming from New Bedford. Except for military service in 1918, he was a regular through 1924. He was playing manager of the Cubs in 1925 and was released by the Dodgers in 1926. After a year at Rochester,

Rabbit Maranville

he returned to regular status for the next six seasons. Leaving the Braves in 1935, Maranville managed in the minors through 1941, making occasional playing appearances. In later years he became director of the *New York Journal-American*'s baseball school. On January 5, 1954, at age 62, he died of a heart attack at his New York City home. Maranville was posthumously elected to the Hall of Fame in 1954. (*Sporting News; Total Baseball; Deadball Stars of the National League; New York Times*)

Cliff Markle had trials with the Yankees in 1915–16, and 1924 and with the Reds in 1921–22. In all he worked just over 234 innings, winning 12. Markle began at Morristown in 1913, leading the Appalachian League in strikeouts. In 1914 he led the Virginia League with 31 wins and 265 strikeouts. In military service during World War I, he was a reported casualty. He earned his shot with the Reds after pitching for Salt Lake City and Atlanta. Returned to St. Paul, he gained a final trial with the Yankees in 1924. The native of Lincoln Plains, PA, was still pitching in the Texas League in 1928. He died at Temple City, CA, on May 24, 1974, at age 80. According to Bill Lee, Markle "was a warehouse foreman for Westinghouse-Parker for ten years." (*Hall of Fame file; Baseball-Reference.com; Atlanta Constitution; New York Times; Baseball Necrology*)

Richard (Rube) Marquard won 201 games in 18 seasons, but his Hall of Fame reputation rests on three monster seasons of 1911–13 when he went 24–7, 26–11 and 23–10 for the champion Giants, leading the NL in strikeouts in 1911 and in victories in 1912. In that season he also beat the Red Sox twice in the World Series, giving up only one earned run in 18 innings. He had come to the Giants at the end of 1908 after a 28-win, 250-strikeout performance at Indianapolis. Traded to Brooklyn in 1915, he helped the Dodgers to two pennants. In 1916 he compiled a 1.58 ERA while winning 13 games. Finishing with the Braves in 1925, Marquard pitched and

Rube Marquard

managed in the minors through 1933. In 1930 the Cleveland native moved to Baltimore, where he became a pari-mutuels clerk at a racetrack. Elected to the Hall of Fame in 1971, he died at Baltimore on June 1, 1980, at age 90. (*Baseball's Best; Baseball-Reference.com; Deadball stars of the National League; New York Times*)

Armando Marsans, "the Cuban Ty Cobb," hit .317 and .297 as a regular outfielder for the Reds in 1912–13. In 1916 he finished second to Ty Cobb in stolen bases while playing for the Browns. Marsans, along with fellow Cuban Rafael Almeida, was signed by the Reds in 1911 from New Britain. After jumping to the Federal League in 1914, he was awarded to the Browns in 1916. He played eight seasons in the majors before a broken leg forced him back to the minors,

Christy Mathewson

his career figures showing a .269 average and 171 stolen bases. Player-manager in the minors at Elmira, NY, he later managed in Mexico. At the time of his death, he was regarded as one of the five greatest players Cuba ever produced. Marsans died of cancer in Havana on September 3, 1960, at age 74. (*Times of Havana; Hall of Fame file; Total Baseball*)

Joe Mathes spent 68 years in professional baseball, but played in only 32 games in the majors. Signed from the St. Louis sandlots as a $60-a-month infielder in 1910, he went on to play 4 games with the 1912 A's, 26 with the 1914 St. Louis Federals and 2 with the 1916 Braves. He first entered the majors from Butte of the Union Association. After playing and managed in the minors until 1936, Mathes then became a Cardinal scout. With the Cardinals he often served as "scouting supervisor or head of minor league playing personnel." At the time of his death he was still scouting for the Cubs and was believed to be the "oldest active man in baseball." He died at St. Louis on December 21, 1978, at age 87. (*Sporting News; Total Baseball; Washington Post*)

Christy Mathewson won 20 or more games 13 times and 30 or more games four times en route to a NL record 373 career wins. Among other career accomplishments were 80 shutouts and a 2.13 ERA. He led the NL four times in wins and shutouts and five times in strikeouts and ERA. A big money pitcher, he had 10 complete games, four shutouts and a 1.15 ERA in World Series play. While a student a Bucknell, Mathewson began playing professional baseball, being promoted from Norfolk to the Giants before his 20th birthday. A year later he was a 20-game winner. In a monster 1908 season he won 37 games, 11 by shutout, with a 1.43 ERA. After World War I he was in ill health for a number of years because of inhaling lethal gas in France. He later developed tuberculosis but died of pneumonia at Saranac Lake, NY, on October 7, 1925, at age 45. Mathewson had managed the Reds and coached the Giants; at the time of his death he was President of the Braves. A younger brother Henry pitched briefly for the Giants. (*Sporting News; Total Baseball; New York Times; SABR Collegiate Database; Deadball Stars of the National League*)

Erskine Mayer (James Erskine) was nicknamed "Eelskin Mayer" by the Dodgers because of his slippery sidearm curve. He won 91 games in eight big league seasons, including back-to-back 21-win seasons with the Phillies in 1914–15. The 6'1", 150-pounder lost a 2–1 duel to Rube Foster in Game 2 of the 1915 World Series, and closed his major league career with an inning of relief for the White Sox in the 1919 World Series. A native of Atlanta, he had attended Georgia Tech before entering professional baseball. He came to the Phillies at the end of 1912 after leading the Virginia League with 26 victories at Portsmouth. Pitching more than 595 innings over a two-year period took its toll on his arm. While he won 16 games in 1918, he was traded to the Pirates and by 1919 was through as a major league pitcher and by 1920 was out of baseball. At the time of his death, Mayer operated a cigar stand in Los Angeles. He died of a heart attack there on March 10, 1957, at age 68. (*Sporting News; Total Baseball; Deadball Stars of the National League; Encyclopedia of Minor League Baseball; SABR Collegiate Database*)

Carl Mays compiled Hall of Fame numbers for his 15 major league seasons. The right-handed submariner had five 20-win seasons and 208 career wins with a 2.92 ERA, but he was always tarred with having thrown the pitch that killed Ray Chapman. Despite Ban Johnson's prediction that he would never throw another pitch, Mays had a league leading 27 wins and seven saves the following season. Five years later he led the NL with 24 complete games. He also had 5 complete games in seven World Series starts (2.35 ERA) for the Red Sox and Yankees. As a rookie in 1915 Mays made 32 relief appearances, leading the AL in saves. He closed his career with the 1929 Giants in much the same role — 29 relief appearances, 7 wins and 4 saves. The Kentucky native remained in baseball, scouting for Cleveland and Milwaukee and Kansas City. He died at El Cajon, CA, on April 4, 1971. (*San Diego Union; Baseball-Reference.com; Atlanta Constitution; New York Times*) **Photograph on page 58**

James (Ike) McAuley had four trials as a shortstop with the Pirates, Cardinals and Cubs, over a twelve-year period. He played 15 games with the Pirates in 1914 and 37 games for the Cubs in 1925. Overall the Wichita native played in 64 games, hitting .246. Minneapolis released him as a player after the 1927 season so that he could become manager of Des Moines of the Western Association. During spring training McAuley became ill with the flu and developed pneumonia. He died a month later on April 6, 1928, at age 36. (*Sporting News; Chicago Daily Tribune; Los Angeles Times; Baseball Encyclopedia*)

George McBride, a Milwaukee semi-pro, played shortstop for the original Milwaukee Brewers when they entered the American League on September 12, 1901. He returned to the majors with Pittsburgh in 1905 and was traded to St. Louis in 1906. Sent down to Kansas City because of weak hitting, he was purchased by the Senators for 1907. Despite his career .218 average, he spent 16 years in the majors, 11 as a regular shortstop. A fine fielder, he led AL shortstops in double plays six times and in fielding five times. McBride managed the Senators to a 4th place finish in 1921 and coached for the Tigers in 1925–26 and 1929. Because of investments he was able to live the life of a retired athlete, a member of the Milwaukee Athletic Club. He died on July 2, 1972, at age 92. (*Milwaukee Journal; Washington Post; Baseball Encyclopedia; Boston Daily Globe; information supplied by Ronald Bliffert*)

George McBride

Tim McCabe got off to a promising start with the Browns in 1915. The 20-year-old rookie completed all four of his starts with a 2.38 ERA, and in the following season he

Lew McCarty

had 13 successful relief appearances. Subsequent trials in 1917 and 1918 totaled fewer than four innings. He came to the Browns from Decatur of the Three-I League. Sent down to Salt Lake City in 1917, he was sold to Louisville in 1919. McCabe pitched in the minors until 1920 when arm injuries forced him to retire. Returning to his hometown of Ironton, MO, he became mill superintendent at Hanna Mining Company. McCabe died at Ironton on April 12, 1976, at age 82. (*Mountain Echo [Ironton]; Total Baseball; Washington Post; Sporting News*)

Alex McCarthy was the Pirates regular second baseman in 1912, hitting .277. But in eight seasons the Notre Dame product hit .229. After playing football and baseball at Notre Dame, he went to South Bend and was sold to the Pirates in October 1910. Sold to the Cubs in 1915, he was released to Kansas City in 1916, only to receive another trial with the Pirates. After leaving the Pirates in 1917, he played and managed in the minors until 1927. The Chicago native then moved to Salisbury, MD, where he was "employed in road construction and the building trade." Until he retired in 1965, he also tended bar at the William Penn Hotel in Salisbury. McCarthy died at a Salisbury nursing home on March 12, 1978, at age 88. (*Hall of Fame file; Atlanta Constitution; New York Times; Total Baseball; SABR Collegiate Database*)

Lew McCarty averaged 80 games per season as a catcher for the Dodgers and Giants 1914–19. After hitting .359 in 40 games for Newark in 1913, he was promoted to the Dodgers at the end of the season. A .266 hitter for his nine-year career, he reached .339 in 1916. McCarty played for the Cardinals in 1920 and in 1921 was sold to Kansas City. He also he played for Baltimore and Reading and managed Piedmont in 1927. Upon retiring from baseball, McCarty operated a hotel in Reading, PA. He died of cerebral embolus on June 19, 1930, at Reading. He was 41 years old. (*Pennsylvania Certificate of Death; Baseball; Reference.com; Reading Eagle; New York Times; Hall of Fame File*)

George McConnell, a tall right-hander from Tennessee, posted a 25–10 record for the Chicago Whales in 1915, leading the FL in wins and winning percentage. His major league record otherwise shows only 16 wins for three full seasons and parts of two others with the Yankees and Cubs. He came to the majors as a first baseman, playing 14 games there in 1909. With the Yankees in 1912 and 1913, McConnell played with the Cubs briefly in 1914 and in 1916. Sold to Kansas City in 1917, he left baseball in 1918. McConnell and his brother opened a photographic studio in Chattanooga, TN, which he operated until his death. He died at Chattanooga on May 10, 1964, at age 86. (*Sporting News; Baseball-Reference.com; New York Times; Chicago Daily Tribune*)

Lee McElwee joined the A's in 1916 after graduating from Bowdoin College. Debuting in July of that year, the Californian

George McConnell

appeared in 54 games—primarily as a third baseman—hitting a respectable .265. McElwee served in the U.S. Navy during World War I and then became a public accountant, operating services in Rockland, ME, and Union, ME. On February 8, 1957, he died at Union at age 62. (*Courier-Gazette [Rockland, ME]; Total Baseball; SABR Collegiate Database*)

Marty McHale was described by Damon Runyon as "probably the most versatile chap that ever followed the business of baseball." A two-sport star at the University of Maine, he signed with the Red Sox directly from college in 1910. Before joining the Air Force in 1917, McHale compiled a 12–20, 3.57 ERA career record. Most of his record came in 1914 when he pitched 191 innings for the Yankees, managing a 6–16, 2.97 ERA record. He sang in vaudeville to supplement his baseball earnings, wrote a weekly column for the *New York Sun*, formed his own film company, Athletic Feature Films, and finally founded his own investment securities company in New York City. He died at Hempstead, NY, on May 7, 1979, at age 90. (*Hall of Fame file; New York Times; SABR Collegiate Database; Total Baseball*)

John (Stuffy) McInnis was the first baseman on the famous "$100,000 infield" of the 1911–14 A's. A superb fielder, he led the AL in fielding five times, in 1921 making just one error in 1652 chances. He also had 2406 hits for a career .308 average, hitting over .300 ten times in 14 seasons as a regular. Along the way McInnis helped five teams win league championships—the 1911, 1913, and 1914 A's, the 1918 Red Sox and the 1925 Pirates. Connie Mack originally signed him as a shortstop from Haverhill of the New England League in 1909. After managing the Phillies in 1927 and Salem, MA, in 1928, he spent the next 26 years coaching at Norwich College, Brooks School, and Harvard University. He died at Ipswich, MA, on February 16, 1960, at age 69. (*Chicago Daily Tribune; Baseball Encyclopedia; Atlanta Constitution; New York Times*)

Bill McKechnie was a statistically average major league player for 1916, playing in 11 seasons, four as a regular third baseman, and hitting .251. In his best season he hit .304 at Indianapolis while leading the FL in total chances, assists and double plays. From the Pittsburgh suburb of Wilkinsburg, McKechnie had a trial with the Pirates in 1907. When his playing career ended at Minneapolis in 1921, he began the managerial career that eventually led him to the Hall of Fame in 1962. McKechnie managed from 1922 through 1946, winning pennants with the

Bill McKechnie

Pirates (1925), the Cardinals (1928), and the Reds (1939–40). After coaching Cleveland 1946–49, he retired to Florida, where he did well in land and oil investments. He died at Bradenton, FL, on October 29, 1965, at age 78. (*Chicago Daily Tribune; New York Times; Baseball Encyclopedia*)

Raymond (Red) McKee caught four seasons with the Tigers, hitting .254 in 186 games, but he spent 28 years (1910–37) in organized baseball. He joined the Tigers from Battle Creek in 1913, hitting .283 in 67 games. This was his most productive season. In 1920–21 he managed and played for the local Saginaw team of the Michigan-Ontario League. In 1942 McKee went to work for Eaton Manufacturing Co in its Plant Protection squad, a position he held until he retired in 1958. He lived most of his life in Saginaw, MI, dying there on August 5, 1972, at age 82. (*Hall of Fame file; Baseball Encyclopedia; Encyclopedia of Minor League Baseball*)

Frank (Limb) McKenry pitched in 27 games over a two-year period for the Reds, winning six and losing six. The *Los Angeles Times* heralded him as a second Walter Johnson when he entered the PCL in 1913, yielding only one run in his first two starts. The 6'4" right hander came to the Reds in June 1915 from Victoria and won 5 games. During the 1916 season, the Tennessee native quit the club and moved to California to operate a fruit farm. However, he was still pitching in the PCL as late as 1926. Suffering from arthritis, the 68-year-old McKenry killed himself with a shotgun on November 1, 1956. (*Sporting News; Los Angeles Times; Total Baseball*)

Fred McMullin was one of the eight White Sox players banned from organized baseball after the 1920 season. After a one-game trial with the Tigers in 1914, McMullin spent five seasons (1916–20) in Chicago as a utility infielder. Overall he hit .256 in 304 games, but he hit .294 for the AL champions in 1919. McMullin was a native of Scammon, KS, but his family moved to Los Angeles when he was 14, and this was his home for the rest of his life. He always maintained his innocence in the fix of the 1919 World Series but knew of it, and so was banned. In later years McMullin worked as a deputy in the office of the U.S. Marshal in Los Angeles. He died in Los Angeles on November 21, 1952, at age 61. (*Sporting News; 1919Black Sox.com; baseball-reference.com*)

Mike McNally became the first player to steal home in a World Series game on October 5, 1921. A cousin of the O'Neill brothers, he spent 10 seasons in the majors as a utility infielder with the Red Sox, Yankees and Senators. In his busiest season he hit .256 in 93 games for the Red Sox in 1920. Only a .238 career hitter, he was regarded as an exceptionally fine third baseman and base runner. Early in his career he was used frequently as a pinch runner. After finishing his major league career with Washington in 1925, McNally began a career as a minor league manager at Binghamton, Wilkes-Barre, and Williamsport. He scouted for the Indians and later became their Farm Director. Retiring in 1960, he remained with the Indians as a "roving goodwill ambassador." A resident of Cleveland, McNally died of an apparent heart attack while visiting in Bethlehem, PA, on May 29, 1965. He was 71 years old. (*Bethlehem Globe-Times; Total Baseball; Washington Post; Encyclopedia of Minor League Baseball*)

George McQuillan, at age 23, won 23 games for the Phillies with a 1.53 ERA. He had been promoted on the basis of work at Providence. Two years later, in 1910, he led the NL with a 1.60 ERA. But he refused "to take care of himself," and his ten-year totals show 85 wins. In 1911 the Phillies dealt him to Cincinnati, who sent him to Columbus. He came back with the Pirates in 1915, was passed back to the Phillies in 1916, and finished with Cleveland in 1919. Subsequently he played for and managed seven minor league clubs before ending his involvement with organized baseball in 1926. The Brooklyn native then became "affiliated with the F. & R. Lazarus Company" in Columbus, OH. He died of a heart attack at his home there on March 30, 1940, at age 54. (*Sporting News; Deadball Stars of the National League; Baseball-Reference.com; New York Times*)

Bill (Pudge) McTigue had trials with the Braves in 1911 and 1912 and with the Tigers in 1916, pitching 77 innings with two wins. He was only 20 years old when he joined the Braves from New Bedford in 1911, but after 14 games and a 0–5 record, he was optioned to Montreal and recalled in 1912, winning two games. He pitched in 3 games for the Tigers and finished with Providence in 1917. Leaving baseball due to ill health, he died of tuberculosis in Nashville, TN, on May 11, 1920, at age 29. (*Sporting News; Boston Daily Globe; Total Baseball*)

Pudge McTigue

Lee Meadows was the first major leaguer to wear glasses. In his first 13 seasons (1915–27), the right-hander won 187 games with the Cardinals, Phillies and Pirates, winning at least 10 games 11 times and leading the NL with 20 wins in 1926. For the NL champion Pirate teams of 1925 and 1927, Meadows won 19 games each season and lost one start in each World Series. He won 13 games as a Cardinal rookie, coming directly from Durham of the North Carolina State League. After pitching little in 1928 because of a sore arm, he was optioned to Indianapolis in 1929. Remaining in baseball until 1938, he pitched and managed in the minors. Then the North Carolina native became an IRS employee, moving to Daytona Beach, FL. He died at Daytona Beach following a stroke on January 29, 1963, at age 68. (*Sporting News; Baseball-Reference.com; Chicago Daily Tribune; Washington Post; New York Times*)

Mike Menosky was a regular outfielder for five seasons with the Senators and Red Sox. A career .278 hitter for nine seasons, he had back-to-back .297 and .300 seasons in 1920–21. He played at Indiana (PA) Teachers in 1913 and joined the Pittsburgh Federals in 1914–15. The Senators selected him from Minneapolis in 1916, and he became a regular in 1917. After service in France in World War I, he had his best years. The *Washington Post* deemed him "one of the speediest players in the American League." After leaving the Red Sox in 1923, he played at Vernon and Columbus. By 1928 he is described as "being in business in Detroit." Menosky later became a probation officer in Detroit. He died there on April 11, 1983, at age 88. (*Sporting News; SABR Collegiate Database; Washington Post; Los Angeles Times; Chicago Daily Tribune*)

Fred Merkle played 16 major league seasons—11 as a regular first baseman—but is forever remembered for his failure to touch second base, costing the Giants the 1908 NL championship. The 18-year-old Merkle joined the Giants in September 1907 from Tecumseh. He became the regular first baseman in 1910, hitting .292. The career .273 hitter hit .309 in 1912 and .297 for the Cubs in 1918. In 27 World Series games with the Giants, Dodgers and Cubs, he hit .239. He played for Rochester (1921–24) and coached for the Yankees (1925–26), but suffered the loss of most of his baseball earning during the Depression. Before World War II, he obtained work in WPA projects; after the war he became "a partner in a small business that manufactured fishing equipment." He died at Daytona Beach, FL, on March 2, 1956, at age 67. (*Sporting News; Deadball Stars of the National League; Baseball-Reference.com*)

Billy Meyer hit .236 in 113 games as a catcher for the White Sox (1913) and A's (1916–17). The Knoxville, TN, native played one game for the White Sox late in 1913, coming from Davenport, IA. Purchased by Connie Mack in 1916, Meyer played very sparingly in Philadelphia through 1917. Sold to Louisville in 1918, he took over as manager there in 1926. He managed in the New York Yankee farm system through 1947, winning eight pennants — three in Kansas City. In 1948 Meyer accepted the managerial job with Pittsburgh, winning a Manager of the Year award in 1948. He later scouted for the Pirates through 1955 when he suffered a heart attack. Continuing heart problems and a kidney infection resulted in his death on March 31, 1957, at age 65. (*Sporting News; New York Times; Baseball-Reference.com*)

John (Chief) Meyers, a Jacarata Indian from California, caught on the great Giants teams of 1910–14. Having attended Dartmouth College for a year, he was already 28 years old before he caught a major league game. He came to the Giants at the end of 1908 from St. Paul and went on to hit .291 in nine seasons while catching 925 games. He also hit .290 in 18 World Series games and threw out 12 base runners in the 1911 World Series. In 1911, 1912, and 1913 Meyers hit .332, .358, and .312. Crossing town, he also shared catching duties for the 1916 NL champion Dodgers. When he left the majors in 1917, he managed at New Haven for a time and then became employed by the Bureau of Indian Affairs. However even at age 50, he was still able to catch for an old-timers all-star team on a nationwide tour. He died at San Bernardino, CA, on July 25, 1971, at age 90. (*The

Chief Meyers

Glory of their Time; Deadball Stars of the National League; Total Baseball; New York Times)

Clyde (Deerfoot) Milan led the AL with 88 steals in 1912 and 75 steals in 1913. In 14 seasons as the regular centerfielder for the Senators, Milan hit over .300 four times on his way to a .285 average. He reached .322 in 1920 and .315 in 1911. Because of his great speed, "he played center field more shallow than any man in baseball," according to Clark Griffith. Milan finished his major league career in 1922, playing in 11 games while managing the Senators. The Tennessee native then played and managed in the

Clyde Milan

minors through 1936, winning a Southern Association championship with Birmingham in 1931. In 1937 he returned to the Senators as a coach, a position he held until his death. On March 3, 1953, Milan died of a heart attack, suffered during spring training at Orlando, FL. He was 65 years old. His younger brother Horace was also an outfielder for the Senators. (*Sporting News; New York Times; Total Baseball; Encyclopedia of Minor League Baseball*)

Elmer Miller hit .298 while playing centerfield for the AL champion Yankees in 1921. A three-time regular, he hit .243 in seven seasons with the Cardinals, Yankees and Red Sox. He entered the majors with the Cardinals in 1912, having played at Duluth in 1911. The Yankees purchased him from Mobile in 1915, and he stayed with them off and on through 1922, when he was sold to the Red Sox. Miller left the Red Sox in 1923 to work for Fairbanks Morse & Co of Beloit, WI, and play for the Beloit Fairies of the independent Midwest League. After five seasons as a player and two more as manager, he retired from baseball, but remained a Fairbanks Morse employee. He died from a heart attack on November 28, 1944, at age 54. (*Beloit Daily News; Sporting News; Baseball-Reference.com*) **Photograph on page 23**

Frank (Bullet) Miller won 52 games in five full seasons as a starter with the Pirates and Braves. Originally the property of the White Sox, he reached the majors at the end of 1913, coming from San Francisco. Sent down to Montreal, he returned with the Pirates in 1916. In his best season, the right-hander from Salem, MI, won 13 games for the 1919 Pirates. He sat out the next two seasons after suffering diphtheria. After finishing with the Braves in early 1923, he retired from baseball and purchased a farm near Allegan, MI, which he operated until he retired. He died at Allegan on February 19, 1974, at age 87. (*Allegan County News and Gazette; information supplied by Melvin F. Miller; Baseball Encyclopedia; Chicago Daily Tribune; New York Times; Washington Post*)

John (Dots) Miller joined the Pirates in 1909 as the regular second baseman, helping them to a World Championship. By 1912 he had become the regular first baseman. In 12 seasons with the Pirates, Cardinals and Phillies, Miller hit .263 and led the NL in fielding twice. In his best season he hit .290 for the Cardinals in 1914. Finishing his major league career in 1921, he hit .297 in 84 games with the Phillies. Miller became manager of the San Francisco Seals of the PCL in 1922 but contracted tuberculosis. He died at a sanitarium at Saranac Lake, NY, on September 5, 1923, at age 36. (*Sporting News; Total Baseball; New York Times*)

Lawrence (Hack) Miller, one of the strongest men ever to play major league baseball, hit .323 in six seasons with the Dodgers, Red Sox and Cubs, using a 47-ounce — and at times a 65-ounce — bat. Despite his lofty average, he held regular status as a Cubs outfielder only in 1922 and 1923. The son of a professional wrestler and strongman, Miller took his nickname from wrestling great Hackenschmidt. He played in three games for the Dodgers in 1916, coming from Winnipeg. He spent the next five seasons–except for a 12-game trial with the Red Sox in 1918 — with Oakland before joining the Cubs in 1922. Miller led the PCL in hits in 1918 and 1920 and in average in 1921. After spending 15 years in professional baseball, he became a longshoreman on the San Francisco–Oakland waterfront, serving as a crew boss. Miller died of a pulmonary embolism at Oakland on September 17, 1971. He was 77 years old. (*Hall of Fame file; Sporting News; Los Angeles Times; Encyclopedia of Minor League Baseball*)

Otto (Moonie) Miller, a Nebraska native, caught 13 seasons for the Dodgers (1910–22) and stayed on to become a Brooklynite for life. The Dodgers drafted him from Duluth in 1910, and he became their first string catcher in 1912. A career .245 hitter, he hit .255 in 73 games for the 1916 NL champions and .289 in 90 games for the 1920 champs, when he also led NL catchers in fielding. Miller later worked for a while on Wall Street, coached for the Dodgers, and managed a bar near Ebbets Field. Following unsuccessful surgery to remove a cataract from his left eye, he apparently leaped to his death from the fourth floor of the hospital on March 29, 1962, at age 72. (*Hall of Fame file; New York Certificate of Death; Total Baseball; New York Times*)

Ward (Windy) Miller reached stardom in the Federal league, where he hit .294 and .306 for the St. Louis Terriers. The left-handed hitting outfielder spent eight seasons in the majors—three as a regular—hitting .278. He played baseball at Northern Illinois University before joining the Pirates in 1909 and leading the NL with 11 pinch hits in 1910. The speedy outfielder—he was timed in 3.2 seconds in getting to first base after a bunt—joined the Cubs in 1912 from Montreal. In 1914 he jumped to the Federal League and in 1916 was awarded to the Browns. A native of Mt. Carmel, IL, he became police chief for the state school at Dixon, IL, after leaving baseball. He died from heart failure at Dixon on September 4, 1958, at age 74. (*Illinois Certificate of Death; Sporting News; SABR Collegiate Database; Baseball Encyclopedia*)

Clarence Mitchell threw his slippery elm bark–aided spitter until 1932, the only lefty among those legally entitled to throw it after 1920. He won 125 games in 18 major league seasons, his high of 13 coming with the 1931 Giants. He also pitched in two World Series, hitting a line drive to Bill Wambsganns in 1920 to start the only unassisted triple play in series history. Mitchell pitched in five games for the Tigers in 1911 and returned to the majors with Cincinnati in 1916. With time out to serve with the U.S. Army in France in 1918, he also pitched for Brooklyn, the Phillies, and Cardinals. After leaving the majors, Mitchell continued to pitch in the minors until he was 49 years old and also managed in the minors. Out of baseball, he operated a tavern at Aurora, NE, and raised greyhounds. The heart condition, which caused him to lose both legs, ultimately resulted in his death at Grand Island, NE, on November 6, 1963, at age 72. (*Sporting News; Total Baseball; New York Times; Washington Post*)

Willie Mitchell, a left-handed Mississippian, won 83 games for the Indians and Tigers in eight full seasons and parts of three others. After graduating from Mississippi A&M—now Mississippi State—in June 1909, he set a Texas League record in August by striking out 20 batters in one game while pitching for San Antonio. By season's end he had completed all three starts for the Indians. In 1913 he posted a 14-8 record with a 1.74 ERA. Released to the Tigers in 1916, he went 12-8 (2.19 ERA) in 1917 before serving in the U.S. Army. When he left baseball, he became an agent for Standard Oil in Meridian and later in Sardis, MS. He died at Sardis on November 23, 1973, at age 83. (*Southern Reporter [Sardis, MS]Total Baseball; SABR Collegiate Database; Encyclopedia of Minor League Baseball; information supplied by Mrs. Daisy Mitchell*)

Ralph Mitterling joined the A's in 1916 directly from Ursinus College, where he was a teammate of Jing Johnson. The outfielder played in 13 games, hitting .154. He served in the Army in World War I before finishing his baseball career at Springfield in 1919. Completing graduate studies at Springfield College and NYU, Mitterling became a teacher and coach. He coached baseball at East Stroudsburg Normal School 1927–36. In 1939 he became baseball coach at the University of Pittsburgh, a position he held until his death. Mitterling died of a stroke at the Veterans Administration hospital in Pittsburgh on January 22, 1956. He was 65 years old. (*Hall of Fame file; New York Times; Baseball Encyclopedia; East Stroudsburg Athletic History*)

Danny Moeller

Dan Moeller came to the majors by way of Millikin University, where he played in 1906–07. He was the Senators regular right fielder for four of his seven big league seasons, reaching a .276 batting average in 1912. A year later he stole 62 bases despite a .236 batting average and a league-leading 103 strikeouts. Before the 1914 season he sold his automobile because the club thought owning it hampered his performance. Released by Cleveland after the 1916 season, he spent five seasons in the minors before retired from baseball in 1921. Ironically, Moeller then began to work for companies manufacturing automobile parts. A native of Iowa, he had begun work at the Muscle Shoals Auto Parts Company in Florence, AL. Following a two-day illness, he died at Florence on April 14, 1951, at age 66. (*Sporting News; Washington Post; SABR College Database; Baseball Encyclopedia*)

George Mogridge, a thin lefthander, emerged at age 32 as one of the strong men of the Washington pitching staff, winning 65 games between 1921 and 1924. For the 1924 World Champions Mogridge went 16–11 with a World Series win. In 15 major league seasons, he posted a 132–131 record, leading the AL in games (45) and saves (7) in 1918. Mogridge joined the White Sox from Galesburg in August, 1911. The Yankees brought him up to stay in 1916, sending him to Washington in 1921. When he left baseball, Mogridge returned to his native Rochester, NY, where he operated an inn and later a sporting goods store. After 1943 he became an employee of Weathermaster, a manufacturer of storm windows. He died in Rochester of a heart attack on March 4, 1962, at age 72. (*Hall of Fame file; Rochester Democrat and Chronicle; Chicago Daily Tribune; Baseball-Reference.com; Baseball Necrology*)

Frederick (Fritz) Mollwitz was the only German-born player among the Men of '16. He was the regular first baseman for the Reds in 1915, for the Reds and Cubs in 1916, and for the Pirates in 1918, leading the NL in fielding in 1915. The Cubs drafted him from

Green Bay in September 1913, traded him to the Reds in 1914, and got him back on waivers in 1916. After seven seasons Mollwitz closed his major league career in 1919 with a .241 batting average. At Sacramento of the PCL, beginning in 1920, he played first, and "there perhaps is none better in this league." He continued to play and manage in the minors until 1929, then left baseball to join the police force at Shorewood, WI. Mollwitz died at Bradenton, FL, on October 3, 1967, at age 77. (*Sporting News; Total Baseball; Chicago Daily Tribune; Washington Post; Los Angeles Times*)

Ray Morgan was the Senators regular second baseman for six of his eight major league seasons, twice leading the AL in double plays. A .254 career hitter, he reached .272 in 1913. The Senators acquired him in 1911 from Danville, and he played the last 25 games of the season at third base. Waived to the Phillies in 1919, he refused to report and was sold to Baltimore. Following a disagreement with Orioles management, he was sold to Akron and retired in 1920. Morgan was a native of Baltimore, where he operated a café after leaving baseball. On February 15, 1940, he died in a Baltimore hospital from a heart ailment and pneumonia. He was 50 years old. (*Sporting News; Baltimore Evening Sun; Baseball Encyclopedia; Washington Post*)

George Moriarty is better known for his 22 years as an American League umpire (1917–26) and 1929–40) than as a player, but he was a regular first or third baseman for the Yankees (1907–08) and Tigers (1909–14). In 13 major league seasons he hit .251 and played in the 1909 World Series. Moriarty spent more than fifty years in organized baseball as player, manager, umpire and scout. The Cubs picked him up from the sandlots of Woodstock, IL, and he made brief appearances for them in both 1903 and 1904. The Yankees acquired him from Toledo in 1906 after he stole 51 bases there. He finished as a player with the White Sox in 1916 and later managed the Tigers (1927–28). When he retired as an umpire, he worked in public relations for the AL, then became a "master scout" for the Tigers, a position he held until 1959. Moriarty died at Miami, FL, on April 8, 1964, at age 80. His older brother Bill played briefly with the Reds. (*Sporting News; New York Times; Total Baseball; Washington Post*)

Bill Morrisette had trials with the A's in 1915 and 1916 and with the Tigers in 1920. In all, the right-hander spitballer pitched in 13 games with a 3–1, 3.35 ERA record. He was a native of Baltimore and pitched college baseball at Mount St. Mary's. Morrisette began his professional career at Richmond in 1915, moving from there to the A's. Sent down after one game in 1916, he pitched at Baltimore, Mobile, and Jersey City before earning a return trip to the majors. Upon leaving baseball, Morrisette became a U.S. Civil Service employee and moved to Virginia Beach, VA. He died in a nursing home there on March 25, 1966, at age 71. (*Virginia Pilot [Virginia Beach, VA]; Total Baseball; Washington Post*)

Guy Morton won 98 games for the Indians in 11 seasons. After coming to the Indians from Waterbury in June of 1914, he turned in a 1–13 record. He won at least 10 games in each of the next four seasons,

Ray Morgan

topped by a 16-win, 2.14 ERA season in 1915. After working only 137 innings for the 1920 World Champions, Morton did not appear in the World Series that year. He went 14–9 in 1922 but drew his release in early 1924. He continued to pitch in the American Association, the Southern Association, and the Piedmont League until early 1932, when he became an employee of the Tennessee Valley Authority. Only forty years old at the time of his death, Morton died of a heart attack at his home in Sheffield, AL, on October 18, 1934. A son Guy, Jr. made a pinch hitting appearance for the Red Sox in 1954. (*Sporting News; Total Baseball; Atlanta Constitution; Chicago Daily Tribune*)

Earl Moseley began by throwing rocks at squirrels on an Ohio farm and went on to win games in all three major leagues. He won 34 games for Indianapolis/Newark in the Federal league, eight with the Red Sox and 7 with the Reds. The Central League strikeout leader in 1912 at Youngstown, Moseley was sold to the Red Sox. Jumping to Indianapolis in 1914, he led the FL with a 1.91 ERA in 1915. After serving overseas in World War I, he pitched in the minors until 1922, when he became baseball coach at Mount Union College, later serving in the Maintenance Department there. He also owned a clothing store in Mount Union. Moseley died of cancer at Alliance, OH, on July 1, 1963, at age 78. (*Alliance Review; Encyclopedia of Minor League Baseball; Total Baseball; Washington Post*)

Harry (Mike) Mowrey was the regular third baseman for the Reds, Cardinals, Pirates, Pittsburgh Federals and Dodgers during his 13-year major league career, leading a league three times in double plays and twice in fielding. A career .256 hitter, he hit .282 in 1910. Mowrey began his professional career with Savannah in 1905 and was promoted to the Reds at the end of the season. Awarded to the Dodgers after the FL folded, he helped them win the 1916 NL championship, and finished with the club in 1917.

After World War I he played for and managed minor league teams in Hagerstown, MD, and his hometown of Chambersburg, PA, until 1923. When Mowrey left baseball, he was employed as a night watchman at Wilson College and later at Letterkenny Ordinance Depot. He died of heart disease at Chambersburg on March 20, 1947, at age 62. (*Hall of Fame File; Sporting News; Baseball Encyclopedia; Public Opinion [Chambersburg]; Pennsylvania Certificate of Death*)
Photograph on page 45

Charlie Mullen was the regular first baseman for the Yankees in 1914, hitting .260 in 93 games. A great Seattle schoolboy and University of Washington star, he was signed originally by the White Sox for whom he played in 1910–11. Arriving directly from campus, he got into 41 games, hitting .191. In 1914 the Yankees claimed him from Lincoln and he played with them through 1916. In five major league seasons, Mullen hit .247. After serving as a Second Lieutenant in the Army in World War I, he managed Seattle and Tacoma of the PCL in 1919–20. In 1922 he joined H. M. Herrin & Co., a Seattle securities firm. Mullen later became president of the Seattle Stock Exchange. He died in Seattle on June 6, 1963, at age 75. (*Seattle Times; Washington Post; Total Baseball; Chicago Daily Tribune*)

Eddie Mulligan was the regular third baseman for the White Sox in 1921–22. Overall he spent 5 seasons in the majors over a 14-year period, hitting .232 for 351 games. The St. Louis native played at Saint Louis University and joined the Cubs as a shortstop in late 1915. He played in 58 games in 1916 but hit only .153 and was released to Kansas City. The White Sox then acquired him from Salt Lake City. He finished his major league career playing 27 games for the Pirates in 1928. Beginning in 1922 he played in the PCL for 17 seasons. Mulligan became a club owner in 1939, and in 1956 he began a 20-year term as President of the California League. Suffering from emphysema, he died on March 15, 1982, at San Rafael, CA, at age

Eddie Murphy

87. (*Sporting News; Total Baseball; SABR Collegiate Data Base; Chicago Daily Tribune; Los Angeles Times*)

Eddie Murphy joined the A's as a 20-year-old outfielder from Villanova University in 1912, hitting .317 in 33 games. He was a regular with their championship teams of the next two years, hitting .295 and .272 (but only .227 and .188 in World Series play). Traded to the White Sox in 1915, he played on two championship teams there, holding regular status in 1915 and 1918. After the "Black Sox" scandal, he acquired the nickname "Honest Eddie," because he was not involved. In 11 seasons the left-handed Murphy hit .287. After last playing in the majors with Pittsburgh in 1926, he served in the WPA as a recreation supervisor; during World War II he was in the USO, and later worked as a clerk at Grumman Aircraft for a number of years. Murphy died of prostate cancer at Dunmore, PA, on February 21, 1969. He was 77 years old. (*Hall of Fame file; Washington Post; Total Baseball; SABR Collegiate Database*)

Mike Murphy caught in one game for the Cardinals in 1912 and played in 14 games for the A's in 1916, hitting .111. He had played at Villanova prior to entering organized baseball and came to the Cardinals via Dallas. After being sent down to Binghamton in mid-1916, he continued to play in the minors until 1924, returning as an umpire in the New York–Pennsylvania League in 1926. Murphy spent the last 33 years of his life in Johnson City, NY, where he worked as a machinist for the Ozalid Corporation. He died of a cerebral hemorrhage at Johnson City on October 26, 1952, at age 64. (*Sporting News; New York Certificate of Death; SABR Collegiate Database; Baseball-Reference.com*)

Elmer Myers won 14 games in 1916, 39 percent of the A's total of 36. He joined the A's from Raleigh, "the moonshine hills of North Carolina," in October 1916. Even though he was gassed while serving as a stretcher-bearer at the end of World War I, he remained a strong AL pitcher through 1921, posting an 11-5, 3.27 ERA record in 1920. His career totals show 55 wins and a 4.06 ERA in 8 seasons with the A's, Indians and Red Sox. After leaving the Red Sox in 1922, he pitched in the PCL, the Southern Association, and the American Association. In ill health, a delayed effect of the gassing, Myers first tried selling for a pork packing concern, but he found the work too difficult. He and his wife then opened a cigar and confectionery store in Atlantic City, NJ. He died at Collingwood, NJ, on July 29, 1976, at age 82. (*Hall of Fame file; Chicago Daily Tribune; Washington Post; Los Angeles Times; Total Baseball*)

Henry (Hy) Myers was a speedy centerfielder on two NL champion Dodger teams. He first came to the Dodgers in August 1909 from Anderson, SC, and joined them to stay in 1914, holding regular status through 1922 before finishing his 14-year career with the Cardinals and Reds. A career .281 hitter, he hit as high as .307 in 1919 when he led the NL in triples, RBI's and slugging. He also led in triples the following season when he hit .304.

Traded to St. Louis in 1923, he finished his major league career in 1925. A native of Ohio, Myers owned an automobile agency in Kensington, OH, and later worked in a bank there. He died suddenly at Minerva, OH, on May 1, 1965, at age 76. (*Minerva Leader; Atlanta Constitution; Total Baseball; New York Times*)

Jack Nabors compiled a 1–20 record for the 1916 A's, despite a 3.47 ERA. The A's scored 2 or fewer runs behind him 14 times. Nabors came to the A's in August 1915 from the Georgia-Alabama League, where he had a 12–1 record. Sent down to Indianapolis in 1917, he left the majors with a 1–25 record for three seasons. He spent what was to be his last year in organized baseball with Sioux City in 1918. Nabors enlisted in the army, where he came down with a severe case of the Spanish flu, leading to tuberculosis. He spent the remainder of his life in and out of a sick bed, dying at Wilton, AL, on October 29, 1923, at age 36, a delayed casualty of World War I. (*Hall of Fame file; Total Baseball; Encyclopedia of Minor League Baseball; Anniston Star*)

Alfred (Greasy) Neale had an 8-year major league career—five as a regular—as an outfielder for the Reds and Phillies. A career .259 hitter, he hit .294 in 1917 and .357 in the 1919 World Series. The Reds acquired him in 1916 from Wheeling, and he became an instant regular, playing through 1924. But he is best remembered as a football player and coach. As a college player he helped tiny West Virginia Wesleyan College defeat the University of West Virginia. And he began coaching at his alma mater at the same time he began his major league baseball career. He also played professional football under the alias of "Foster." As a college coach, he led Washington and Jefferson into the 1922 Rose Bowl. As a professional coach, he led the Philadelphia Eagles to NFL titles in 1948 and 1949. A native of Parkersburg, WV, he died at Lake Worth, FL, on November 2, 1973, at age 81. He is a member of the football Hall of Fame. (*Sporting News; SABR Collegiate Database; Total Baseball; Los Angeles Times*)

Art Nehf, a lefty with pinpoint control, won 184 games with four NL teams. He had a league leading 28 complete games for the Braves in 1918 and back-to-back 20-win seasons for the Giants in 1920–21. With the great Giants teams of 1921–24, he made six World Series starts, winning four—including a 1–0 victory over the Yankees in the final game of the 1921 Series. Over his career Nehf averaged just over 2 walks per nine innings; in 1920 he walked only 45 batters in 281 innings. He had graduated from Rose Polytechnic Institute, with a degree in electrical engineering, before entering baseball and is a member of that school's Hall of Fame. He reached the majors with the Braves in August 1915, coming from Terre Haute. When he left the majors in 1929, he moved to Phoenix where he managed a hotel for Cubs owner Phil Wrigley. Nehf later became very successful in real estate. He died of cancer in Phoenix on December 18, 1960, at age 68. (*Sporting News; Dictionary of American Sport: Baseball; SABR Collegiate Database; Total Baseball; New York Times*)

Jack Ness had a 12-game trial as a first baseman with the Tigers in 1912, joining the club from Williamsport. He then hit .267 in 75 games with the White Sox at the end of 1916. Ness earned his way back to the majors with a 49-game hitting streak for Oakland in 1915. Refusing to take a pay cut in 1917, the Chicago native retired when he was sent down to Columbus, preferring to begin training as a mechanic while playing independent ball in the Midwest League. Ness later became a purchasing agent for Strom Ball Bearing Company. He was found dead in his home in DeLand, FL, on December 4, 1957, an apparent heart attack victim. He was 72 years old. (*Hall of Fame file; Los Angeles Times; Baseball-Reference.com; Sporting News*)

Bert Niehoff played second base for the pennant winning Phillies in 1915, one of his

Les Nunamaker

four seasons as a regular. He joined the Reds at the end of 1913, becoming the regular third baseman in 1914. A career .240 hitter, he still led the NL with 42 doubles in 1916. In all Niehoff spent more than 50 years in baseball. After closing with the Giants in 1918, he played for Los Angeles and then in 1922 became player-manager of Mobile. He managed 11 different minor league clubs, coached the Giants and scouted for the Yankees and Angels, retiring in 1969 at age 85. He died at Inglewood, CA, on December 8, 1974, at age 90. (*Sporting News; Baseball-Reference.com; Atlanta Constitution; Los Angeles Times; Washington Post; Encyclopedia of Minor League Baseball*)

Al Nixon played nine seasons in the majors, three as a regular outfielder with the Braves and Phillies. A career .277 hitter, he hit .293 with the 1926 Phillies. The Dodgers bought Nixon from Beaumont in September 1915 but returned him to Beaumont for most of 1916. He played in six games for the Dodgers in 1918 and was released back to Beaumont in 1919, from where he was purchased by the Braves for 1921. He played independent ball in 1924–25 and finished his major league career with the Phillies in 1928. After leaving the majors in 1928, he managed at Lake Charles in the Cotton States League, was one of the founders of the Opelousas club of the Evangeline League and was also an Evangeline League umpire. After a long illness he died at Opelousas, LA, on November 9, 1960, at age 74. (*Sporting News; Total Baseball; Atlanta Constitution; Washington Post*)

Les Nunamaker caught 70 or more games five straight seasons with the Yankees and Browns. For his career he hit .268 for 12 seasons, but in 1916 he reached .296 in 91 games. The Red Sox drafted him from Bloomington in 1911 and released him to the Yankees in 1914. He went to the Browns in 1918 and the Indians in 1919. After leaving the Indians in 1922, Nunamaker began a career as playing manager for minor league teams at Chattanooga, Saginaw, Corsicana, and Lincoln. He retired from active baseball after the 1931 season and two years later moved to Hastings, NE, where he joined his brother in operating a meat market while serving as director of the Nebraska Sportsmen's Association. In failing health for several months, he died on November 14, 1938, at age 49. (*Hastings [NE] Daily Tribune; Sporting News; Aurora[NE] Republican-Register; Total Baseball*)

Ray O'Brien played briefly as an outfielder for Pittsburgh in 1916, hitting .211 in 16 games. The Pirates acquired him from Davenport of the Three-I League and returned him to Davenport in that same season because he "failed to deliver." The St. Louis Trolley League product spent almost 20 years in organized baseball, playing in the minors until 1932. He saw service in Nashville, Fort Worth, Omaha, Wichita Falls, Denver and St Joseph. O'Brien was a native of St. Louis, and at the time of his death, he was a grocer there. He died on March 31, 1942, at age 49. (*Sporting News; Baseball Encyclopedia; Washington Post; Boston Daily Globe*)

John (Bucky) O'Connor caught in one game for the Cubs on September 16, 1916 and, like the legendary Moonlight Graham, did not receive a turn at bat. According to *Baseball-Reference.com* O'Connor attended the University of Illinois prior to playing professional baseball. However, according to Hall of Fame documents, the Irish-born O'Connor was a graduate of St. Anselm's Prep and Fordham University. He became a career navy man, remaining in the reserves through the Korean War. His death certificate lists his occupation as "Chief Yeoman (retired), U.S. Navy." O'Connor died at a nursing home in Bonner Springs, KS, on May 30, 1982, at age 90. (*Hall of Fame file; Baseball-Reference.com; Kansas Certificate of Death*)

Joe Oeschger is most remembered for the 26-inning 1–1 tie he pitched for the Braves against Leon Cadore and the Dodgers in 1920. The Chicago native had earned a degree in civil engineering from St. Mary's College before entering professional baseball. The Phillies signed him from campus for a $5,000 bonus in 1914. In his best season with the Phillies, he went 15–14 in 1917. At different times he pitched for the Giants (twice), the Braves (for whom he went 20–14 in 1921), the Phillies (again) and Dodgers. In all he won 82 games in a 12 year NL career. After leaving baseball in 1925, Oeschger earned a teaching degree from Stanford and spent the next 27 years teaching physical education and hygiene in junior high school. Following a stroke, he died at Rohnert Park, CA, on July 28, 1986, at age 94. (*Sporting News; Total Baseball; SABR Collegiate Database*)

Bob O'Farrell was the NL's Most Valuable Player in 1926, when he hit .293 and caught 146 games for the world champion Cardinals. He hit .304 in the World Series that year. Over his 21-year career he hit .273, going over .300 four times. O'Farrell also led NL catchers in putouts and assists twice each. He was only 19 years old when he joined the Cubs in September 1915 from the amateur ranks. But it was 1920 before he became their regular catcher. In 1925 he was traded to the Cardinals, and by 1927 he had been appointed player/manager. O'Farrell also played for the Giants, the Cardinals (three times), the Cubs (twice) and Reds. After leaving the majors in 1935, he played and managed three years in the minors, then devoted the rest of his life to operating his bowling lanes in Waukegan, IL, his hometown. He died at Waukegan on February 20, 1988, at age 91. (*Sporting News; Baseball Encyclopedia; Chicago Daily Tribune; New York Times*)

Robert (Rube) Oldring was the centerfielder behind the "$100,000 infield" at Philadelphia. Originally a third baseman, he was shifted to the outfield because of his strong throwing arm (and also his propensity to overthrow first base). Oldring began in the majors with the Yankees at the end of

Rube Oldring

1905, joining the A's in 1906. He was a regular from 1907 to 1915, including the glory years of 1910–14. A career .270 hitter for 13 seasons, he hit .308 in 1910, but missing the World Series that year because of an injury. Traded to the Yankees in 1916, he left baseball to farm. Oldring tried a comeback with the A's in 1918 and then played and managed in the minors until 1923, when he became public relations director for a canning company. He died at Bridgeton, NJ, on September 9, 1961, at age 77. He had been hospitalized earlier for a heart condition. (*Sporting News; New York Times; Baseball Encyclopedia; Washington Post; Los Angeles Times*)

Ivan (Ivy) Olson played shortstop on the Dodgers NL champions of 1916 and 1920. A second-generation Swede, born in Kansas City, he spent 14 seasons (1911–24) with Cleveland and the Dodgers, ten as a regular. He hit a modest .258 for his career, but hit .293 in 12 World Series games and led the NL in hits in 1919 while batting only .278. Cleveland purchased Olson from Portland, where he had helped the Beavers win the 1910 PCL championship. Sent to the Reds in 1914, Olson hit only .232 and was sold to Brooklyn. After retiring as an active player, Olson managed in the minors and coached Brooklyn and the Giants. He then spent 20 years as a customer serviceman for a Buick agency in Inglewood, CA. He died there of heart disease on September 1, 1965, at age 79. (*Sporting News; New York Times; Total Baseball; Los Angeles Times; California Certificate of Death*)
Another photograph on page 45

Ollie O'Mara, a St. Louis sandlot player, entered the majors in 1912 as a one-day replacement for striking Detroit Tigers players. He returned in 1914 to play four seasons with the Dodgers, hitting .231 in 412 games. He was the regular shortstop in 1915 and regular third baseman in 1918. A .202 average in 1916 sent him to Atlanta for 1917. Sent down again in 1919, O'Mara jumped from Indianapolis in 1920 to play independent ball until 1928. Moving to Kenosha, WI, he ran a billiards parlor and managed a semi-pro baseball club, before retiring to Nevada. He died at 98 on October 24, 1989, in Reno, NV. (*Sporting News; Total Baseball; Washington Post*)

Ivy Olson

Ollie O'Mara

Steve O'Neill was one of four brothers from an Irish family who played in the majors. His older brothers Jack, a catcher, and Mike, a pitcher, were born in Ireland. Steve and his younger brother Jim, an infielder, were born in Minooka, PA. Steve caught more than 100 games nine consecutive seasons for the Indians. While his career batting totals show a modest .263, he had three seasons over .300. He hit .321 in 148 games for the pennant-winning Indians in 1920, followed by a .333 World Series average. A genial Irishman, he remained in baseball. He managed at Toronto (1929–31), Toledo (1934–35), Cleveland (1935–37), Detroit (1943–48), the Red Sox (1950–51), and the Phillies (1952–54). All 14 seasons of major league managing were winning seasons. He also coached at Toledo (1932), Cleveland (1935, 1949), Detroit (1941), and the Red Sox (1950). In addition, he scouted for Cleveland. O'Neill died in Cleveland on January 26, 1962, at age 70. (*Total Baseball; New York Times; Washington Post; Los Angeles Times*)

Gene Packard, a lefthander from Colorado, had 85 wins with a 3.01 ERA in eight major league seasons. 40 of those wins came in two seasons with the FL Kansas City Cowboys. The Reds had drafted Packard from Columbus in 1912. After a 7–11 season in 1913, he jumped to the Federal League and became the property of the Cubs when the FL folded. He was praised as a "master of mound craft" with five different pitching motions—including a particularly nasty cross fire delivery. Packard was traded to the Cardinals—for whom he won 12 games in 1918—and finished with the Phillies in 1919. After leaving baseball, he moved to Riverside, CA, where he was employed as a stock clerk in a men's clothing store. He died at Riverside following a heart attack on May 18, 1959, at age 71. (*California Certificate of Death; Total Baseball; Washington Post; Chicago Daily Tribune*)

Emilio Palmero, a Cuban-born lefthander, was brought to the United States by John McGraw in 1913 and debuted at the end of 1915. Over the next 14 years he had five major league trials—with the Giants (1915–16), Browns (1921), Senators (1926), and Braves (1928)—compiling a 6–15 record. But near the end of his career he become the ace of the staff at Toledo, where he made his home, helping the Mud Hens win the 1927 American Association championship and the Junior World Series. After a short stint at managing in the Ohio State League in 1937, Palmero spent 20 years as an order assembler for the DeVilbliss Company in Toledo. He died of uremia at Toledo on July 15, 1970, at age 75. (*Toledo Blade; Total Baseball; New York Times; Ohio Certificate of Death*)

Jim Park graduated from the University of Kentucky in 1915 and was pitching for the Browns before the season was over. His three-year record with the Browns was 4–5 with a 3.02 ERA for 122 innings. But in the meantime, he had pitched his way through law school, graduating in 1920. He then became a partner in a prominent law firm in Lexington. Entering politics, he was elected County Attorney and later Commonwealth Attorney for Fayette County, KY, and once made an unsuccessful run for the U.S. Senate. He died of "Cerebral vascular insufficiency" at Lexington, KY, on December 17, 1970, at age 78. (*Hall of Fame file/SABR Collegiate Database; Information provided by James Park, Jr.; Total Baseball*)

James (Rube) Parnham had two complete games in three starts after joining the A's from Raleigh in 1916. His two-year major league totals show a 2–2 record for 35.2 innings, but he went on to become an International League star with Baltimore. Beginning in 1917 he turned in victory totals of 16, 22, and 28. After two seasons in independent baseball, Parnham returned to the Orioles with records of 16–10 and 33–7 in 1922 and 1923. A final fling with the Orioles in 1926 brought 13 more victories. Parnham finished his professional baseball career in 1927. A native of Heidelberg, PA, he resided in McKeesport, PA, where he died of a heart attack on November 25, 1963, at age 69. His death certificate lists his occupation as "laborer." (*Sporting News; Hall of Fame file; Total Baseball; New York Times*)

George (Dode) Paskert had a 15-year major league career with the Reds, Phillies and Cubs, hitting .268 in 1695 games. An outstanding defensive centerfielder, he led NL outfielders in total chances twice and in fielding, putouts and double plays once each. He had 17 putouts in the five-game World Series of 1915. The Reds had picked up Paskert from Atlanta in September 1907. Traded to the Phillies in 1911, he hit .315 in 1912 and helped the Phillies win the 1915 NL championship. Traded to the Cubs in 1918, he helped them win the 1918 NL championship. After finishing with the Reds in 1921, Paskert played in the minors, finishing with Nashville in 1927 when he was 46 years old. He later became an inspector for the Gabriel Snubber Company of Cleveland, his hometown. Following a heart attack, he died there on February 12, 1959, at age 77. (*Sporting News; Deadball Stars of the National League; Baseball Encyclopedia; Atlanta Constitution*)

Gene Paulette was banned for life after the 1920 season for accepting gifts from St. Louis gamblers during the 1919 season. He first joined the Giants in 1911, "dug up in the west," according to the *New York Times*. In 1916 the Browns acquired him from Nashville, and in 1917 he became the regular first baseman of the Cardinals, holding regular status for the Cardinals and Phillies through 1920. A career .269 hitter, he reached .288 for the Phillies in his last season. When his ban was announced, Paulette signed to play independent ball for Massillon, OH, but the league rejected his contract. Paulette was a native of Centralia, IL, but spent most of his life in Little Rock, AR, where he became a yardmaster for the Missouri Pacific Railroad Lines. He died at Little Rock on February 8, 1966, at age 73. (*Arkansas Gazette; Bill James Historical Baseball Abstract; Total Baseball; New York Times; Atlanta Constitution*)

George Pearce (Pierce) twice won 13 games for the Cubs in a six-year major league career. The lefty from Aurora, IL, had 14 complete games and a 2.31 ERA in 1913. The Cubs acquired Pearce on waivers from the Giants in 1912, but Pearce spent most of that season at Scranton. After three years as a starting pitcher, he was sent to Toledo early in 1916. Pearce last pitched for the Cardinals in early 1917 before being sent to Kansas City. Released to Atlanta in 1918, he refused to report. In 1918 he moved to Plainfield, IL, where he purchased a pool and billiards hall and pitched independent ball in the Chicago-based Midwest League. Following an operation, he died on October 11, 1935, at a hospital in Joliet IL. He was 47 years old. (*Plainfield [IL] Enterprise; Sporting News; Baseball Encyclopedia; Chicago Daily Tribune*)

Charles Pechous had three trials as a third baseman with his local Chicago Whales and Cubs, hitting .181 in 53 games. He had attended St. Ignatius (Loyola) college for one year and was selected from the Chicago amateur ranks to accompany the Whales on a September trip to the East, playing in 18 games. Awarded to the Cubs in 1916, he split time over the next two seasons between the majors and Peoria, before ending up in Toledo. Returning to college, he graduated from Loyola Medical School in 1925, where he also coached baseball. Pechous then served as a general practitioner in Kenosha, WI, from 1928 until his retirement in 1973. Following a three-month illness, he died on September 13, 1980, at age 83. (*Kenosha News; SABR Collegiate Data Base; Chicago Daily Tribune; Baseball Encyclopedia*)

Roger Peckinpaugh was the regular shortstop for the Yankees and Senators from 1913 through 1925, standing 10th on the all-time list for games played at that position. A career .259 hitter, he had only one .300 sea-

Roger Peckinpaugh

son, but he led AL shortstops in double plays 5 times and in assists 4 times. Only 19 years old, Peckinpaugh played in 15 games for the Indians in 1910 before being sent down to Sacramento. Traded to the Yankees in 1913, he hit .268. Helping the Senators win back-to-back AL championships, Peckinpaugh hit .417 in the 1924 World Series and received the AL Most Valuable Player award in 1925 after hitting .294. He later managed the Indians on two separate occasions—1928–33 and 1941 and served as vice president and general manager from 1942 trough 1946. In 1935–38 he had been part of the American League promotion team which worked with college campuses. He died at Cleveland on November 17, 1977, at age 86. (*Sporting News; Baseball Encyclopedia; Los Angeles Times; New York Times*)

Ken Penner had two major league trials 13 years apart, pitching 12.7 innings for the 1916 Indians and 12.7 innings for the 1929 Cubs. After leading the Central Association with a 1.41 ERA while playing with Marshalltown, Penner arrived in Cleveland in September 1916. Then for more than a decade Penner pitched in the PCL, the Texas League and the American Association, before being purchased by the Cubs at the end of 1929. Overall the Booneville, IN, native spent 43 years in organized baseball—pitching (1914–33), managing and coaching (1934–43), and scouting (1944–57). His scouting reports on Ted Williams were instrumental in Cardinal success against him in the 1946 World Series. Stricken with ALS, he died at his home in Sacramento, CA, on May 28, 1959, at age 63. (*Sporting News; Baseball-Reference.com; New York Times; Los Angeles Times*)

Herb Pennock, a stylish lefthander, joined the Yankees in 1923 and helped them win five AL championships while posting a 5–0 record in World Series play. He had reached the majors as an 18-year-old with the A's in 1912, moving directly from high school. For the AL champions of 1914, he posted 11 wins. In 22 seasons with the A's, Red Sox and Yankees, Pennock won 240 games with a 3.61 ERA. Returning from naval service in World War I, Pennock went 16–8, 2.71 ERA for the Red Sox in 1919. For the Yankees he had 23–11, 21–9, 19–6, 19–8 and 17–6 records. Despite his frail 160-pound frame, he logged more than 200 innings for ten consecutive seasons, including a league leading 277 in 1925. He spent the rest of his life in baseball as club president of Charlotte, coach and later farm director for the Red Sox and general manager of the Phillies. Pennock died of a cerebral hemorrhage in New York

Herb Pennock

City on January 30, 1948. He was 53 years old. Later in 1948 he was elected posthumously to the Hall of Fame. (*Sporting News; Total Baseball; New York Times; Washington Post*)

William (Pol) Perritt had a 17–7, 1.88 ERA record for the NL champion Giants in 1917. His 92 career wins include five straight seasons (1914–18) of 12 or more victories, topped by two 18-win seasons. The Arcadia, LA, native joined the Cardinals at the end of 1912 from Greenwood. Traded to the Giants in 1915, he turned in his best seasons with them. In the 1917 World Series, he relieved three times, working 8.1 innings with a 2.16 ERA. He was sent down in 1920 but pitched for the Tigers in 1921 and for Minneapolis in 1922 before retiring. Returning to his home state of Louisiana, Perritt became an oil operator, an occupation he held until his death. "After a long illness" he died in Shreveport on October 15, 1947, at age 55. (*Sporting News; Baseball Encyclopedia; New York Times*)

Scott Perry won 20 games with a 1.98 ERA for a 1918 A's club that won only 52 times. That year he led the AL in starts, complete games, innings and losses. In 1920 he again led the AL with 25 losses. In all, he compiled a 40–68 record, largely with last place clubs. The Browns purchased him from Louisville in 1915 but returned him after one game. The Cubs acquired him from Atlanta in September 1916 but returned him to Atlanta the following April. Perry pitched in four games with the Reds and was sold to Boston, but did not pitch. In 1918 The A's purchased his contract from Atlanta. A dispute between the A's and Braves for Perry's services led to the resignation of the president of the National League. In 1919 Perry jumped from the A's to play semi-pro ball at Franklin, PA, but was reinstated for 1920. Suspended in 1921, Perry again left the A's, pitching semi-pro ball for a number of years. A native of Corsicana, TX, he moved to Kansas City, where he was employed as a cook. After a month-long illness, he died in Kansas City on October 27, 1959, at age 68. (*Sporting News; Total Baseball; Chicago Daily Tribune; Atlanta Constitution; Washington Post; New York Times*

Edward (Jeff) Pfeffer struck out more than 225 batters 7 times. In 13 seasons with the Dodgers, Cardinals and Pirates he won 158 games, 10 or more eight times. He won 67 games in a three-year period (1914–16), including a 25–11 record for the NL champion Dodgers of 1916. He had a trial with the Browns in 1911, and after a league leading 25 wins at Grand Rapids in 1913, he was signed by the Dodgers. After closing his major league career with the Pirates in 1924, Pfeffer remained in baseball through 1933, pitching, coaching, and umpiring in the minors. *Sporting News* includes later entries that he was "running a restaurant in Chicago" and that he was "employed by the Hotel Morrison in Chicago." A native of Seymour, IL, he died at Chicago of a heart attack on August 16, 1972, at age 84. Pfeffer was the younger brother of Francis Xavier (Big Jeff) Pfeffer, a right-handed pitcher for the Braves and Cubs. (*Hall of Fame file; Illinois Certificate of Death; Sporting News; Baseball Encyclopedia; Deadball Stars of the National League; Encyclopedia of Minor League Baseball*)

Val Picinich joined the A's straight from Princeton Prep in 1916. The 19-year-old caught 37 games, hitting .195. Sent down to Atlanta in 1917, he returned to the majors with Washington in 1918. In 18 seasons with the A's, Senators, Red Sox, Reds, Dodgers and Pirates, he hit .258 and played in 1037 games, catching 935. His best season was 1928 when he hit .302 in 96 games for the Reds. He also caught no-hit games behind Bullet Joe Bush (1916), Walter Johnson (1920) and Howard Ehmke (1923). After leaving the majors in 1933, Picinich managed in the minors until 1940, when he became a poultry farmer at Nobleboro, ME. During World War II, he worked in the electrical department at the Bath Iron Works, where he became director of personal services and morale. Stricken with bronchial influenza, Picinich died of pneumonia at Nobleboro on December 5, 1942. He was 46 years old. (*Sporting News; Baseball-Reference.com; New York Times; Atlanta Constitution*)

Charlie Pick played six seasons—three as a regular infielder—for the Senators, A's, Cubs and Braves, hitting .261. In his fifth season of organized baseball, Pick joined the Senators in September 1914, coming from Toronto. Although he played in only 29 games for the Cubs in 1918, he hit .326 and then hit .389 in the World Series that year, leading both teams with 7 hits. Sold by the Braves to Sacramento in 1921, the Virginian played in the minors through 1927. In later years he served as attendance officer for the Rustville, VA, School District. He died of a heart attack at Lynchburg, VA, on June 26, 1954, at age 65. (*Sporting News; Baseball-Reference.com; New York Times; Washington Post*)

Wally Pipp is forever remembered as the man who lost his job to Lou Gehrig. Actually he was a regular for the Yankees and Reds for 12 of his 15 seasons, hitting .281, while twice leading the AL in homers. A solid fielder, he led his league in double plays and putouts five times, in total chances per game four times and in fielding 3 times. After a 12-game trial with the Tigers in 1913, Pipp joined the Yankees from Rochester in 1915. He helped the Yankees win three AL championships in 1921–23 and a World Championship in 1923, hitting .296, .329 and .304 for those teams. Traded to the Reds in 1926, he hit .291 and then led NL first basemen in fielding in 1927. Pipp played one season in the minors and then tried his hand at publishing, at broadcasting and at script writing before "becoming a manufacturer's agent in the automotive supply field" in Kalamazoo, MI. He was a native of Chicago and had attended Catholic University before entering professional baseball. Following a series of strokes, he died at Grand Rapids, MI, on January 11, 1965, at age 71. (*Sporting News; Baseball Encyclopedia; SABR Collegiate Database; New York Times*)

Eddie Plank joined the A's straight from Gettysburg College in 1901. The left-hander won at least 15 games for 16 straight seasons and 20 games eight times to amass 326 career victories. Over his career he had 410 complete games (529 starts) 69 shutouts and a 2.35 ERA. He had 26 wins in 1904 and a 1.71 ERA in 1909. A particularly tough World Series competitor, he had six complete games in six starts, and a 1.32 ERA. In the 1913 Series he lost to Christy Mathewson in 10 innings in Game 2 and then defeated Mathewson with a two-hitter in Game 6. He jumped to the St. Louis Federals in 1915 and finished his career with the Browns in 1917. Plank "entered the garage business" when he retired from baseball, and he also served as a guide at Gettysburg battlefield. Having suffered "a stroke of paralysis," the 50-year-old Plank died at Gettysburg on February 24, 1926. In 1946 Plank was elected to the Hall of Fame. (*Sporting News; Total Baseball; SABR Collegiate Database; New York Times*)

Derrill (Del) Pratt was a 13-year regular at second base for the Browns, Yankees, Red Sox and Tigers. A career .292 hitter, he had six .300 seasons, headed by a .324 in 1921. Pratt led the AL with 103 RBI's in 1916. A fine fielder, he led the AL in putouts and total chances five times and in double plays and assists three times. Prior to entering professional baseball, Pratt had captained the University of Alabama football and baseball teams. In 1912 he came to the Browns from Montgomery, where he had led the Southern Association in average, runs and hits. After leaving the Tigers in 1924, he managed in the Texas League for 11 seasons before retiring after 1935. Pratt made his home in Galveston, TX, where he coached high school football, managed a semi-pro baseball team, and operated a bowling alley and later a service station. He died at Texas City, TX, on October 7, 1977, at age 89. (*Hall of Fame file; information supplied by Donald Pratt; Baseball*

Bill Rariden

Encyclopedia; SABR Collegiate Database; Encyclopedia of Minor League Baseball)

Mike Prendergast won 41 games with a 2.74 ERA in 6 major league seasons with the Chicago Federals, Cubs and Phillies. In his two best seasons he compiled a 14–12 record for the 1915 Federals and a 13–14 record for the 1918 Phillies, in both seasons working more than 250 innings. Prendergast joined the Chi-Feds in 1914 from Peoria of the Three-I League, winning five games as a rookie. He retired from baseball rather than report to the minors in 1919, though he pitched in the Western League in 1922 and 1923. A native of Arlington, IL, he moved to Omaha, where he worked as a salesman for Falstaff Brewing Co. Prendergast died of pneumonia at Omaha on November 18, 1967, at age 79. (*Sporting News; Nebraska Certificate of Death; Total Baseball; Chicago Daily Tribune; Atlanta Constitution*)

Pat Ragan averaged 24 starts and 12 complete games annually over seven seasons (1912–18). In an 11-year major league career with seven clubs, he won 76 games, including a 17–12, 2.34 ERA season with the Dodgers and Braves in 1915. The product of Blanchard, IA, had attended Simpson and Cornell colleges before entering professional baseball. He advanced to the Reds from Omaha in 1909, also pitching for the Braves, Giants and White Sox before being sent down in 1919. After a final fling with the Phillies in 1923, he managed in the minors through 1926, when he became a guard at an aircraft corporation. On September 4, 1956, he died in Los Angeles of a carcinoma on the kidneys at age 67. (*Hall of Fame File; California Certificate of Death; Total Baseball; Sporting News; SABR Collegiate Database*)

William (Bedford Bill) Rariden caught 100 games for four consecutive seasons 1914–17. A .235 hitter for his career, he hit .271 for the Pennant-winning Giants in

1917, going on to hit .385 in the World Series that year. As a catcher he led the FL or NL in putout and assists three times. The Bedford, IN, native began his major league career with the Braves in 1909, coming from Canton. Jumping to the Federal League in 1914, he hit .270 for Newark in 1915. The Giants traded him to the Reds, and he shared catching duties with Ivy Wingo and Nick Allen on the 1919 World Champions. Sent down to Atlanta in 1921, Rariden retired from baseball and returned to Bedford, where he operated a service station until his health began to fail. He died at Bedford on August 28, 1942, at age 54. (*Sporting News; Baseball-Reference.com; Boston Daily Globe; Los Angeles Times*)

Del Pratt

Carl Ray, a left-handed pitcher from Stokes County, NC, had trials with the Philadelphia A's in 1915 and 1916, starting (and losing) a game each season. Prior to joining the A's, he had led the Carolina League with 28 wins and 317 strikeouts at Winston-Salem. Ray returned to Stokes County, and, like many other former professional baseball players, became a law enforcement official, serving at times as county sheriff and as a policeman at Walnut Cove, NC. For the last ten years of his life he suffered from a crippling illness, from which he died on April 3, 1970, at age 81. (*Danbury [NC] Reporter; Encyclopedia of Minor League Baseball; Baseball Encyclopedia*)

Ed Reulbach completed 28 of 29 starts (1.42 ERA) for the Cubs in 1905. Over the next three years he compiled a 60–15 record, leading the NL in winning percentage each year, as the Cubs won three straight pennants. In 13 seasons he fashioned a 182–106, 2.28 ERA career record and pitched in four World Series. Reulbach held university degrees in engineering (Notre Dame), and medicine (Vermont). He joined the Cubs directly from Vermont, posting an 18–14 record as a 22-year-old rookie. As a founding member of the Baseball Players Fraternity, he was released by the Dodgers in 1914, going 21–10 for the Newark Federals in 1915. After finishing with the Braves in 1917, Reulbach lived in Montclair, NY, where he had an interest in the stock market. He also worked for a piano manufacturer, started a tire business, and later worked for a construction company. He died at Glen Falls, NY, following a heart attack on July 17, 1961, at age 78. (*Sporting News; Dictionary of American Sport: Baseball; Deadball Stars of the National League; Total Baseball; New York Times*) **Photograph on page 122**

Edgar (Sam) Rice retired at age 44, just 13 hits short of 3,000, a fact that delayed his election to the Hall of Fame until 1963. Already 25 years old, Rice came to the Senators as a pitcher in 1915 from the Virginia State League. By June of 1916 he was being spoken of as a dangerous pinch hitter; by July he has been given a place in the outfield, hit-

Ed Reulbach

ting .299 for the season. After hitting .302 in 1917, he spent most of 1918 in military service. In 20 major league seasons, he hit .322, leading the AL in hits twice. In 1925 he hit .350, helping the Senators to an AL championship, and in the World Series he had a record 12 hits. Described as "one of the fastest men in baseball," he led the AL in stolen bases in 1920 and in triples in 1923, and he became "one of the best outfielders in the country." In 1930 at age 40, he hit .349, his highest average. After Rice retired in 1934, he operated a chicken farm in Ashton, MD. He died at Rossmor, MD, on October 13, 1974, at age 84. (*Baseball's Best; Total Baseball; Washington Post; New York Times*)

Jack Richardson, a big right-hander from Illinois, had trials with the A's in both 1915 and 1916. He made three starts in 1915 and pitched less than an inning in relief in 1916, leaving the majors with an 0–1 record. After serving in World War I, he became an insurance salesman at Edwardsville IL. Having suffered from arteriosclerotic heart disease for a number of years, Richardson died at the Veterans Administration Hospital in Marion, IL, on January 18, 1970. He was 77 years old. (*Illinois Certificate of Death; Total Baseball*)

Art Rico, a promising young catcher, played in 17 games for the Braves in 1916–1917, hitting .222. The Boston area schools star joined the Braves from the semi-pro ranks. In 1916 he split time between the Braves and Providence and in 1917 between the Braves and Springfield. Rico served in the U.S. Navy during World War I. While preparing for the 1919 season, he was discovered to have a ruptured appendix. On January 3, 1919, Rico died "of peritonitis superinduced by appendicitis." He was 22 years of age. (*Boston Evening Globe; Sporting News; Baseball-Reference.com*)

William (Hank) Ritter had four major league trials with the Phillies and Giants, but only in 1915 did he spend an entire season. His career marks show a 4–1 record with a 3.96 ERA for 77.1 innings. The graduate of Albright College made his major league debut with the Phillies in August, 1912 from East Liverpool. He returned to the majors with the Giants in 1914 and was returned to the minors early in 1916. After serving in World War I, Ritter left baseball to enter the coal business. He became head of the Wreitz Coal Co., president of the Central Pennsylvania Coal Association and director of the National Coal Association. Ritter later moved to Akron, OH, where he became director and public relations advisor for the Ruhlin Construction Company. He died at Akron on September 3, 1964, at age 70. (*Sporting News; Total Baseball; New York Times*)

Eppa Rixey, a 6'5" lefty from Virginia, won 266 games for the Phillies and Reds, despite the fact that those clubs finished in the second division for 12 of his 21 seasons. He had four 20-win seasons topped by a league-leading 25 wins in 1922 and won at least 10 games 14 times. In 1916 he had 22 wins and a 1.85 ERA for the Phillies. Before entering baseball, he had graduated from the University of Virginia, where he starred in baseball and basketball. He joined the Phillies directly from campus, winning ten games the remainder of the season. He missed 1918 entirely, serving with the Chemical Warfare Division in Europe. While still active with the Reds, Rixey began an insurance business in the suburbs of Cincinnati, and after leaving baseball in 1933, he became one of the most successful insurance executives in the city. One month after being elected to the Hall of Fame, he died of a sudden heart attack on February 28, 1963, at age 71. (*Sporting News; Total Baseball; Deadball Stars of the National League; SABR Collegiate Database*)

Dave Robertson twice led the NL in homers (1916–17) with twelve each year. The left-handed hitting outfielder had a .287 batting average in 9 major league seasons with the Giants, Cubs and Pirates. In the 1917 World Series he produced 11 hits, a record that stood until 1953. Before entering baseball, he had been a four-sport star at North Carolina State and was signed by the Giants as a pitcher in 1912. Converted to an outfielder, he led the Southern Association in homers at Mobile in 1913 before returning to the Giants. Robertson sat out 1918 refusing to play for John McGraw, and was traded to the Cubs in 1919 and to the Pirates in 1921, finishing back with the Giants in 1922. Since Robertson had attended veterinary school at Wake Forest, he became a Virginia game warden, a position he held for thirty years. He also managed in the Virginia League, operated a sporting goods store and an insurance business, and sold real estate. He died at Virginia Beach, VA, on November 5, 1970, at age 81. (*Virginia Pilot[Virginia Beach, VA]; Baseball Encyclopedia; SABR Collegiate Database; New York Times; Atlanta Constitution*)

Bill Rodgers played second base for the Indians, Red Sox and Reds in 1915–16, hitting .243 in 102 games. He came to the Indians from Portland, where he was team

Sam Rice

Henri Rondeau

captain, and returned to Portland after leaving the Reds. Rodgers was a native of Ohio, but early in his baseball career he bought a ranch at Berclair in south Texas, where he hunted in his off-season. According to his son Tom K. Rodgers, he never really got out of baseball. He scouted for the Senators and then became "owner and manager" of the local professional team at Sinton, TX. He died at Berclair on December 26, 1978, at age 91. (*Hall of Fame file; Goliad [TX] Advance-Guard; Los Angeles Times; information supplied by Tom K. Rodgers; Total Baseball*)

Jose (Silent Joe) Rodriguez played 58 games as a Giants infielder in 1916–18, hitting .166. Signed as a 20-year-old in 1916, he was "rated as the best first baseman in the Cuban National League." One of six Cubans playing in the majors in 1916, Rodriguez spent his life in baseball; he managed various clubs in the Cuban league, "cooperated considerably" in the Havana Cubans' entry in the Florida International League, and "introduced" baseball to Venezuela. In 1947 Rodriguez is described as the "commissioner of the Junior Baseball League" in Cuba. In his last managerial post in the United States, he managed Sherman, TX, to the championship of the Big State League in 1948. The 58-year-old Rodriguez died in Havana after a long illness on January 21, 1953. (*Havana Post; Baseball-Reference.com; New York Times; Hall of Fame file; Encyclopedia of Minor League Baseball*)

Henri Rondeau, brought up originally by the Red Sox, first played in the majors as a catcher/first baseman with the Tigers in 1913. He returned from Minneapolis in 1915 as an outfielder with the Senators. In three seasons, totaling 99 games, Rondeau hit .206. Released by Washington to Minneapolis in 1916, he played in the minors until 1927 with time out for work in a defense plant during World War I. After he retired, Rondeau operated a cafe in Woonsocket, RI. The cause of his death on May 28, 1943, was thought to "date back to an attack of sunstroke he suffered while playing for Boston." He was 56 years old. (*Sporting News; Total Baseball; Washington Post; Los Angeles Times*)

Robert (Braggo) Roth played eight seasons in the American League, six as a regular outfielder with six different clubs. He debuted with the Chicago White Sox in 1914, coming from Kansas City, and was traded to Cleveland the following year. A remarkably consistent .284 hitter over his career, he led the AL with 7 homers in 1915. Roth missed most of the 1921 season with a knee injury and was released by the Yankees in 1922. Until 1928 he played minor league and independent ball (Beloit Fairies). Roth then returned to his home in Burlington, WI, where he "enjoyed life fishing, playing golf and visiting with friends." At age 44, he was killed in an auto accident in Chicago on September 11, 1936. An older brother Frank caught in the majors for six seasons. (*Burlington Free Press; Sporting News; Baseball Encyclopedia; Chicago Daily Tribune; New York Times*)

Edd Roush was the highest paid player in the NL in 1920, making $10,000. He later reached $70,000 for a three-year contract with the Giants in 1927. Swinging a 48-

Edd Roush

ounce bat, the left-handed hitting outfielder had eleven .300 seasons, two NL batting titles, and a career .323 average for 18 seasons. He first came to the majors with the White Sox in 1913 from Evansville. Sent down to Lincoln at the end of the season, he jumped to the Federal League. Assigned to the Giants in 1916, Roush played little and was sent to Cincinnati, where he became a star, helping the Reds win the 1919 World

Championship. Sold back to the Giants in 1927, he played three seasons and then held out for the entire 1930 season. In 1931 he played one final season for the Reds and then retired for good. His baseball earnings and modest lifestyle allowed him to spend his life watching and talking baseball. The Veterans Committee voted him into the Hall of Fame in 1962. Roush died at Bradenton, FL, of a massive heart attack on March 21, 1988, at age 94. (*Sporting News; Deadball Stars of the National League; Total Baseball; New York Times*)

Harland Rowe played three years at the University of Maine before joining the A's in June 1916. Appearing in 17 games as an outfielder/third baseman, he hit .139. After serving in World War I, he returned to his hometown of Springvale, ME, where he played independent baseball for 15 years. Rowe became a cashier in the Springvale National Bank, a position he held for 48 years. He died at Springvale on May 26, 1969, at age 73. (*Journal Tribune [Biddeford, ME]; SABR Collegiate Database; Baseball Encyclopedia*)

George (Nap) Rucker, described as the Dodgers' greatest lefthander before Sandy Koufax, had 116 victories by age 27 when his arm went bad. Drafted from Augusta after a 27–9 season in 1907, the big Georgian averaged more than 300 innings and 16 wins over the next seven seasons for Dodger teams that finished near the bottom of the NL. Overall he won 134 games with a 2.42 ERA (NL average 2.87) in ten seasons and was out of baseball by age 31. Rucker pitched in 21 1–0 games, winning 11, and 28 percent of his wins were shutouts. Almost unhittably fast as a young pitcher, he later developed an almost unhittable knuckleball. In 1916, when he was reduced to part time pitching, the Dodgers finally won a pennant, and Rucker got to pitch in a World Series game. He returned to his plantation near Rosewell, GA, where he supervised cotton plantations and owned a wheat mill. He also scouted for the Dodgers and served as mayor and city water commissioner for Rosewell, Rucker died at Alpharetta, GA, on December 19, 1970, at age 86. (*Sporting News; New York Times; Deadball Stars of the National League; Total Baseball*)

Dick Rudolph turned in a monster 26–10, 2.36 ERA season for the "Miracle Braves" in 1914, adding two complete game victories over the A's in the World Series that year. In 13 seasons he won 121 games with a 2.66 ERA. Rudolph was a native of New York City, where he attended Fordham University. He first enters the majors with the Giants at the end of 1910, coming from Toronto. After pitching briefly in both 1910 and 1911, he was returned to Toronto from where the Braves acquired him in 1913. He remained a strong pitcher through 1919, but the strain of 300-plus inning seasons told on his arm so that by 1920 he worked only 89 innings. He served as pitching coach through 1927, retiring with 121 career victories. After leaving baseball, he helped his brother in the undertaking business and later worked for Stevens Brothers as a supervisor of concessions at the Polo Grounds and Yankee Stadium. Rudolph died in New York City on October 20, 1949, at age 62. He is a member of the Fordham University Hall of Fame. (*Sporting News;*

Dick Rudolph

Deadball Stars of the National League; Total Baseball; New York Times; SABR Collegiate Database)

Bill Rumler was one of a group of players—including Pete Alexander, Sam Crawford, Clarence Mitchell, Les Nunamaker, Otto Miller and Tom Seaton—who came from small towns in Nebraska to the majors before World War I. He joined the Browns as a catcher in 1914, and after a season at Atlanta, rejoined them as an outfielder in 1916, leading the AL with 16 pinch hits in 1917. Three major league trials resulted in 128 games and a .251 batting average. Given an opportunity to play regularly, he blossomed at Salt Lake City, leading the PCL in hitting in 1919. He was suspended and later banned from organized baseball for five years as a result of betting on games. After playing outlaw baseball, he returned to the PCL with the Angels in 1929, hitting .386. A broken ankle ended his baseball career there in 1930. Rumler then returned to Milford, NE, where he served as "police and fire chief, justice of the peace, and city marshal." He died at Lincoln, NE, on May 26, 1966, at age 74. (*Sporting News; Atlanta Constitution; Los Angeles Times; Total Baseball; Encyclopedia of Minor League Baseball*)

Allen Russell may have been the first "full-fledged fireman" in the major leagues. He made 233 relief appearances in 11 seasons with the Yankees, Red Sox and Senators. Russell pitched in 52 games for the Senators in 1923, leading the AL with 9 relief wins and 9 saves. His statistics for the AL champions of 1924 resemble those of a modern day closer: 37 games—all in relief—5 wins and 8 saves. He came up with the Yankees in September 1915 from Richmond as a starting pitcher. By 1919 his relief appearances exceed his starts; by 1923 he is used almost exclusively in relief. His death certificate lists his occupation as "Retired Clerk" for U.S. Steel. Following a heart attack, Russell died at Baltimore on October 20, 1972. He was 79 years old. An older brother, Lefty, pitched for the A's. (*Hall of Fame file; Maryland Certificate of Death; New York Times; Washington Post; Baseball Encyclopedia*)

Ewell (Reb) Russell threw 316 innings and won 22 games as a rookie for the White Sox in 1913, only one season removed from Class D Bonham, TX. He went 15–5 with a 1.95 ERA for the AL champions in 1917. But in 1918, after 81 major league victories, his arm went bad, and he was sent down. Known as a control pitcher, he yielded only 1.85 walks per nine innings over his major league career. At Minneapolis he switched to the outfield, becoming the American Association RBI champion in 1921. Called up by the Pirates in 1922, he hit .368 and drove in 75 runs in 60 games. The Pirates released him in 1923, even though he was hitting .289 after 94 games. Russell played in the minors for 10 more years, winning the American Association batting crown in 1928 at age 39. He then went to work for an Indianapolis meatpacking firm, from which he retired in 1959. Russell died at Indianapolis on September 30, 1973, at age 84. (*Indianapolis Star; Total Baseball; Atlanta Constitution; Encyclopedia of Minor League Baseball*)

George Herman (Babe) Ruth led the AL in homers 12 times and in slugging 13 times, including a record .847 in 1920. He also led the AL in runs scored 8 times and in 1924 led with a .378 batting average. A career .342 hitter, he still holds major league records for bases on balls, home run percentage and slugging percentage. In 41 World Series games he hit .326 with 15 home runs. Ruth also was on his way to a Hall of Fame career as a pitcher, having compiled a 67–34 record after just three full seasons, before making the transition to the outfield. In his one World Series start in 1916 he outdueled the Dodgers Sherry Smith 2–1 in 14 innings. The Baltimore native joined the Red Sox in 1914 from the Baltimore Orioles and was traded to the Yankees in 1920. After finishing his 22-year career with the Braves in 1935, he lived the life of an international celebrity in New York City, living from his baseball earnings. He also did a coaching stint for the Dodgers in 1938 and played himself in the movie *Pride of the Yankees*. Ruth was in the first group of players inducted into the Hall of Fame in 1936. At age 53, he died of throat cancer on August 16, 1948, in New York City. (*Baseball's Best; Total Baseball; Baseball Encyclopedia; New York Times*) **Photograph on page 58**

Vic Saier was the Cubs first baseman from the time he arrived in 1911 through 1916. In 1910 he led the Southern Michigan League with 175 hits while playing at Lansing. When Frank Chance was hurt early in 1911, the 20-year-old Saier became the regular first baseman. He had back-to-back .288 and .289 seasons in 1912–13, but settled for a .263 average for his eight-year career. Saier suffered a broken leg six games into 1917, worked in a defense plant during all of 1918, and ended his major league career by hitting .223 in 58 games for the Pirates in 1919. He was a life-long resident of East Lansing, MI, where he worked as manager of City Club. He died of cancer at East Lansing on May 14, 1967, at age 76. (*Michigan Certificate of Death; Deadball Stars of the National League; Total Baseball; Chicago Daily Tribune*)

Slim Sallee

Harry (Slim) Sallee, a tall left-handed sidearmer, who weighed less than 150 pounds, won 174 games with a 2.56 ERA in 14 seasons with the Cardinals, Giants and Reds. He had nine seasons with at least 10 wins. After going 18–7 for the NL champion Giants in 1917, he helped the Reds win the NL flag by turning in a 21–7 record two years later. His career totals also show 168 relief appearances, resulting in 24 wins and 35 saves. The Cardinals acquired him from Williamsport in 1908, sold him to the Giants in 1916, who sold him to the Reds in 1919. Dropped by the Giants at the end of the 1921 season, he made one brief minor league stop at Toledo before returning to Higginsport, OH, and using his baseball earnings to acquire an ice plant, a restaurant and a service station. Losing everything in an Ohio River flood, he began again, tending bar and finally purchasing "Slim's Café" in Higginsport, which he operated until his death of a heart attack on March 22, 1950. He was 65 years old. (*Sporting News; Baseball Encyclopedia; Deadball Stars of the National League; New York Times*)

Vic Saier

Carl (Huck) Sawyer hit .222 in 26 games as a Senators infielder in 1915–16. He made it to the Senators after a strong year at Des Moines. One of the first baseball comedians, Sawyer teamed with Nick Altrock in Washington to entertain fans. In 1917 he had to choose between a baseball contract with the Senators and a movie contract with Keystone Films. He chose baseball but was sent down to Minneapolis before the season began. The Seattle native continued to play and coach in the minors until 1939, when he left baseball "to devote full time to the printing and office equipment business." His obituary lists him as "vice president of Stationers Inc." On January 18, 1957, the 66-year-old Sawyer died of cancer in Los Angeles. (*Sporting News; Los Angeles Times; Baseball Encyclopedia; Washington Post*)

Herman (Germany) Schaefer hit .334 as the Senators first baseman in 1911. Overall he hit .257 in a 15-year career with six clubs, for whom he played every position except catcher. The Chicago native came to the Cubs from St. Paul at the end of 1902. Sent down in 1903 he played at Milwaukee and returned in 1905 as the regular second baseman of the Tigers. He was an infielder on the AL champion Tiger teams of 1907–08 and was traded to Washington in 1909. There he developed into one of baseball's greatest comedians, joining with Nick Altrock and Al Schacht to entertain fans. After finishing with the Indians in 1918, Schaefer was then employed by the New York Giants as a scout. He died on May 16, 1919, of "a hemorrhage due to a sudden coughing spell." The 41-year-old Schaefer was riding on a train near Saranac Lake, NY, at the time. (*Sporting News; Chicago Tribune; Washington Post; New York Times; Baseball Encyclopedia*)

Ray Schalk caught more than 100 games for the White Sox 12 times in a 13 year span, averaging more than 78 percent of their games—despite weighing only 165 pounds. His career total of 1727 games caught ranks him 10th on the all-time list. He also ranks first in career double plays, second in assists and 8th in total chances. A career .253 hitter, he led the Sox to two AL championships, hitting .282 for the 1919 "Black Sox." Chicago acquired Schalk from Milwaukee for $10,000 and two players in August, 1912, and he caught 125 games the following season. He finished his major league career as a playing coach for the Giants in 1929. After that, he scouted and managed in the minors, operated a successful bowling alley in Chicago, and for 18 years was an assistant baseball coach at Purdue. Schalk was elected to the Hall of Fame in 1955. On May 19, 1970, he died of cancer at Chicago at age 77. (*Baseball's Best; New York Times; Baseball Encyclopedia; Chicago Daily Tribune*)

Wally Schang caught 32 World Series games for six AL champion teams—the 1913–14 A's, the 1918 Red Sox, and the 1921–23 Yankees. The A's acquired him in draft from Buffalo in 1913. After he hit .357 in the World Series, Connie Mack said of him, "I think Schang is the greatest young catcher that ever broke into the major leagues." His major league career covered 19 seasons, in six of which he hit above .300, his lifetime mark being .284. In World Series games Schang hit .287. He caught at least 80 games nine times and 100 or more five times. Playing for the Browns, he hit .330 in 1926 and led AL catchers in fielding in 1929. Schang ended his major league career with the Tigers in 1931, but played in the minors and later coached Cleveland (1936–38). After leaving baseball, he operated a farm near Dixon, MO. He died at St. Louis on March 6, 1965, at age 75. (*Sporting News; Chicago Daily Tribune; Total Baseball; New York Times*) **Photograph on page 130**

Alexander (Rube) Schauer (Dimitri Ivanovich Dmitrihoff), a Russian-born right-hander, posted a 10–29 record in five seasons with the Giants and A's. Schauer entered baseball "because he failed to make good as a minister of the gospel." With less than six months of professional baseball, he was able to jump from Superior of the Class C Northern League to the Giants in 1913. Described as coming from the "Wisconsin

Wally Schang

cornstalks," Schauer won only three games in four seasons with the Giants and was sent to Louisville in 1916, from where he returned to the A's. He logged more than half of his major league innings in 1917, when he went 7–16 for the A's. Having attended Mankato Teachers College for two years before entering professional baseball, Schauer became a deputy clerk in the county auditor's office in Minneapolis after finishing his playing career there in 1922. He died of a heart attack in Minneapolis on April 15, 1957, at age 66. (*Hall of Fame File; Baseball Encyclopedia; Boston Daily Globe; New York Times*)

Walter Schmidt had a dream season in 1921, leading NL catchers in putouts, assists, double plays, total chances and fielding, while hitting .282. In 10 major league seasons—nine with the Pirates—he hit .257, holding regular status five times. He and his older brother "Boss" Schmidt, a Tiger catcher, were natives of Arkansas. Already 29 years old, Walter came to the Pirates from the PCL in 1916. He returned to the PCL when he left the Cardinals in 1925, playing for Mission and Seattle and managing Mission. By this time Schmidt had moved to the Modesto, CA, area, where he had a successful career in real estate. He maintained ties with baseball as a scout and a friend of Casey Stengel and through involvement with the PCL and Modesto baseball. He died at Modesto on July 4, 1973, at age 86. (*Modesto Bee; Total Baseball; Encyclopedia of Minor League Baseball; Chicago Daily Tribune;* information supplied by Mrs. Janice Thiry)

Pete Schneider won 20 games with a 1.98 ERA for the 1917 Reds. His six-year big league career shows 162 starts and a 2.62 ERA. It also shows three consecutive seasons of 19 losses and two seasons of leading the NL in walks. Schneider had compiled a 12–2 record at Seattle when he was sold to Cincinnati in June 1914. The Reds sold him to the Yankees at the end of 1918, and they released him to Vernon in 1919. There he ruined his arm and later became a slugging outfielder, who in one game in 1923 hit five homers and a double in six at bats. A lifelong resident of Los Angeles, he died of a heart attack on June

1, 1957, at age 61. His death certificate lists no occupation other than "Baseball Player — Pro. Sportsman." (*Hall of Fame file; Total Baseball; California Certificate of Death; Sporting News*)

Frank (Wildfire) Schulte won the Chalmers Award in 1911 as the National League Most Valuable Player. That season he led the NL with 21 homers and 121 RBI's while hitting .300. In a 15-year career, 12 with the Cubs, he hit .270 and played with four NL championship clubs. In 21 World Series games, he hit .309. Schulte came to the Cubs from Syracuse in 1904, hitting .286 in 20 games. He remained with the Cubs until 1916, when he was traded to the Pirates. He finished his major league career with the Senators in 1918 but continued in the minors through 1923. In 1913, while still an active player, he purchased a 637-acre plantation north of Atlanta, where he harvested crops of peaches and cotton. This burned in 1918. Schulte finally settled in Oakland, CA. An invalid for a number of years, he died there on October 2, 1949, at age 67. (*Hall of Fame file; Deadball Stars of the National League; Total Baseball*).

Joe Schultz played with every NL club except the Giants in an 11-year major league career. He was only 18 years old when he joined the Braves at the end of 1912, coming from Akron. Schultz reached regular status as a Cardinal outfielder in 1920 after the Cardinals had traded eight players to get him. A career .285 hitter — helped by his ability to hit left-handed pitching — he reached .314 with the Cardinals in 1922. After ending his major league career in 1925, he then played with Minneapolis and Mobile and managed Topeka, Danville, Houston and Springfield, IL. Starting in 1934 he scouted for the Cardinals, Sacramento and the Pirates. At the time of his death Schultz was head of the Pirate farm system. He died on April 13, 1941, in Columbia, SC, of the effects of ptomaine poisoning. He was 47 years old. A son, Joe, Jr., caught for the Pirates and Browns. (*Sporting News; Columbia [SC] News; Total Baseball; New York Times*)

Al Schulz won 21 games for the Buffalo Federals in 1915. In five seasons the left-hander compiled a 48–61 record with the Yankees, Buffalo and the Reds. He first pitched in the majors in 1913 with the Yankees, coming from Savannah, where he had won 25 games and struck out 318. He jumped to Buffalo in 1914 and was awarded to the Reds when the FL folded. Despite an 8–19, 3.14 ERA season, he was sent down to Toledo, where he pitched in 1917–18 before retiring from baseball. Schulz worked as a salesman in his hometown of Toledo until his mind "became crazed with fits." In July 1931 he was admitted to the hospital for epileptics at Gallipolis, OH, where he died on December 14, 1931. He was 42 years old. (*Hall of Fame file; Encyclopedia of Minor League Baseball; Total Baseball; Sporting News; Toledo Blade*)

Ferdinand Schupp led NL pitchers in winning percentage in 1917 when he turned in a 21–7, 1.95 ERA record for the Giants. He capped that season by shutting out the White Sox in Game Four of the World Series. In the previous season he had compiled a 0.90 ERA for 140 innings. Schupp joined the Giants in

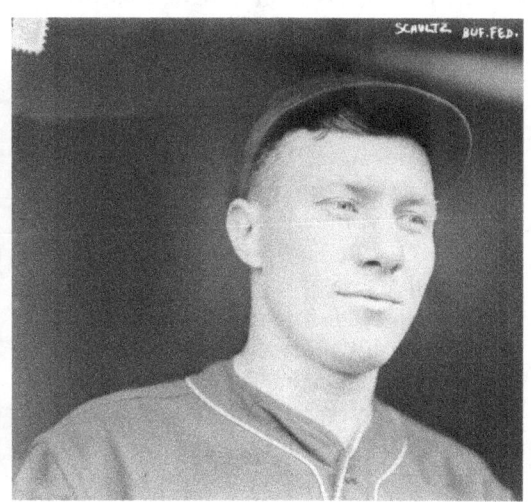

Al Schulz

Ferdinand Schupp

1913 from Decatur, with a reputation of being able to throw a rising fastball. In 10 seasons with the Giants, Cardinals, Dodgers and White Sox, the lefthander won 61 games. The Louisville native pitched eight more seasons in the American Association. He lived in the Los Angeles area after 1932, dying there on December 16, 1971, at age 90. His obituaries, appearing in the *Los Angeles Times*, listed no post-playing career; however, *Sporting News* gives a 1934 address of "care of Shell Oil Company," suggesting that he was employed by that company. (*New York Times; Sporting News; Los Angeles Times; Total Baseball*)

Everett (Deacon) Scott held the major league record for playing in consecutive games (1307), broken by Lou Gehrig. In 13 seasons—eleven as a regular—he led AL shortstops in fielding for 8 consecutive seasons. While he hit only .249 for his career, Scott played for five AL championship teams: Boston (1915, 1916, 1918) and New York (1922, 1923), appearing in 27 World Series games. He joined the Red Sox in 1914 from St. Paul and was a regular in his first season. He also played for the Senators, White Sox and Reds before leaving the majors in 1926. A national-tournament-class bowler, Scott operated a bowling alley in Fort Wayne, IN, after retiring from baseball. He died in Fort Wayne on November 2, 1960, at age 68. (*Sporting News; Baseball Encyclopedia; Washington Post*)

Jack Scott won 103 games in a checkered major league career. He joined the Pirates in September 1916 from Macon and then pitched for the Braves 1917–21, winning 15 games in 1921. Released by the Reds in 1922 because of a sore arm, he signed with the Giants, helping them win the Pennant and pitching a 3-hit shutout in Game 3 of the World Series. Twice he was returned to the minors after successful seasons—in 1924, following a 16–7 record, and in 1928, after leading the NL in games pitched with the Phillies! Closing his playing career with the Giants in 1929, he became police chief in

Everett Scott

Jack Scott

Jim Scott

victories. The Deadwood, SD, native attended Nebraska Wesleyan College before entering professional baseball. Drafted by the White Sox from Wichita after the 1908 season, he immediately compiled a 12–12 record in 1909. The second major leaguer to enter military service in 1917, he attained the rank of Captain in the infantry. After World War I Warrenton, NC, a position he held for 30 years. While undergoing emergency surgery, He died at Durham, NC, on November 30, 1959, at age 67. (*Sporting News; New York Times; Total Baseball*)

Jim (Death Valley) Scott turned in 22–20 and 24–11 records during a 9-year career with the White Sox, which ended with 107

Tom Seaton

he played independent ball (Beloit Fairies), and minor league ball (PCL and Southern Association), quitting to become an umpire. Scott umpired through 1932, the last two years in the National League. At the conclusion of his baseball career, he was employed as a studio technician by Republic and RKO. Scott died of a heart attack at Palm Springs, CA, on April 7, 1957, at age 68. (*Sporting News; Chicago Daily Tribune; SABR Collegiate Directory; Baseball Encyclopedia*)

Tom Seaton led the NL in innings pitched, strikeouts and wins in 1913, while pitching for the Phillies. He followed that 27–12 record with a 25–14 season with the Brooklyn Federals in 1914. Drafted by the Phillies from Portland in 1912, the Nebraskan went 16–12 in his first season. By 1915 his win total had dropped to 13 and his ERA had ballooned to 3.81. Back in the NL, he managed only 11 more victories for the Cubs and Reds before being sold to San Francisco, leaving the majors with 92 victories. In 1920 he was officially released by San Francisco "for the good of baseball." He also was later denied a contract to play for Little Rock. In 1921 Seaton moved to El Paso TX, where he played semi-pro ball and became "foreman at the cottrell and arsenic plants of the smelter there." Following a long illness, he died on April 10, 1940, at age 52. (*Sporting News; Total Baseball; New York Times; Los Angeles Times; Atlanta Constitution*)

Harry (Socks or Sox) Seibold first came to the talent-poor A's in 1915 as a shortstop, hitting .115 in 10 games. He rejoined the A's in 1916 as a pitcher, compiling a 7–21 record through 1919, when he quit rather than play for such a bad club. After bouncing around in the minors and retiring twice because of arm trouble, Seibold returned to the majors with the Braves in 1929, winning 37 games in the next three seasons. He had led the IL with 22 victories in 1928 to earn his ticket back. Seibold returned to the minors in 1934, leaving a major league mark of 48–86. He later managed in the Eastern Shore League and scouted for the Phillies and Giants. Seibold was a Philadelphia native and a World War I veteran. He died in Philadelphia on September 21, 1965, at age 69. (*Sporting News; Baseball-Reference.com; Washington Post*)

Hank Severeid caught 100 or more games seven times during his 15-year major league career, catching 125 or more four times. A career .289 hitter, he had five consecutive seasons over .300, while also leading AL catchers in fielding three times. In 1921 he threw out 51 of 53 base runners attempting to steal. After a long career with the Browns, he finished with two AL champions—the 1925 Senators and the 1926 Yankees, catching every game of the 1926 World Series. Sent down in 1927, Severeid played the next five seasons in the PCL, hitting between .301 and .367 each year and making the all-star team in 1929. He continued to play and manage in the minors until 1937, when he was 46 years old. In all he caught 2357 major and minor league games. After that Severeid coached and scouted for the Reds. The Story City, IA, native died of a heart attack at San Antonio, TX, on December 17, 1968. He was 77 years old. (*Sporting News; Total Baseball; Encyclopedia of Minor League Baseball; New York Times; Los Angeles Times*)

Howard Shanks hit .302 in 1921, led the AL with 19 triples and led AL third-basemen in fielding, putouts and double plays. The Senators drafted Shanks from Youngstown, and he began his major league career in 1912 as their regular left fielder, before shifting to shortstop in 1917 and to third base in 1921. In 14 seasons—11 as a regular—he hit .253. Shanks played for the Red Sox in 1923–25 and for the Yankees in 1926. After leaving the majors, he played one season in the minors, coached for the Indians until 1932 and managed Beaver Falls, PA, in 1938. Outside of baseball he became head of the Real Estate Department in Beaver County, PA. Following a heart attack, Shanks died at Monaca, PA, on July 30, 1941. He was 50 years old. (*Sporting News; Baseball-Reference.com; Washington Post; New York Times*)

James (Grunting Jim) Shaw led the AL in games and innings pitched while posting a 17–17 record in 1919. In seven full seasons with the Senators, Shaw, a product of the Pittsburgh sandlots, won 84 games. The 19-year-old joined the Senators from York of the Tri-State League at the end of 1913. In five of the next seven seasons he won at least 10 games. In 1918 he posted a 16–12, 2.42 ERA record. An operation in 1921 to correct a hip ailment was unsuccessful, so he was forced to retire from baseball at age 28. Shaw then became a federal prohibition agent and later an agent for the Internal Revenue Service, stationed outside Washington, DC. After a long illness, he died at Georgetown Hospital on January 27, 1962, at age 68. (*Washington Star; Baseball-Reference.com; Washington Post*)

Bob Shawkey joined the A's in 1913 from Baltimore and went on to win 196 games in 15 seasons with the A's and Yankees. The

Jim Shaw

Bob Shawkey

Slippery Rock Teachers product had four 20-win seasons, topped by a 24–14 record in 1916 and an AL leading 2.45 ERA in 1920. Service in the U.S. Navy during World War I caused him to miss almost all of the 1918 season, costing him perhaps 20 victories. Shawkey pitched for five AL champions, making five World Series starts for a 1–3 record. In 1930 he succeeded Miller Huggins as Yankee manager for one season and later managed at Jersey City, Scranton and Newark before becoming baseball coach at Dartmouth College. After a long illness he died at the Veterans Administration Hospital in Syracuse, NY, on December 31, 1980, at age 90. (*Hall of Fame File; Total Baseball; SABR Collegiate Data Base; New York Times*)

Arthur (Marty) Shay had two major league trials, totaling 21 games, eight years apart. He played in two games at shortstop for the 1916 Cubs after hitting .380 at Goddard Seminary. Shay served in the U.S. Navy in World War I and then played at New Haven and Worcester before moving to the Braves for 19 games in 1924. His major league totals show a .240 average for 75 at bats. After leaving baseball, he was employed by Parker and Harper Mfg. Co. as a "helper." Shay died at his home in Worcester, MA, on February 20, 1951, of myocardial degeneration. He was 54 years old. (*Hall of Fame file/Massachusetts Certificate of Death/New York Times; Baseball Encyclopedia*)

Tom Sheehan won 17 and lost 39 in six major league seasons, his record hurt considerably by a 1–16 record for the 1916 A's. He helped Atlanta win the Southern Association before serving with the American Expeditionary Force in France in World War I. After a brief trial with the Yankees in 1921, Sheehan won 26 and 31 games for St. Paul, helping the Saints win the 1922 AA championship and earning himself a trial with the Reds. In his best major league season, he compiled a respectable 9–11, 3.24 ERA record with the 1924 Reds. Traded to Pittsburgh, Sheehan ended his major league playing career there. He later helped Kansas City win the 1929 AA championship and pitched in the PCL with Hollywood. After his playing days ended, Sheehan became a hotel detective, but in 1948 the Giants hired him as a super scout and later, in 1960, as manager. He died in Chillicothe, OH, on October 29, 1982, at age 87. (*Sporting News; Total Baseball; Atlanta Constitution; Los Angeles Times; Baseball-Reference.com*)

Urban Shocker (Urbain Schockeor) won 187 games in 13 seasons with the Yankees and Browns. He won 20 games four consecutive seasons, including a league-leading 27 in 1921. He also led the AL in strikeouts in 1922. A 19-game winner for the AL champion Yankees in 1926, he lost Game 2 of the World Series that year to Pete Alexander. Shocker came to the Yankees in 1916 from Ottawa, where he led the Canadian League in wins and strikeouts. Traded to the Browns in 1918, he became a starter in 1919. In 1928 Shocker retired from baseball because of an athletic heart, the result of putting "everything he had into the game." Before his retirement he had begun to operate a radio shop. Less than a year after his retirement, he died at Denver on September 9, 1928. He was 38 years old. (*Sporting News; Denver Post; Total Baseball; New York Times; Chicago Daily Tribune*)

Ray Shook was a pinch runner for the White Sox on April 16, 1916, his only major league appearance. The 155-pound catcher had joined the White Sox from Racine toward the end of 1915 but saw no action. Early in 1916 he was sent down to Rockford. Shook later played for Beloit Fairbanks-Morse in the independent Midwest League. A native of Perry, OH, he lived in South Bend, IN, where he became owner of F & S Transit Co. He died of congestive heart failure at South Bend on September 16, 1970, at age 79. (*Indiana Certificate of Death; baseball-reference.com; Chicago Daily Tribune*)

Ernie Shore won 58 games for the Red Sox in four seasons (1914–17) before torn ligaments in his pitching arm cut short his career. The 6'4" right-hander posted a 19-8, 1.64 ERA record in 1915 and had a 1.82 ERA for four World Series starts in 1915–16. A graduate of Guilford College, Shore pitched one inning for the Giants in 1912 and is described as "Long" Shore and as being "so thin he doesn't make a shadow." After serving in the U.S. Navy during World War I, Shore was traded to the Yankees in 1919, finishing his major league career in 1920. After pitching in the PCL, he became sheriff of Forsyth County, North Carolina, a post he held for 34 years, retiring when he was 80. He died at Winston-Salem, NC, on September 4, 1980, at age 89. (*Hall of Fame file; Total Baseball; SABR Collegiate Data Base; New York Times*) **Photograph on page 58**

Charles (Chick) Shorten spend half a century in organized baseball as a player and scout. In eight seasons he hit .275 with the Red Sox, Tigers, Browns and Reds and led the AL in pinch-hitting in 1921. With the Red Sox in 1916, the left-handed hitting outfielder went 4 for 7 in the World Series, driving in two runs. During World War I, he attended naval training school in Cambridge. In 1919 Shorten hit .315 for the Tigers. Send down to St. Paul in 1923, he refused to report. He finished his major league career with the Reds in 1924 and then played at Reading and Newark. Shorten then became a scout for the Indians, a post he held until 1959. A life-long resident of Scranton, PA, Shorten died there on October 23, 1965, at age 73. (*Sporting News; Total Baseball; New York Times*)

Burt Shotton was a regular outfielder with the Browns and Senators for eight years (1911–18). Reaching .297 in 1913, he settled for a .270 average for his 14 seasons in the majors. He first joined the Browns from Wheeling at the end of 1909. In 1919 he joined the Cardinals, becoming Branch Rickey's "Sunday Manager" in addition to playing outfield. Shotton coached the Cardinals, managed the Phillies (1928–34), managed Cardinal farm teams, scouted for

Burt Shotton

1915 World Series opening day pitchers Ernie Shore (left) of the Red Sox and Pete Alexander of the Phillies.

the Indians, and in 1947 became manager of the Dodgers. In four seasons with the Dodgers, he guided them to NL championships in 1947 and 1949 and was replaced after finishing second in 1950. In Jackie Robinson's first year with the Dodgers, Shotton was his manager. He died at his home in Lake Wales, FL, on July 29, 1972, at age 77. (*Sporting News; New York Times; Total Baseball*)

Eddie Sicking was still a teenager when he played in one game with the Cubs in 1916 and was within a day of being the youngest player in the majors that year. With time out for military service in World War I, he played 15 seasons of professional baseball, five as a utility infielder in the majors, hitting .226 in 203 games. In his last major league trial, he played in six games for the Pirates in 1927. Sicking later played for Indianapolis and Minneapolis. After his retirement from baseball, he operated the Sportsman's Cafe in his hometown of St. Bernard, OH, a Cincinnati suburb. After a long illness he died there on August 30, 1978, at age 81. (*Cincinnati Post; Total Baseball; Washington Post*)

Wesley (Paddy) Siglin had three trials with the Pirates, totaling 23 games. In these the second baseman hit .180. After leading the Central Association in hitting in 1914, the Iowa native joined the Pirates in September of that year, hitting .154 in 14 games. After serving in the U.S. Army Medical Corps in World War I, he enjoyed a productive career in the Pacific Coast League — first with Portland, then with Salt Lake City, Sacramento and San Francisco. In 1921 he led the PCL in runs, hits and home runs. After 22 years in baseball he became the owner of an orange orchard and later operated a bar. His death certificate lists his occupation as "watchman-janitor." Siglin died of cancer at Oakland, CA, on August 5, 1956, at age 64. (*Hall of Fame File; Baseball Encyclopedia; Sporting News; California Certificate of Death*

George Sisler came to the Browns as a pitcher in 1915 and was converted into a first baseman, good enough to lead the AL in assists six times and to be "considered one of the two finest defensive first basemen in baseball history." But the University of Michigan graduate is best remembered as a hitter. His major league record 257 hits stood for 74 years, and he had two AL batting crowns — .407 in 1920 and .420 in 1922. Sisler finished with a career .340 average, a figure that surely would have been higher had he not suffered from sinus poisoning, which caused him to miss the 1923 season entirely and limited his vision thereafter. He was player manager for the Browns 1924–26 before finishing his career with the Boston Braves in 1929, hitting only .326. He loaned his name to a sporting goods and printing firm, managed softball parks, served as ABC commissioner and finally scouted for the Browns. Sisler was elected to the Hall of Fame in 1939. He died at St. Louis on March 26, 1973, at age 80. Two of his sons — Dick, a first baseman, and Dave, a pitcher — played in the majors. (*Baseball's Best; New York Times; Total Baseball*)

Smejkal *see* **Smykal**

Clarence (Pop Boy) Smith had trials with the White Sox in 1913 and with Cleveland in 1916–1917. The former concession stand worker (hence the nickname) pitched in 26 games, compiling a 1-4 record. On the strength of a very good curve, the 20-year-old Smith came to the White Sox after turning in an 18-6 record at Birmingham in 1912. Sold to Venice of the PCL in 1914, he moved on to New Orleans and was sold to Cleveland in 1916. The right hander continued to pitch until 1921, when he retired because of ill health. Smith managed minor league teams

Pop Boy Smith

at Sweetwater, TX, and Clovis, NM, dying of tuberculosis at Sweetwater on February 16, 1924. He was 31 years old. (*Sporting News; Total Baseball; Chicago Daily Tribune; Atlanta Constitution; Encyclopedia of Minor League Baseball*)

Earl Smith hit .306 in 103 games as a Browns third baseman/outfielder in 1920. In seven seasons with the Cubs, Browns and Senators, he averaged 70 games per year, hitting .272. The Cubs purchased him from Omaha in September 1916. Returned to Omaha, he was bought by the Browns in July 1917. Released by the Senators in 1922, he played in the minors until 1932 and later managed and umpired in the minors through 1938. Afterwards Smith worked as a salesman for Standard Brewing Co, but at the time of his death, he was working as a plumber and pipe fitter at a war plant near Portsmouth, OH. He died at Portsmouth on March 14, 1943, at age 52. (*Sporting News; Total Baseball; Boston Daily Globe; Washington Post; Chicago Daily Tribune*)

Elmer Smith hit the first grand slam homer in World Series history in 1920, a season in which he hit .316 and drove in 103 runs. He played ten major league seasons, eight as a regular outfielder, hitting .276. Smith came to the Indians at the end of 1914 from Waterbury. Traded to the Senators in 1916, he returned to Cleveland in 1917, also playing for the Red Sox, Yankees and Reds in a major league career lasting until 1925. He later played for Portland and Minneapolis, hitting .332 with the Millers in 1930. Following his baseball days, he worked as a salesman/route man for a Cleveland brewery and later as a stock manager for a trenching company there. He died at a nursing home at Columbia, KY, on August 3, 1984, at age 91. (*Sporting News; Total Baseball; information supplied by Mrs. Sally Nell; Washington Post*)

George (Columbia George) Smith joined the Giants directly from Columbia University in 1916 and won his only start — plus two more in relief. In eight seasons he won 41 games for the Giants (four trials), Phillies (4 trials) Dodgers (two trials), and Red (one trial) — including 13 in 1920; but he also lost 81 — including a league-leading 20 in 1921. Cut by the Dodgers after the 1923 season, Smith became a mathematics teacher at Greenwich (CT) High School, becoming head of the department before he retired in 1957. He died at Greenwich on January 7, 1965, at the age of 72. (*Sporting News; New York Times; Total Baseball; SABR Collegiate Database*)

Jack Smith (Jan Smitka), born in Chicago of Bohemian parents, was the regular right fielder of the Cardinals and Braves for 10 of his 15 major league seasons. The left-handed batter hit higher than .300 six times and finished with a career .287 average. He came to the Cardinals from Seattle in September 1915, served in the military during part of 1918, and was traded to Boston in 1926. Leaving baseball in 1929 as the Great Depression hit, he worked at a service station for a while and then went to work for International Harvester, Co in plant security, a position from which he retired. Smith died suddenly from a heart attack at Westchester, IL, on May 2, 1972, at age 76. (*Hall of Fame file; Total Baseball; Los

Elmer Smith

Red Smith

Angeles Times; information supplied by Mrs. Yvonne Schroeder)

James Carlisle (Red) Smith hit .314 after joining the Braves in August 1914 to help them to the NL championship. In nine major league seasons with the Dodgers and Braves—seven as a regular third baseman—Smith hit .278 while leading the NL in assists and errors four times each. The Auburn University product first joined the Dodgers from Nashville in September 1911. He was hitting only .245 when he was traded to the Braves in 1914. A broken leg on the last day of the season kept him out of the World Series that year. After leaving the Braves in 1919, he played and managed in the minors for several years. Smith then became a tax investigator for the city of Atlanta. He died in Atlanta of heart disease on October 10, 1966, at age 76. (*Hall of Fame File; Atlanta Constitution; Baseball-Reference.com; SABR Collegiate Database; Sporting News*)

Jimmy Smith joined the Chicago Federals as a 19-year-old in 1914, becoming their regular shortstop in 1915, his only year as a regular. In 8 seasons with the Federals, Pirates, Giants, Braves, Red, and Phillies, he hit .219. Smith spent 1920 at Indianapolis before finishing with the Phillies. Having attended Duquesne University in his native Pittsburgh, he became general manager of the National Distilleries Company when the Phillies released him in 1923. Later he founded the Hillcrest Coal Co. and still later worked in the Pennsylvania State Inheritance Tax office. Smith was the father-in-law of light-heavyweight boxing champion Billy Conn. He died at Pittsburgh on January 1, 1974, at age 78. (*Pittsburgh Post-Gazette; Washington Post; Baseball-Reference.com*)

Paul Smith played ten games as an outfielder for the Reds in 1916, hitting .227. He was first signed by the Cubs in 1910 but was sent to Louisville without appearing in a game. In 1914 the Senators acquired him from Adrian, where he had hit .331, but sent him down before the season began. In 1918 the Red Sox obtained him from Montreal, but again he did not play. The 200-pounder was an outstanding football player at Millikin University—even after playing professional baseball. After serving in World War I, Smith was employed by the U.S. Fish and Wildlife Service, retiring in 1951. A native of Mt. Zion, IL, he died of a heart attack at Decatur, IL, on July 3, 1958, at age 70. (*Sporting News; Chicago Daily Tribune; Washington Post; SABR Collegiate Database; Baseball-Reference.com*)

Sherry Smith, a lefthander with what base runners called a "miracle move" to first base, won 114 games in 14 seasons with the Pirates, Dodgers and Indians. Smith lost Game 2 of the 1916 Series to Babe Ruth 2–1

Frank Smykal (Smejkal) joined the Pirates as a 27-year-old infielder in August 1916, hitting .300 in 6 games. He had started the season at Chattanooga, was dropped to Ottawa, KS, and promoted to the Pirates. After service in World War I, the Chicago native played in the independent Midwest League. A graduate of the University of Illinois, he played baseball for the Illini between 1908 and 1914. In the on-line *Philadelphia Athletics Historical Society Guestbook*, his daughter Carol Pastoret asserts that he was a civil engineer graduate; however, his death certificate lists his occupation as "physician and surgeon." Smykal died of "cerebral vascular hemorrhage" on August 11, 1950, at the Veterans Administration Hospital in Chicago. He was 60 years old. (*Illinois Certificate of Death; Baseball-Reference.com; Atlanta Constitution; Chicago Daily Tribune*)

Sherry Smith

in 14 innings, but overall in World Series play, he allowed only three earned runs in 30.1 innings. In 1920 he won the third game 2–1 and lost a 1–0 duel to Duster Mails in Game 6. He first pitched in the majors with Pittsburgh in 1911, coming from Jacksonville, and he came to stay with the Dodgers in 1915 when he went 14–8. In 11 seasons as a starting pitcher he won at least 10 games 7 times. He led the AL in complete games and innings in 1925. After being released by the Indians in 1928, he managed in the minors through 1932, when he returned to his native Georgia to become a deputy sheriff in Newton County. At the time of his death, Smith worked at Tattnall State Prison. He died at Reidsville, GA, on September 12, 1949, at age 58. (*Sporting News; Baseball Encyclopedia; Los Angeles Times; New York Times*)

James (Red) Smyth, born in Mississippi of Irish parents, had four major league trials with the Dodgers and Cardinals. Used as both an outfielder and an infielder, he hit .191 in 118 games. Smyth joined the Dodgers from Fort Wayne in 1915 and was shipped to Montreal and later traded to the Cardinals in 1917. After service in World War I, he played at Milwaukee until 1922. When he left professional baseball, Smyth became a bookkeeper for Simmons Mattress Company at Kenosha, WI. Sixty-five years old and suffering from Parkinson's Disease, Smyth died of bronchopneumonia at Inglewood, CA, on April 14, 1958. (*California Certificate of Death; Sporting News; Baseball-Reference.com; New York Times; Boston Daily Globe*)

Fred Snodgrass, like teammate Fred Merkle, is always remembered for a crucial error. He dropped an easy fly ball in the 10th inning of Game 7 of the 1912 World Series, contributing to a Giants loss. But he played nine seasons in the majors—seven as the regular center fielder for the Giants and Braves. A career .275 hitter, he helped the Giants win three straight NL championships, hitting .296 in 1911 and .291 in 1913. He was a catcher

Fred Snodgrass

for St. Vincent's College (now Loyola-Marymount), but when he arrived in New York in 1908, John McGraw converted him to an outfielder. After leaving the majors in 1916 — still only 28 years old — he played one year in the PCL and then retired from baseball. Snodgrass settled in Oxnard, CA, where he operated an electrical appliance business and grew citrus fruit while serving as mayor of the city. He died at Ventura, CA, on April 5, 1974, at age 86. (*Sporting News; New York Times; Baseball-Reference.com; Los Angeles Times; Baseball Necrology; Deadball Stars of the National League*)

Frank Snyder was an iron man catcher for the Cardinals and Giants. Except for the war year of 1918, he averaged catching 99 games per year from 1914 through 1924. He was a regular on four consecutive NL championship teams in New York, hitting .364 in the 1921 World Series and as high as .343 in

Frank Snyder

the 1922 season. The Cardinals acquired him from Flint at the end of 1912 and traded him the Giants in 1919. After leaving the majors in 1927, Snyder played and managed in the minors through 1931 and coached for the Giants through 1937. When he left baseball, he became a salesman for a brewery. Snyder was a native of San Antonio and died there of a brain tumor on January 5, 1962, at age 68. (*Hall of Fame file; Texas Certificate of Death; Total Baseball; New York Times*)

Tris Speaker hit 793 career doubles, more than anyone else who ever played the game. In 22 major league seasons he collected 3515 hits, fifth on the all time list. His career .344 batting average ranks seventh, and his 1881 runs ranks eighth. A tremendous fielder, he also is career leader in double plays started by an outfielder and is tied for leadership in assists per game. From 1910 to 1915 he played between Harry Hooper and Duffy Lewis in what is generally regarded as a peerless outfield. As player-manager of the Indians 1919–26, Speaker led them to one pennant in 1920. Before turning professional, he played one season at Texas Wesleyan University. After leaving the majors in 1928, Speaker managed in the minors for two years, spent two years as a radio announcer in Chicago and two years as part owner of the Kansas

Tris Speaker

City Blues before returning to announcing. He was among the second group of players elected to the Hall of Fame in 1937. After retiring to Florida, Speaker became a goodwill ambassador for baseball. Suffering from deteriorating health, he died of a heart attack at Lake Whitney, TX, on December 8, 1958, at age 70. (*Baseball Encyclopedia; Baseball's Best; New York Times*)

Edward (Tubby) Spencer had two major league careers. Joining the Browns in 1905 from Waco, he was a talented but undisciplined catcher who, by 1912, had eaten and caroused his way out of baseball. He hit .265 in 1907 but was down to .162 when the Red Sox sent him to St. Paul in 1909. At a low point in his career, he was remanded to the workhouse in Indianapolis for drunkenness. After working in a lumber camp in the Northwest, he returned to baseball via the Pacific Coast League. Hitting .277 at Vernon, he came back to the Tigers in August 1916 and played well through 1918. His career totals show a .225 average for 449 games. Spencer went back to the PCL in 1919 with Salt Lake City and later Los Angeles. Leaving professional baseball, he became a "sleuth" for the Auto Club, for whom he played on weekends. Spencer retired to San Francisco, where he died of a cerebral hemorrhage on February 1, 1945. He was 60 years old. (*Hall of Fame file; Total Baseball; Sporting News; Los Angeles Times*)

Henry (Heinie) Stafford was signed by John McGraw from Tufts University, where he had majored in chemistry and had had an outstanding baseball career. On the last day of the 1916 season, he made an unsuccessful pinch hitting appearance for the Giants. Married, Stafford joined Cannon Textiles as a chemist the following year to increase his earnings. Eventually he became a vice president in the company. In 1941 Stafford retired to his native Vermont to do experimental farming. While on vacation, he died at Lake Worth, FL, on January 29, 1972. He was 80 years old. (*Total Baseball; SABR Collegiate Database; information supplied by Ms. Irene Stafford*)

Oscar Stanage held or shared first-string catching duties with the Tigers for 12 seasons. He caught more than 100 games 4 times, topped by a 141-game season in 1911. A career .234 hitter, he reached .261 in 1912. After playing one game for the Reds in 1906, he was sent down to Newark. Detroit acquired him in time to help them win the 1909 pennant, as he hit .262 in 77 games. Dropped by the Tigers at the end of the 1920 season, Stanage remained in baseball through 1931, playing in the PCL, coaching for the Tigers and Pirates and managing in the Three-I League. A native of Tulare, CA, he made his home in Detroit, where he died of staphylococcal pneumonia on November 11, 1964. He was 81 years old. His death certificate lists his occupation as "Baseball Player (Ret.)."(*Sporting News; Hall of Fame File; Baseball-Reference.com; New York Times; Los Angeles Times; Washington Post*)

Bob Steele, a Canadian lefty, seems to have been especially unfortunate in his clubs. He was traded from the last place Cardinals—for whom he was 5–15 in 1916—to the last place Pirates—for whom he was 6–14 in 1917. Despite a respectable 3.05 ERA, he had a 16–38 record in just over 3 seasons. Steele came to the Cardinals from St. Paul in 1916. After finishing his professional career at Indianapolis in 1919, he pitched independent ball in Franklin, PA, and later in the Chicago-based Midwest League. In 1918 the New York Giants roster describes him as a teacher in the off season; when he moved to Burlington, WI, he went into business, owning two bowling alleys and a motel. Steele died of a heart attack at Ocala, FL, on January 27, 1962, at age 67. (*Burlington Free Press; Total Baseball; New York Times; Chicago Daily Tribune*)

Bill Stellbauer hit .271 in 25 games after joining the Philadelphia A's as an outfielder in 1916. He was a native of Bremond, TX, and played at Baylor University in 1914 and 1915. In 1917 the A's released him to Houston of the Texas League. Stellbauer later lived in Houston, where he worked for an oil company. He died at Houston on February 16, 1974, at age 79. (*Baseball Encyclopedia; SABR Collegiate Database; Washington Post; Houston Chronicle; information supplied by Billy Stellbauer*)

Casey Stengel attended Western Dental College, trying to become a left-handed dentist, but he spent almost all of his adult life in baseball. He played 14 seasons—eight as a regular outfielder—for five NL clubs, hitting .284. He hit .316 and led the NL is slugging in 1914 and hit .368 as a part timer in 1922. In 12 World Series games with the Dodgers and Giants, he hit .393. The Kansas City native reached Brooklyn from Montgomery in late 1912 and finished with Boston in 1925. He played and managed in the minors, coached the Dodgers, and managed the Dodgers and Braves, but is best remembered for his twelve seasons with the Yankees (1949–60) when his teams won 10 AL championships and 7 World Series. After a year spent as Director of Valley National Bank in Glendale, CA, Stengel returned to manage the hapless New York Mets for four seasons. He died at Glendale, CA, on September 19, 1975, at age 85. Stengel was elected to the Hall of Fame in 1966. (*Baseball's Best; Deadball Stars of the National League; Total Baseball; New York Times*)

John (Stuffy) Stewart played in 176 major league games spread over 14 seasons, opening with nine games for the Cardinals in 1916 and closing with 22 games for the 1929 Senators. In between he had trials with Pittsburgh and the Dodgers. He came to the Cardinals from Jacksonville, played for Birmingham on eight occasions, and finished with Tyler, TX, in 1932. He hit only .238 for his career, but once beat Ty Cobb in a foot race and led a minor league in stolen bases seven times. Stewart had attended Columbia College in Lake City, FL, but when he left baseball, he worked "as an employee at an illegal race track in New Jersey ... worked for Gulf Oil Co. for ten years and was a judge for the Florida Racing Commission." For a time

Milt Stock

Overall Stock spent 40 seasons in professional baseball, serving as a manager and business manager in the minors and as a coach for the Cubs, Dodgers, and Pirates when his playing days had ended. He died at Montrose, AL, on July 16, 1977, at age 84. He was the father-in-law of major league player/manager Eddie Stankey. (*Hall of Fame file; Sporting News; Total Baseball/New York Times*)

Ralph (Sailor) Stroud compiled 20 wins with a 2.94 ERA in three trials with the Tigers and Giants. He joined the Tigers in 1910, but after a 5–9 record was sent to Buffalo. In 1915 the Giants acquire him from Sacramento, and he went 12–9 that year. After a 3–2 record in 1916, Stroud returned to the Pacific Coast League where he pitched for the 1926 champion Los Angeles Angels. The New Jersey native later became a shop worker for the railroad. Suffering from heart disease, he died of pneumonia at Stockton, CA, on April 11, 1970. He was 84 years old. (*California Certificate of Death; Los Angeles Times; New York Times; Total Baseball; Washington Post*)

Amos Strunk played centerfield for five AL championship teams—the Philadelphia A's of 1910–11 and 1913–14 and the 1918 Boston Red Sox. As a teenager he played briefly for the A's in 1908 and 1909. On loan

he also operated a restaurant, gas station and trailer park business. He died at Lake City on December 30, 1980, at age 86. (*Lake City Reporter; information supplied by Mrs. John Blaine; Total Baseball; Washington Post; Atlanta Constitution*)

Milt Stock overcame partial deafness to become a regular National League third baseman for 12 seasons. A career .289 hitter, he had five .300 seasons, topped by a .328 in 1925. The graduate of St. Ignatius College joined the Giants in 1913 from Mobile. Traded to the Phillies in 1915, he helped them win the NL championship, hitting .118 in the World Series. He also played for the Cardinals and finished with Brooklyn in 1926.

Amos Strunk

to Milwaukee for most of 1909, he came up to stay in 1910. Although a leg injury limited him to 16 games that season, he had five hits in the World Series. In all Strunk spent 17 seasons in the majors, eleven as a regular, hitting .283. In his best season he hit .332 for the 1921 White Sox; two years later he led the AL with 12 pinch hits. His speed on the base paths often allowed him to advance two bases on a sacrifice bunt. His speed made him a very good outfielder, leading the AL four times in fielding. After leaving baseball in 1924, the Philadelphia native became an insurance advisor and broker in Llanerch, PA. He died there on July 22, 1979, at age 89. (*Philadelphia Inquirer; Washington Post; Baseball Encyclopedia*)

Billy Sullivan caught the first AL game ever played on April 24, 1901. He had originally joined the Boston Braves from Grand Rapids in September 1899. When the AL was formed, he jumped to the White Sox, becoming a nine-year regular with the club and leading AL catchers in fielding four times. A light hitter (.212 career average), he helped them become world champions in 1906 as the "Hitless Wonders," his two homers leading the club. Catching all six World Series games, Sullivan went hitless. He managed the White Sox in 1909 and served as a player/coach for both the White Sox and Tigers before retiring in 1916. In retirement Sullivan operated a "walnut and filbert farm" near Newberg, OR. He died there of a heart ailment on January 28, 1965, just four days short of his 90th birthday. His son, Billy, Jr., was also an AL catcher. (*Sporting News; Total Baseball; Washington Post; Chicago Daily Tribune*)

Zeb Terry weighed less than 130 pounds, but hit .280, .275, and .286 in three years as a regular second baseman for the Cubs. In seven seasons with the White Sox, Braves, Pirates and Cubs, he was a regular four times. Only the second man to earn four letters in baseball at Stanford, he shifted to the Los Angeles Angels after his 1914 graduation and was acquired by the White Sox for 1916. After hitting .190 as a rookie, he was returned to the PCL, from where he returned to the Braves. After service in World War I, he achieved regular status with the Pirates, leaving the majors in 1922 at age 31. At the time of his retirement, he was "busily engaged in selling acres of valuable real estate." A "Down Memory lane" column in *The Sporting News* described him as being "in the bonding business in Los Angeles." Bill Lee describes him as "self-employed in the oil leasing business." He died in Los Angeles on March 14, 1988, at age 96. (*Sporting News; Los Angeles Times; Chicago Daily Tribune; SABR Collegiate Database; Baseball Necrology*)

Charles (Jeff) Tesreau "threw a spitball with the speed of Walter Johnson's fastball," allowing him to win 115 games for the Giants in just over 6 seasons. The Giants purchased him from Shreveport at the end of 1910, and after a year at Toronto, he became a starting pitcher, going 17–7 in 1912. That year he hooked up with Joe Woods three times in the World Series, losing 3–1 and 4–3 and winning 11–4. The Missouri native had a NL-leading 1.96 ERA in 1912 and posted 22–13 and 26–10 records in 1913 and 1914, leading the league in complete games each season. Only 29 years old when he left the majors in 1918 after a feud with John McGraw, Tesreau

Jeff Tesreau

Pinch Thomas

pitched in the Bethlehem Steel Baseball League. He later became baseball coach at Dartmouth, a position he held until the time of his death. On September 25, 1946, he died at Hanover, NH, the result of a stroke that had paralyzed one side of his body. He was 57 years old. (*Sporting News*; *Deadball Stars of the National League*; *Total Baseball*; *New York Times*)

Chester (Pinch) Thomas was first-string catcher for the AL champion Red Sox in 1915 and 1916. In a 10-year major league career with the Red Sox and Indians, he hit .237 but led AL catchers in fielding in 1917. He came to the Red Sox in 1912 from Sacramento. After the 1916 World Series he made the society pages by marrying a Chicago cabaret dancer. At the conclusion of naval duty during World War I, he was a player/coach for the Indians and later coached the Browns and managed in the SALLY League. In 1920 he expected "to be connected with a movie picture company." The native of Camp Point, IL, died at Modesto, CA, on December 24, 1953. His death certificate lists the cause of death as "pulmonary edema" occurring two days after surgery to amputate his left leg. His occupation is listed as "Baseball player." He was 65 years old and had suffered from psychosis for the past 19 years. (*Hall of Fame file*; *Baseball Encyclopedia*; *New York Times*; *Los Angeles Times*; *Chicago Daily Tribune*)

Claude Thomas spent 18 seasons (1910–1927) in professional baseball, but part of only one season in the majors. Joining the Senators from Des Moines in August 1916, he appeared in 7 games, making 4 starts with a 1–2 record. He was optioned to Minneapolis in 1917 and served in the military in World War I. The much-traveled left-hander pitched for Seattle, Los Angeles and Vernon of the PCL after the war, ultimately finishing his playing career back at Des Moines. Moving to Nevada in 1927, Thomas became a law enforcement official, serving as a deputy sheriff and as a staff member for the El Reno Reformatory. In 1940 he returned to his native Oklahoma as a co-coordinator of the Oklahoma Selective Service headquarters. Thomas died at the Veterans Hospital at Sulphur, OK, on March 6, 1946. He was 55 years old. (*Sporting News*; *Baseball Encyclopedia*; *Washington Post*; *Los Angeles Times*)

James (Shag) Thompson began his professional career in 1913 as a Durham Bull after playing at the University of North Carolina. Acquired by the A's in 1914, he played parts of three seasons as a utility outfielder, hitting .203 in 48 games. Later he played for Bloomington of the Three-I League and Columbus of the American Association. After leaving baseball, Thompson became president of General Building Products of Asheville, NC. He died at Black Mountain, NC, on January 7, 1990, at age 96. (*Asheville Citizen*; *The BULLetin*; *Total Baseball*; *SABR Collegiate Database*; *Washington Post*)

Frank (Buck) Thrasher, a left-handed hitting outfielder, had two trials with the A's in 1916 and 1917, totaling 30 games. After winning the batting championship in the Virginia League in 1914, he was promoted to Atlanta for 1915 and from the Crackers to the A's at the end of 1916. Returned to Atlanta in 1917, he again played for the Crackers and later New

Orleans. Thrasher played for and managed semi-pro teams in the South while operating a drug store. In 1934 he returned to Cleveland, TN, and became a cotton buyer for Anderson-Clayton Co. At age 49 he suffered two heart attacks, the second one fatal on June 12, 1938. (*Sporting News; Cleveland [TN] Daily Banner; Total Baseball; Atlanta Constitution*)

Ben Tincup, "a 100% Cherokee Indian" from Oklahoma, posted an 8–10, 2.61 ERA record as a Phillies rookie in 1914, but was 0–1 in four subsequent trials with the Phillies and Cubs. The side-arm right-hander came to the Phillies from Sherman of the Texas-Oklahoma League, where the struck out 233 batters in 1913. Describing himself as the "Indian who owns land where they didn't find oil," he spent forty years in baseball. After leaving the majors, he played, managed and umpired in the minors. In addition Tincup scouted for the Braves, Pirates and Phillies (1946–58) and coached for the Yankees in the early 1960's. He died at Claremore, OK, on July 5, 1980, at age 89. (*Hall of Fame file; Total Baseball; Sporting News; Washington Post; Atlanta Constitution*)

Joe Tinker, the shortstop of the famous Tinker-to-Evers-to-Chance double play combination, was a regular for 13 seasons with the Cubs, Reds and FL Chicago Whales. A .264 career hitter, he led shortstops in fielding four times, in total chances four times, in assists three times, but curiously only once in double plays. The Cubs acquired Tinker from Portland in 1902. Between 1906 and 1910, he helped the Cubs to four pennants, playing in 21 World Series games. When his playing career ended in 1916, he remained in baseball as a minor league club owner and manager until 1930. Having invested heavily in Florida land, he lost a million dollars during the Depression. Tinker then operated a billiards parlor, opened a bar after the repeal of prohibition, and traveled for a brewery. During World War II he worked at the Orlando airfield. Tinker was elected to the Hall of Fame in 1946. In 1947 his left leg was amputated, the result of diabetes. He died of respiratory complications on July 27, 1948, his 68th birthday. (*Sporting News/Baseball's Best; Deadball Stars of the National League; Total Baseball; New York Times*)

Jack Tobin was one of the best drag bunters in baseball, producing more than 200 hits four times and hitting over .300 six times. A career .309 hitter, Tobin joined Baby Doll Jacobson (career .311) and Ken Williams (career .319), to form the famous "Garden Party" outfield of the St. Louis Browns from 1920 through 1924. He began his professional career with the St. Louis Federals in 1914, leading the FL with 184 hits in 1915, before being awarded to the Browns. He spent 1917 at Salt Lake City before returning to wear out AL pitching. After finished his major league career in 1927 by hitting only .310 for the Red Sox, he played or managed in the minors until 1930. Before returned to the Browns as a hitting coach in 1949, he coached in the sandlots of his native St. Louis. Tobin died of pneumonia in the St. Louis suburb of Creve Coeur on December 10, 1969. He was 77 years old. (*Sporting News; Hall of Fame file; Total Baseball; New York Times*)

Fred Toney was the winning pitcher in a double no-hitter in 1917, when he out dueled the Cubs Hippo Vaughn 1–0 in ten innings. A massive right-hander, Tony won 137 games in 12 seasons with the Cubs, Reds, Giants and Cardinals. In 1917 he compiled a 24–16 record for the Reds, working more than 339 innings, and also had a 21-win season for the Giants in 1920. He arrived with the Cubs in 1911, coming from Winchester. The Reds acquired him from Louisville in 1915, and he responded with a 17–6, 1.58 ERA season. Before the 1918 season he was in trouble for giving false information to his draft board and for violation of the Mann Act. Still his win totals read 12, 13, 21 and 18 over the next four seasons. After winning 11 games for the Cardinals in 1923, Tony left the majors and finished his career with Nashville, his home town, in 1925. In later years Toney operated a sandwich stand, served as a guard at an aircraft factory, and was employed in the sheriff's office in Nashville. He died of a heart ailment on March 11, 1953, at age 64. (*Sporting News; Total Baseball; Deadball Stars of the National League; New York Times*)

Walt Tragesser caught 98 games for the Braves in 1917, hitting .222. In seven seasons with the Braves and Phillies, he hit .215 in 272 games. He was baseball captain-elect at Purdue University but left after one year. Prior to joining the Braves, Tragesser played at Birmingham of the Southern Association. After serving in the U.S. Navy during World War I, he was traded to the Phillies. A lifetime resident of Lafayette, IN, he joined the Indiana Gas Co. in 1924, becoming a superintendent of the service department. In 1925 he also became assistant baseball coach at his alma mater. Tragesser died on December 14, 1970, at age 83. (*Lafayette Journal and Courier; Baseball Encyclopedia; Washington Post; Chicago Daily Tribune*)

Terry Turner was a regular for the Indians in 11 of his 17 big league seasons, leading AL shortstops and third basemen in fielding three times each. Only a .253 hitter over his career, he hit .308 in 1912 and specialized in headfirst slides on the base paths. The Pennsylvanian had a 2-game trial with the Pirates in 1901; then Cleveland outbid the Reds and the Senators to gain him from Toledo in 1904. The *Atlanta Constitution* reported that Toledo received the highest price ever paid for a minor league player up to that time — and split the money with Turner. After 15 seasons with the Indians, Turner played for the A's in 1919 and retired from baseball after playing part of 1920 in the minors. A resident of Cleveland, he became chief superintendent for the Cleveland Street Department. Turner died at Cleveland, following a stroke on July 18, 1960. He was 79 years old. (*Sporting News; Baseball Encyclopedia; Washington Post*)

Howard (Twink) Twining pitched two innings for the Reds in 1916, following his graduation from Swarthmore College. After serving in the Army in World War I, he graduated from Hahneman Hospital in Philadelphia and received training in dermatology at Vienna. Twining enlisted in the Navy during World War II and then became Chief of Dermatology at Hahneman. He also served on the staff of other Philadelphia hospitals when he returned to his home town, Lansdale, PA. Following a 10-month illness, he died there on June 14, 1973, at age 79. (*Lansdale Reporter; SABR Collegiate Database; New York Times; Baseball Encyclopedia*)

George Twombly played parts of five seasons in the majors as an outfielder for the Reds, Braves and Senators, hitting .211 in 150 games. Developed by the Baltimore Orioles, Twombly reached the majors with the Reds in 1914, when he played in 68 games, hitting .233. Returned to the Orioles, Twombly hit

Terry Turner

over .300 and was sold to the Braves in 1917. After serving in World War I, he had a one-game trial with the Senators. Then he became president of C.E. Twombly Co., "the world's largest distributors of diversified paper products." He also authored inspirational literature. A native of Boston, Twombly died at Lexington, MA, on February 17, 1975, at age 82. A younger brother, Babe, was an outfielder for the Cubs. (*Boston Herald-American; Hall of Fame file; Washington Post; New York Times; Total Baseball*)

George (Lefty) Tyler led the NL with 28 complete games in 1913 and averaged more than 22 from 1912 through 1918. He posted 127 wins in 12 seasons, helping the 1914 Braves and the 1918 Cubs to NL championships. His best seasons were 19–8, 2.00 ERA for the 1918 Cubs and 17–9, 2.02 ERA for the 1916 Braves. He had one win and a 1.91 ERA for 4 World Series starts. The product of Derry, New Hampshire joined the Braves from Lowell in 1910. Released by the Cubs to Rochester in 1921, Tyler finished his playing career in 1926 and later umpired in the New England League (1928–30) and the

Lefty Tyler

Eastern League (1931–32). After leaving baseball, he worked for the New England Power Company, and later became a shoe cutter for Haverhill's. He died unexpectedly at his home in Lowell, MA, on September 29, 1953, at age 63. His younger brother Fred was a catcher for the 1914 Braves. (*Manchester Union Leader; Sporting News; Total Baseball; Deadball Stars of the National League; New York Times*)

Hippo Vaughn

James (Hippo) Vaughn gained his nickname from his lack of foot speed, but he had a very quick left arm. In 13 seasons, he won 178 games—20 or more five times—all with the Cubs. He had a career 2.49 ERA, going under 2.0 three times. He also led the NL twice in strikeouts, twice in innings pitched and once in shutouts. In a remarkable 1918 season, he led the NL in six categories and had three complete games with a 1.0 ERA in the World Series. Originally a Yankee, Vaughn entered the majors from Hot Springs in 1908. Over the next five seasons he bounced around among the Yankees, Washington and the minors, to suddenly emerge in 1914 as the best lefthander in baseball. Only 33 years old when he left the majors, Vaughn pitched independent ball in the Chicago-based Midwest League until he was 47. A native of Texas, he made his home in Chicago, where he worked as "an assembler for a refrigeration products company." Vaughn died in Chicago on May 29, 1966, at age 78. (*Biographical Dictionary of American Sport: Baseball; Deadball Stars of the National*

League; *Total Baseball; New York Times; Sporting News*)

Bobby Veach played alongside Ty Cobb, Sam Crawford and later Harry Heilmann in an all-star Detroit outfield. In 14 seasons, twelve with the Tigers, Veach hit .310, leading the AL in RBI's three times and in doubles twice. In 1919 he led the AL in hits on his way to a .355 average; in 1921 he hit .338 with 16 homers and 128 RBI's. The Island, KY, native reached the Tigers in August 1912 from Indianapolis, hitting .342 in 23 games. He ended his major league career with the Senators in 1925, qualifying for his only World Series. After playing in the minors through 1930, Veach retired and "entered the coal business in Detroit." After a long illness, he died on August 7, 1945. He was 57 years old. (*Sporting News; Total Baseball; New York Times; Chicago Daily Tribune*)

Jim Viox was the regular second baseman for the Pirates from 1913 through 1915. He hit .273 during his five-year career, topped by a .317 average in 1913. The Pirates purchased Viox from Lexington, KY, in 1912. Released to Los Angeles near the end of the 1916 season, he played triple-A ball for several years and later managed in the Virginia, Piedmont and Blue Grass leagues. After leaving baseball, Viox worked as a parts man for General Motors. A native of Cincinnati, he made his home at Erlinger, KY, where he died of lung cancer on January 6, 1969, at age 78. (*Sporting News; Kentucky Certificate of Death; Total Baseball; Boston Daily Globe; Encyclopedia of Minor League Baseball*)

Ossie Vitt hit only .238 in ten major league seasons with the Tigers and Red Sox, but was an extremely fine third baseman, who set major league records for chances and assists in 1916 and led the AL in fielding three times. He came to the Tigers in 1912 from San Francisco, a 22-year-old weighing less than 130 pounds. He ultimately reached 150 pounds and hit .254 in 1917. In 1921, his final major league season, he served as player-coach for the Red Sox. After obtaining his release, he played in the Pacific Coast League until 1928 and continued to manage in the minors until 1938, when he was named Cleveland manager. In three seasons the Indians finished 3rd, 3rd, and 2nd, and Vitt was let go—primarily because of a player revolt against his leadership. After two more years managing in the PCL, Vitt retired from organized baseball and spent the remainder of his life teaching baseball on the sandlots. A native of the Bay Area, He died at Oakland, of complications following a stroke, on January 31, 1963, at age 72. (*Sporting News; New York Times; Baseball Encyclopedia; Los Angeles Times*)

Alfred (Fritz) Von Kolnitz had three major league trials with the Reds and White Sox. He graduated from the University of South Carolina Law School in 1913 and joined the Reds in 1914. His major league totals show a .212 average for 115 games, played at five positions. In 1917 he entered the U.S. army, reaching the rank of major. Returning to Charleston, he became a vice president and treasurer of a real estate and insurance firm, athletic director for College of Charleston—where he had also attended college—and chairman of the city board of commissioners of parks and playgrounds. Von Kolnitz also served in World War II, becoming a lieutenant colonel in the Air Force. He died following a heart attack at Mount Pleasant, SC, on March 18, 1948. He was 54 years old. Von Kolnitz is a member of the Hall of Fame at both the University of South Carolina and College of Charleston. (*Charleston Evening Post; Total Baseball; SABR Collegiate Database*)

Bill Wagner had five trials as a catcher with the Pirates and Braves, hitting .207 in 93 games. He entered professional baseball as a 19-year-old in 1913 and made it from Burlington to Pittsburgh for three games the following season. In 1917, his only full season in the majors, he played in 53 games with the Pirates. Released by the Braves early in 1918, he played in the minors until 1920,

Heinie Wagner

when he jumped to Steelton in the Pennsylvania Oil League. After retiring from baseball, he became a boilermaker with the Illinois Railroad Shops in Waterloo, IA, near his hometown of Jessup. He died at Waterloo of an adrenal tumor on January 11, 1951, at age 57. (*Sporting News; Hall of Fame file; Total Baseball; Iowa Certificate of Death*)

Charles (Heinie) Wagner came from the New York City sandlots to become the regular shortstop of the Boston Red Sox. A career .250 hitter, he hit .274 for the World Champions in 1912, but went hitless in the World Series. In 12 major league seasons, he led AL shortstops in total chances per game three times. Originally a Giant in 1902, he came to the Red Sox in 1906 from Waterbury and achieved regular status in 1907. In 1916 Wagner became manager at Hartford, but returned to the Red Sox as a coach later in the season and remained through 1919. He also coached the Red Sox from 1921 through 1929 and was appointed manager in 1930. After one year, in which the Red Sox finished in the cellar, he resigned. A resident of New Rochelle, NY, Wagner became superintendent of a lumberyard there and coached local amateur baseball teams. He died at New Rochelle on March 20, 1943, at age 60. (*Sporting News; Baseball Encyclopedia; Washington Post; New York Times*)

John Peter (Honus) Wagner led the NL in hitting eight times—still a record—and finished a 21-year major league career with 3418 hits, seventh on the all-time list. He also finished 3rd in career triples, 6th in career stolen bases, and 7th in career doubles. The 200-pounder also led NL shortstops in double plays four times, and in fielding and total chances per game three times each. For these accomplishments, he was named as one of the charter members of the baseball Hall of Fame. As a 23-year-old rookie he hit .338 with Louisville in 1897; as a 43 year old he played in 74 games for the Pirates in 1917, hitting .265. Wagner retired from the Pirates following the 1917 season, going into the sporting goods business. He

Honus Wagner

him from Kansas City in 1913 and traded him to the Red Sox in 1916. His last six years were with the A's. Walker played, umpired and managed in the minors until 1940, when he became a Tennessee highway patrolman. At age 72 he died at Unicol, TN, on September 20, 1959. (*Erwin[TN] Record; Sporting News; Total Baseball; SABR Collegiate Database*)

Rhoderick (Bobby) Wallace, in 1953, became the first AL shortstop to be voted into the Hall of Fame. Only a .267 hitter during his career, he stands fifth on the all-time fielding list in chances per game, handling more than 900 per season five times. He jumped from semi-pro ball to the Cleveland Spiders in 1894. By 1897 he had become the regular third baseman and two years later,

also held two political offices — Sergeant-at-Arms in the Pennsylvania legislature and state Fish Commissioner — and coached at Carnegie Tech. When the depression ruined his sporting goods venture, Wagner accepted a position as a coach of the Pirates in 1933, a post he held until illness forced him to retire in 1951. He died at Carnegie, PA, on December 6, 1955, at age 76. His older brother Albert (Butts) Wagner played for Brooklyn and Washington in 1898. (*Deadball Stars of the National League; Sporting News; Baseball Encyclopedia*)

Clarence (Tilly) Walker, a rifle-armed outfielder, led the AL in assists four times during his 13 big league seasons. When Boston traded Tris Speaker to Cleveland, Walker took over in centerfield, helping the Red Sox win the 1916 World Championship. In 1918, at age 31, he emerged as a power hitter: tying Babe Ruth for the AL lead with 11 homers and reaching 37 homers in 1922, his last year as a regular. After attending Washington (MD) College, he reached the majors with the Senators in 1911, his second year in organized baseball. The Browns acquired

Tilly Walker

when he had been transferred to St. Louis, had made the conversion to a shortstop. In 1902 Wallace jumped to the American League Browns, whom he managed in 1911. In all he spent 63 years in organized baseball, 25 as a major league player. He umpired briefly in the AL, managed both major and minor league teams, and coached before becoming a scout for the Reds. On November 3, 1960, the day before his 87th birthday, Wallace died at Torrance, CA. He had earlier suffered a heart attack. (*Sporting News; Baseball Encyclopedia; New York Times*)

Ed Walsh

Edward (Big Ed) Walsh, a miner's son, found pitching harder than mining. He joined the White Sox from Newark in 1904. By 1906 he had mastered the spitter and begun an amazing 7-year period in which he won 168 games. In one monster season of 1908, he worked a record 464 innings, winning 40 games and throwing 11 shutouts. One of his losses that season was a 1–0 duel with Cleveland's Addie Joss, who threw a perfect game. By 1913 his arm had gone dead, and he ultimately left the majors with 195 career victories but the lowest career ERA (1.82) in history. After finishing with the Braves in 1917, Walsh tried managing in the minors, umpiring, and coaching (one season with Notre Dame, two stints with the White Sox). Moving to Connecticut in 1930, he worked at the Meriden Water Plant. Walsh was named to the Hall of Fame in 1946. He died of cancer at Pompano Beach, FL, on May 26, 1959, at age 78. His son Ed also pitched for the White Sox. (*Cooperstown; Total Baseball; Baseball Library; SABR Collegiate Database*)

Jimmy Walsh, an Irish-born outfielder, was an AL regular four times despite an anemic .231 career batting average. He played professional baseball for 28 years — six in the majors for the A's, Yankees and Red Sox — qualifying for two World Series — with the 1914 A's and the 1916 Red Sox. After playing at Niagara University, he joined the A's in 1912 from Baltimore. During World War I, Walsh served in the U.S. Navy, ending his major league career. However, in a 13-season career in the International League he hit .325, leading the league in batting in both 1925 and 1926. After leaving baseball in 1931, he became a foreman in the Department of Public Works for the City of Syracuse. Walsh died of a heart attack on the golf course on July 3, 1962, at age 73. (*Hall of Fame file; Washington Post; Total Baseball; SABR Collegiate Database; Encyclopedia of Minor League Baseball*)

Jimmy Walsh

Alfred (Roxy) Walters caught for 11 seasons in the majors, hitting .222 for the Yankees, Red Sox and Indians. He came to the Yankees from Waco in 1915, catching in two games in September. In 1916–18 he split catching duties in New York with Les Nunamaker and Truck Hannah. Traded to the Red Sox, he enjoyed his most productive season in 1920, playing in 88 games. After leaving the Indians in 1925, the San Francisco product returned to California and played in the PCL through 1929. In later years, Walters managed an apartment building, painted buildings and did other "odd jobs." He died of arteriosclerosis at Alameda, CA, on June 3, 1956. He was 63 years old. (*Hall of Fame File; Baseball Encyclopedia; Sporting News*)

Bill Wambsganss is remembered as the only player to perform an unassisted triple play in a World Series game. But he played 13 seasons in the majors, 11 as a regular second baseman for the Indians and Red Sox, leading the AL in errors four times. A career .259 hitter, he hit .295 in 1918 and .290 in 1923. Coming to the Indians in August 1914, he immediately became a regular. Following his playing career, he managed at Springfield, IL, and Ft. Wayne, IN. During World War II, he managed in the All-American Girls Professional Baseball League. Wambsganss then became a salesman for a hardware manufacturer in the Cleveland suburb of Lakewood. He died there from heart failure on December 8, 1985, at age 91. (*Sporting News; Washington Post; New York Times; Total Baseball*)

Wallace (Cy) Warmoth, a lefty from Bone Gap, IL, had three trials with the Cardinals and Senators, compiling an 8–5 record, seven of those wins coming in 1923 when he worked 105 innings. Called up by the Cardinals at the end of 1916, he pitched in three games. The Senators acquired him from Little Rock at the end of 1922 and in 1924 transferred him back to the Southern League, where he pitched for Memphis and Atlanta. Though Warmouth is listed at 5'11" and 158 pounds, the *Constitution* notes that his "great heft" stood in the way of his becoming a great pitcher. After his playing days ended, Warmoth became a switchman for the New York Central Railroad. He died at Mt. Carmel, IL, on June 20, 1957, at age 64. (*Mt. Carmel Register; Baseball-Reference.com; Washington Post; Atlanta Constitution*)

Hoke (Hooks) Warner hit .228 in 67 major league games. The Pirates purchased him from Dayton in August 1916, and he became the regular third baseman for the remainder of that season. Sent to Wilkes-Barre after three games in 1917, he spent 1918 in the army. The Pirates once again sent him down in 1919, and he finished his major league career with the Cubs in 1921. Warner then managed a restaurant in Pittsburgh. The Del Rio, TX, native died of a cerebral hemorrhage at San Francisco on February 19, 1947. He was 52 years old. (*Sporting News; Total Baseball; Baseball-Reference.com; Atlanta Constitution; Boston Daily Globe*)

Milt (Mule) Watson joined the Cardinals in July 1916 from Paris of the Western Association. He was described as having been "dug up ... from the wilds of Texas" and as being "unsophisticated in the ways of the world." In four seasons with the Cardinals and Phillies he posted a 21–30 record with a 3.57 ERA. In his best season (1917) he won 10 games. In 1919 he left the Phillies to play independent ball, although he remained the property of Sacramento into the 1930's. Milt Watson's career overlapped that of John Watson who pitched for the A's, Braves and Giants (1918–24) and who was also known as "Mule." This fact makes some newspaper references confusing. Bill Lee identifies Milt Walson as "a guard at the Jacksonville (AR) Ordinance Plant and a fireman at the Pine Bluff Arsenal." Watson died at Pine Bluff on April 20, 1962, at age 72. (*Hall of Fame file; Total Baseball; Baseball Necrology; Atlanta Constitution; Boston Globe*)

George (Buck) Weaver was reportedly the only third baseman that Ty Cobb would not bunt against. He began with the White Sox as a shortstop in 1912, making the conversion to third base in 1916. He was a .272 hitter over his nine-year career with the White Sox, but over the last four years he hit .284, .300, .296 and .333. He also hit .327 in 14 World Series games. Only thirty years old when he was forced out of organized baseball in 1920, as a result of the Black Sox scandal, Weaver always maintained his innocence. Despite a petition signed by 30,000 Chicago fans asking for his reinstatement, his appeal was denied in 1927. He turned to semi-pro ball, and later in life worked in the parimutuel department of Chicago racetracks. Weaver collapsed on the street while walking to consult a tax expert, dying on January 31, 1956, at age 64. (*Sporting News; Eight Men Out; Baseball Encyclopedia; Chicago Daily Tribune; Bill James Historical Baseball Abstract*)

Harry Weaver had five trials with the A's and Cubs between 1915 and 1919, resulting in a 3–6 record for 81.2 innings worked. He was a graduate of Edinboro (Pennsylvania) State College and worked as a school principal for three years before entering professional baseball. After serving in World War I, Weaver played in the minors until 1925. He then had a successful business career, holding positions with Union Petroleum, Atwater Kent Radio Corp., RCA, and Beckwith Chandler Corp. For many years he was manager of the finishing division at Taylor Instrument Co. When Weaver "retired" in 1965, he became a process engineer for Max Russer, the sausage maker. He died in a Rochester, NY, nursing home on May 30, 1983, at age 91. (*Hall of Fame file; Sporting News; Total Baseball; Chicago Daily Tribune*)

Carl Weilman (Weilenmann), a 6'6" lefthander, won 63 games for the Browns in the four-year period 1913–16. He missed the next two seasons, following an operation to remove one kidney and retired as an active player after the 1920 season. Weilman first came to the Browns in August 1912 from Maysville. He won 18 games in 1915, and turned in a 2.08 ERA in 1914, his career figures showing 85 wins and a 2.67 ERA. After leaving the playing ranks, he scouted for the Browns. The 34-year-old Weilman died on May 25, 1924, in his hometown of Hamilton, OH. He had "suffered an attack of influenza," and his death was thought to be "directly attributable to a kidney condition which grew out of the influenza attack." (*Sporting News; Baseball Encyclopedia; New York Times; Washington Post*)

Harry Budson (Bud) Weiser played in 41 games as an outfielder for the Phillies in 1915–16, hitting .162. The Phillies had acquired him from Charlotte, where he had led the North Carolina League in hits, runs and average. Weiser was the only rookie retained by the Phillies in 1915. He remained in baseball as a minor league player and manager until 1928. The native of Shamokin, PA, returned there and became a deputy tax collector. Following a two-year illness, he died at Shamokin on July 31, 1961, at age 70. (*Sporting News; Baseball-Reference.com; Washington Post; Encyclopedia of Minor League Baseball*)

Ollie Welf appeared as a pinch runner for the Indians on June 15, 1916, and then left the majors without a turn at bat or a fielding chance. A native of Cleveland, he graduated from Ohio State with a degree in veterinary medicine. After Army service in World War I, he attended John Marshall Law School, graduating in 1928. Upon receiving his degree, Welf became a legal counsel for the Workman's Compensation division of the Industrial Commission of Ohio, a position he held for 36 years. He died at Cleveland on June 15, 1967, at age 78. (*Cleveland Plain Dealer; Baseball Encyclopedia; SABR Collegiate Database*)

Lew Wendell had five trials as a catcher with the Giants and Phillies between 1915 and 1926. He had already left organized baseball when the Giants acquired him from the

Zack Wheat

semi-pro ranks in 1915. Sent down in 1916, he spent 8 years in the minors before the Phillies acquired him in 1924. His career totals show a .180 average for 100 games. Released by the Phillies in June 1926, Wendell signed with the Indians, who sent him to Portland, where he retired as a player in 1927. Having suffered from heart disease for twenty years, he died of a heart attack on July 11, 1953, at age 61. He was a resident of the Bronx, and his death certificate lists his occupation as "Ball player — retired." (*Sporting News/The Johns Hopkins University Department of Chronic Diseases; Baseball-Reference. com*)

McKinley (Mack) Wheat, the younger brother of Hall of Fame outfielder Zack Wheat, spent parts of seven seasons in the majors, catching for the Dodgers and Phillies. In 1920, his most productive season, he played in 78 games for the Phillies, hitting .226. A year later the Phillies released him unconditionally, and he signed with the Los Angeles Angels. In 1945 Wheat moved to Los Banos, CA, where he became manager of the Pacific Gas & Electric office there. He died at Los Banos on August 14, 1979, at age 86. (*Los Banos Enterprise; Baseball Encyclopedia; New York Times; Los Angeles Times*)

Zack Wheat was the first Dodger ever to be voted into the Hall of Fame in 1959. In 19 major league seasons — 18 in Brooklyn — the Hamilton, MO, native amassed 2884 hit for a .317 average, won the NL batting title in 1918, and helped the Dodgers win two NL championships in 1916 and 1920. He had back-to-back .375 seasons in 1923 and 1924. The Dodgers drafted him from Mobile in August 1909, and he immediately hit .304. Released in 1927, he played one more season with the A's, hitting .324. While still an active player, Wheat successfully operated a farm in Caldwell County, MO, but lost it in the Great Depression. He later ran a bowling alley in Kansas City and served on the Kansas City police force. Following a severe auto accident, he operated a hunting and fishing resort on the Lake of the Ozarks; during World War II he worked at a defense plant in Wichita. Wheat died at Sedalia, MO, on March 11, 1972, at age 83. (*Baseball's Best; Deadball Stars of the National League; Baseball Encyclopedia; New York Times*)

Walt (Doc) Whittaker pitched two innings in relief for the Philadelphia A's on July 6, 1916, giving up 3 hits and one earned run. He joined the A's directly from Tufts University, where he had played for three years, a teammate of Doc Carroll (later with the A's) and Heinie Stafford (later with the Giants). Born in Chelsea, MA, he then became a dentist at Somerville, MA. Whittaker died of an apparent heart attack on August 7, 1965, while traveling to his summer home at Bryantville, MA. He was 71 years old. (*Brockton [MA] Daily Enterprise;*

Washington Post; Baseball-Reference.com; SABR Collegiate Database)

George (Possum) Whitted, the center field for the "Miracle Braves" of 1914, was an outfielder/first baseman for the pennant-winning Phillies a year later. The Cardinals purchased him from Jacksonville in August 1912 and traded him to the last-place Braves on July 4, 1914. The Braves sent him to the Phillies in February 1915. Whitted also played for the Pirates and Dodgers. In eleven seasons — eight as a regular — he hit .270. After leaving the majors in 1922, he managed in the minors and also was a club owner for his hometown Durham Bulls. Whitted had served in World War I, and during World War II he was athletic director for the Wilmington, NC, shipyard; following the war he worked for the city of Wilmington in both the street department and the parks and recreation department. On October 16, 1962, he died at Wilmington of complications following a hip injury. He was 72 years old. (*Sporting News; Baseball-Reference.com; Washington Post; Encyclopedia of Minor League Baseball*)

Joe Wilhoit hit in 71 consecutive games while playing at Wichita in 1919. Following his graduation from DePaul University, he played for the Vernon Tigers of the PCL in 1915. Sold to the Braves, he became the regular right fielder in 1916, hitting .230 in 116 games. The following season he hit .340 in 34 games to help the Giants win the NL championship, making two pinch hitting appearances in the World Series. After playing six games with the Braves in 1919, he returned to the minors at Wichita, where he hit .422. Wilhoit finished his baseball career at Salt Lake City in 1923. Prior to his retirement, the Hiawatha, KS, native had purchased a trunk shop in Santa Barbara, CA, and renamed it Wilhoit Luggage Shop. Wilhoit died at Santa Barbara on September 25, 1930, following a two-month illness. He was 44 years old. (*Santa Barbara Morning Press; Los Angeles Times; Total Baseball; SABR Collegiate Database*)

Possum Whitted

Alva (Buff) Williams, a catcher/first baseman from Carthage, IL, hit .265 in 493 major league games. Described as "exceedingly awkward and excessively earnest," he began in the majors with the Red Sox in 1911, coming from Buffalo. As highlights of his seven-year career in the American League, he played in 95 games with the Red Sox that first year and hit .318 for the Senators in 1912. Traded to Baltimore in 1917, he was suspended by the club in July and signed by the Indians for 1918. Leaving the Indians in June 1918, Williams retired to a farm near Hamilton, IL. He died in a hospital at Keokuk, IA, on July 23, 1933, at age 51. (*Sporting News; Washington Post; Atlanta Constitution; Baseball Encyclopedia*)

Claude (Lefty) Williams won 82 games in seven seasons — four as a full-time starting pitcher — including a 23–11 record for the AL champion White Sox in 1919 and a 22–14 in 1920. After brief trials with the Tigers in 1913 and 1914, Williams won 33 games with Salt Lake City in 1915 to earn a place with the White Sox in 1916. The losing pitcher in games 2 and 5 of the 1919 World Series, Williams was scheduled to pitch the final game. The night before he was visited by a professional hitman named Harry F. who "persuaded" him to lose the game, which he did, lasting just a third of an inning and giving up four runs. Banned from baseball in 1920 at age 27, Williams remained in Chicago "eking out a sparse living with his poolroom, then moved to Laguna Beach, CA, where he managed a garden-nursery business." After an extended illness, he died at Laguna Beach on November 4, 1959, at age 66. (*Eight Men Out; Sporting News; Baseball-Reference.com; New York Times*)

Fred (Cy) Williams, an outfielder with the Cubs and Phillies, was one of the NL's great power hitters of the deadball era. In 19 seasons—14 as a regular—Williams hit .292 and led the NL in homers four times, with a high of 41 in 1923. He left the majors in 1930 with 251 homers, an NL record for the time. From the tiny town of Wadena, IN — also the hometown of Doc Crandall — Williams became a three-sport star at Notre Dame, graduating with a degree in architecture. He went directly from Notre Dame to the Cubs in 1912 but did not become a regular until 1915. Traded to the Phillies in December 1917, he developed into a batter who hit for both power and average. The speed that would have allowed him to compete in the hurdles and long jump in the Stockholm Olympics made him "about the best fly catcher in the league." He left the majors in 1930, played one year in the minors, and then retired to a farm in Wisconsin. Williams worked in construction, building the structures he designed as an architect. He died at Eagle River, WI, on April 23, 1974, at age 86. (*Who's Who in Baseball; Deadball Stars of the National League; Total Baseball; SABR Collegiate Database*)

Ken Williams became the first 30–30 man in major league history in 1922 when he led the AL with 39 homers and 155 RBI's while also stealing 32 bases. Without a homer until he was 30 years old, Williams finished with 196 in just 9 seasons as a regular. The Browns leftfielder also carried a career .319 batting average. He first played for the Reds in 1915, coming from Spokane. Returned to Spokane in 1916, he played two years for Portland to earn a return trip — this time to the Browns at the end of 1918. He hit .300 in 1919 to set up the good years to come, hitting as high as .357 in 1923 and hitting at least 10 homers for 8 straight seasons. Williams closed by hitting .303 and .345 for the Red Sox. After leaving the majors in 1929, he played two years for Portland in the PCL and then returned to his native Grants Pass, OR, where he served as a policeman, also owning a tavern and later a billiards parlor. He died of a heart condition on January 22, 1959, at age 68. (*Grants Pass [OR] Daily Courier; Total Baseball; Los Angeles Times; Atlanta Constitution*)

Marsh Williams, a right-hander from Faison, NC, pitched in 10 games for the A's in 1916, compiling a 0–6, 7.89 ERA record. He joined the A's after graduating from the University of North Carolina. Earlier he had played at Presbyterian College in South Carolina. A career Army officer, he reached the rank of major and was on the retired list at the time of his death. Bill Lee asserts that Williams "was gassed during the war and died from the effects of that gassing." Only

Steamboat Williams

42 years old, he died at his home in Tucson, AZ, on February 22, 1935. (*Arizona Daily Star[Tucson, AZ]; Washington Post; SABR Collegiate Database; Baseball Necrology*)

Rees (Steamboat) Williams pitched in 36 games for the Cardinals in 1916, compiling a 6–7, 4.20 ERA record. An earlier 5-game trial with the Cardinals in 1914 had produced no wins. He later pitched for Milwaukee and St. Paul, helping the Saints win the 1919 American Association championship. The only Montana-born player among the "Men of '16," Williams became a 54-year resident of Deer River, MN, where he owned a resort. He died there on June 29, 1979, at age 87. (*Deer River Western Itasca Review; Baseball Encyclopedia*)

Art Wilson put together .291 and .305 seasons catching for the Chicago Federals in 1914–15; in 14 seasons he hit .261 in 812 games. After brief trials with the Giants in 1908–10, he shared catching duties with Chief Meyers on three consecutive NL championship New York teams (1911–13). He held regular status with the Chi-Feds, Pirates, Cubs and Braves from 1914 through 1918, finishing with the Indians in 1921. He managed at Pittsfield in 1923. A native of Macon, IL, Wilson became a Chicago resident in 1920. When he died there of heart disease on June 12, 1960, neither his obituary nor his death certificate mentions an occupation other than former major league baseball player. He was 74 years old. (*Hall of Fame file/ Chicago Daily Tribune; Total Baseball; New York Times*)

Owen (Chief) Wilson set a still-standing major league record in 1912 when he hit 36 triples—22 more than he hit in any other season. The left-handed hitting Texan was a nine-year regular outfielder with the Pirates and Cardinals. When he joined the Pirates from Des Moines in 1908, he hit only

Art Wilson

.227. A career .269 hitter, he had back-to-back .300 seasons in 1911 and 1912 and led the NL in RBI's in 1911. Possessed of a strong throwing arm, Wilson led the NL with 34 assists in 1914 and in fielding in 1914 and 1915. After leaving the majors in 1916, Wilson played one more season in the minors before retiring to his ranch near Bertram, TX. On February 22, 1954, he died suddenly of a heart attack while working on that ranch. He was 70 years old. (*Sporting News; Hall of Fame file; Total Baseball; Deadball Stars of the National League*)

Ivey (Ivy) Wingo caught at least 100 games five times and at least 75 games ten times in a 17-year career with the Cardinals and Reds. The NL assist leader three times, he also led NL catchers in errors six times. Wingo joined the Cardinals in 1911, coming from Greenville of the Carolina Association. After hitting .300 for the Cardinals in 1914, he was traded to the Reds. Sharing catching duties with Bill Rariden on the 1919 World Champions, Wingo hit .571 in the World Series. He became a Reds coach in 1926, a position he also held in 1928, 1929, and 1936, managing at Columbus in 1927. A doctor's son from Norcross, GA, he retired there after the 1936 season. After an illness of more than a year, he died on March 1, 1941, at age 50. A younger brother, Al, was an outfielder for the A's and Tigers. (*Hall of Fame file; Sporting News; Baseball Encyclopedia; Deadball Stars of the National League*) **Photograph on page 85**

Whitey Witt (Ladislaw Waldemar Wittkowski) did "most of the work in the outfield" when he played center between Babe Ruth and Bob Meusel from 1922 through 1924. While he hit only 18 career homers, he hit .297, .314 and .297 as a Yankee regular and finished a ten-year major league career with a .287 average. Connie Mack signed the 19-year-old Witt as a shortstop in 1916, after his freshman year at Bowden College. He played five seasons for the A's, with time out for naval service in World War I, hitting .315 in 1921. He finished his major league career with Brooklyn in 1926. After leaving baseball, Witt owned a farm in New Jersey and at different times operated a package liquor store and a tavern. Following a heart attack, He died at Alloway Township, NJ, on July 14, 1988, at age 92. (*Sporting News; Total Baseball; SABR Collegiate Database; Boston Daily Globe*)

Mellie Wolfgang compiled a 9–5, 1.89 ERA record for the White Sox as a rookie in 1914. But in four subsequent seasons, the small right-hander managed only six more victories, finishing with a 15–14, 2.18 ERA career record. Wolfgang earned his trial with the White Sox by fashioning a 16–12 record at Denver in 1913. He finished with the White Sox in 1918 and retired from baseball in 1919. He was a lifelong resident of Albany, NY, where, according to his grandson, he supported his family for more than twenty years as a professional gambler, operating a numbers game called Policy. He died of a stroke brought on by heart disease on June 30, 1947, at age 57. (*Hall of Fame file; information supplied by Mel Wolfgang III; Baseball Encyclopedia; New York Times; Sporting News*)

William (Chuck) Wortman is listed as the regular shortstop for the Cubs in both 1916 and 1917, though he played in only 69 and 75 games respectively. His three-year major league totals show a .181 average in 161 games. The Cubs purchased Wortman from Kansas City in 1916. He made his final major league appearance in the 1918 World Series. Sold to Columbus, he elected to leave organized baseball to play independent ball in Baltimore. The Baltimore native moved to Las Vegas, where he became a post office clerk. Following a heart attack, he died in Las Vegas on August 19, 1977, at age 85. (*Nevada Certificate of Death; Total Baseball; Chicago Daily Tribune; Washington Post*)

Ceylon (Cy) Wright played in eight games as a shortstop for the White Sox in 1916, going hitless in 18 at bats. He joined the White Sox directly from the amateur ranks, from the "White Giants of the Chicago City League." Wright later served in World War I. A native of Minneapolis, he became a resident of Chicago, where he worked as a bank clerk and continued his involvement in baseball, playing in the independent Midwest League. He died of pneumonia at the Veterans Administration hospital at Hines, IL, on November 7, 1947, at age 54. (*Illinois Certificate if Death; Chicago Daily Tribune; Hall of Fame file; Baseball Encyclopedia*)

John Weldon Wyckoff was a pitcher who suffered because of the management of Connie Mack. Wyckoff posted an 11–7 record for the AL champions of 1914 and relieved in the first game of the World Series. In 1915 when the A's plummeted to last place, Wyckoff won 10 games—almost a quarter of the team total—but led the AL with 22 losses. Traded to the Red Sox in 1916, the 24-year-old never won another major league game, retiring in 1918. He left the majors with a 23–34 record. Wyckoff came to the A's by way of Bucknell University and the semi-pro ranks. A native of Williamsport, PA, Wyckoff worked as a saw operator for Special Machinery Manufacturers. He later moved to Sheboygan Falls, WI, where he died

Steve Yerkes

Weldon Wyckoff

following a heart attack on May 7, 1961, at age 67. (*Sporting News; Hall of Fame file; New York Times*)

Steve Yerkes is remembered for driving home the winning run in the last game of the 1912 World Series. But he was a regular at shortstop or second base for five of his seven major league seasons with the Red Sox, Pittsburgh Federals, and Cubs, hitting .268. Yerkes had a trial with the Red Sox at the end of 1909, coming from Wilson (Eastern Carolina). Sent down to Worcester, he returned as a regular in 1911. Hitting only .218 in 1914, he was released by the Red Sox and signed by Pittsburgh, for whom he hit .338. Yerkes, who played at the University of Pennsylvania, was appointed freshman baseball coach at Yale in 1940. He also owned and managed Glenside Bowling Lanes in Glenside, PA. Yerkes died at Lansdale, PA, on January 31, 1971, at age 81. (*Philadelphia Enquirer; Baseball Encyclopedia; Washington Post; New York Times; SABR Collegiate Database*)

Ralph (Pep) Young, a 5'5" second baseman joined 5'6" shortstop Donie Bush to form one of the majors' smallest double play combinations in Detroit. Young was the regular second baseman for the Tigers (1915–21) and A's (1922). He had a 1913 trial with the

Rollie Zeider

Yankees before arriving at Detroit via Sacramento. Only a .247 hitter over his career, he put together back-to-back .291 and .299 seasons in 1920 and 1921. The AL assist leader in 1917, he also twice led AL second basemen in errors. Before entering professional baseball, Young played at Washington (MD) College, where he was a teammate of Red Sox outfielder Tilly Walker. The Philadelphia native coached baseball at Temple and at St. Joseph's when his playing career had ended. He died at Philadelphia on January 24, 1965, at age 76. (*Sporting News; SABR Collegiate Database; Baseball Encyclopedia; Los Angeles Times*)

Rollie Zeider held regular status throughout his 9-year major league career with the White Sox, Yankees, Chicago Federals and Cubs, but he did not have a regular position. He averaged 104 games each season — about a third each at second base and third base, the rest split among shortstop, first base and the outfield. His career .240 average was helped considerably by a .274 season in the Federal league. Zeider first entered the majors in 1910, coming from San Francisco, where he had led the PCL in runs and stolen bases. He left the Cubs after the 1918 season and played and managed in the minors through 1924. Returning to his hometown of Garrett, IN, he operated a tavern until he retired. Zeider died at Garrett on September 12, 1967, at age 83. (*Hall of Fame file; Total Baseball; Los Angeles Times; Encyclopedia of Minor League Baseball*)

Henry (Heinie) Zimmerman hit .372 for the Cubs in 1912, leading the NL in hits, doubles, homers, RBI's, average and slugging. In 13 seasons he hit .295 while leading the NL three times in RBI's and participating in three World Series. He, along with Hal Chase, was quietly dropped from the Giants roster in late

Heinie Zimmerman

1919 and was later accused of throwing games and attempting to bribe fellow Giants to throw games. While he denied the charges, he never attempted to clear his name officially, and so was banned for life. The New York City native joined the Cubs from Wilkes-Barre in 1907 and by 1910 had become a regular who could hit for both average and power. In 1916 Zimmerman was traded to the Giants and helped them win the 1917 pennant. After leaving baseball, he worked as a plumber and steamfitter. For a time he also operated a speakeasy in partnership with racketeer Dutch Schultz. Zimmerman died at New York City on March 14, 1969, at age 82. (*Sporting News; Total Baseball; Deadball Stars of the National League; New York Times; Bill James Historical Baseball Abstract*)

Edward (Dutch) Zwilling led the Federal League with 15 homers in 1914 and with 94 RBI's in 1915 while playing with Chicago. The tiny left-handed-hitting centerfielder hit .313 and .286 during those seasons. Trials with the White Sox in 1910 and the Cubs in 1916 resulted in .184 and .113 averages. In all, Zwilling spent almost 60 years in baseball. He came to the White Sox from Battle Creek. Returned to St. Joseph, he jumped to the Federal League. After leaving the Cubs, he played in the minors until 1927; managed the Kansas City Blues, Oakland, Birmingham, Sioux City and Quincy; coached for the Indians; and scouted for the Indians, Yankees and Mets, retiring in 1971. A native of St. Louis, he died at La Crescenda, CA, on March 27, 1978, following a long illness. He was 89 years old. (*Hall of Fame file; Total Baseball; Encyclopedia of Minor League Baseball; Sporting News*)

Appendix A: The 1916 Season

According to attendance records, 6,503,519 fans watched major league baseball games during the 1916 season, an average of about 5,300 per game. They saw good pennant races in both leagues. In the American League the Red Sox, despite trading Tris Speaker and losing Smoky Joe Woods to a season-long holdout, edged the White Sox by two games and the Tigers by four. In the National League the Dodgers finished three games ahead of the Phillies.

In the World Series Red Sox pitching limited the Dodgers to 13 runs in five games in winning four games to one. Included in the package were complete game victories by Babe Ruth (a 14-inning six-hitter in Game 2), Ernie Shore (a three-hitter in Game 5) and Dutch Leonard (a five-hitter in Game 4).

Speaker earned his $18,000 salary by out-hitting Cobb .386 to .371 to win the AL batting championship. Yankee first baseman Wally Pipp hit 12 home runs, beating out his infield mate Home Run Baker by two. Walter Johnson, despite twenty losses, led AL pitchers in wins (25) and strikeouts (228). Ruth led in ERA with 1.75.

Reds first baseman Hal Chase hit .339 to win the NL batting championship. Dave Robertson of the Giants and Cy Williams of the Cubs each hit 12 home runs. Grover Cleveland Alexander made a clean sweep of NL pitching laurels, leading in wins (33), ERA (1.55), shutouts (16), and strikeouts (167).

Two hundred major league positions had vanished on December 21, 1915, when the owners of the two-year-old Federal League and the National and American League owners reached an agreement ending the Federal League. When 1916 training camps opened, 61 "graduates" of the Federal League joined or rejoined established clubs, increasing the competition for roster places. On clubs such as the Chicago Cubs and St. Louis Browns—inheritors of complete rosters of the Chicago Whales and St. Louis Terriers—competition was especially keen.

Many of the graduates found that their 1916 stats did not reach their Federal League promise. Batting champion Benny Kauff dropped from .342 at Brooklyn to .264 with the Giants; first baseman Ed Konetchy hit .310 at Pittsburgh and .260 with the Phillies; outfielder Max Flack dropped from .314 in Chicago to .258 with the Browns; promising outfield star Jack Tobin, who led the Federal League with 186 hits for the Terriers, managed only 32 hits as a Browns part-timer. Pitchers also suffered. Lefty Gene Packard dropped from 20 wins (Kansas City) to 10 (Cubs). Another lefthander, Al Schulz, went from 21 wins (Buffalo) to 8

(Reds); Frank Allen dropped from 23 wins (Brooklyn) to 8 (Braves). None fell so far as the tall Tennessean George McConnell, whose 4 wins for the 1916 Cubs were 21 fewer than he recorded with the 1915 Whales.

With Federal League additions, 527 players passed through the major leagues in 1916. For some, such as future Hall of Fame members Christy Mathewson, his long-time pitching rival Three Finger Brown, Joe Tinker and Larry Lajoie, 1916 was their valedictory season as players. A twenty-year-old Texan named Rogers Hornsby was in his first full season as the Cardinal third baseman, and Ruth, just barely voting age, was a pitching star for the Red Sox. Cobb, Speaker, Johnson and Alexander were all under 30 and in their prime.

All told, 39 members of the Men of '16 would eventually make the Hall of Fame, including the entire inaugural group of 1936 — Cobb, Ruth, Johnson, Mathewson and Honus Wagner. Ruth was joined on the world champion Red Sox by left fielder Harry Hooper and another young left-handed pitcher named Herb Pennock. The AL runner-up White Sox featured second baseman Eddie Collins and catcher Ray Schalk along with pitchers Red Faber and Ed Walsh. Cobb was joined on the third-place Tigers by outfielders Sam Crawford and Harry Heilmann. Baker was the third baseman for the fourth-place Yankees; 23-year-old George Sisler was established as the first baseman on the fifth-place Browns, whose roster also included 40-year-old pitcher Eddie Plank and 42-year-old infielder Bobby Wallace. Speaker was the new center fielder for the sixth-place Indians, supporting the pitching of Stan Coveleski. Sam Rice, a utility outfielder and pitcher, joined Johnson on the seventh-place Senators, and the 40-year-old Nap Lajoie was the regular second baseman on an A's team that set a major league record by losing 117 games that year.

Zack Wheat and Casey Stengel played in the outfield for the NL champion Dodgers, and Rube Marquard was a starting pitcher. Alexander headed the pitching staff of the runner-up Phillies, which also included Eppa Rixey and Chief Bender; Dave Bancroft was their shortstop. The double-play combination at third-place Boston was Johnny Evers and Rabbit Maranville. Twenty-year-old first baseman George Kelly, third baseman Bill McKechnie and a young outfielder named Edd Roush joined Mathewson on the fourth-place Giants; Tinker managed the fifth place Cubs, for whom he and Brown played bit roles. The 42-year-old Wagner was still the regular shortstop in sixth-place Pittsburgh, where Max Carey led the league in stolen bases and Burleigh Grimes was mastering slippery elm bark. When Mathewson became manager of seventh-place Cincinnati in July, McKechnie and Roush also were part of the deal. Hornsby and player-manager Miller Huggins helped the Cardinals tie the Reds for seventh place.

In addition to Stengel, Huggins and McKechnie, all of whom made the Hall of Fame primarily for their managerial careers, three future Hall of Fame members managed teams in 1916: John McGraw in New York, Connie Mack in Philadelphia, and Wilbert Robinson in Brooklyn.

Among the Men of '16 was one pitcher who had once won 40 games (Walsh) and five thirty-game winners — Mathewson (four times), Alexander (three times), Johnson (twice), Jack Coombs and Jim Bagby, Sr. (once each). There were also six men who hit .400 for a season: Ty Cobb and Rogers Hornsby (three times each), George Sisler (twice); Larry Lajoie, Shoeless Joe Jackson and Harry Heilmann (once each).

Within two years the war in Europe would reach the lives of a number of the Men of '16. While it did not have the impact that World War II would have on a later generation of players, it did affect the lives and careers of a number of the players. One hundred three of the Men of '16 lost major league playing time by volunteering, being drafted or working in defense plants. This figure does not include those who were already out of the majors by 1918. Two players — Newt Halliday and Larry Chappell — died of the Spanish flu while undergoing military training. A third, Jack Nabors, was so ravaged by the flu that he was never a well man again, dying in 1923, a delayed casualty of the war. Christy Mathewson breathed poison gas during a training accident in France, hastening the tuberculosis that killed him in 1925. Athletics pitcher Elmer Myers, a stretcher-bearer, was gassed at Verdun in 1918. Though he was able to pitch until 1921, his constitution was so wrecked that he was unable to do manual work thereafter. Ed Klepfer, 14–4 with the Indians in 1917, was gassed and never won another major league game. But probably no player was affected more by the war than Pete Alexander. He entered World War I following three straight 30-win seasons. While serving with an artillery unit in France, he was wounded by shrapnel, he lost much of his hearing, his epilepsy worsened and he developed the alcoholism that cut into his effectiveness later in his career. Before the war he had 190 victories in 7+ seasons; after the war he had 181 victories in 11+ seasons.

The darker side of major league baseball in 1916 was the number of men playing who would ultimately bring discredit to the game. Baseball historian Bill James calls the Black Sox scandal "merely the largest and ugliest wart of a disease that had infested baseball at least a dozen years earlier and grown, unchecked, to ravage the features of a generation" (134). More than 20 of the Men of '16 were either officially banned or quietly dropped from rosters, a fairly common practice when allegations of fixing were believed but could not be proved. Some of those are listed below. Six of the "Eight Men Out"— pitchers Eddie Cicotte and Lefty Williams, outfielders Shoeless Joe Jackson and Happy Felsch and infielders Buck Weaver and Fred McMullin — had already assembled in Chicago. Their ringleader, first baseman Chick Gandil, was playing for Cleveland. These seven would be banned from organized baseball for life in 1920 for their part in the fix of the 1919 World Series. In the aftermath of that scandal, Browns third baseman Joe Gedeon and Giants pitcher Jean Dubuc were banned for having advance knowledge of the fix and not reporting it, though Dubuc later managed in the minors. Another Giants pitcher, Rube Benton, was alleged to have made $1,500 betting on the Reds because of advance knowledge. Dropped by the Giants in 1921, and rejected by the American League, he was signed by the Reds and pitched until 1925. Giants first baseman Hal Chase reportedly made $40,000 betting on the Reds in the series and was dropped quietly by the Giants. Another 1916 player, Billy Maharg, served as a go-between in the negotiations between gamblers and players. He was already out of baseball. Attempts to fix games in the National League involved Chase, third baseman Heinie Zimmerman, and outfielder Lee Magee of the Giants, along with pitcher Paul Carter and first baseman Gene Paulette of the Cubs. Zimmerman, Magee and Paulette were banned for life; Carter was dropped as was another Cubs pitcher, Claude Hendrix.

Following a similar scandal in the Pacific Coast League in 1919, four members of the Men of '16 were sent packing — either officially or unofficially: Chase, pitcher Tom Seaton, first baseman Babe Borton, and pitcher Gene Dale. Outfielder Bill Rumler drew a five-year suspension.

In an unrelated case, Giants outfielder Benny Kauff was given a lifetime suspension from organized baseball — less for participating in a stolen car ring than for consorting with the kind of people who did.

The rosters of 1916 also contain the names of three men who did not play that season, their stories reminding us of the vanity of human wishes. Yankee right-hander King Cole, a 20-game winner for the Cubs in 1910, died in January 1916 at age 29. Bill James, a 26-game winner for the Braves in 1914 and the hero of the World Series that year, was already out of baseball by 1916, his arm gone at age 23. A comeback trial in 1919 lasted one game. Smoky Joe Wood, with 116 wins at age 26, never won another major league game. The smoke that had allowed him to win 34 games in 1912 gone, he held out the entire 1916 season before beginning a second career as an outfielder for the Indians.

Appendix B:
What Manner of Men Were These?

Ethnic Background

There were, of course, no blacks on the 1916 rosters. There were six "light-skinned" Cubans: Merito Acosta, Angel Aragon, Mike Gonzales, Armando Marsans, Emilo Palmero and Jose Rodriguez. When some fans questioned the presence of Marsans on the Cincinnati roster, the owner assured them that he was "as pure white as Castille soap" (*Baseball: An Illustrated History* 112). There was one Mexican-American — Charlie Hall. There were also four Native Americans: Albert (Chief) Bender, a half Chippewa from Minnesota; John (Chief) Meyers, a Cahuilla from California; and two Cherokees from Oklahoma — Jim Bluejacket (James Smith) and Ben Tincup. In general, the rest were Caucasians of North European descent.

In many individual cases, it is now impossible to determine ethnic background precisely. Even when information is available, the American "melting pot" may blur it. Consider the case of Milo Allison. In his file in the Hall of Fame Library are two statements concerning his background. There is a 1956 statement from an "old friend" stating, "Allison is a Swede and they are quite clannish." But on the library questionnaire his widow filled out in 1957, she lists him as "English, Scotch."

For the most part, then, we are left with names as indexes of national origin. For players born in the last quarter of the 19th century, when Americans were closer to their European roots, names can be a fairly reliable indicator of paternal national origin — especially in the case of names such as Ulatowski, Ryan or Hoernschemeyer. We need to remember, however, that both individuals and families changed names. Hall of Fame outfielder Zack Wheat and his brother Mack, a Dodger catcher, were from Caldwell County, Missouri, a county settled by people of English origin. Wheat certainly appears to be an English name. But in *Caldwell County, Missouri, History*, we learn that Zack and Mack's father was born Basil DuBoise and had changed his name to Wheat when he came to the United States, so that it would "sound more American" (263). At least fifteen of the Men of '16 altered their own names, generally for the reason DuBoise did, to seem more American.

About 80 percent of the players bear names that appear in Elsdon Smith's *American Surnames*. Of these 191 (44 percent) bear traditional English surnames; an additional 26 Scot and

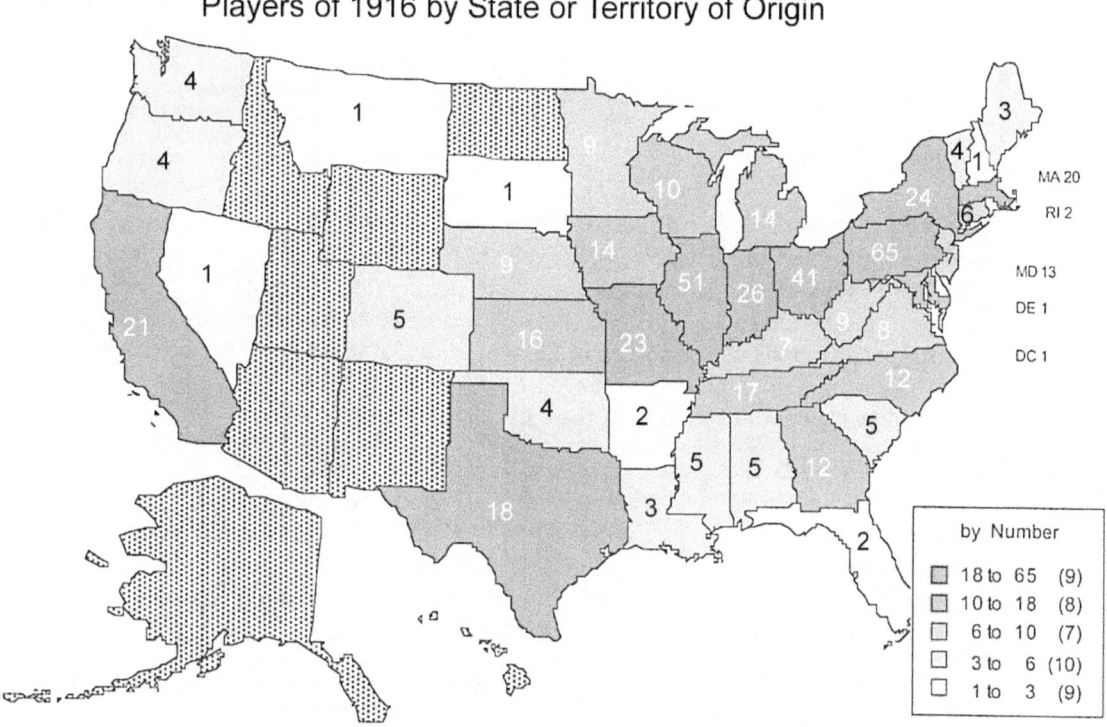

Players of 1916 by State or Territory of Origin

18 Welsh names raise the percentage to 55 percent for the British Isles. But since British names appear to be "American," these figures are probably inflated for reasons given above. Ninety-seven German names make up almost a quarter (23 percent); another 56 names (13 percent) are Irish. There is also a scattering of Scandinavian and French Canadian names (10 of each). Finally six names suggest East European ancestry: Kowalewski, Ulatowski, Wittkowski, Smitka, Smejkal, and Baranowski, the respective family names of Stan and Harry Coveleski, Count Clements, Whitey Witt, Jack Smith, Frank Smykal and Frank Fuller.

STATE OR COUNTRY OF ORIGIN

Twenty of the 527 players (3.8 percent) were foreign born. Ten of these were born in Europe, six in Cuba, and four in Canada. Of the Europeans, three were Irish and two were Swedish; one Dane, one German, one Russian, one Scot and one Welshman completed the group.

The map above shows the distribution of the 507 players born in the United States. Forty states, the District of Columbia, and the Oklahoma and South Dakota territories are represented. The most striking feature of this map is the concentration of players in a band of states extending from Massachusetts across the upper Midwest. Seven states—Missouri, Illinois, Indiana, Ohio, Pennsylvania, New York and Massachusetts—together produced 250 players, 47.5 percent of the total. Another 45 players came from Kansas, Iowa and Michigan. When we compare this distribution pattern with that of 1876, when 77.5 percent of the players were from the Atlantic rim, we can see that by 1916 professional baseball had developed strong Midwestern roots.

From today's perspective, when college baseball is dominated by teams from the Sun Belt and major league rosters are filled with Californians, we may note the relative unimportance of those areas in the production of players in 1916. Only 117 players (23 percent) came from Dixie and the Sun Belt combined.

URBAN OR RURAL?

According to Geoffrey Ward (*Baseball: An Illustrated History* 4), baseball had developed as a sport of urban youth, with roots specifically in New York City. Therefore, it is not surprising that in 1916, 259 of the 506 American-born players (51.2 percent) came from multiplayer areas. Eleven metro areas produced 104 players, almost 20 percent of the total. These figures suggest that baseball was still an urban sport and that requisite skills were best developed through competition on the sandlot.

The following counties producing the most players on 1916 rosters:

Cook, IL (Chicago)	21	Baltimore, MD (city)	7
Allegheny, PA (Pittsburgh)	16	Suffolk, MA (Boston)	7
New York City	13	Hamilton, OH (Cincinnati)	5
St. Louis, MO (city)	11	Cuyahoga, OH (Cleveland)	5
Philadelphia, PA	8	Northumberland, PA (Shamokin)	5
San Francisco, CA	7		

On the other hand, 247 players (48.8 percent) were the sole representatives of their county on a major league roster, providing some evidence that by this time baseball had also developed small town and rural roots. The way such players were viewed by their urban teammates can be seen in the number of derogatory nicknames indicating country bumpkin. There were no fewer than seven players nicknamed "Rube" and three nicknamed "Cy." There was also a "Hick" and an "Ike." Needless to say, most recipients of these names were from small towns.

To some extent geographical distribution is linked to ethnic considerations. As shown above, the largest ethnic minority — at least by names — is German. Apparently by 1916 professional baseball had become a vehicle of upward mobility for the sons of German immigrants, just as it had been for the sons of Irish immigrants in 1896 and would be for impoverished Southern whites in 1936, and for blacks and Latin Americans in subsequent groups of players.

There is a close relationship between the presence of a large number of players of German origin and the large numbers of players from the Midwest. *The Historical Atlas of the United States* points out that the largest influx of German immigrants — a quarter of a million — arrived around 1882 when overpopulation in German states led to mass emigration. Upon arriving in the United States, they fanned out across the Midwest, becoming "farmers, brewers, factory workers and shopkeepers" (National Geographic Society 53). Their sons began arriving in the majors around the beginning of World War I. Almost every Midwestern state produced a group of players whose names suggest Germanic origins. These players include the following:

Iowa: Joe Lotz, Danny Moeller, and Bill Wagner.
Kansas: Claude Hendrix and Joe Wilhoit.
Minnesota: Bullet Joe Bush and Joe Fautsch
Missouri: Charlie Grimm, Walter Holke, Solly Hofman, Casey Stengel, and Dutch Zwilling.
Illinois: Fred Brainerd, Max Flack, Red Gunkel, Joe Oescheger, Jake Pfeffer, Germany Schaeffer, and Ray Schalk.

Indiana: Paddy Baumann, Joe Benz, Al Bergman, Frank Boehler, Hooks Dauss, Emil Huhn, Grover Lowdermilk, Art Nehf, Walt Tragesser, and Rollie Zeider.
Michigan: Jesse Altenburg, Harry Heilmann, Ernie Koob, Ed Reulbach, and Vic Saier.
Ohio: Bill Batsch, Zinn Beck, Bob Bescher, Bruno Betzel, Frank Emmer, Clyde Engle, Heinie Groh, Benny Kauff, Lee Magee (born Leopold Hoernschemeyer), Al Schulz, Ray Shook, Eddie Sicking, George Sisler, Bill Wambsganss, Carl Weilmann, and Ollie Welf.
Pennsylvania: Rube Bressler, Jake Daubert, Gus Getz, George Hesselbacher, Bill Hinchman, Ed Klepfer, Brad Kocher, Otto Knabe, Elmer Knetzer, Jack Lapp, Howie Lohr, Ralph Mitterling, Hank Ritter, Joe Schultz, Honus Wagner, and Bud Weiser.
Wisconsin: Happy Felsch, Fred Luderus, Fred Merkle, and Braggo Roth.
Maryland: Buck Herzog, Fritz Maisel, George Maisel, Babe Ruth, and Chuck Wortman.
New York: Howard Ehmke, Bill Fischer, Wildfire Schulte, Heinie Wagner, Mellie Wolfgang, and Heinie Zimmerman.

States such as Ohio, Pennsylvania and New York with large populations and considerable ethnic diversity are always among the leaders in production of major league players, so for them the Germans were just one of a series of upwardly mobile minorities. But states such as Indiana, and to some extent Wisconsin and Iowa, have never since attained the importance as player-producing states that they achieved in 1916.

AGE

In terms of player age, 1916 was a relatively normal year. There was no 15-year-old Joe Nuxhall trying to make the leap from junior high school. There was no 57-year-old Minnie Minoso making a token appearance of the decade. On opening day 1916, six players had passed their fortieth birthday. Eddie Plank was just 40; Napoleon Lajoie and Billy Sullivan were both 41; Honus Wagner, Bobby Wallace and Harry Davis had already passed age 42. Wagner hit .287 as the regular shortstop for the Pirates; Wallace appeared in only 14 games for the Browns. Davis, an A's coach, made one pinch hitting appearance. He was the oldest of the group, achieving his forty-third birthday in July.

Sixteen players were still teenagers on opening day—several of them perhaps still in school that day. The youngest, A's outfielder Charlie Grimm, was only 17 when he made his major league debut in July. Six of the 16—A's outfielder Don Brown, A's infielder Lew Malone, Cubs catcher Bob O'Farrell, Cubs third baseman Charlie Pechous, Cardinals infielder Rogers Hornsby and Senators outfielder Merito Acosta—were veterans, having played in the majors in 1915. In fact, Acosta was in his fourth season. Hornsby was the only regular among the teenagers, hitting .313 for the Cardinals, though Val Picinich caught 40 games for the A's.

Between these two groups, the Men of '16 were—as we would suspect—a young crowd. Between Harry Davis and Charlie Grimm, the median player was Reds catcher Ivy Wingo, born July 8, 1890. On opening day, he would have been just over 25 years and nine months of age.

SIZE

Height

The tallest player in the majors in 1916 was New York Yankee left-hander Slim Love, who stood 6' 7". The Browns' Dave Davenport and the Reds' Fred Toney, two massive right-handers, both went 6' 6". Hall of Famer right-hander Eppa Rixey of the Phillies and lanky left-hander Carl Weilmann of the Browns both topped 6' 5". Giants first baseman George Kelley joined six more pitchers—Ernie Shore, Grover Lowdermilk, Bill James, Wheezer Dell and Shorty DesJardien—at the 6' 4" mark.

The vertically challenged players—those 5' 6" or shorter—tended to be infielders. The shortest player was Billy Maharg, a 5' 4" outfielder and third baseman. Hall of Fame shortstop Rabbit Maranville joined Tiger second baseman Ralph Young and Yankee utility player Angel Aragon at the 5' 5" mark. Young's double-play partner Donie Bush, Hall of Fame second baseman and manager Miller Huggins, and Senator third baseman Eddie Foster were among the nine players who stood tall at 5' 6".

Between Maharg's 5' 4" and Love's 6' 7", the median height for players of 1916 was 5' 11", a height achieved by 113 players (21.5 percent). Two-thirds of the players stood between 5' 9" and 6' 0".

Weight

Twenty-five players (fewer than 5 percent) weighed 200 pounds or more. Outfielders Shoeless Joe Jackson and Bob Bescher, catchers Tubby Spencer, Bill Killefer and Mike Gonzales, and Shortstop Honus Wagner were among these. But as with height, the list was headed by the pitchers. Fred Toney was tops at 245 pounds. He was followed by Death Valley Jim Scott at 235, Dave Davenport and Ernie Shore at 220 and Jeff Tesreau at 218.

Of the fourteen players weighing less than 150 pounds, eleven were primarily infielders. The lightest was Cub second baseman Johnny Evers, who weighed only 125 pounds. Fellow Windy City infielder Zeb Terry of the White Sox also could not make 130 pounds. Other infield lightweights were Miller Huggins, Donie Bush, Eddie Foster, Bobby Byrne, and Deacon Scott.

Between Evers' 125 pounds and Toney's 245 pounds, the median weight of 1916 players was 172 pounds. Heights and weights are taken from *The Baseball Encyclopedia*. The weight of any individual player would fluctuate over the course of a career, so listed weights are career *averages*.

Appendix C: Career Baseball Statistics

Questions we sometimes ask about a professional sports career concern duration and impact. Upon entering the majors, what percentage of players will enjoy an extended career, will attain a status of acknowledged solid performer? What percentage will have a career curtailed by injuries, by some external factors such as war, by talent found to be short of major league standards, or by an inability to take care of themselves? Some time after he retired from baseball, Cy Young reportedly told a fan, "I won more games than you'll ever see." A career of 511 wins and 7356 innings pitched testifies that Young enjoyed the talent, the attitude and the support required for a Hall of Fame. On the other hand, the movie *Field of Dreams* introduced audiences to the career of the legendary Archibald (Moonlight) Graham, who played half an inning for the Giants in 1911, leaving the majors without so much as a turn at bat. In his case, whatever his talent level, his priorities took him out of baseball into a professional career in medicine.

Is a player entering the majors more likely to enjoy a Cy Young career or a Moonlight Graham career? Among the Men of '16, there were a fair number of both with many in-between cases.

YEARS OF SERVICE

A quick look at years of service will provide a partial answer to the question of career duration.

Forty of the 527 players (7.5 percent) appeared in games only in the 1916 season. One hundred eighty players (34 percent) had major league careers that did not exceed five years. The median figure was 8 years. However 210 players (40 percent) played in 10 or more seasons; ninety (17 percent) played in 15 or more seasons. 21 players reached or exceeded 20 seasons. Eddie Collins and Bobby Wallace were both quarter-century men; Ty Cobb lasted 24 seasons; Rogers Hornsby and Rabbit Maranville played in 23; Babe Ruth, Tris Speaker, Herb Pennock, Harry Davis, and Sam Jones reached 22; Walter Johnson, Larry Lajoie, Bob O'Farrell, Eppa Rixey and Honus Wagner made 21. Pete Alexander, Max Carey, Red Faber, Charlie Grimm, Joe Judge and Sam Rice all played in 20 seasons.

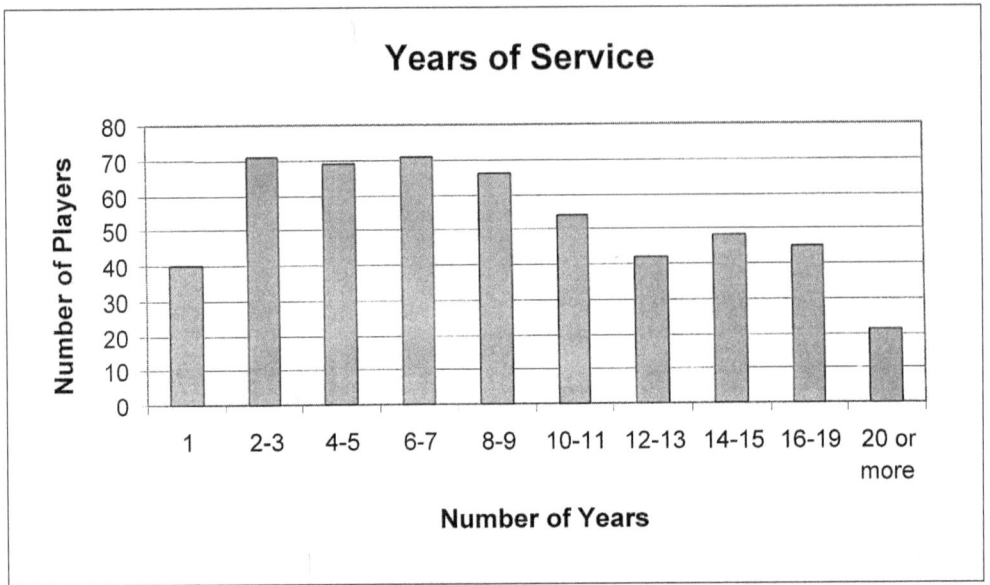

The median figure is eight years.

The obvious limitation of this statistic is that while it tells us how many years a given players appeared in major league games, it will not tell us how much he played in any of those seasons. For example, Harry Davis lasted 22 seasons—seemingly an exemplary career. However, in seven of those seasons, he played in fewer than 10 games and in another he played in only 18 games. While he had a solid 13 seasons as a regular, the "years of service" contains fluff. Let us look at some performance indicators to gain a more precise look at impact.

Pitchers

In 1916 the 80 frontline pitchers—5 for each team—put up these statistics. On average, each pitched 218 innings in 38 games, won 13 games, saved 2 more, and struck out 95 batters while compiling a 2.62 ERA. We perhaps can use these statistics as an index for discussing the career achievements of the 185 men who pitched in 1916. If a pitcher lasted 8 years as a frontline performer, he would pitch 1750 innings in 300 games, win 100, save 16, and strike out 750 batters, while maintaining the 2.62 ERA.

Games Won

The "Career Wins" chart is set up along the 13-win criteria. So it measures a pitcher's career against the above standard. Note first that 48 of 185 pitchers (almost 26 percent) did not exceed in their career what an average front line pitcher of the era would have won in one season. In fact eighteen pitchers won no games at all. These include Carl Ray, Mike Driscoll, Les Lanning, George Hasselbacher, Marsh Williams, Jack Richardson, Axel Lindstrom, and Doc Whittaker of the A's; Shorty Des Jardien and Red Gunkel of the Indians; Bill Fincher of the Browns; Molly Craft of the Senators; Jess Buckles of the Yankees; Murphy Currie and Joe Lotz of the Cardinals; Twink Twining of the Reds; Paul Carpenter of the Pirates; and Gary Fortune of the Phillies.

On the positive side, 36 pitchers (19.4 percent) won at least 143 games—more than an average front line pitcher would have won in 11 seasons. Several of these put up Cy Young–like

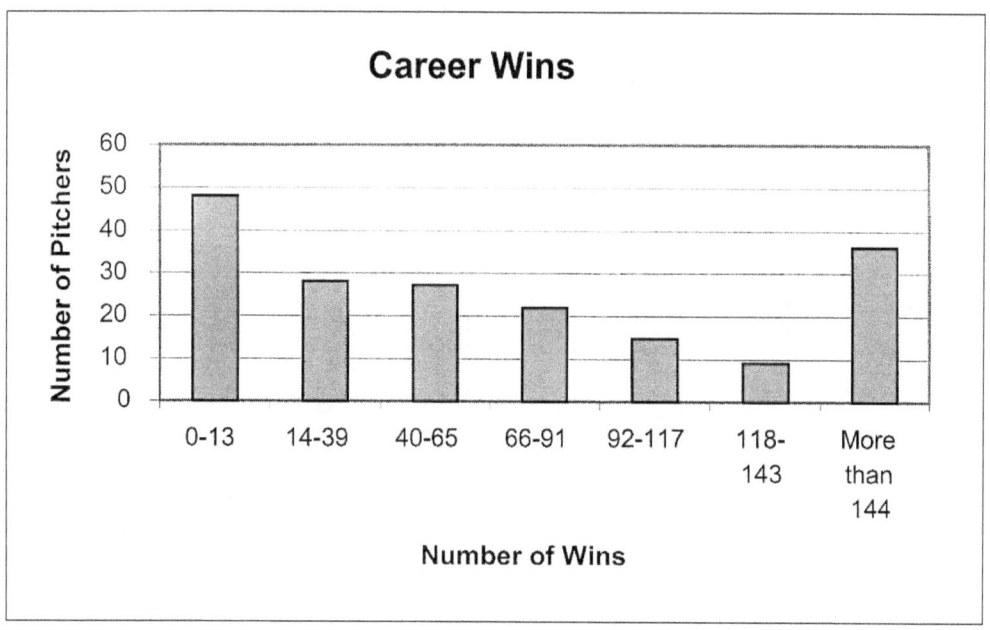

numbers. One pitcher, Walter Johnson, won more than 400 games. In his 21 seasons with the Senators, Johnson turned in 417 — almost exactly 20 per season. Three other are members of the 300 Club. Pete Alexander and Christy Mathewson are forever linked at 373. Connie Mack's ace Eddie Plank turned in 327 despite being older than 25 when he entered the majors.

An additional thirteen pitchers logged more than 200 wins. Burleigh Grimes with 270 leads seven Hall of Fame pitchers — right handers Eppa Rixey (266), Red Faber (254), Herb Pennock (240), Three-Finger Brown (239), Stan Coveleski (215) and Chief Bender (208) and lefthander Rube Marquard (201). Non–Hall of Fame members of the 200 Club are Sam Jones (229), Hooks Dauss (223), Wilber Cooper (215), Eddie Cicotte (209) and Carl Mays (208).

Hall of Fame member Ed Walsh (195), along with Bullet Joe Bush (196), Bob Shawkey (195) and Babe Adams (194), heads a group of 36 pitchers who exceeded 100 career wins. In all 53 pitchers (29 percent) reached the 100 career wins circle.

The median figure for the 185 pitchers was 57 career victories, a total achieved by right hander Harry Harper and left hander Nick Cullop.

Innings Pitched

Statistics for career innings pitched generally resemble those for wins. Two pitchers — Johnson and Alexander — worked more than 5000 innings. Five more — Mathewson, Plank, Grimes, Faber and Rixey — exceeded 4000. Thirteen more exceeded 3000 — Jones, Pennock, Cooper, Dauss, Marquard, Cicotte, Ames, Brown, Bush, Coveleski, Mays, Bender, and Lee Meadows. Babe Adams and Wild Bill Donovan along with Walsh and Shawkey lead 27 more who were members of the 2000-inning club Fifty-two pitchers reached the 1750 mark, almost exactly the same group as the 100-win group. Only Joe Oeschger worked at least 1750 innings without winning 100 games.

Statistics for the lower end also appear consistent. Eight pitchers — Gunkel, Des Jardien, Twining, Whittaker, Lindstrom, Buckles, Driscoll, and Carpenter — had major league careers of less than a complete games. Twenty-eight pitchers threw fewer than 100 innings. Forty-one (22 percent) threw fewer than 218 innings.

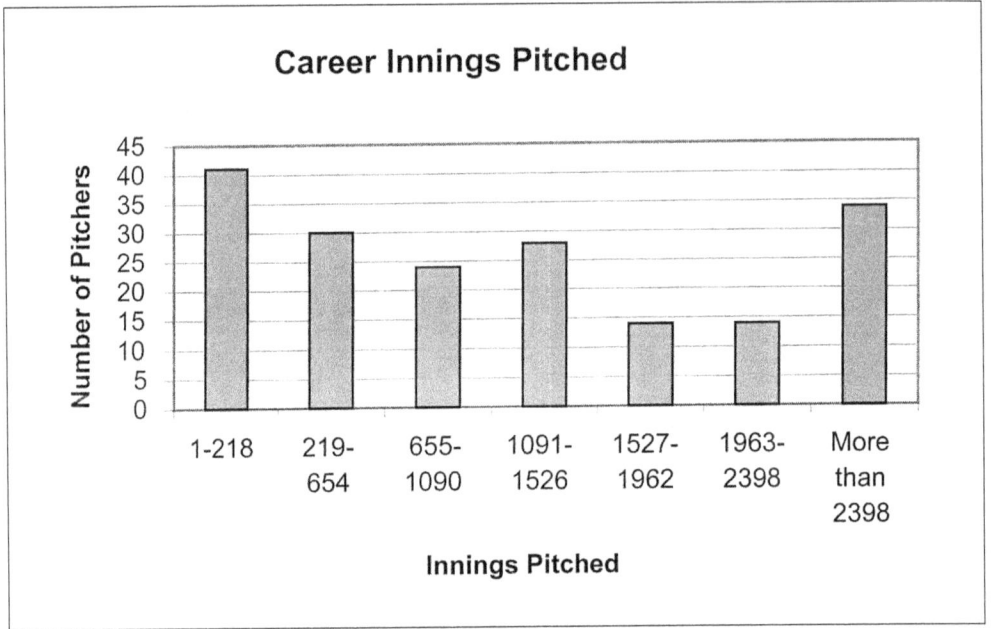

The median pitcher in career innings was Tiger right hander Bernie Boland, who threw 1062 before a broken arm ended his career.

Games Pitched

In general, statistics for games pitched show the same pattern. Once again Johnson leads with 802 games—almost 40 per season for 21 seasons. Eight pitchers headed by Alexander worked in more than 600 games. Five more reached 500. These are all pitchers who also won at least 200 games. Seventeen more reached 400 games; 23 reached 300 games—the figure our "average" frontline pitcher would have reached in eight seasons. Note that the total of

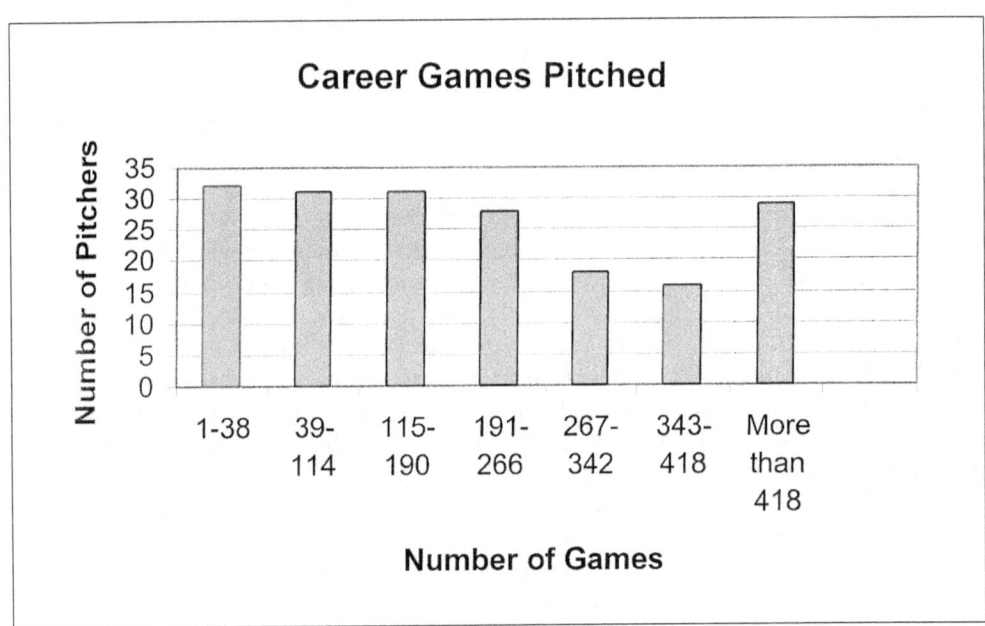

pitchers who reached this figure — 55 — is almost exactly the same as the number who reached 100 wins and 1750 innings. Jeff Tesreau, Ray Fisher and Dick Rudolf won 100 games without appearing in 300; Joe Oeschgar, Allan Russell, Jim Bagby and Guy Morton appeared in 300 games without winning 100.

At the lower end of the scale, thirty-two pitchers (17 percent) worked in fewer than 38 games. Six — Driscoll, Lindstrom, Whittaker, Twining, Gunkel and Des Jardien — appeared in only one game, and Buckles made two appearances.

The median between Johnson and Driscoll was Lefty Williams who appeared in 189 games before being banned from baseball at age 27.

Saves

This category does not yield the same stats as games, innings and wins. Relief pitching was not a specialty of the deadball era though Allan Russell, who made 233 career relief appearances, may have been the beginning of the breed. Some of those with strong credentials as starters were also strong in saves. On one side of Chicago, Three Finger Brown made 149 career relief appearances, saving 49 and leading the NL four times. On the South side Ed Walsh made 115 appearances, leading the AL five times for a total of 35 saves. Except for Russell (42 saves), Doc Crandell (168 appearances, 25 saves) and the dentist Dave Danforth (174 appearances, 23 saves) the career save leaders among the Men of '16 are pretty much starters — Alexander, Johnson, Bender, Pennock, Mays, Dauss, Red Ames, Slim Sallee, and Sam Jones — taking a busman's holiday. However, only 35 pitchers recorded as many as 16 saves. Many of those pitchers who were strong in wins, games and innings posted mediocre numbers in saves. For example, hard-firing lefthander Hippo Vaughn saved only 5 games in thirteen seasons.

On the other hand, 38 pitchers recorded no saves at all. And 57 pitchers (30.8 percent) recorded no more saves (2) than a frontline pitcher should have recorded in one season.

The median for the entire group is 5 saves.

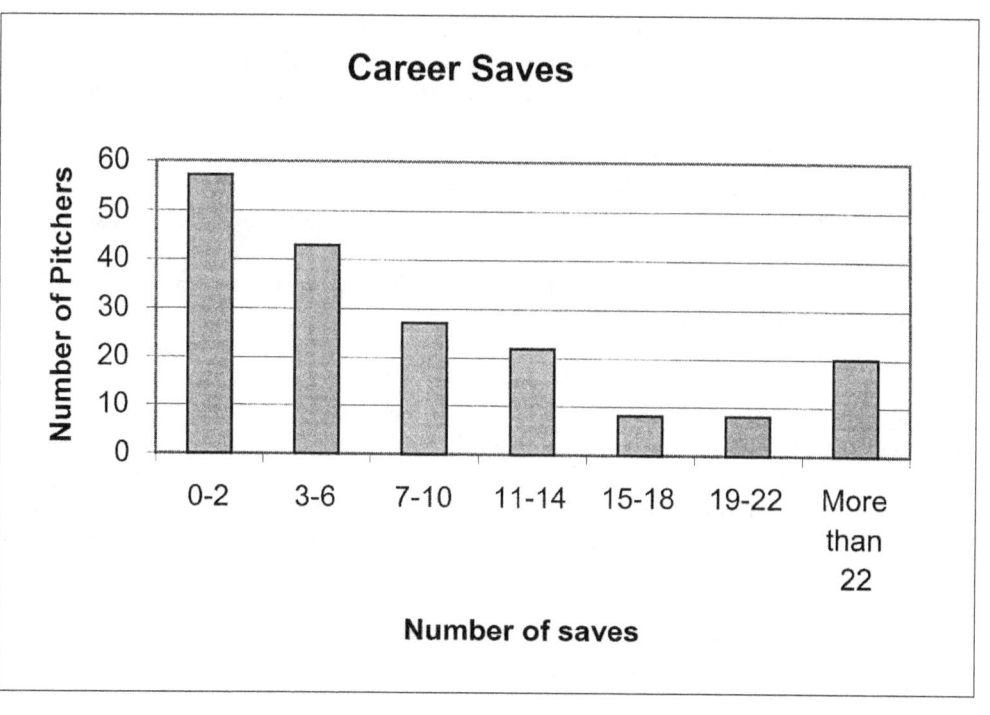

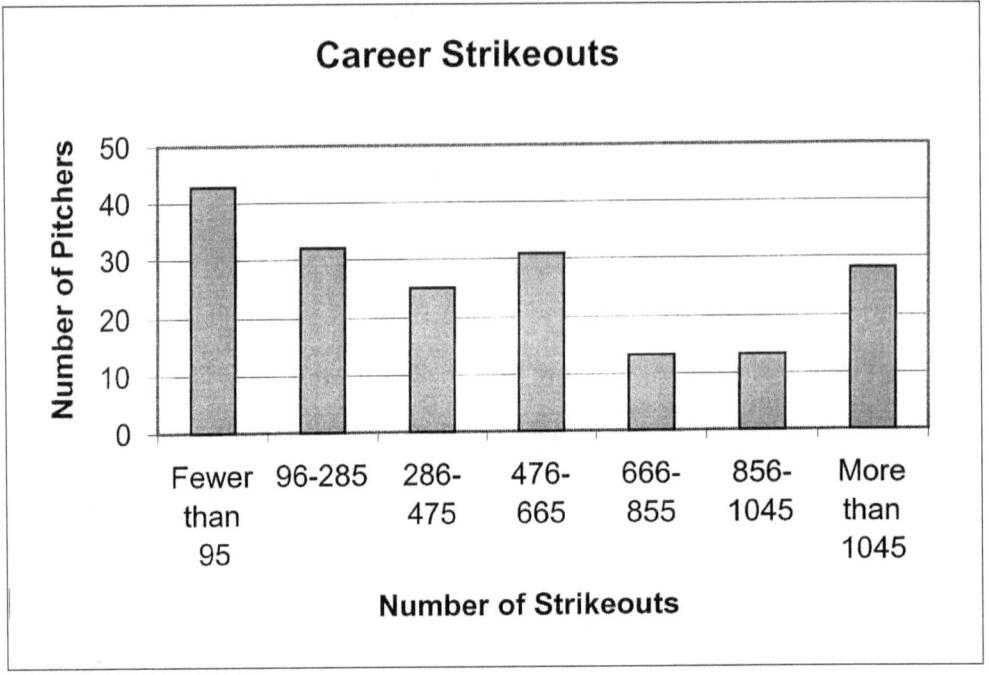

Strikeouts

Statistics for career strikeouts fall between wins and saves. Walter Johnson struck out 3509 batters—over a thousand more than his closest rival. Over his entire career he averaged more than 165 per season. Not surprisingly his closest rivals were Mathewson, Alexander and Plank—all over 2000. Six more—Walsh, Bender, Ames, Marquard, Donovan, and Grimes—topped 1500. Twenty-three more passed 1000. Forty-eight pitchers in all (25.9 percent) topped 750, our threshold figure. Again the list included many of the same names as previous lists. However Willie Mitchell, and Jim Shaw were strong strikeout pitchers who, because of shortened careers, missed 100 wins. On the other hand, Sherry Smith struck out only 428 in 2052 innings, 1.87 per nine innings. He would stand as an example of those who were successful pitchers without being strikeout pitchers.

At the lower end 44 pitchers struck out fewer than 100 batters in their careers. Of these Twining, Driscoll, Des Jardien and Whittaker struck out none. Gunkel and Lindstrom got one each.

The median career in strikeouts actually was Smith, whose 428 was matched by Elmer Myers in 950 fewer innings.

Earned Run Average

In general earned run averages were lower for the deadball era than those recorded by pitchers today. The median for the 80 frontline pitchers of 1916 was 2.62. Red Gunkel pitched one scoreless inning in 1916, leaving the majors with a 0.00 ERA. Paul Carpenter gave up one earned run in seven innings, leaving with 1.17. The lowest "career" ERA was Walsh with an eye-popping 1.82; Brown was right behind with 2.06, Mathewson finished with 2.13 and Johnson with 2.17.

Fifteen more frontline pitchers had career ERA's of less than 2.5. These include Ruth and Ed Reulbach (2.28), Death Valley Jim Scott (2.3), Reb Russell (2.33), Plank 2.35, Rube Foster (2.36), George McQuillan and Cicotte (2.38), Harry Coveleski (2.39), Nap Rucker (2.42),

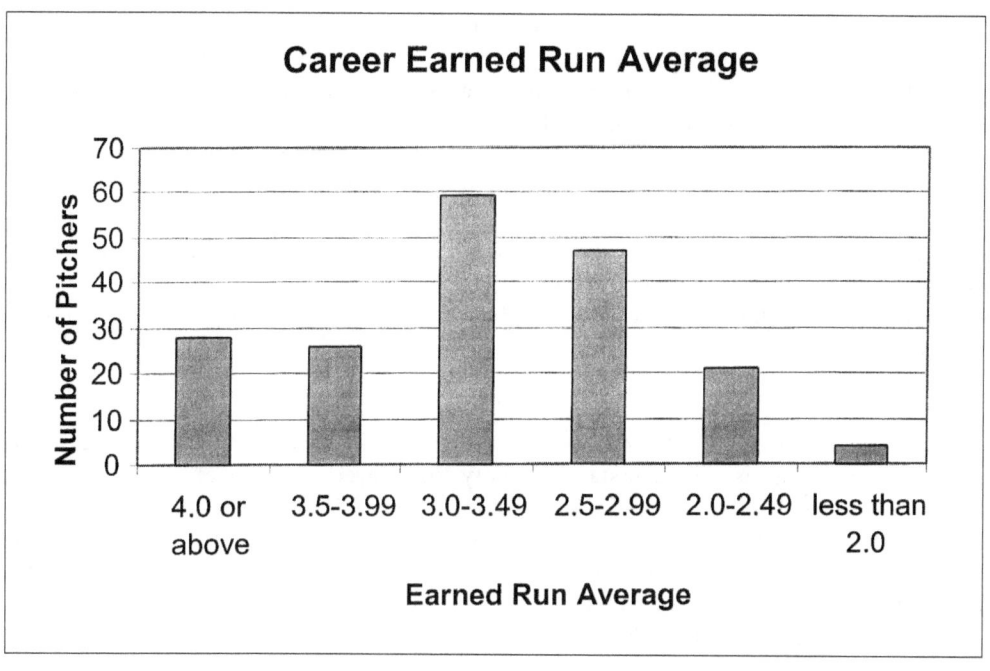

Joe Benz and Jeff Tesreau (2.43), Bender (2.46), Ernie Shore (2.47) and Vaughn (2.49). Only 25 full career pitchers had ERA's below 2.62. The median was 3.11.

Des Jardien gave up two earned runs in one major league inning and Twining gave up three in two innings, both resulting in inflated career ERAs. Only three pitchers who worked at least 1000 innings had career ERA's above 4. Socks Siebold had 4.43, Clarence Mitchell 4.12 and Elmer Myers 4.06.

Career Performance Figures

Nine pitchers turned in career figures exceeding the threshold in all six categories of games, innings, wins, saves, strikeouts and ERA. These include Johnson, Mathewson, Alexander, Plank, Brown, Bender, Cicotte, Walsh and Sallee. Twenty more exceeded the threshold in 5 of the six categories. Grimes, Faber, Pennock, Jones, Dauss, Stan Coveleski, Mays, Marquard, Bush, Shawkey, Shocker, Ames, Doak, Benton, Hendrix, and Cheney had career ERA's above 2.62; Reulbach, Vaughn, Rucker and Jim Scott had fewer than 16 saves. Seventeen more pitchers headed by Rixey exceeded the figures in four categories. All seventeen missed on ERA; fourteen missed on saves; George Mogridge, Sherry Smith and Jack Scott missed on strikeouts. Seven pitchers met three of the categories; six more met at least two of the six.

On average across the categories 45 pitchers (24 percent) achieved the eight-year performance standards. Almost exactly the same number (44) failed to exceed the one-year performance standards. Another way of translating these statistics is to say that upon entering the majors one pitcher in four might be likely to enjoy a relatively long and productive career; about one pitcher in four would likely have a one- or two-line career.

BATTING PERFORMANCE

Again it may be helpful to look at the statistics compiled by the 128 position players in 1916 to establish performance standards. On average each of the 128 regulars that year played in 130 games in which he managed 120 hits, scored 55 runs, hit 3 home runs, drove in 45 runs, and hit .258. So once again we might define a "solid" field player as one who lasted 8 years, thus playing in roughly 1040 games, making 960 hits, scoring 440 runs, hitting 24 home runs, driving in 360 runs and batting .258.

There were 346 field players in 1916. This list includes Babe Ruth, Rube Bressler and Reb Russell, pitchers who later made career shifts to field positions. It does not include good-hitting pitchers such as Ray Caldwell and Doc Crandall who occasionally played a field position throughout their careers. It does include the A's Les Lanning, who split a 19-game career almost evenly between the outfield and pitching mound.

Many of these players far exceeded the above figures; an equally large number fell woefully short.

Games

Not surprisingly Ty Cobb led the Men of '16 by playing in 3034 games, the equivalent of more than 23 seasons of regular status. Twenty-four players played in at least 2000 games. In addition to Cobb these players include Collins, Speaker, Wagner, Maranville, Crawford, Ruth, Lajoie, Carey, Wheat, Rice, Wallace, Hooper, Hornsby, Heilmann, Sisler, Milan, and Roush. The other eight were Joe Judge, Charlie Grimm, Stuffy McInnis, Sherry Magee, Ed Konetchy, Jake Daubert, Roger Peckinpaugh and Cy Williams.

One hundred twenty-one players (almost 35 percent) played in at least 1040 games—8 years of regular status.

At the other end of the scale, 13 field players joined Moonlight Graham in having one-game careers. Six of the thirteen made one pinch-hitting appearance: Bill Batsch, Wilbur Fisher, and Gene Madden for the Pirates; Joe Fautsch for the White Sox; Ray Kennedy for the Browns; and Heinie Stafford for the Giants. Five more played in the field. Phillies outfielder Bob Gandy batted twice; Dodger catcher Artie Dede and Pirate first-baseman Newt Halliday each got one turn at bat; neither Cub catcher Bucky O'Connor nor Giant catcher Duke Kelle-

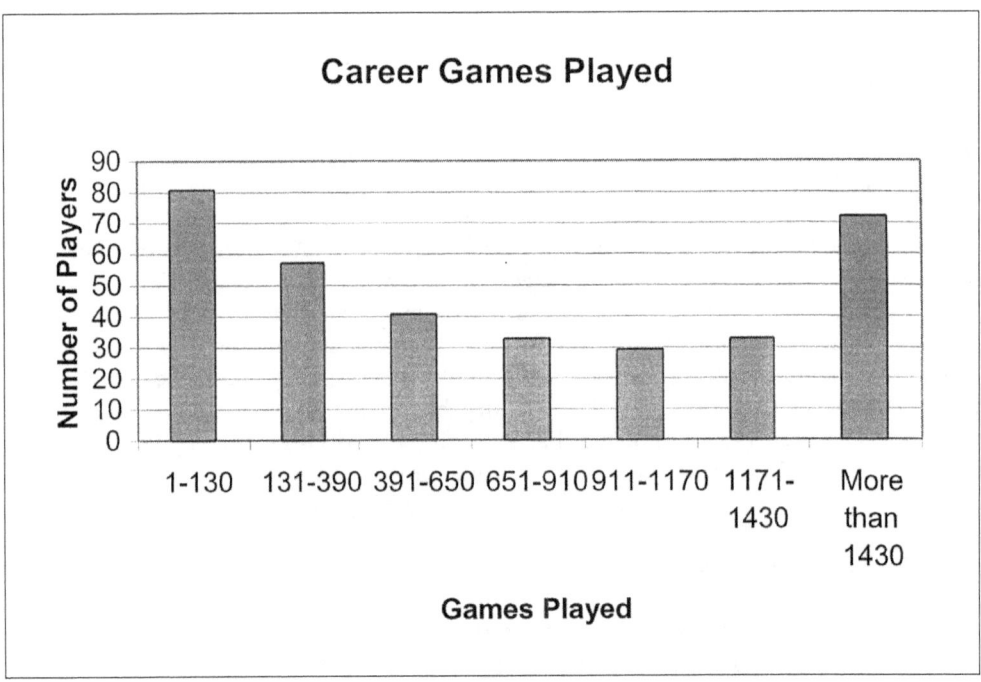

her had a turn at bat. Two other players—Ray Shook of the White Sox and Ollie Welf of the Indians—appeared only as pinch runners.

In all 81 players (23 percent) played in fewer than 130 games (130)—the one year average for a 1916 regular.

The median player between Ty Cobb and Ollie Welf is St. Louis Browns third baseman Joe Gedeon, who appeared in 581 games, the equivalent of just over four seasons of regular service. One of the fallout victims of the Black Sox scandal, Gedeon was banned from organized baseball after the 1920 season for admitting knowledge of the fix, thus seeing his career end at age 27.

Hits

Cobb, of course, again led the Men of '16 with 4191 career hits, the equivalent of almost 35 seasons of regular service for the average major leaguer of the era. Twenty-nine players made over 2000 hits. In addition to Cobb, Speaker (3515), Wagner (3418), Collins (3311), and Lajoie (3244) were members of the 3000-hit club. Rice, Crawford, Hornsby, Wheat, Ruth, Sisler, Carey, Heilmann, and Maranville topped 2500. In the 2000-hit club were Hooper, McInnis, Edd Roush, Judge, Jake Daubert, Wallace, Grimm, Sherry Magee, Hal Chase, Konetchy, Clyde Milan, George Burns, Bobby Veach, Tioga George Burns, and Dave Bancroft.

One hundred fifteen players (33 percent) reached the 8-year standard of 960 hits.

At the low end, sixteen of the field players left the majors without a single hit. The thirteen one-game players listed above were joined by Cleveland catcher Jack Bradley and Phillies outfielder Billy Maharg, both hitless in two games, and by White Sox shortstop Cy Wright, hitless in 8 games. In all 101 players (29 percent) left the majors with fewer hits than an average regular would have reached in one season.

Between Cobb and Wright, the median player was Cincinnati shortstop Bob Fisher. A regular for only two of his six seasons, Fisher managed 480 career hits.

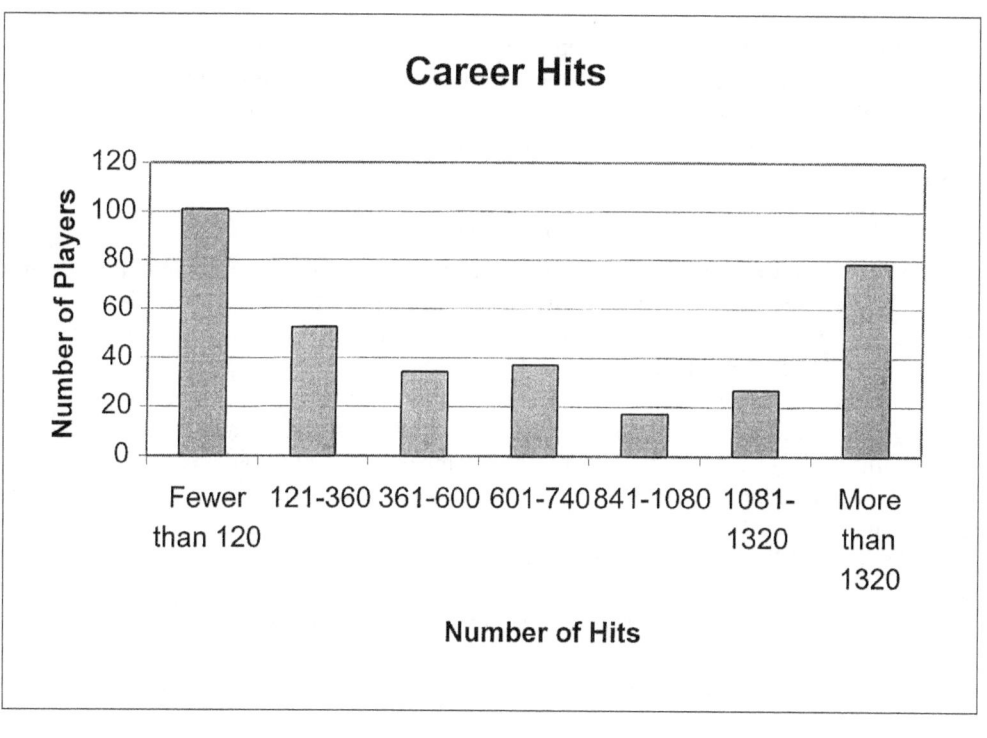

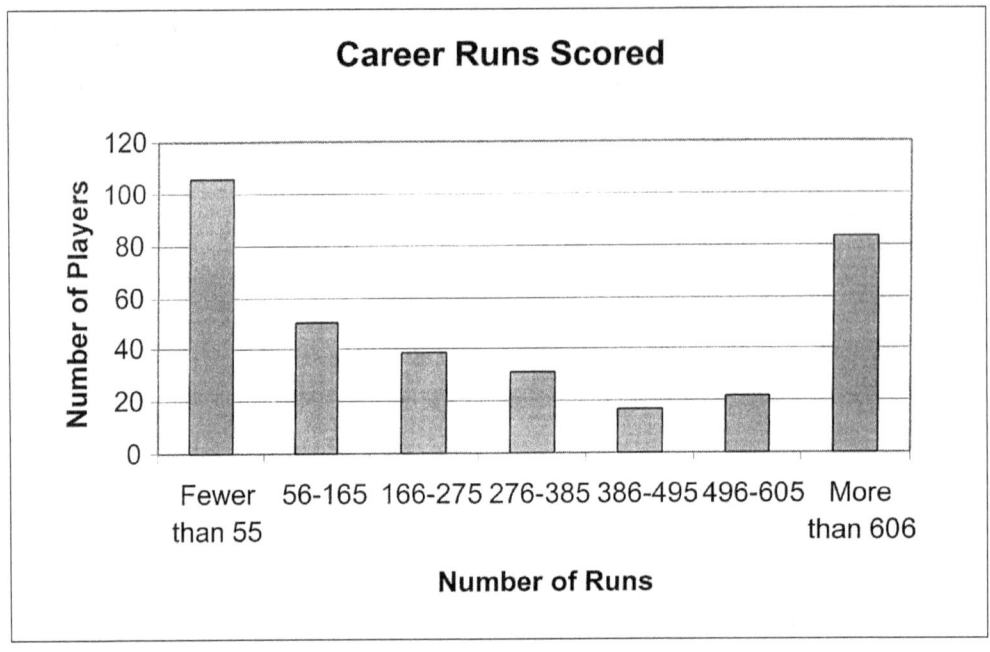

Runs

Cobb scored 2245 runs in his career, beating out Babe Ruth by 81 runs. Cobb's number is especially impressive when we realize that it would require more than 40 seasons for the average regular of his era to reach that figure. There were 27 members of the 1000-run club — most familiar names. Behind Cobb and Ruth were Speaker, Collins, Wagner, Hornsby, Carey, Rice and Lajoie — all with 1500 runs. Tiger shortstop Donie Bush ranked 15th with 1280 runs and Senator outfielder Charlie Jamieson ranked 22nd with 1062.

One hundred sixteen players (33.5 percent) scored at least 440 runs — the eight year threshold.

At the lower end, 106 players (30 percent) scored fewer than 55 career runs. Seventeen field players left the majors without crossing the plate at all — the sixteen hitless players plus catcher Mike Murphy, who failed to score in 15 games over two seasons with the Cardinals and A's.

The median player is Braves outfielder Joe Connolly, who reached 202 runs in just four seasons, three as a regular.

Home Runs

The year 1916 was a dead-ball year to an extent that is hard to comprehend today. Only three major league *clubs* hit as many as 40 homers, headed by the Cubs with 46. Seven American League clubs hit fewer than 20. The Washington Senators had a club total of 12 and the World Champion Red Sox had only 14.

In this context, Babe Ruth's 714 career homers is an Everest. Only 14 of 346 players hit as many as 100 career homers and only three — Ruth, Hornsby (301) and Phillies outfielder Cy Williams (251) — had as many as 200. Other members of the 100-homer clubs were Browns outfielder Ken Williams (196), Heilmann (183), George Kelly (148), White Sox first baseman Jack Fournier (136), Wheat (132) Phillies outfielder Gavvy Cravath (119), Cobb (118), Red Sox outfielder Tilly Walker (118), Speaker (117), Wagner (101) and Sisler (100). Home Run Baker had only 90.

Only eighty-three players (23.9 percent) hit 24 or more career homers — the eight-year threshold.

Of the six offensive categories, home runs has the largest number in the lowest group.

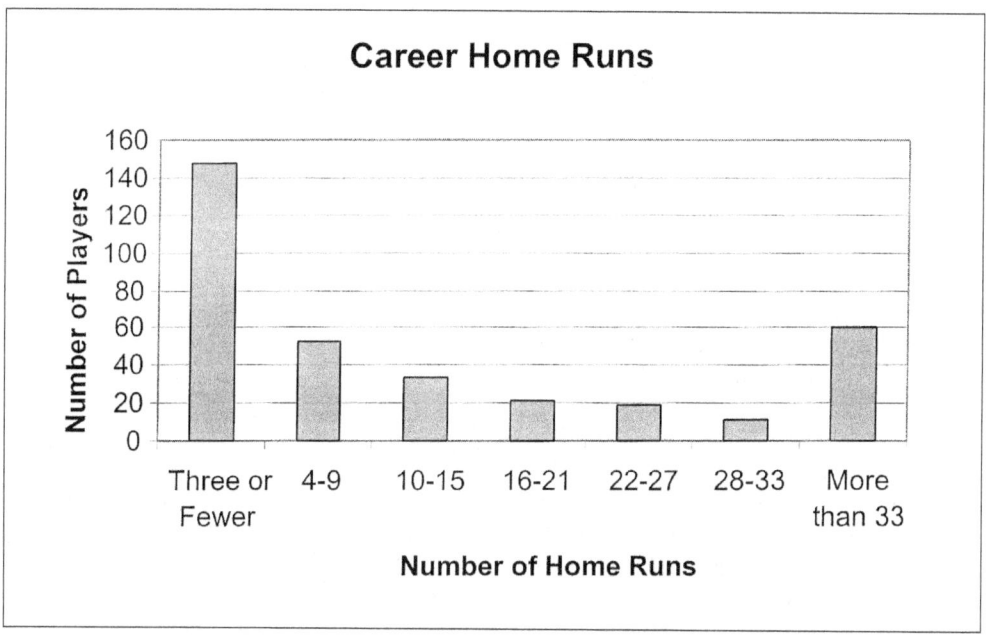

146 players (42 percent) had three or fewer career homers. Eighty-four players left the majors without a single homer. Catcher Roxy Walters was the frustration leader here, going 498 games and 321 hits without a round tripper. Twenty-nine players hit one homer; 20 hit two; 13 hit three. The median figure for the players of 1916 was six homers. The chart below shows the distribution of 1916 players by home runs.

Runs Batted In

Babe Ruth, of course, led the Men of '16 with 2211 runs batted in, the only player in the 2000 club. Cobb finished with 1961, good enough for fourth place on the all-time list. Wag-

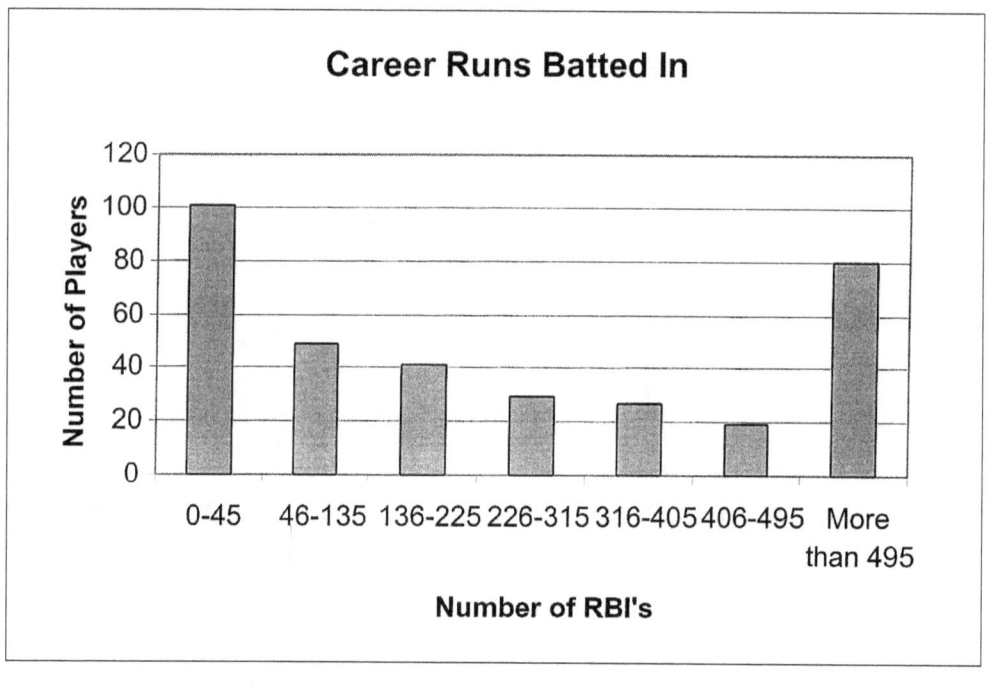

ner, Lajoie, Hornsby, Speaker, Heilmann, and Crawford also finished over 1500. These eight led 21 players over 1000, the remaining names being Collins, Wheat, Sherry Magee, Sisler, Veach, Wallace, Rice, Grimm, McInnis, Judge, Kelly, Baker and Cy Williams.

A solid eight-year career would yield around 360 RBI's, a figure reached by 113 players (32.6 percent).

At the lower end, 20 players finished with no RBI's at all. Topping this list was Milo Allison, an outfielder with the Cubs and Indians, who failed to drive in a run in 49 games. One hundred one players (29 percent) drove in no more than the one-year standard of 45 runs.

The median player between Ruth and Allison was Tommy Clarke, a catcher for the Reds and Cubs. In a ten-year career, he drove in 191 runs.

Batting Average

The Men of '16 included some of the greatest hitters of all time. Twenty-eight players (8 percent) had career averages of .300 or higher. Cobb (.367), Hornsby (.358), and Jackson (.356) are the top three on the all-time list. Speaker (.344), Ruth (.342), Heilmann (.342), Sisler (.340), Lajoie (.338), Collins (.333), Wagner (.327), Roush (.323) and Rice (.322) are all in the top forty. Lost among this group of great and near great are Brooklyn outfielder Hack Miller (.323), Giant outfielder Benny Kauff (.311), and Tiger outfielder George Harper (.303).

Average, of course, is not a cumulative figure. But 93 field players who qualified in at least one other category (i.e. drove in at least 360 runs) also hit .258 or higher.

The sixteen players without hits were also men with batting averages of .000. But they had company in the lower ranges. The A's Doc Carroll finished at .097. A total of 47 players hit below .200 for their career.

Between Cobb and Ollie Welf the median players were two third basemen. Mike Mowrey, a 13-year NL veteran, and Fred McMullin, a utility player with the White Sox, both had career averages of .256. The "Career Batting Averages" chart shows the distribution of players by average.

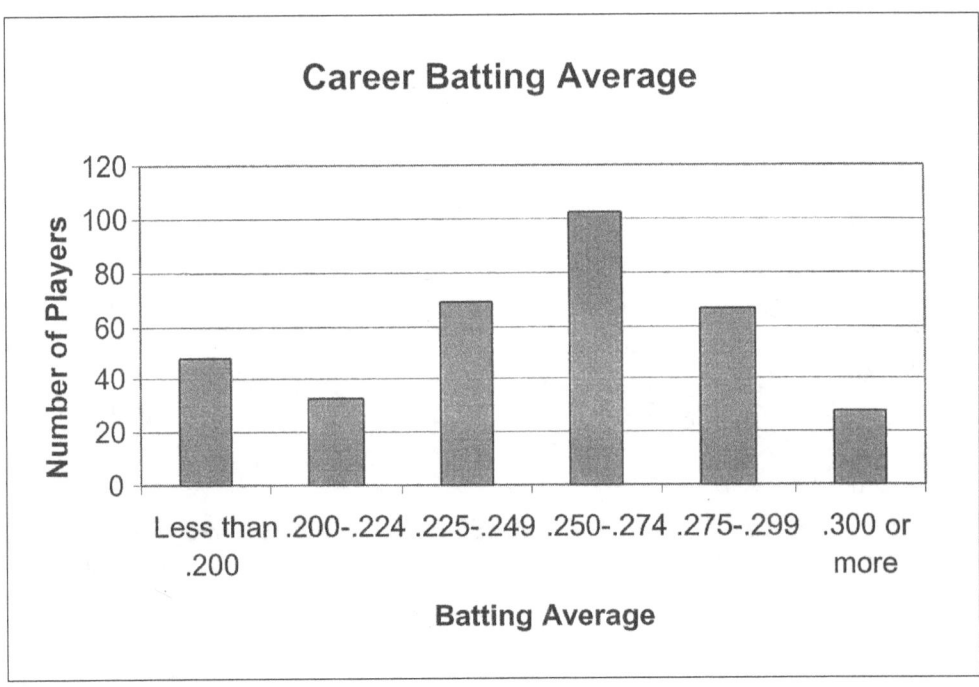

Career Performance Figures

Sixty-eight field players achieved the eight-year standards in all six categories: games, hits, runs, home runs, RBI's and average. An additional 21 achieved five of the six, usually falling short in home runs. Twenty-two more attained four of the categories. Six players made at least three of the six and sixteen reached career figures in two categories. On average 107 field players (31 percent) met or exceeded the eight-year performance standards. As with pitchers, exactly the same number of field players (107) failed to exceed in their careers the one-year marks established by 1916 regulars. Again we might interpret these statistics in this way: for a new player entering the majors, the odds are about one in three that his career will be distinguished, average or less than ordinary.

Factors Impacting Career Statistics

One hundred three of both field players and pitchers lost major league playing time—primarily in 1918—because of military service or war-related work. This figure includes only players who were part of a major league roster at the time. And since 450 games were cancelled at the end of 1918 as "nonessential," all players active at the time lost those opportunities from their career statistics. Among field players, Sam Rice stands out as a career casualty. He had 177 hits in 1917 and 179 in 1919 but only eight before going into service in 1918, so he lost roughly 170 career hits and a chance for 3150 instead of 2987. Among pitchers, Pete Alexander had 31 wins in 1917 and 28 in 1919, so he lost close to 30 career wins and a chance for 400 instead of 373. Shawkey, Lefty Williams, Rube Benton, Jeff Pfeffer, Howard Ehmke, Herb Pennock and Ray Fisher are others who probably lost at least 10 wins. Players such as Alexander, Elmer Myers and Ed Klepfer were wounded or gassed in the war, also hampering post-war performances.

On the other hand, a number of both batters and pitchers benefited from two years of Federal League competition. By increasing the number of "major leaguers" from 400 to 600, the league surely diluted the talent level while creating opportunities. Among pitchers Claude Hendrix had 45 FL victories, followed by Gene Packard (41), Tom Seaton (40), Knetzer (37), Nick Cullop (36), Earl Moseley (35), Crandall (34), Fred Anderson (32) and Al Schulz (31). In Moseley's case FL wins constituted two thirds of his career totals. Among batters, Benny Kauff rang up 376 FL hits, 72 percent of his 521 career hits. Dutch Zwilling had 332 FL hits out of 351 total. While Jack Tobin's 329 is only 17 percent of his 1908 career total, Bill McKechnie's 289 is 40 percent of his total.

As noted above, the odds on a field player enjoying a significant career are better than those for a pitcher. Two issues emerge. First, pitching more than 200 innings a year often places a strain on the arm, leading to overuse injuries and shortened careers. Ed Walsh, Harry Coveleski. Nap Rucker, and Erskine Meyer stand as examples of Men of '16 whose arms simply wore out early.

The second issue is the change in the game after 1920. In the introduction to Eliot Asinof's *Eight Men Out,* Steven Jay Gould points out that one of the effects of the Black Sox scandal (and also of the death of Ray Chapman) was to force changes to attract fans back to the game. The spitball was banned. Dirty or scuffed balls were removed from play. The result was more home runs and more runs scored (Asinof xvii–xviii). In 1916 the NL as a league hit .247 while the AL hit a point higher at .248. By 1925 both leagues hit .292. In 1916 NL pitchers had a league ERA of 2.61; the AL 2.82. By 1925 NL pitchers had a bloated 4.27 ERA and their AL counterparts had an even worse 4.39. For those hitters whose careers extended into the 1920s, their chances of reaching the 1916 career goals were enhanced considerably; for pitchers, the opposite was true.

Appendix D: Occupational and Mortality Data

Career Direction

When we ask whatever happened to Jack Dalton, we generally want to know what he has done with his life since we last saw him in the major leagues. Underlying the question is a sense that a major league experience should have a special meaning that continues to shape the life of the person. Before attempting this summary, I think that three preliminary remarks are in order.

First, few of the Men of '16 made a lot of money in baseball. Ruth, Cobb, Roush, and Bancroft—stars who lasted into the more lush salaries of the 1920s—retired relatively well-to-do. But, according to Eliot Asinof's *Eight Men Out*, outstanding players such as Joe Jackson and Eddie Cicotte never reached the $6,000 mark (16, 18). The Federal League temporarily inflated salaries, but as soon as it folded, NL and AL owners tried to recoup losses by slashing salaries. The Red Sox attempted to cut Tris Speaker's salary from a decade high of $18,000 to $9,000 before dealing him to Cleveland. The Pirates dropped Honus Wagner's salary from $10,000 to $5,700 (*Baseball: An Illustrated History* 123).

Salaries were also low relative to other employment. The gap between the salary of the player in the field and that of the fan in the stands was quite narrow. For example, a Ford worker on the "$5/day" plan would have an annual salary of $1200 to $1250; David Quentin Voigt's research showed that the effect of the Federal League was to "make $70,000 the average sum for a twenty-five man major league team" (66). This would make an average salary around $3,000, with fringe players making considerably less. No one—especially the Dodgers—seemed surprised when Hall of Fame outfielder Zack Wheat held out in 1918, alleging that he could make more money on his farm than the Dodgers were offering. *The Sporting News* labeled the claim "probably true," and the Dodgers agreed, offering Wheat a $500 pay increase. Fringe players were more susceptible to lures from outside the sport. Reds outfielder Larry Kopf left baseball in 1918 to accept a position as sales director for a rubber company, which, according to *The Sporting News*, "from all accounts pays better than baseballing."

Second, many of the Men of '16 would have been at the head of the employment line. At a time when, according to the Bureau of the Census, only 7.4 percent of males graduated from high school, 155 of 527 players (29.4 percent) had attended college. This level of education helped many to find suitable careers once they left baseball.

Third, however, the Men of '16 could hardly have been born at a worse time economically. On average, they were 39 years old when the Great Depression hit. They left baseball in time to join the rest of the nation's unemployed in seeking whatever work was available. Unlike today's players, they faced this challenge without the safety net of a major league pension plan or unemployment insurance. The daughters of Jack Smith and Elmer Smith both spoke of the difficulties their fathers faced in finding any work at all after leaving baseball. Two players who died in the 1930s—Rowdy Elliott and Murphy Currie—were unemployed and in Elliott's case, at least, destitute. On the other hand, Eugene Madden, Jr., spoke with pride of his father's being able to start up a business manufacturing automobile springs in the depths of the Depression.

Occupational information does not lend itself well to statistical analysis. In several cases players had multiple careers; in other cases the record is incomplete or imprecise; at times the categories seem to overlap. But I hope that the following classification and summary of occupations will give a sense of the post-playing life of the Men of '16. The largest number (37.8 percent) remained in baseball in some capacity—as players, managers, coaches, scouts, executives or even umpires—for at least five years after leaving the majors. Like Gene Madden, 18.4 percent started or bought into a business. Eleven percent found blue collar jobs; 10.1 percent were employed by the government; 8.1 percent were in management, 7 percent listed farming as their occupation; 6.6 percent entered law enforcement; 5.6 percent entered sales, 5 percent were in the professions; and 3.9 percent held clerical positions.

A quick glance through this biographical dictionary would suggest that the majority of players did relatively well after leaving baseball—especially considering the economic conditions of the times. However, as we look at the relationship between major league careers and post-playing careers, we might make four rough-and-ready categories of these players. Each player might be more or less an Art Nehf, more or less a Fritz Von Kolnitz, more or less an Elmer Myers or more or less a Pete Alexander.

The Art Nehf group consists of those players for whom major league baseball was a relatively successful period of their lives. These players used their experience as a springboard to move into productive post-playing careers in some field. Perhaps a quarter of the players would fit into this category.

The Fritz Von Kolnitz group consists of those players for whom major league baseball was a relatively short and relatively minor interval in their lives before going on to highly successful careers—generally outside of baseball. This would be a smaller group than the Nehf group.

The Elmer Myers group consists of all those men whose playing careers for whatever reasons fell short of excellence and who went on to make the best they could of life afterwards with the tools and opportunities at hand. Probably half of the players would be here.

The Pete Alexander group consists of those players for whom a major league baseball career—however successful—was essentially an end in itself. Like John Updike's "ex–basketball player" Flick Webb, their post-game lives were largely anticlimactic. This is a relatively small group.

MORTALITY STATISTICS

The question of whatever happened to Jack Dalton may also be one of mortality. When we ask it, we really want to know when, where, and how Jack Dalton died. This section summarizes some mortality data for the Men of '16.

Appendix D

I began collecting biographical data on the Men of '16 in the chronological order of their deaths; as a result, I concluded that the life of the average player was short and tragic. I quickly saw that the ability to snap off a curve or hit one well did not exempt these men from the accidents, epidemics and physical malfunctions that shortened life for the general run of mankind.

Twenty-five players had died by 1930, forty-nine by 1940 and 113 — more than a fifth of the total — by 1950. Put another way, 6 players (1.1 percent) died in their twenties; 12 players (2.2 percent) died in their thirties; 29 players (5.5 percent) died in their forties, and 62 players (11.8 percent) died in their fifties.

Born on average in 1890, surviving players had generally reached the age of 60 by 1950. After 1950 we notice that heart attacks — by far the leading cause of death for these players — and other diseases associated with aging are replacing accidents and epidemics as causes of death. We also note that 80 percent of the players are still living. Then we begin to see that as in many of the indicators of success, major league baseball players do better than the rest of the population in the longevity sweepstakes.

Statistics from the Bureau of the Census show that a twenty-year-old male in 1909–1911 (the age of the average member of the Men of '16) could expect to live another 42.7 years — or until age 62.7. The group as a whole bettered that figure by almost 10 years. The median death age was 72. Four hundred sixteen players (almost 80 percent) reached the age of 60. Of these, 113 players (21.5 percent) died in their sixties, and 152 players (28.9 percent) died in their seventies. These figures leave 151 players (28.7 percent) who lived to become octogenarians, and of these 36 (6.9 percent) lived into their nineties. So far as we know Ollie O'Mara, who died at age 98, holds the longevity record for the group.

If Jack Dalton and Don Brown — the two players missing from the above statistics — are alive today (2006), they are 121 and 109 years of age, respectively.

Selected Bibliography

Apple, Martin, and Burt Goldblatt. *Baseball's Best: The Hall of Fame Gallery.* New York: McGraw, 1977.

Asinof, Eliot. *Eight Men Out: The Black Sox and the 1919 World Series.* Introduction by Stephen Jay Gould. New York: Holt, 1983.

Baseball: An Illustrated History. Narrative by Geoffrey C. Ward. Based on a documentary filmscript by Geoffrey C. Ward and Ken Burns. New York: Knopf, 1994.

The Baseball Encyclopedia: The Complete and Official Record of Major League Baseball. 8th ed. New York: Macmillan, 1990.

Caldwell County (MO) Historical Society. *Caldwell County, Missouri History.* 2 vols. Caldwell County Historical Society, 1994.

"The Colleges." *Baseball Almanac.* http://www.baseball-almanac.com.

Douchant, Mike. *Encyclopedia of College Basketball.* Detroit: Gale, 1995.

Forman, Sean L. Baseball-Reference.com. Major League Statistics and Information. http://www.baseball-reference.com/.

Gould, Stephen Jay. Introduction to *Eight Men Out* by Eliot Asinof. New York: Holt, 1983.

James, Bill. *The Bill James Historical Baseball Abstract.* Text designed and illustrated by Mary A. Worth. New York: Villard, 1986.

Johnson, Lloyd, and Miles Wolff, eds. *The Encyclopedia of Minor League Baseball: The Official Record of Minor League Baseball.* 2nd ed. Durham, NC: Baseball America, 1997.

Karst, Gene, and Martin J. Jones, Jr. *Who's Who in Professional Baseball.* New Rochelle, NY: Arlington House, 1973.

Lee, Bill. *The Baseball Necrology: The Post-Baseball Lives and Deaths of Over 7,600 Major League Players and Others.* Jefferson, NC: McFarland, 2003.

National Geographic Society (U.S.). *Historical Atlas of the United States.* Centennial ed. Washington, DC: National Geographic Society, 1988.

Neft, David S., Richard M. Cohen, and Rick Korch. *The Football Encyclopedia: The Complete History of Professional Football from 1892 to the Present.* New York: St. Martin's, 1994.

"Obit Listings." *The Deadball Era: Where Every Player Is Safe at Home.* http://www.thedeadballera.com.

Porter, David L., ed. *Biographical Dictionary of American Sport: Baseball.* New York: Greenwood, 1987.

Reidenbaugh, Lowell. *Cooperstown: Where Baseball Legends Live Forever.* Edited by Joe Hoppel. St. Louis: Sporting News, 1983.

Ritter, Lawrence. *The Glory of Their Times: The Story of the Early Days of Baseball Told by the Men Who Played It.* New York: Morrow, 1984.

Shatzkin, Mike, ed. *The Ballplayers: Baseball's Ultimate Biographical Reference.* New York: Arbor House/Morrow, 1990.

Smith, Elsdon C. *American Surnames.* Philadelphia: Chilton, 1969.

Snelling, Dennis. *The Pacific Coast League: A Statistical History, 1903–1957.* Jefferson, NC: McFarland, 1995.

Society for American Baseball Research. *SABR Collegiate Database.* http://www.ncaa-baseball.com/sabr/database.

Thorn, John, Pete Palmer, Michael Gershman, and David Pietrusza, with Matthew Silverman and Sean Lahman, eds. *Total Baseball: The Official Encyclopedia of Major League Baseball.* 6th ed. New York: Total Sports, 1999.

Tompkins, Vincent, ed. *American Decades 1910–1919.* Detroit: Gale, 1994.

Turkin, Hy, and S. C. Thompson. *The Official Encyclopedia of Baseball.* Rev. ed. New York: Barnes, 1956.

United States, Bureau of the Census. *Historical Statistics of the United States, Colonial Times to 1970.* Bicentennial ed. Washington, DC: U.S. Department of Commerce, Bureau of the Census, 1975.

Vitale, Dick. Foreword ("Hoop Heaven") to *Encyclopedia of College Basketball* by Mike Douchant. Detroit: Gale, 1995.

Voigt, David Q. *American Baseball. Vol. 2, From the Commissioners to Continental Expansion.* Foreword by Allan Nevins. Norman: University of Oklahoma Press, 1966.

Index

The index below is arranged alphabetically by subject (in small and large capital letters) and includes persons, places, teams, and colleges. Rather than citing page numbers, this index is arranged to provide a useful context by citing the pertinent individual biographical entries themselves.

Players who are the primary subject of an entry in the dictionary are listed in the index only when their names appear in at least one other entry.

ABERDEEN, WA Egan, Dick
ADRIAN, MI Gilhooley, Frank; Smith, Paul
AKRON, OH Doak, Bill; Good, Wilbur; Morgan, Ray; Schultz, Joe
ALABAMA Allen, Frank; Cruise, Walton; Long, Tommy; Moeller, Danny; Morton, Guy; Nabors, Jack; Stock, Milt
ALBANY, NY Evers, Johnny
ALBRIGHT COLLEGE Ritter, Hank
ALEXANDER, PETE Cheney, Larry; Killefer, Bill; Leonard, Dutch; Maharg, Billy; Rumler, Bill
ALL-AMERICAN GIRLS PROFESSIONAL BASEBALL LEAGUE Carey, Max; Wambsganss, Bill
ALL-STAR BASEBALL SCHOOL Billings, Josh
ALLEN, NICK Rariden, Bill
ALMEIDA, RAFAEL Marsans, Armando
ALTROCK, NICK Sawyer, Carl; Schaefer, Germany
AMHERST COLLEGE Henry, John
ANDERSON, SC Myers, Hy
ARAGON, JACK Aragon, Angel
ARIZONA Grimm, Charlie; Henry, John; Nehf, Art; Williams, Marsh
ARKANSAS Davenport, Dave; Ellison, Bert; Harper, George; Paulette, Gene; Schmidt, Walter; Watson, Milt

ASHEVILLE, NC Fortune, Gary
ATLANTA, GA Archer, Jimmy; Barber, Turner; Bressler, Rube; Chapman, Harry; Dumont, George; Hughes, Tom; Lee, Billy; Long, Tommy; Love, Slim; Markle, Cliff; O'Mara, Ollie; Paskert, Dode; Pearce, George; Perry, Scott; Picinich, Val; Rariden, Bill; Rumler, Bill; Sheehan, Tom; Thrasher, Buck; Warmoth, Cy
AUBURN UNIVERSITY Smith, Red
AUGUSTA, GA Cobb, Ty; Huhn, Emil; Rucker, Nap
AUSTIN, TX Brainerd, Fred; Cook, Doc

BAGBY, JIM, JR. Bagby, Jim
BALL, PHIL Lavan, Doc
BALTIMORE, MD Barber, Turner; Bentley, Jack; Crowell, Cap; Hartzell, Roy; Jacobson, Merwyn; Kopf, Larry; Lawry, Otis; Magee, Sherry; Maisel, Fritz; Maisel, George; McCarty, Lew; Morgan, Ray; Morrisette, Bill; Parnham, Rube; Ruth, Babe; Shawkey, Bob; Twombly, George; Walsh, Jimmy; Williams, Buff
BALTIMORE FEDERALS (TERRAPINS) Doolan, Mickey; Hickman, Jim; Knabe, Otto
BARANOWSKI, IGNATZ Fuller, Frank

BARNES, VIRGIL Barnes, Jesse
BATON ROUGE, LA/CLARKSVILLE, MS Billings, Josh; Love, Slim
BATTLE CREEK, MI Compton, Pete; Koob, Ernie; McKee, Red; Zwilling, Dutch
BATTLEAXES, VA (AMATEUR) Boehling, Joe
BAYLOR UNIVERSITY Danforth, Dave; Stellbauer, Bill
BEAUMONT, TX Appleton Ed; Baker, Del; Dell, Wheezer; Jasper, Hi; Nixon, Al
BED-MAKERS (SIMMONS MATTRESS), WI Dyer, Ben
BERGMAN, ARTHUR Bergman, Al
BETHANY COLLEGE Batsch, Bill
BINGHAMTON, NY Fischer, Bill; Kennedy, Ray; McNally, Mike; Murphy, Mike
BIRMINGHAM, AL Brottem, Tony; Caldwell, Ray; Elliott, Rowdy; Grimes, Burleigh; Hill, Carmen; Johnston, Jimmy; Long, Tommy; Milan, Clyde; Smith, Popboy; Stewart, Stuffy; Tragesser, Walt; Zwilling, Dutch
BLOOMINGTON, IN Bluejacket, Jim; Nunamaker, Les; Thompson, Shag
BONHAM, TX Russell, Reb
BOSTON BRAVES Allen, Frank; Bailey, Fred; Bancroft, Dave; Barbare, Walter; Barnes, Jesse; Blackburn, Earl; Chap-

pell, Larry; Coleman, Bob; Collins, Zip; Compton, Pete; Connolly, Joe; Cruise, Walton; Deal, Charlie; Dugey, Oscar; Elliott, Rowdy; Evers, Johnny; Fitzpatrick, Ed; Fournier, Jack; Getz, Gus; Gonzales, Mike; Gowdy, Hank; Griffith, Tommy; Grimes, Burleigh; Grimm, Charlie; Hughes, Tom; Keating, Ray; Kelleher, John; Kelly, George; Kelly, Joe; King, Lee; Konetchy, Ed; Kopf, Larry; Lewis, Duffy; Magee, Sherry; Mann, Les; Maranville, Rabbit; Mathes, Joe; Mathewson, Christy; Mays, Carl; McTigue, Pudge; Miller, Frank; Nehf, Art; Nixon, Al; Oeschger, Joe; Palmero, Emilio; Perry, Scott; Pick, Charlie; Ragan, Pat; Rariden, Bill; Reulbach, Ed; Rico, Art; Rudolph, Dick; Ruth, Babe; Schultz, Joe; Scott, Jack; Seibold, Socks; Shay, Marty; Smith, Jack; Smith, Jimmy; Smith, Red; Snodgrass, Fred; Stengel, Casey; Sullivan, Billy; Terry, Zeb; Tincup, Ben; Tragesser, Walt; Twombly, George; Tyler, Lefty; Wagner, Bill; Whitted, Possum; Wilhoit, Joe; Wilson, Art
BOSTON COLLEGE Henriksen, Olaf
BOSTON RED SOX Anderson, Fred; Baker, Del; Barbare, Walter; Barry, Jack; Burns, George; Cady, Hick; Carrigan, Bill; Cicotte, Eddie; Coleman, Bob; Collins, Eddie; Collins, Shano; Coumbe, Fritz ; Cravath, Gavvy; Daly, Tom; Dumont, George; Ehmke, Howie; Engle, Clyde; Fortune, Gary; Foster, Eddie; Foster, Rube; Fuller, Frank; Gainer, Del; Gardner, Larry; Gilhooley, Frank; Gregg, Vean; Haley, Pat; Hall, Charley; Harper, Harry; Hartley, Grover; Hendryx, Tim; Henriksen, Olaf; Hoblitzell, Dick; Hooper, Harry; Hunter, Herb; Janvrin, Hal; Johnson, Ernie; Jones, Sam; Leibold, Nemo; Leonard, Dutch; Lewis, Duffy; Mays, Carl; McHale, Marty; McInnis, Stuffy; McNally, Mike; Menosky, Mike; Miller, Elmer; Miller, Hack; Moseley, Earl; Myers, Elmer; Nunamaker, Les; O'Neill, Steve; Pennock, Herb; Picinich, Val; Pratt, Del; Rodgers, Bill; Rondeau, Henri; Russell, Allan; Ruth, Babe; Schang, Wally; Scott, Deacon; Shanks, Howard; Shore, Ernie; Shorten, Chick; Smith, Elmer; Smith, Paul; Speaker, Tris; Spencer, Tubby; Strunk, Amos; Thomas, Pinch; Tobin, Jack; Vitt, Oscar; Wagner, Heinie; Walker, Tilly; Walsh, Jimmy; Walters, Roxy; Wambsganss, Bill; Williams, Buff; Williams, Ken; Wyckoff, Weldon; Yerkes, Steve
BOWDEN COLLEGE McElwee, Lee; Witt, Whitey
BRIDGEPORT, CT Boehling, Joe; Lobert, Hans
BROOKLYN DODGERS Allen, Frank; Appleton Ed; Baird, Doug; Barber, Turner; Barnes, Jesse; Betzel, Bruno; Boehler, George; Bressler, Rube; Cadore, Leon; Carey, Max; Cheney, Larry; Coombs, Jack; Cooper, Claude; Crane, Sam; Cutshaw, George; Dalton, Jack; Daubert, Jake; Deberry, Hank; Dede, Arte; Dell, Wheezer; Doak, Bill; Donovan, Bill; Doolan, Mickey; Egan, Dick; Elliott, Rowdy; Fabrique, Bunny; Fischer, Bill; Fisher, Bobby; Fournier, Jack; Getz, Gus; Griffith, Tommy; Grimes, Burleigh ; Griner, Dan; Groh, Heinie; Harper, Harry; Hickman, Jim; Jacobson, Merwyn; Janvrin, Hal; Johnston, Jimmy; Kelleher, John; Kelly, George; Knetzer, Elmer; Konetchy, Ed; Magee, Lee; Mails, Duster; Malone, Lew; Mamaux, Al; Maranville, Rabbit; Marquard, Rube; McCarty, Lew; Merkle, Fred; Meyers, Chief; Miller, Hack; Miller, Otto; Mitchell, Clarence; Mowrey, Mike; Myers, Hy; Nixon, Al; Oeschger, Joe; Olson, Ivy; O'Mara, Ollie; Pfeffer, Jeff; Picinich, Val; Ragan, Pat; Reulbach, Ed; Rucker, Nap; Ruth, Babe; Schupp, Ferdie; Shotten, Burt; Smith, George; Smith, Red; Smith, Sherry; Smyth, Red; Stengel, Casey; Stewart, Stuffy; Stock, Milt; Wheat, Mack; Wheat, Zack; Whitted, Possum; Witt, Whitey
BROOKLYN FEDERALS (TIP-TOPS) Bluejacket, Jim; Cooper, Claude; Hofman, Solly; Magee, Lee; Seaton, Tom
BROWN UNIVERSITY Crowell, Cap; Kelleher, Jack
BUCKNELL UNIVERSITY Doolan, Mickey; Mathewson, Christy; Wyckoff, Weldon
BUFFALO, NY Archer, Jimmy; Groh, Heinie; Jamieson, Charlie; Judge, Joe; Schang, Wally; Stroud, Sailor; Williams, Buff
BUFFALO FEDERALS (BUFFEDS) Allen, Nick; Anderson, Fred; Dalton, Jack; Ehmke, Howie; Engle, Clyde; Louden, Baldy; Schulz, Al
BURLINGTON, IA Hale, George; Jacobs, Elmer; Wagner, Bill
BUSH, BULLET JOE Picinich, Val
BUTTE, MT Grover, Roy; Mathes, Joe

CADORE, LEON Oeschger, Joe
CALIFORNIA Adams, Jack; Agnew, Sam; Austin, Jimmy; Billings, Josh; Bohne, Sammy; Borton, Babe; Buckles, Jess; Burns, Ed; Chappell, Larry; Chase, Hal; Corhan, Roy; Coumbe, Fritz; Craft, Molly; Crandall, Doc; Cravath, Gavvy; Crawford, Sam; Cutshaw, George; Deal, Charlie; Dell, Wheezer; Demaree, Al; Des Jardien, Shorty; Egan, Dick; Elliott, Rowdy; Ellison, Bert; Gandil, Chick; Gedeon, Joe; Gould, Al; Guisto, Lou; Hall, Charley; Hamilton, Earl; Heilmann, Harry; Hooper, Harry; Hughes, Tom; James, Bill; Johnson, Bill; Johnson, Ernie; Kantlehner, Elmer; Keating, Ray; Kelly, George; Killefer, Red; Leonard, Dutch; Lewis, Duffy; Lotz, Joe; Lynn, Byrd; Mails, Duster; Mamaux, Al; Mann, Les; Markle, Cliff;

Mayer, Erskine; Mays, Carl; McElwee, Lee; McKenry, Limb; McMullin, Fred; Meyers, Chief; Miller, Hack; Mulligan, Eddie; Niehoff, Bert; Oeschger, Joe; Olson, Ivy; Packard, Gene; Penner, Ken; Ragan, Pat; Sawyer, Carl; Schmidt, Walter; Schneider, Pete; Schulte, Wildfire; Schupp, Ferdie; Scott, Jim; Siglin, Paddy; Smyth, Red; Snodgrass, Fred; Spencer, Tubby; Stanage, Oscar; Stengel, Casey; Stroud, Sailor; Terry, Zeb; Thomas, Pinch; Vitt, Oscar; Wallace, Bobby; Walters, Roxy; Wheat, Mack; Wilhoit, Joe; Williams, Lefty; Zwilling, Dutch

CANADA Daly, Tom; Gibson, George; Graney, Jack; Steele, Bob

CANTON, OH Rariden, Bill

CANTWELL, TOM Cantwell, Mike

CARNEGIE INSTITUTE OF TECHNOLOGY Lobert, Hans

CARROLL, DOC Whittaker, Walt

CASTRO, FIDEL Gonzales, Mike

CATHOLIC UNIVERSITY Pipp, Wally

CAVENEY, JIMMY Bohne, Sammy

CHALMERS AWARD Daubert, Jake; Doyle, Larry; Evers, Johnny; Schulte, Wildfire

CHAMBERSBURG, PA Mowrey, Mike

CHANCE, FRANK Evers, Johnny; Saier, Vic; Tinker, Joe

CHAPMAN, RAY Mays, Carl

CHARLOTTE, NC Carpenter, Paul; Pennock, Herb; Weiser, Bud

CHASE, HAL Dubuc, Jean; Zimmerman, Heinie

CHATTANOOGA, TN Benton, Rube; Cunningham, George; Gleason, Bill; Johnston, Doc; Johnston, Jimmy; Nunamaker, Les; Smykal, Frank

CHEYENNE INDIANS, WY Hendrix, Claude

CHICAGO ART INSTITUTE Demaree, Al

CHICAGO CUBS Allen, Nick; Allison, Milo; Archer, Jimmy; Barber, Turner; Beebe, Fred; Blackburn, Earl; Brown, Three Finger; Carter, Paul; Chapman, Harry; Cheney, Larry; Clarke, Tommy; Clemens, Count; Cooper, Wilbur; Daly, Tom; Deal, Charlie; Doolan, Mickey; Dugey, Oscar; Elliott, Rowdy; Evers, Johnny; Fischer, Bill; Fisher, Bobby; Flack, Max; Fournier, Jack; Gibson, George; Gonzales, Mike; Good, Wilbur; Griffith, Tommy; Grimes, Burleigh; Grimm, Charlie; Hagerman, Rip; Hendrix, Claude; Herzog, Buck; Hofman, Solly; Hornsby, Rogers; Hunter, Herb; Jacobs, Elmer; Jacobson, Merwyn; Johnston, Jimmy; Kelleher, John; Kelly, George; Kelly, Joe; Killefer, Bill; Knabe, Otto; Lavender, Jim; Lobert, Hans; Luderus, Fred; Magee, Lee; Maisel, George; Mann, Les; Maranville, Rabbit; Mathes, Joe; McAuley, Ike; McCarthey, Alex; McConnell, George; Merkle, Fred; Miller, Hack; Miller, Ward; Mollwitz, Fritz; Moriarty, George; Mulligan, Eddie; O'Connor, Bucky; O'Farrell, Bob; Packard, Gene; Paskert, Dode; Pearce, George; Pechous, Charles; Penner, Ken; Perry, Scott; Pick, Charlie; Prendergast, Mike; Reulbach, Ed; Robertson, Dave; Saier, Vic; Schaefer, Germany; Schulte, Wildfire; Seaton, Tom; Shay, Marty; Sicking, Eddie; Smith, Earl; Smith, Paul; Stock, Milt; Terry, Zeb; Tincup, Ben; Tinker, Joe; Toney, Fred; Tyler, Lefty; Vaughn, Hippo; Warner, Hooks; Weaver, Harry; Williams, Cy; Wilson, Art; Wortman, Chuck; Yerkes, Steve; Zeider, Rollie; Zimmerman, Heinie; Zwilling, Dutch

CHICAGO FEDERALS (CHI-SOX/WHALES) Clemens, Count; Fischer, Bill; Flack, Max; Hendrix, Claude; McConnell, George; Pechous, Charles; Prendergast, Mike; Smith, Jimmy; Tinker, Joe; Wilson, Art; Zeider, Rollie; Zwilling, Dutch

CHICAGO WHITE SOX Allen, Nick; Austin, Jimmy; Beall, Johnny; Bender, Chief; Benz, Joe; Borton, Babe; Bush, Donie; Byrne, Bobby; Chappell, Larry; Cicotte, Eddie; Clemens, Count; Collins, Eddie; Collins, Shano; Corhan, Roy; Cravath, Gavvy; Daly, Tom; Danforth, Dave; Evers, Johnny; Faber, Red; Fautsch, Joe; Felsch, Happy; Fournier, Jack; Gandil, Chick; Good, Wilbur; Hasbrook, Ziggy; Jackson, Joe; Jacobs, Elmer; James, Bill; Jasper, Hi; Johnson, Ernie; Johnston, Jimmy; Jourdan, Ted; Klepfer, Ed; Lapp, Jack; Leibold, Nemo; Lowdermilk, Grover; Lynn, Byrd; Mayer, Erskine; McMullin, Fred; Meyer, Billy; Mogridge, George; Moriarty, George; Mullen, Charlie; Mulligan, Eddie; Murphy, Eddie; Ness, Jack; Ragan, Pat; Roth, Braggo; Roush, Edd; Russell, Reb; Schalk, Ray; Schupp, Ferdie; Scott, Deacon; Scott, Jim; Shook, Ray; Smith, Popboy; Strunk, Amos; Sullivan, Billy; Terry, Zeb; Von Kolnitz, Fritz; Walsh, Ed; Weaver, Buck; Williams, Lefty; Wolfgang, Mellie; Wright, Cy; Zeider, Rollie; Zwilling, Dutch

CHILLICOTHE, OH Carpenter, Paul

CINCINNATI REDS Allen, Nick; Ames, Red; Bagby, Jim; Beall, Johnny; Benton, Rube; Bescher, Bob; Blackburn, Earl; Bluejacket, Jim; Bohne, Sammy; Bressler, Rube; Burns, George; Bush, Donie; Chapman, Harry; Clarke, Tommy; Coumbe, Fritz; Crane, Sam; Crawford, Sam; Dale, Gene; Daubert, Jake; Davenport, Dave; Doak, Bill; Doolan, Mickey; Egan, Dick; Emmer, Frank; Fisher, Bobby; Fisher, Ray; Fournier, Jack; Gonzales, Mike; Goodwin, Marv; Gowdy, Hank; Griffith, Tommy; Grimes, Burleigh; Griner, Dan; Groh, Heinie; Hall, Charley; Heilmann, Harry; Hinchman, Bill; Hobbs, Bill; Hoblitzell, Dick; Hornsby, Rogers; Huggins, Miller; Huhn, Emil; Johnston, Doc; Kelly, George; Killefer, Red; Knetzer, Elmer; Kopf, Larry; Lobert, Hans; Lohr, Howie; Louden, Baldy;

Magee, Lee; Magee, Sherry; Markle, Cliff; Marsans, Armando; Mathewson, Christy; McKenry, Limb; McKechnie, Bill; McQuillan, George; Mitchell, Clarence; Mollwitz, Fritz; Moseley, Earl; Mowrey, Mike; Myers, Hy; Neale, Greasy; Niehoff, Bert; O'Farrell, Bob; Olson, Ivy; Packard, Gene; Paskert, Dode; Perry, Scott; Picinich, Val; Pipp, Wally; Ragan, Pat; Rariden, Bill; Rixey, Eppa; Rodgers, Bill; Roush, Edd; Sallee, Slim; Schneider, Pete; Schulz, Al; Scott, Deacon; Scott, Jack; Seaton, Tom; Severeid, Hank; Sheehan, Tom; Shorten, Chick; Smith, Elmer; Smith, George; Smith, Jimmy; Smith, Paul; Stanage, Oscar; Tinker, Joe; Toney, Fred; Twining, Twink; Twombly, George; Von Kolnitz, Fritz; Wallace, Bobby; Williams, Ken; Wingo, Ivy
CLARKE, FRED Bigbee, Carson
CLEVELAND, TN Griner, Dan
CLEVELAND INDIANS Adams, Jack; Allison, Milo; Bagby, Jim; Baker, Del; Barbare, Walter; Beall, Johnny; Bergman, Al; Bescher, Bob; Betzel, Bruno; Billings, Josh; Boehling, Joe; Bradley, Jack; Burns, George; Caldwell, Ray; Carter, Paul; Chapman, Ray; Chappell, Larry; Coleman, Bob; Coumbe, Fritz; Coveleski, Stan; Cullop, Nick; Daly, Tom; Davis, Harry; Deberry, Hank; Des Jardien, Shorty; Engle, Clyde; Evans, Joe; Farmer, Jack; Gandil, Chick; Gardner, Larry; Getz, Gus; Good, Wilbur; Gould, Al; Graney, Jack; Gregg, Vean; Guisto, Lou; Gunkel, Red; Hagerman, Rip; Hartley, Grover; Hendryx, Tim; Hinchman, Bill; Howard, Ivan; Jackson, Joe; James, Bill; Jamieson, Charlie; Jasper, Hi; Johnson, Walter; Johnston, Doc; Jones, Sam; Kavanaugh, Marty; Klepfer, Ed; Kopf, Larry; Lajoie, Larry; Lambeth, Otis; Leibold, Nemo; Leonard, Joe; Lohr, Howie; Mails, Duster; Mays, Carl; McKechnie, Bill; McNally, Mike; McQuillan, George; Mitchell, Willie; Moeller, Danny; Morton, Guy; Myers, Elmer; Nunamaker, Les; Olson, Ivy; O'Neill, Steve; Peckinpaugh, Roger; Penner, Ken; Rodgers, Bill; Roth, Braggo; Schaefer, Germany; Schang, Wally; Shanks, Howard; Shorten, Chick; Shotten, Burt; Smith, Elmer; Smith, Popboy; Smith, Sherry; Speaker, Tris; Thomas, Pinch; Turner, Terry; Vitt, Oscar; Walters, Roxy; Wambsganss, Bill; Welf, Ollie; Wendell, Lew; Williams, Buff; Wilson, Art; Zwilling, Dutch
CLEVELAND SPIDERS Wallace, Bobby
CLEVELAND TELLINGS, OH (AMATEUR) Divis, Moxie
CLOVIS, NM Smith, Popboy
COBB, TY Crawford, Sam; Jackson, Joe; Kauff, Benny; Kocher, Brad; Leonard, Dutch; Marsans, Armando; Stewart, Stuffy; Veach, Bobby; Weaver, Buck
COBB EDUCATIONAL FOUNDATION Cobb, Ty
COLBY COLLEGE Coombs, Jack
COLLEGE OF CHARLESTON Von Kolnitz, Fritz
COLLEGE OF THE HOLY CROSS Barry, Jack; Carrigan, Bill; Carroll, Doc
COLLINS, SHANO Leibold, Nemo
COLORADO Bradley, Jack; Hartzell, Roy; Hughes, Tom; Packard, Gene; Shocker, Urban
COLORADO SCHOOL OF MINES Hartzell, Roy
COLUMBIA, SC Betzel, Bruno
COLUMBIA COLLEGE (FL) Stewart, Stuffy
COLUMBIA UNIVERSITY Collins, Eddie; Smith, George
COLUMBUS, OH Bailey, Fred; Bradley, Jack; Brown, Don; Cooper, Wilbur; Hall, Charley; Hamilton, Earl; Hartley, Grover; Hasbrook, Ziggy; Hinchman, Bill; Leonard, Joe; McQuillan, George; Menosky, Mike; Ness, Jack; Packard, Gene; Thompson, Shag; Wingo, Ivy; Wortman, Chuck
COMISKEY, CHARLES Cicotte, Eddie; Doolan, Mickey; Hartley, Grover
CONCORDIA SEMINARY Carey, Max
CONN, BILLY Smith, Jimmy
CONNECTICUT Keating, Ray; Lanning, Les; Smith, George; Walsh, Ed
CORNELL COLLEGE Ragan, Pat
CORSICANA, TX Nunamaker, Les
COVELESKI, HARRY O'Neill, Steve
COVELESKI, STAN Coveleski, Harry; O'Neill, Steve
CRANDALL, DOC Williams, Cy
CRAWFORD, SAM Harper, George; Rumler, Bill; Veach, Bobby
CREIGHTON UNIVERSITY Lotz, Joe
CROOKSTON, MN Boone, Luke
CUBA Acosta, Merito; Aragon, Angel; Gonzales, Mike; Marsans, Armando; Palmero, Emilio; Rodriguez, Joe
CUBAN SPORTS HALL OF FAME Acosta, Merito
CUBAN STARS Gonzales, Mike
CUMBERLAND COLLEGE Farmer, Jack

DALLAS, TX Billings, Josh; Bluejacket, Jim; Brainerd, Fred; Dale, Gene; Murphy, Mike
DANVILLE, VA Morgan, Ray; Schultz, Joe
DARTMOUTH COLLEGE Meyers, Chief; Tesreau, Jeff
DAVENPORT, IA Barnes, Jesse; Meyer, Billy; O'Brien, Ray
DAVIDSON COLLEGE Anderson, Fred
DAYTON, OH Bescher, Bob; Brottem, Tony; Hobbs, Bill; Warner, Hooks
DAYTONA BEACH, FL Hartley, Grover
DECATUR, IL McCabe, Tim; Schupp, Ferdie
DELAWARE Killefer, Bill; Lobert, Hans
DENISON TX Hornsby, Rogers
DENMARK Henriksen, Olaf
DENVER, CO Beall, Johnny; Compton, Pete; Dyer, Ben; Hartzell, Roy; Kelleher, John; O'Brien, Ray; Wolfgang, Mellie
DEPAUL UNIVERSITY Wilhoit, Joe
DES MOINES, IA Benz, Joe; Dal-

Index

ton, Jack; Faber, Red; Hasbrook, Ziggy; Jasper, Hi; Leonard, Joe; McAuley, Ike; Sawyer, Carl; Thomas, Claude; Wilson, Owen
DETROIT TIGERS Archer, Jimmy; Ayers, Doc; Baker, Del; Baumann, Paddy; Boehler, George; Boland, Bernie; Burns, George; Bush, Donie; Cicotte, Eddie; Cobb, Ty; Coleman, Bob; Coombs, Jack; Coveleski, Harry; Crawford, Sam; Cunningham, George; Cutshaw, George; Dalton, Jack; Dauss, Hooks; Deal, Charlie; Donovan, Bill; Dubuc, Jean; Dyer, Ben; Ehmke, Howie; Ellison, Bert; Erickson, Eric; Fournier, Jack; Fuller, Frank; Gainer, Del; Hall, Charley; Harper, George; Heilmann, Harry; High, Hugh; James, Bill; Jones, Deacon; Kavanaugh, Marty; Kennedy, Ray; Killefer, Red; Kocher, Brad; Leonard, Dutch; Louden, Baldy; Love, Slim; Lowdermilk, Grover; Maharg, Billy; Maisel, George; McBride, George; McKee, Red; McMullin, Fred; McTigue, Pudge; Mitchell, Clarence; Mitchell, Willie; Moriarty, George; Morrissette, Bill; Ness, Jack; O'Mara, Ollie; O'Neill, Steve; Perritt, Pol; Pipp, Wally; Pratt, Del; Rondeau, Henri; Schaefer, Germany; Schang, Wally; Shorten, Chick; Spencer, Tubby; Stanage, Oscar; Stroud, Sailor; Sullivan, Billy; Veach, Bobby; Vitt, Oscar; Williams, Lefty; Young, Ralph
DICKINSON COLLEGE Bender, Chief
DISTRICT OF COLUMBIA Cantwell, Mike; Foster, Eddie; Judge, Joe; Leonard, Joe; Shaw, Jim
DORAIS, GUS Bergman, Al
DOYLE, LARRY Hooper, Harry
DRAUGHTON BUSINESS COLLEGE Fletcher, Art
DUBUQUE, IA Jasper, Hi
DUKE UNIVERSITY Coombs, Jack
DULUTH, MN Miller, Elmer; Miller, Otto
DUQUESNE UNIVERSITY Mamaux, Al; Smith, Jimmy

DURHAM, NC Meadows, Lee; Thompson, Shag; Whitted, Possum

EARNSHAW, GEORGE Grimes, Burleigh
EAST LIVERPOOL, OH Ritter, Hank
EAST STROUDSBURG STATE NORMAL SCHOOL Mitterling, Ralph
EBBETS, MAIE Cadore, Leon
"EDDIE SULLIVAN" Collins, Eddie
EDINBORO NORMAL SCHOOL Weaver, Harry
EHMKE, HOWARD Picinich, Val
ELMIRA, NY Marsans, Armando
ELON COLLEGE Evans, Bill
EVANSVILLE, IN Roush, Edd
EVERS, JOHNNY Tinker, Joe

FAIRBANKS-MORSE FAIRIES, BELOIT, WI Allison, Milo; Gharrity, Pat; Gunkel, Red; Miller, Elmer; Roth, Braggo; Scott, Jim; Shook, Ray
FAIRMOUNT COLLEGE (WICHITA STATE) Hendrix, Claude
FARGO, ND Allen, Nick; Dumont, George
FLINT, MI Snyder, Frank
FLORIDA Acosta, Merito; Ainsmith, Eddie; Alexander, Walt; Beck, Zinn; Betzel, Bruno; Bush, Joe; Carey, Max; Cheney, Larry; Clemens, Count; Clemons, Vern; Doak, Bill; Doolan, Mickey; Dubuc, Jean; Emmer, Frank; Fisher, Bobby; Gandy, Bob; Good, Wilbur; Hartley, Grover; Hunter, Herb; Kennedy, Ray; Lajoie, Larry; McKechnie, Bill; Meadows, Lee; Merkle, Fred; Mollwitz, Fritz; Moriarty, George; Neale, Greasy; Ness, Jack; Roush, Edd; Shotten, Burt; Speaker, Tris; Stafford, Heinie; Stewart, Stuffy; Tinker, Joe
FONSECA, LOU Bohne, Sammy
FORD, HOD Carroll, Doc
FORD, RUSS Corhan, Roy
FORDHAM UNIVERSITY Egan, Dick; Kopf, Larry; O'Connor, Bucky; Rudolph, Dick
FORT WAYNE, IN Wambsganss, Bill Smyth, Red
FORT WORTH, TX Cooper, Claude; Konetchy, Ed O'Brien, Ray

"FOSTER" Neale, Greasy
FOSTER, RUBE Mayer, Erskine
FRATERNITY OF PROFESSIONAL BASE BALL PLAYERS Clemens, Count; Reulbach, Ed
"FRED BRADY" Kopf, Larry

GALESBURG, IL Mogridge, George
GALVESTON, TX Madden, Gene
GEHRIG, LOU Pipp, Wally; Scott, Everett
GEORGETOWN UNIVERSITY Cantwell, Mike; Judge, Joe
GEORGIA Alexander, Walt; Bagby, Jim; Baird, Doug; Carter, Paul; Cobb, Ty; Fincher, Bill; Lavender, Jim; Mayer, Erskine; Rucker, Nap; Schulte, Wildfire; Smith, Red; Smith, Sherry; Wingo, Ivy
GEORGIA SCHOOL OF TECHNOLOGY Lavender, Jim; Mayer, Erskine
GERMANY Mollwitz, Fritz
GETTYSBURG COLLEGE Plank, Eddie
GIPP, GEORGE Bergman, Al
GIRARD COLLEGE Davis, Harry
GODDARD SEMINARY Shay, Marty
GONZAGA COLLEGE Cadore, Leon
GRAFTON, ND Gainer, Del
GRAHAM, "MOONLIGHT" O'Connor, Bucky
GRAND RAPIDS, MI Pfeffer, Jeff; Sullivan, Billy
GREEN BAY, WI Mollwitz, Fritz
GREENSBORO, NC Crane, Sam
GREENVILLE, NC Beck, Zinn; Jackson, Joe; Wingo, Ivy
GREENWOOD, MS Perritt, Pol
GREGG, DAVE Gregg, Vean
GRIFFITH FAMILY Beck, Zinn; Milan, Clyde
GROVE, LEFTY Grimes, Burleigh
GUILFORD COLLEGE Shore, Ernie
GULFPORT, MS Evans, Joe
GUNKEL, RED Bradley, Jack

HACKENSCHMIDT Miller, Hack
HAGERSTOWN, MD Mowrey, Mike
HAMILTON, OH Hobbs, Bill
HANNAH, TRUCK Walters, Roxy
HARRISBURG, PA Bressler, Rube; Egan, Dick
"HARRY F." Williams, Lefty
HARTFORD, CT Bailey, Fred; Butler, Art; High, Hugh; Wagner, Heinie

Index

HARVARD UNIVERSITY Costello, Dan; McInnis, Stuffy
HAVANA, CUBA Acosta, Merito; Gonzales, Mike; Rodriguez, Joe
HAVERHILL, MA McInnis, Stuffy
HEILMANN, HARRY Veach, Bobby
HERMANN, AUGUST Fisher, Ray
HIGH, ANDY High, Hugh
HIGH, CHARLIE High, Hugh
HINCHMAN, HARRY Hinchman, Bill
HOLLYWOOD, CA Sheehan, Tom
HOOPER, HARRY Henriksen, Olaf; Lewis, Duffy; Speaker, Tris
HOT SPRINGS, AR Vaughn, Hippo
HOUSE OF DAVID Alexander, Pete
HOUSTON, TX Compton, Pete; Foster, Rube; Goodwin, Marv; Killefer, Bill; Schultz, Joe; Stellbauer, Bill
HUGGINS, MILLER Fletcher, Art; Shawkey, Bob
HUNTINGTON, WV Mamaux, Al

IDAHO Cadore, Leon
ILLINOIS Allen, Nick; Archer, Jimmy; Beebe, Fred; Benz, Joe; Bluejacket, Jim; Brainerd, Fred; Brottem, Tony; Cadore, Leon; Cady, Hick; Chappell, Larry; Clemens, Count; Cutshaw, George; Demaree, Al; Doyle, Larry; Dyer, Ben; Faber, Red; Flack, Max; Fletcher, Art; Foster, Eddie; Gleason, Bill; Grimm, Charlie; Groom, Bob; Gunkel, Red; Haley, Pat; Halliday, Newt; Hamilton, Earl; Hendryx, Tim; Howard, Ivan; Johnson, Bill; Johnson, Ernie; Leonard, Joe; Lowdermilk, Grover; McCarthey, Alex; Miller, Ward; Moriarty, George; Ness, Jack; Oeschger, Joe; O'Farrell, Bob; Paulette, Gene; Pearce, George; Pechous, Charles; Pfeffer, Jeff; Pipp, Wally; Prendergast, Mike; Richardson, Jack; Schaefer, Germany; Schalk, Ray; Smith, Jack; Smith, Paul; Smykal, Frank; Stock, Milt; Thomas, Pinch; Vaughn, Hippo; Warmoth, Cy; Weaver, Buck; Williams, Buff; Williams, Lefty; Wilson, Art; Wright, Cy

INDIANA Baumann, Paddy; Benz, Joe; Bergman, Al; Boehler, George; Brown, James Donaldson; Brown, Three Finger; Bush, Donie; Carey, Max; Coleman, Bob; Coveleski, Stan; Crandall, Doc; Dauss, Hooks; Hartley, Grover; Hill, Carmen; Penner, Ken; Rariden, Bill; Russell, Reb; Scott, Everett; Shook, Ray; Tragesser, Walt; Williams, Cy; Zeider, Rollie
INDIANA (PA) NORMAL SCHOOL Menosky, Mike
INDIANA UNIVERSITY Beebe, Fred; Mann, Les
INDIANAPOLIS, IN Baird, Doug; Betzel, Bruno; Blackburn, Earl; Bush, Donie; Carter, Paul; Cicotte, Eddie; Connolly, Joe; Hill, Carmen; Holke, Walter; Kantlehner, Erving; Kelly, Joe; Marquard, Rube; Meadows, Lee; Nabors, Jack; O'Mara, Ollie; Sicking, Eddie; Smith, Jimmy; Steele, Bob; Veach, Bobby
INDIANAPOLIS FEDERALS (HOOSIERS) Kauff, Benny; McKechnie, Bill; Moseley, Earl
IOWA Cady, Hick; Clemons, Vern; Faber, Red; Gould, Al; Haley, Pat; Hasbrook, Ziggy; Lotz, Joe; Moeller, Danny; Ragan, Pat; Severeid, Hank; Wagner, Bill; Williams, Buff
IRELAND Archer, Jimmy; O'Connor, Bucky; Walsh, Jimmy

JACKSON, JOE Klepfer, Ed
JACKSON, MI Deal, Charlie
JACKSONVILLE, FL Cruise, Walton; Fisher, Bobby; Smith, Sherry; Stewart, Stuffy; Whitted, Possum
JACOBSON, BABY DOLL Tobin, Jack
JAMES, BILL James, Bill
JAMES MILLIKIN UNIVERSITY Moeller, Danny; Smith, Paul
JAPANESE BASEBALL Hunter, Herb
JERSEY CITY, NJ Barney, Ed; Donovan, Bill; Foster, Eddie; Gilhooley, Frank; Jamieson, Charlie; Janvrin, Hal; Jourdan, Ted; Lawry, Otis; Lobert, Hans; Morrisette, Bill; Shawkey, Bob

JOHN MARSHALL LAW SCHOOL Welf, Ollie
JOHNSON, BAN Leonard, Dutch; Mays, Carl
JOHNSON, DON Johnson, Ernie
JOHNSON, JING Mitterling, Ralph
JOHNSON, WALTER Ainsmith, Eddie; Bentley, Jack; Bigbee, Carson; Bush, Bullet Joe; Gallia, Bert; McKenry, Limb; Picinich, Val
JOHNSTON, JIMMY Johnston, Doc
JOPLIN, MO Dalton, Jack; Engle, Clyde
JOSS, ADDIE Walsh, Ed

KALAMAZOO, MI Killefer, Red; Koob, Ernie
KANSAS Barnes, Jesse; Billings, Josh; Chapman, Harry; Cheney, Larry; Des Jardien, Shorty; Hagerman, Rip; Hale, George; Hendrix, Claude; Jones, Deacon; Lambeth, Otis; McAuley, Ike; McMullin, Fred; O'Connor, Bucky
KANSAS CITY, MO Billings, Josh; Butler, Art; Carter, Paul; Compton, Pete; Evans, Bill; Gallia, Bert; Good, Wilbur; Knabe, Otto; Lambeth, Otis; Lavan, Doc; Leonard, Joe; Love, Slim; McBride, George; McCarthy, Alex; McCarty, Lew; McConnell, George; Meyer, Billy; Mulligan, Eddie; Pearce, George; Roth, Braggo; Sheehan, Tom; Speaker, Tris; Walker, Tilly; Wortman, Chuck; Zwilling, Dutch
KANSAS CITY FEDERALS (COWBOYS) Agnew, Sam; Cullop, Nick; Packard, Gene
KELLY, REN Kelly, George
KENTUCKY Chapman, Ray; Harper, George; Hobbs, Bill; Mays, Carl; Park, Jim; Schupp, Ferdie; Smith, Elmer; Veach, Bobby; Viox, Jim
KERR, DICKIE Fisher, Ray
KILLEFER, BILL Killefer, Red
KILLEFER, RED Killefer, Bill
KOUFAX, SANDY Rucker, Nap

LACROSSE, WI Konetchy, Ed
LAJOIE, LARRY Connolly, Joe
LAKE CHARLES, LA Nixon, Al
LANSING, MI Saier, Vic
LAWRENCE, MA Ainsmith,

Eddie; Keating, Ray; Knetzer, Elmer
LEIBOLD, NEMO Collins, Shano
"LEW RYAN" Malone, Lew
LEWIS, DUFFY Henrikson, Olaf; Hooper, Harry; Speaker, Tris
LEXINGTON, KY Viox, Jim
LINCOLN, NE Cicotte, Eddie; Lavan, Doc; Mullen, Charlie; Nunamaker, Les; Roush, Edd
LITTLE ROCK, AR Chapman, Harry; Fincher, Bill; Grimm, Charlie; Seaton, Tom; Warmoth, Cy
LOBERT, FRANK Lobert, Hans
LOGAN SQUARES Gunkel, Red
LONG BRANCH CUBANS, NJ Aragon, Angel
LORAS COLLEGE Faber, Red
LOS ANGELES, CA Billings, Josh; Butler, Art; Chase, Hal; Cravath, Gavvy; Crawford, Sam; Daly, Tom; Fabrique, Bunny; Gedeon, Joe; Hamilton, Earl; Howard, Ivan; Jacobs, Elmer; Keating, Ray; Love, Slim; Niehoff, Bert; Rumler, Bill; Spencer, Tubby; Stroud, Sailor; Terry, Zeb; Thomas, Claude; Viox, Jim; Wheat, Mack
LOUISIANA Davenport, Dave; Farmer, Jack; Fincher, Bill; Harmon, Bob; Jourdan, Ted; Nixon, Al; Perritt, Pol
LOUISVILLE, KY Acosta, Merito; Betzel, Bruno; Brottem, Tony; Bush, Donie; Cheney, Larry; Clemons, Vern; Herzog, Buck; Koob, Ernie; McCabe, Tim; Meyer, Billy; Perry, Scott; Schauer, Rube; Smith, Paul; Toney, Fred
LOUISVILLE COLONELS Davis, Harry; Wagner, Honus
LOWDERMILK, LOU Lowdermilk, Grover
LOWELL, MA Daly, Tom; Tyler, Lefty
LYTER, DELLA Crane, Sam

MACK, CONNIE Baker, Frank; Barry, Jack; Bender, Chief; Bush, Joe; Crane, Sam; Divis, Moxie; Grimes, Burleigh; Healy, Tom; Lapp, Jack; McInnis, Stuffy; Meyer, Billy; Schang, Wally; Witt, Whitey; Wyckoff, Weldon
MACON, GA Benton, Rube; Scott, Jack
MAILS, DUSTER Smith, Sherry

MAINE Carrigan, Bill; Lawry, Otis; McElwee, Lee; Picinich, Val; Rowe, Harland
MAISEL, FRITZ Maisel, George
MANHATTAN COLLEGE Chalmers, George
MARQUARD, RUBE Leonard, Dutch
MARSHALL COLLEGE Fisher, Wilbur
MARSHALTOWN, IA Des Jardien, Shorty; Penner, Ken
MARYLAND Adams, Babe; Baker, Frank; Beall, Johnny; Bentley, Jack; Brown, Don; Cantwell, Mike; Danforth, Dave; Herzog, Buck; Jacobson, Merwyn; Johnson, Walter; Maisel, Fritz; Maisel, George; Malone, Lew; Marquard, Rube; McCarthey, Alex; Morgan, Ray; Morrissette, Bill; Rice, Sam; Russell, Allan; Ruth, Babe; Wortman, Chuck
MASSACHUSETTS Ainsmith, Eddie; Barry, Jack; Butler, Art; Carroll, Doc; Coleman, Bob; Collins, Eddie; Collins, Shano; Crowell, Cap; Daly, Tom; Donovan, Bill; Driscoll, Mike; Engle, Clyde; Gleason, Bill; Henriksen, Olaf; Henry, John; Hunter, Herb; Janvrin, Hal; Kelleher, John; King, Lee; McInnis, Stuffy; Rico, Art; Shay, Marty; Twombly, George; Tyler, Lefty; Whittaker, Walt
MASSILLON TIGERS Blackburn, Earl
MATHEWSON, CHRISTY Ames, Red; Plank, Eddie
MATHEWSON, HENRY Mathewson, Christy
"MAX TERRY'S TRAVELING ALL-GIRLS TEAM" Bancroft, Dave
MAYS, CARL Chapman, Ray
MAYSVILLE, KY Weilman, Carl
MCGINNITY, IRON MAN Ames, Red
MCGRAW, JOHN Bancroft, Dave; Doolan, Mickey; Egan, Dick; Palmero, Emilio; Robertson, Dave; Snodgrass, Fred; Stafford, Heinie; Tesreau, Jeff
MCKEESPORT, PA Caldwell, Ray
MEDICAL COLLEGE OF VIRGINIA Ayers, Doc
MEDICINE HAT, ALBERTA Buckles, Jess

MEMPHIS, TN Adams, Jack; Allen, Frank; Allison, Milo; Aragon, Angel; Barbare, Walter; Barber, Turner; Cook, Doc; Daubert, Jake; Lohr, Howie; Love, Slim; Warmoth, Cy
MERKLE, FRED Snodgrass, Fred
MEUSEL, BOB Witt, Whitey
MEYERS, CHIEF Wilson, Art
MICHIGAN Altenburg, Jesse; Boland, Bernie; Cicotte, Eddie; Fabrique, Bunny; Fisher, Ray; Fournier, Jack; Fuller, Frank; James, Bill; Kavanaugh, Marty; Killefer, Bill; Killefer, Red; Koob, Ernie; Lavan, Doc; Leibold, Nemo; McKee, Red; Menosky, Mike; Miller, Frank; Pipp, Wally; Saier, Vic; Stanage, Oscar; Veach, Bobby
MIDDLEBURY COLLEGE Fisher, Ray
MILAN, HORACE Milan, Clyde
MILLER, OTTO Rumler, Bill
MILWAUKEE, WI Beall, Johnny; Chappell, Larry; Felsch, Happy; Goodwin, Marv; Leibold, Nemo; Magee, Sherry; Schaefer, Germany; Schalk, Ray; Smyth, Red; Strunk, Amos; Williams, Steamboat
MILWAUKEE BREWERS McBride, George
MINNEAPOLIS, MN Bancroft, Dave; Benton, Rube; Bush, Donie; Craft, Molly; Cravath, Gavvy; Dumont, George; Gharrity, Pat; Hall, Charley; Henry, John; James, Bill; Jourdan, Ted; Killefer, Red; Magee, Sherry; McAuley, Ike; McKechnie, Bill; Menosky, Mike; Perritt, Pol; Rondeau, Henri; Russell, Reb; Sawyer, Carl; Schultz, Joe; Sicking, Eddie; Smith, Elmer; Thomas, Claude
MINNEAPOLIS TWINS Beck, Zinn
MINNESOTA Bender, Chief; Brottem, Tony; Bush, Joe; Cunningham, George; Dumont, George; Fautsch, Joe; Gandil, Chick; Schauer, Rube; Williams, Steamboat; Wright, Cy
MISSION, CA Schmidt, Walter
MISSISSIPPI Evans, Joe; Love, Slim; Mitchell, Willie; Smyth, Red
MISSISSIPPI A&M COLLEGE (MIS-

Index

sissippi State) Mitchell, Willie
Missoula, MT Bush, Joe
Missouri Adams, Babe; Baird, Doug; Byrne, Bobby; Chapman, Harry; Compton, Pete; Dale, Gene; Dauss, Hooks; Graney, Jack; Grimm, Charlie; Harmon, Bob; High, Hugh; Hofman, Solly; Holke, Walter; Jacobs, Elmer; Jasper, Hi; Kelly, Joe; Koob, Ernie; Mathes, Joe; McCabe, Tim; Mulligan, Eddie; O'Brien, Ray; Olson, Ivy; O'Mara, Ollie; Perry, Scott; Schang, Wally; Sisler, George; Stengel, Casey; Tesreau, Jeff; Tobin, Jack; Wheat, Mack; Wheat, Zack; Zwilling, Dutch
Mitchell, Clarence Rumler, Bill
Mobile, CA Allen, Frank; Baker, Del; Demaree, Al; Hasbrook, Ziggy; Hendryx, Tim; Henry, John; Huhn, Emil; Love, Slim; Miller, Elmer; Morrisette, Bill; Niehoff, Bert; Robertson, Dave; Schultz, Joe; Stock, Milt; Wheat, Zack
Montana Williams, Steamboat
Montgomery, AL Pratt, Del; Stengel, Casey
Montreal, Quebec Betzel, Bruno; Burns, Ed; Cadore, Leon; Clarke, Tommy; Connolly, Joe; Dale, Gene; Gilhooley, Frank; Hughes, Tom; Maisel, George; McTigue, Pudge; Miller, Frank; Miller, Ward; Smith, Paul; Smyth, Red
Moose Jaw, Saskatchewan Fournier, Jack
Moriarty, Bill Moriarty, George
Morristown, TN Markle, Cliff
Morton, Guy, Jr. Morton, Guy
Most Valuable Player Burns, George; Hornsby, Rogers; O'Farrell, Bob; Peckinpaugh, Roger; Schulte, Wildfire
Mount St. Mary's College Costello, Dan; Morrissette, Bill
Mount Union College Moseley, Earl
Muscatine, IA Hasbrook, Ziggy

Nashville, TN Boland, Bernie; Farmer, Jack; Lee, Billy; Lindstrom, Axel; O'Brien, Ray; Paskert, Dode; Paulette, Gene; Smith, Red; Toney, Fred
Nebraska Alexander, Pete; Beebe, Fred; Brown, James Donaldson; Crawford, Sam; Mann, Les; Miller, Otto; Mitchell, Clarence; Nunamaker, Les; Prendergast, Mike; Rumler, Bill; Seaton, Tom
Nebraska Wesleyan University Scott, Jim
Nevada Dell, Wheezer; O'Mara, Ollie; Thomas, Claude; Wortman, Chuck
New Bedford, MA Griffith, Tommy; Maranville, Rabbit; McTigue, Pudge
New Britain, CT Marsans, Armando
New England School of Baseball Ainsmith, Eddie
New Hampshire Lewis, Duffy; Tesreau, Jeff; Tyler, Lefty
New Haven, CT Boehling, Joe; Donovan, Bill; Meyers, Chief; Shay, Marty
New Jersey Fitzpatrick, Ed; Getz, Gus; Harper, Harry; Jamieson, Charlie; Lee, Billy; Myers, Elmer; Oldring, Rube; Stroud, Sailor; Witt, Whitey
New London, CT Fortune, Gary
New Mexico Barnes, Jesse; Hagerman, Rip
New Orleans, LA Allison, Milo; Bagby, Jim; Barbare, Walter; Cullop, Nick; Deal, Charlie; Hendryx, Tim; Jackson, Joe; Smith, Popboy; Thrasher, Buck
New York Aragon, Angel; Burns, George; Caldwell, Ray; Chalmers, George; Chapman, Ray; Clarke, Tommy; Collins, Zip; Coumbe, Fritz; Dede, Arte; Donovan, Bill; Dooin, Red; Doyle, Larry; Erickson, Eric; Evers, Johnny; Fischer, Bill; Groh, Heinie; Hickman, Jim; Huggins, Miller; Judge, Joe; Kelleher, Duke; Madden, Gene; Malone, Lew; Maranville, Rabbit; Mathewson, Christy; McHale, Marty; McQuillan, George; Miller, Dots; Miller, Otto; Mogridge, George; Murphy, Mike; Pennock, Herb; Reulbach, Ed; Rudolph, Dick; Ruth, Babe; Schaefer, Germany; Shawkey, Bob; Wagner, Heinie; Walsh, Jimmy; Weaver, Harry; Wendell, Lew; Wolfgang, Mellie; Zimmerman, Heinie
New York Giants Ainsmith, Eddie; Ames, Red; Anderson, Fred; Aragon, Angel; Baird, Doug; Bancroft, Dave; Barnes, Jesse; Bentley, Jack; Benton, Rube; Bescher, Bob; Bluejacket, Jim; Brainerd, Fred; Burns, George; Chase, Hal; Clarke, Tommy; Compton, Pete; Cooper, Claude; Crandall, Doc; Davis, Harry; Deberry, Hank; Demaree, Al; Dooin, Red; Doyle, Larry; Dubuc, Jean; Dyer, Ben; Erickson, Eric; Evers, Johnny; Fletcher, Art; Gibson, George; Gonzales, Mike; Gowdy, Hank; Grimes, Burleigh; Groh, Heinie; Harper, George; Hartley, Grover; Herzog, Buck; Hill, Carmen; Holke, Walter; Hunter, Herb; Jacobson, Merwyn; Kauff, Benny; Kelleher, Duke; Kelly, George; Killefer, Red; King, Lee; Kocher, Brad; Lobert, Hans; Marquard, Rube; Mathewson, Christy; Mays, Carl; McCarty, Lew; Merkle, Fred; Meyers, Chief; Mitchell, Clarence; Nehf, Art; Niehoff, Bert; Oeschger, Joe; O'Farrell, Bob; Olson, Ivy; Palmero, Emilio; Paulette, Gene; Pearce, George; Perritt, Pol; Ragan, Pat; Rariden, Bill; Ritter, Hank; Robertson, Dave; Rodriguez, Joe; Roush, Edd; Rudolph, Dick; Sallee, Slim; Schaefer, Germany; Schalk, Ray; Schauer, Rube; Schupp, Ferdie; Scott, Jack; Seibold, Socks; Sheehan, Tom; Shore, Ernie; Smith, George; Smith, Jimmy; Snodgrass, Fred; Snyder, Frank; Stafford, Heinie; Steele, Bob; Stengel, Casey; Stock, Milt; Stroud, Sailor; Tesreau, Jeff; Toney, Fred; Wagner, Heinie; Wendell, Lew; Wilhoit, Joe; Wilson, Art; Zimmerman, Heinie
New York Journal-American Baseball School Maranville, Rabbit

NEW YORK METS Zwilling, Dutch
NEW YORK SCHOOL OF BASEBALL Ainsmith, Eddie
NEW YORK UNIVERSITY Mitterling, Ralph
NEW YORK YANKEES Alexander, Walt; Aragon, Angel; Austin, Jimmy; Baker, Frank; Barney, Ed; Baumann, Paddy; Bender, Chief; Betzel, Bruno; Boone, Luke; Buckles, Jess; Bush, Joe; Caldwell, Ray; Cantwell, Mike; Chase, Hal; Cook, Doc; Costello, Dan; Coveleski, Stan; Cullop, Nick; Donovan, Bill; Engle, Clyde; Fisher, Ray; Fletcher, Art; Foster, Eddie; Gedeon, Joe; Gilhooley, Frank; Good, Wilbur; Grimes, Burleigh; Grover, Roy; Harper, Harry; Hartzell, Roy; Hendryx, Tim; High, Hugh; Hofman, Solly; Huggins, Miller; Hughes, Tom; Johnson, Ernie; Jones, Sam; Kauff, Benny; Keating, Ray; Klepfer, Ed; Lewis, Duffy; Louden, Baldy; Love, Slim; Magee, Lee; Maisel, Fritz; Markle, Cliff; Mays, Carl; McConnell, George; McHale, Marty; McNally, Mike; Merkle, Fred; Miller, Elmer; Mogridge, George; Moriarty, George; Mullen, Charlie; Niehoff, Bert; Nunamaker, Les; Oldring, Rube; Peckinpaugh, Roger; Pennock, Herb; Pipp, Wally; Pratt, Del; Roth, Braggo; Russell, Allan; Ruth, Babe; Schang, Wally; Schneider, Pete; Schulz, Al; Scott, Deacon; Seveerid, Hank; Shanks, Howard; Shawkey, Bob; Sheehan, Tom ; Shocker, Urban; Shore, Ernie; Smith, Elmer; Stengel, Casey; Tincup, Ben; Vaughn, Hippo; Walsh, Jimmy; Walters, Roxy; Witt, Whitey; Young, Ralph; Zeider, Rollie; Zwilling, Dutch
NEWARK, NJ Appleton Ed; Cady, Hick; Dalton, Jack; Engle, Clyde; Getz, Gus; Kennedy, Ray; Lapp, Jack; Louden, Baldy; Mamaux, Al; McCarty, Lew; Rariden, Bill; Shawkey, Bob; Shorten, Chick; Stanage, Oscar; Walsh, Ed
NEWARK FEDERALS (PEPPERS) Huhn, Emil; Moseley, Earl; Rariden, Bill; Reulbach, Ed
NIAGARA UNIVERSITY Keating, Ray Walsh, Jimmy
NORFOLK, VA Craft, Molly; Mathewson, Christy
NORTH CAROLINA Anderson, Fred; Benton, Rube; Coombs, Jack; Currie, Murphy; Evans, Bill; Fortune, Gary; Lindstrom, Axel; Meadows, Lee; Ray, Carl; Scott, Jack; Shore, Ernie; Thompson, Shag; Whitted, Possum; Williams, Marsh
NORTH CAROLINA STATE COLLEGE Evans, Bill; Robertson, Dave; Williams, Marsh
NORTHERN ILLINOIS STATE NORMAL SCHOOL Miller, Ward
NORWICH COLLEGE McInnis, Stuffy
NOTRE DAME UNIVERSITY Bergman, Al; Clemens, Count; Cutshaw, George; Dubuc, Jean; McCarthey, Alex; Reulbach, Ed; Walsh, Ed; Williams, Cy
NUNAMAKER, LES Rumler, Bill; Walters, Roxy

OAKLAND, Ca Baker, Del; Boehling, Joe; Bohne, Sammy; Cook, Doc; Cooper, Claude; Crandall, Doc; Cutshaw, George; Elliott, Rowdy; Flack, Max; Grover, Roy; Guisto, Lou; Howard, Ivan; Lewis, Duffy; Miller, Hack; Ness, Jack; Zwilling, Dutch
OBERLIN COLLEGE DesJardien, Shorty
OHIO Ames, Red; Batsch, Bill; Bescher, Bob; Betzel, Bruno; Blackburn, Earl; Bressler, Rube; Carpenter, Paul; Daubert, Jake; Divis, Moxie; Dooin, Red; Emmer, Frank; Engle, Clyde; Gilhooley, Frank; Gowdy, Hank; Graney, Jack; Griffith, Tommy; Groh, Heinie; Healy, Tom; Hinchman, Bill; Hobbs, Bill; Huggins, Miller; Jones, Sam; Kauff, Benny; Kopf, Larry; Magee, Lee; Marquard, Rube; McNally, Mike; McQuillan, George; Moseley, Earl; Myers, Hy; O'Neill, Steve; Palmero, Emilio; Paskert, Dode; Peckinpaugh, Roger; Ritter, Hank; Rixey, Eppa; Rodgers, Bill; Sallee, Slim; Schulz, Al; Sheehan, Tom; Shook, Ray; Sicking, Eddie; Smith, Earl; Smith, Elmer; Turner, Terry; Viox, Jim; Wambsganss, Bill; Weilman, Carl; Welf, Ollie
OHIO STATE UNIVERSITY Welf, Ollie
OKLAHOMA Barnes, Jesse; Bluejacket, Jim; Bradley, Jack; Foster, Rube; Klepfer, Ed; Thomas, Claude; Tincup, Ben
OKLAHOMA A&M COLLEGE Billings, Josh
OKLAHOMA CITY, OK Divis, Moxie
OMAHA, NE Austin, Jimmy; Brown, Three-Finger; O'Brien, Ray; Ragan, Pat; Smith, Earl
"$100,000 INFIELD" Baker, Frank; Barry, Jack; Collins, Eddie; McInnis, Stuffy; Oldring, Rube
O'NEILL, JACK McNally, Mike; O'Neill, Steve
O'NEILL, JIM McNally, Mike; O'Neill, Steve
O'NEILL, MIKE McNally, Mike; O'Neill, Steve
O'NEILL, STEVE Daubert, Jake; McNally, Mike
OPELOUSAS, LA Nixon, Al
OREGON Baker, Del; Bigbee, Carson; Egan, Dick; Grover, Roy; Howard, Ivan; Sullivan, Billy; Williams, Ken
OREN, JACK Crane, Sam
OSHKOSH, WI Lotz, Joe
OTTAWA, ONTARIO Shocker, Urban; Smykal, Frank
OTTUMWA, IA Johnston, Jimmy
OWENSBORO, KY Halliday, Newt

PARIS TX Watson, Milt
PAWTUCKET, RI Davis, Harry
PENNSYLVANIA Baumgartner, Stan; Bender, Chief; Boone, Luke; Bressler, Rube; Burns, George; Caldwell, Ray; Cooper, Wilbur; Costello, Dan; Coveleski, Harry; Coveleski, Stan; Crane, Sam; Daubert, Jake; Davis, Harry; Deal, Charlie; Doak, Bill; Doolan, Mickey; Ehmke, Howie; Fitzpatrick, Ed; Getz, Gus; Good, Wilbur; Healy, Tom; Hesselbacher, George; Johnson, Jing; Kennedy, Ray; Knabe, Otto; Knetzer, Elmer; Kocher, Brad; Lapp, Jack;

Lee, Billy; Lobert, Hans; Lohr, Howie; Magee, Sherry; Maharg, Billy; Mamaux, Al; Markle, Cliff; Mathewson, Christy; McCarty, Lew; McKechnie, Bill; McNally, Mike; Mitterling, Ralph; Mowrey, Mike; Murphy, Eddie; O'Neill, Steve; Parnham, Rube; Plank, Eddie; Ritter, Hank; Seibold, Socks; Shanks, Howard; Shorten, Chick; Smith, Jimmy; Strunk, Amos; Twining, Twink; Wagner, Honus; Warner, Hooks; Weiser, Bud; Wyckoff, Weldon; Yerkes, Steve; Young, Ralph

PENNSYLVANIA STATE UNIVERSITY Hesselbacher, George; Klepfer, Ed

PEORIA, IL Flack, Max; Hartzell, Roy; Pechous, Charles; Prendergast, Mike

PFEFFER, "BIG JEFF" Pfeffer, Jeff

PHILADELPHIA A'S Acosta, Merito; Baker, Frank; Barry, Jack; Baumgartner, Stan; Bender, Chief; Betzel, Bruno; Bressler, Rube; Brown, Don; Burns, George; Bush, Joe; Carroll, Doc; Cobb, Ty; Collins, Eddie; Collins, Zip; Coombs, Jack; Coveleski, Stan; Crane, Sam; Crowell, Cap; Danforth, Dave; Davis, Harry; Divis, Moxie; Driscoll, Mike; Ehmke, Howie; Gardner, Larry; Gregg, Vean; Grimm, Charlie; Grover, Roy; Haley, Pat; Healy, Tom; Hesselbacher, George; Jackson, Joe; Jamieson, Charlie; Johnson, Bill; Johnson, Jing; King, Lee; Kopf, Larry; Lajoie, Larry; Lanning, Les; Lapp, Jack; Lawry, Otis; Lindstrom, Axel; Malone, Lew; Mathes, Joe; Mays, Carl; McElwee, Lee; McInnis, Stuffy; Meyer, Billy; Mitterling, Ralph; Morrissette, Bill; Murphy, Eddie; Murphy, Mike; Myers, Elmer; Nabors, Jack; Oldring, Rube; Parnham, Rube; Pennock, Herb; Perry, Scott; Picinich, Val; Pick, Charlie; Plank, Eddie; Ray, Carl; Richardson, Jack; Rowe, Harland; Schang, Wally; Schauer, Rube; Seibold, Socks; Shawkey, Bob;

Sheehan, Tom; Stellbauer, Bill; Strunk, Amos; Thompson, Shag; Thrasher, Buck; Turner, Terry; Walker, Tilly; Walsh, Jimmy; Weaver, Harry; Wheat, Zack; Whittaker, Walt; Williams, Marsh; Witt, Whitey; Wyckoff, Weldon; Young, Ralph

PHILADELPHIA PHILLIES Adams, Jack; Alexander, Pete; Ames, Red; Bancroft, Dave; Baumgartner, Stan; Buckles, Jess; Burns, Ed; Burns, George; Byrne, Bobby; Cady, Hick; Cantwell, Mike; Chalmers, George; Cheney, Larry; Coombs, Jack; Cooper, Claude; Coveleski, Harry; Cravath, Gavvy; Demaree, Al; Donovan, Bill; Dooin, Red; Doolan, Mickey; Dugey, Oscar; Fletcher, Art; Fortune, Gary; Gallia, Bert; Gandy, Bob; Hamilton, Earl; Holke, Walter; Jacobs, Elmer; Kantlehner, Elmer; Killefer, Bill; King, Lee; Knabe, Otto; Konetchy, Ed; Lajoie, Larry; Lavender, Jim; Lobert, Hans; Luderus, Fred; Magee, Sherry; Maharg, Billy; Mayer, Erskine; McInnis, Stuffy; McQuillan, George; Meadows, Lee; Miller, Dots; Mitchell, Clarence; Morgan, Ray; Neale, Greasy; Niehoff, Bert; Nixon, Al; Oeschger, Joe; O'Neill, Steve; Packard, Gene; Paskert, Dode; Paulette, Gene; Pennock, Herb; Prendergast, Mike; Ragan, Pat; Ritter, Hank; Rixey, Eppa; Scott, Jack; Seaton, Tom; Seibold, Socks; Shotten, Burt; Smith, George; Smith, Jimmy; Stock, Milt; Tincup, Ben; Tragesser, Walt; Watson, Milt; Weiser, Bud; Wendell, Lew; Wheat, Mack; Whitted, Possum; Williams, Cy

PINELLI, BABE Bohne, Sammy

PITTSBURGH FEDERALS (REBELS) Allen, Frank; Knetzer, Elmer; Konetchy, Ed; Menosky, Mike; Mowrey, Mike; Yerkes, Steve

PITTSBURGH PIRATES Adams, Babe; Altenburg, Jesse; Archer, Jimmy; Bagby, Jim; Baird, Doug; Barbare, Walter; Barney, Ed; Batsch, Bill; Bigbee, Carson; Blackburn, Earl; Boehler, George; Brottem, Tony; Bush, Donie; Butler, Art; Byrne, Bobby; Carey, Max; Carpenter, Paul; Coleman, Bob; Collins, Zip; Compton, Pete; Cooper, Wilbur; Costello, Dan; Cutshaw, George; Davis, Harry; Evans, Bill; Farmer, Jack; Fischer, Bill; Fisher, Wilbur; Getz, Gus; Gibson, George; Gleason, Bill; Grimes, Burleigh; Grimm, Charlie; Halliday, Newt; Hamilton, Earl; Harmon, Bob; Hartley, Grover; Hendrix, Claude; Hill, Carmen; Hinchman, Bill; Hofman, Solly; Jacobs, Elmer; Johnston, Doc; Kantlehner, Elmer; Kelly, Joe; Kennedy, Ray; King, Lee; Knabe, Otto; Konetchy, Ed; Leonard, Joe; Lobert, Hans; Madden, Gene; Mamaux, Al; Maranville, Rabbit; Mayer, Erskine; McAuley, Ike; McBride, George; McCarthey, Alex; McInnis, Stuffy; McKechnie, Bill; McQuillan, George; Meadows, Lee; Meyer, Billy; Miller, Dots; Miller, Frank; Miller, Ward; Mollwitz, Fritz; Mowrey, Mike; Mulligan, Eddie; Murphy, Eddie; O'Brien, Ray; Pfeffer, Jeff; Picinich, Val; Robertson, Dave; Russell, Reb; Saier, Vic; Schmidt, Walter; Schulte, Wildfire; Schultz, Joe; Scott, Jack; Sheehan, Tom; Sicking, Eddie; Siglin, Paddy; Smith, Jimmy; Smith, Sherry; Smykal, Frank; Stanage, Oscar; Steele, Bob; Stewart, Stuffy; Stock, Milt; Terry, Zeb; Tincup, Ben; Turner, Terry; Viox, Jim; Wagner, Bill; Wagner, Honus; Warner, Hooks; Whitted, Possum; Wilson, Art; Wilson, Owen

PITTSFIELD, MA Collins, Shano; Fortune, Gary; Wilson, Art

POCAHONTAS FUEL, VA Cullop, Nick

PORTLAND, OR Baker, Del; Bancroft, Dave; Coveleski, Stan; Evans, Joe; Farmer, Jack; Fincher, Bill; Graney, Jack; Gregg, Vean; Groom, Bob; Guisto, Lou; Hagerman,

Rip; Heilmann, Harry; James, Bill; Johnson, Ernie; Jones, Deacon; King, Lee; Maisel, George; Olson, Ivy; Rodgers, Bill; Seaton, Tom; Siglin, Paddy; Smith, Elmer; Tinker, Joe; Wendell, Lew; Williams, Ken

PORTSMOUTH VA Gandy, Bob; Mayer, Erskine

PRATT, DEL Lavan, Doc

PRESBYTERIAN COLLEGE Williams, Marsh

"PRIDE OF THE YANKEES" Ruth, Babe

PRINCETON UNIVERSITY Kelleher, Duke

PROVIDENCE, RI Butler, Art; Donovan, Bill; Fabrique, Bunny; Gregg, Vean; Haley, Pat; Kocher, Brad; Lavender, Jim; McQuillan, George; McTigue, Pudge; Rico, Art

PROVIDENCE COLLEGE Connolly, Joe

PURDUE UNIVERSITY Killefer, Red; Tragesser, Walt

QUINCY, IL Zwilling, Dutch

RACINE, WI Shook, Ray

RALEIGH, NC Myers, Elmer; Parnham, Rube

RARIDEN, BILL Wingo, Ivy

RAWLINGS SPORTING GOODS Doak, Bill

READING, PA Dooin, Red; Herzog, Buck; Maisel, George; McCarty, Lew; Shorten, Chick

RHODE ISLAND Connolly, Joe; Crowell, Cap; Driscoll, Mike; Lajoie, Larry; Rondeau, Henri

RICE INSTITUTE Mann, Les

RICHMOND, VA Aragon, Angel; Fautsch, Joe; Morrisette, Bill; Russell, Allen

RICKEY, BRANCH Clemons, Vern; Shotten, Burt

ROBERTSON, WILBERT Mails, Duster

ROBINSON, JACKIE Shotten, Burt

ROCHESTER, NY Dooin, Red; Foster, Eddie; Hughes, Tom; Maranville, Rabbit; Merkle, Fred; Pipp, Wally; Tyler, Lefty

ROCK HILL COLLEGE Cantwell, Mike

ROCKFORD, IL Shook, Ray

ROCKNE, KNUT Bergman, Al

RONDEAU, HENRI Connolly, Joe

ROSE POLYTECHNIC INSTITUTE Nehf, Art

ROTH, FRANK Roth, Braggo

ROUND THE WORLD TOUR Daly, Tom; Doolan, Mickey; Egan, Dick; Faber, Red

RUNYON, DAMON McHale, Marty

RUSIE, AMOS Bush, Bullet Joe

RUSSELL, LEFTY Russell, Allan

RUSSIA Schauer, Rube

RUTH, BABE Agnew, Sam; Smith, Sherry; Witt, Whitey

SACRAMENTO, CA Baker, Del; Jones, Deacon; Keating, Ray; Mails, Duster; Mollwitz, Fritz; Peckinpaugh, Roger; Pick, Charlie; Siglin, Paddy; Stroud, Sailor; Thomas, Pinch; Watson, Milt; Young, Ralph

SAGINAW, MI McKee, Red; Nunamaker, Les

ST. CLOUD, MN Bancroft, Dave

ST. EDWARD'S COLLEGE Killefer, Bill

ST. FRANCIS COLLEGE (NY) Malone, Lew

ST. IGNATIUS COLLEGE (LOYOLA UNIVERSITY) Pechous, Charles; Stock, Milt

ST. JOHN'S UNIVERSITY Gilhooley, Frank

ST. JOSEPH, MO Corhan, Roy; Jourdan, Ted; Kelly, Joe; Zwilling, Dutch

ST. JOSEPH'S COLLEGE (PA) Young, Ralph

ST. LOUIS BROWNS Agnew, Sam; Alexander, Walt; Austin, Jimmy; Baumgardner, George; Billings, Josh; Boehler, George; Borton, Babe; Chapman, Harry; Clemens, Count; Clemons, Vern; Compton, Pete; Crandall, Doc; Cullop, Nick; Danforth, Dave; Davenport, Dave; Evans, Joe; Fincher, Bill; Foster, Eddie; Fournier, Jack; Gallia, Bert; Gedeon, Joe; Gleason, Bill; Groom, Bob; Hale, George; Hamilton, Earl; Hartley, Grover; Hartzell, Roy; Hendryx, Tim; Holke, Walter; Hornsby, Rogers; Howard, Ivan; James, Bill; Kennedy, Ray; Killefer, Bill; Koob, Ernie; Lavan, Doc; Lee, Billy; Lowdermilk, Grover; Magee, Lee; Maisel, Fritz; Maisel, George; Marsans, Armando; McCabe, Tim; Miller, Ward; Nunamaker, Les; Palmero, Emilio; Park, Jim; Paulette, Gene; Perry, Scott; Plank, Eddie; Pratt, Del; Rumler, Bill; Schang, Wally; Severeid, Hank; Shocker, Urban; Shorten, Chick; Shotten, Burt; Sisler, George; Smith, Earl; Spencer, Tubby; Thomas, Pinch; Tobin, Jack; Walker, Tilly; Wallace, Bobby; Weilman, Carl; Williams, Ken

ST. LOUIS CARDINALS Adams, Babe; Ainsmith, Eddie; Alexander, Pete; Ames, Red; Baird, Doug; Beall, Johnny; Beck, Zinn; Beebe, Fred; Bescher, Bob; Betzel, Bruno; Bohne, Sammy; Bressler, Rube; Brottem, Tony; Brown, Don; Brown, Three Finger; Burns, Ed; Butler, Art; Byrne, Bobby; Clemons, Vern; Corhan, Roy; Cruise, Walton; Currie, Murphy; Dale, Gene; Dell, Wheezer; Doak, Bill; Fisher, Bobby; Flack, Max; Fournier, Jack; Gainer, Del; Gilhooley, Frank; Gonzales, Mike; Goodwin, Marv; Grimes, Burleigh; Griner, Dan; Hall, Charley; Harmon, Bob; Harper, George; Hornsby, Rogers; Huggins, Miller; Hunter, Herb; Jacobs, Elmer; Janvrin, Hal; Jasper, Hi; Kavanaugh, Marty; Kelleher, John; Killefer, Bill; Konetchy, Ed; Lavan, Doc; Long, Tommy; Lotz, Joe; Magee, Lee; Maranville, Rabbit; Mathes, Joe; McAuley, Ike; McBride, George; McCarty, Lew; McKechnie, Bill; Meadows, Lee; Miller, Dots; Miller, Elmer; Mitchell, Clarence; Mowrey, Mike; Murphy, Mike; Myers, Hy; O'Farrell, Bob; Packard, Gene; Paulette, Gene; Pearce, George; Penner, Ken; Perritt, Pol; Pfeffer, Jeff; Sallee, Slim; Schmidt, Walter; Schultz, Joe; Schupp, Ferdie; Shotten, Burt; Smith, Jack; Smyth, Red; Snyder, Frank; Steele, Bob; Stewart, Stuffy; Stock, Milt; Toney, Fred; Wallace,

Bobby; Warmoth, Cy; Watson, Milt; Whitted, Possum; Williams, Steamboat; Wilson, Owen; Wingo, Ivy
ST. LOUIS FEDERALS (TERRIERS) Borton, Babe; Chapman, Harry; Compton, Pete; Crandall, Doc; Davenport, Dave; Deal, Charlie; Groom, Bob; Hartley, Grover; Marsans, Armando; Mathes, Joe; Miller, Ward; Plank, Eddie; Tobin, Jack
SAINT LOUIS UNIVERSITY Mulligan, Eddie
ST. MARY'S COLLEGE (CA) Burns, Ed; Guisto, Lou; Heilmann, Harry; Hooper, Harry; Leonard, Dutch; Lewis, Duffy; Mails, Duster; Oeschger, Joe
ST. MARY'S INSTITUTE (TX) Gallia, Bert
ST. MICHAEL'S COLLEGE Archer, Jimmy
ST. PAUL, MN Allen, Nick; Coumbe, Fritz; Dauss, George; Dugey, Oscar; Griner, Dan; Hendryx, Tim; Malone, Lew; Markle, Cliff; Meyers, Chief; Schaefer, Germany; Scott, Deacon; Sheehan, Tom; Shorten, Chick; Spencer, Tubby; Steele, Bob; Williams, Steamboat
ST. VINCENT COLLEGE (LOYOLA MARYMOUNT); Buckles, Jess; Snodgrass, Fred
SALEM, MA McInnis, Stuffy
SALLEE, SLIM Cicotte, Eddie
SALT LAKE CITY, UT Dale, Gene; Gedeon, Joe; Jourdan, Ted; Lynn, Byrd; Markle, Cliff; McCabe, Tim; Mulligan, Eddie; Rumler, Bill; Siglin, Paddy; Spencer, Tubby; Tobin, Jack; Wilhoit, Joe; Williams, Lefty
SAN ANTONIO, TX Davenport, Dave; Fuller, Frank; Henry, John; Mitchell, Willie
SAN DIEGO, CA Baker, Del
SAN FRANCISCO, CA Agnew, Sam; Baker, Del; Bohne, Sammy; Compton, Pete; Corhan, Roy; Dalton, Jack; Ellison, Bert; Erickson, Eric; Gedeon, Joe; Hasbrook, Ziggy; Heilmann, Harry; Hendryx, Tim; Jacobs, Elmer; Johnston, Jimmy; Kantlehner, Erving; Mails, Duster; Maisel, George; Miller, Dots; Miller, Frank; Seaton, Tom; Siglin, Paddy; Vitt, Oscar; Zeider, Rollie
SAN JOSE STATE COLLEGE Grover, Roy
SANTA CLARA UNIVERSITY Chase, Hal; Kantlehner, Erv
SAVANNAH, GA Mowrey, Mike; Schulz, Al
SCHACHT, AL Schaefer, Germany
SCHALK, RAY Lynn, Byrd
SCHMIDT, "BOSS" Schmidt, Walter
SCHULTZ, DUTCH Zimmerman, Heinie
SCHULTZ, JOE, JR. Schultz, Joe
SCOTLAND Chalmers, George
SCRANTON, PA Chalmers, George; Getz, Gus; Maisel, George; Pearce, George; Shawkey, Bob
SEATON, TOM Rumler, Bill
SEATTLE, WA Adams, Jack; Bohne, Sammy; Dell, Wheezer; Emmer, Frank; Fabrique, Bunny; Gregg, Vean; Hall, Charley; Huhn, Emil; Jacobs, Elmer; Johnson, Ernie; Mullen, Charlie; Schmidt, Walter; Schneider, Pete; Smith, Jack; Thomas, Claude
SHERMAN, TX Rodriguez, Joe; Tincup, Ben
SHORE, ERNIE Chalmers, George
SHREVEPORT, TX Byrne, Bobby; Harmon, Bob; Henry, John; Tesreau, Jeff
SIMPSON COLLEGE Ragan, Pat
SINTON, TX Rodgers, Bill
SIOUX CITY, IA Baird, Doug; Bancroft, Dave; Burns, George (Tioga); Zwilling, Dutch
SISLER, DAVE Sisler, George
SISLER, DICK Sisler, George
SLIPPERY ROCK STATE NORMAL SCHOOL Shawkey, Bob
SMITH, ELMER Bagby, Jim
SMITH, SHERRY Ruth, Babe
SNODGRASS, FRED Buckles, Jess
SOUTH BEND, IN Carey, Max; McCarthy, Alex
SOUTH CAROLINA Barbare, Walter; Griner, Dan; Huhn, Emil; Jackson, Joe; Schultz, Joe; Von Kolnitz, Fritz
SOUTH DAKOTA Scott, Jim
SOUTH DAKOTA STATE COLLEGE Gregg, Vean
SOUTHERLAND METHODIST COLLEGE Griner, Dan
SOUTHWESTERN UNIVERSITY (RHODES COLLEGE) Allen, Frank; Carter, Paul
SPEAKER, TRIS Henriksen, Olaf; Hooper, Harry; Leonard, Dutch; Lewis, Duffy; Walker, Tilly
SPOKANE, WA Gregg, Vean; Kelly, George; Williams, Ken
SPRINGFIELD, IL Blackburn, Earl; Doyle, Larry; Hamilton, Earl; Schultz, Joe; Wambsganss, Bill
SPRINGFIELD, MA Collins, Shano; Mitterling, Ralph; Rico, Art
SPRINGFIELD COLLEGE Mitterling, Ralph
STAFFORD, HEINIE Carroll, Doc; Whittaker, Walt
STANFORD UNIVERSITY Oeschger, Joe; Terry, Zeb
STANKEY, EDDIE Stock, Milt
STATE NORMAL SCHOOL AT MANKATO (MN) Schauer, Rube
STEELTON, PA Wagner, Bill
STENGEL, CASEY Schmidt, Walter
SULLIVAN, BILLY, JR. Sullivan, Billy
"SUNDAY MANAGER" Austin, Jimmy; Shotton, Burt
SUPERIOR, WI Schauer, Rube
SWARTHMORE COLLEGE Twining, Twink
SWEDEN Erickson, Eric; Lindstrom, Axel
SWEETWATER, TX Smith, Popboy
SYRACUSE, NY Alexander, Pete; Dubuc, Jean; Ehmke, Howie; Lapp, Jack; Madden, Gene; Schulte, Wildfire

TACOMA, WA Bigbee, Carson; Burns, Ed; Mullen, Charlie
TECUMSEH, MI Merkle, Fred
TEMPLE UNIVERSITY Young, Ralph
TENNESSEE Barber, Turner; Cook, Doc; Cunningham, George; Dalton, Jack; Deberry, Hank; Griner, Dan; Hickman, Jim; Johnston, Doc; Johnston, Jimmy; Love, Slim; McConnell, George; McKenry, Limb; McTigue, Pudge; Meyer, Billy; Milan, Clyde; Thrasher, Buck; Toney, Fred; Walker, Tilly
TERRE HAUTE, IN Nehf, Art

TEXAS Adams, Jack; Appleton Ed; Baker, Del; Baumgartner, Stan; Brainerd, Fred; Compton, Pete; Cook, Doc; Coombs, Jack; Cooper, Claude; Danforth, Dave; Dugey, Oscar; Gallia, Bert; Goodwin, Marv; Hasbrook, Ziggy; Hendryx, Tim; Hornsby, Rogers; Konetchy, Ed; Perry, Scott; Pratt, Del; Rodgers, Bill; Seaton, Tom; Severeid, Hank; Smith, Popboy; Snyder, Frank; Speaker, Tris; Stellbauer, Bill; Vaughn, Hippo; Warner, Hooks; Wilson, Owen
TEXAS CHRISTIAN UNIVERSITY Cooper, Claude
TEXAS WESLEYAN UNIVERSITY Speaker, Tris
TINKER, JOE Evers, Johnny
TOLEDO, OH Aragon, Angel; Barbare, Walter; Carpenter, Paul; Chapman, Ray; Dubuc, Jean; Fabrique, Bunny; Hartley, Grover; Hickman, Jim; Kelly, Joe; King, Lee; Knabe, Otto; Kopf, Larry; Moriarty, George; O'Neill, Steve; Palmero, Emilio; Pearce, George; Pechous, Charles; Sallee, Slim; Schulz, Al; Turner, Terry
TOPEKA, KS Brown, Don; Chapman, Harry; Engle, Clyde; Hagerman, Rip; Jones, Deacon; Lambeth, Otis; Schultz, Joe
TORONTO, ONTARIO Betzel, Bruno; Boehling, Joe; Carrigan, Bill; Costello, Dan; Dalton, Jack; Daly, Tom; Fitzpatrick, Ed; Gibson, George; Kocher, Brad; Maisel, George; O'Neill, Steve; Pick, Charlie; Rudolph, Dick; Tesreau, Jeff
TROY, NY Evers, Johnny
TUFTS UNIVERSITY Carroll, Doc; Stafford, Heinie; Whittaker, Walt
TULSA, OK Allen, Nick Boehler, George
TWOMBLY, BABE Twombly, George
TYLER, FRED Tyler, Lefty
TYLER, TX Stewart, Stuffy

UNION UNIVERSITY Barber, Turner

UNITED STATES MILITARY ACADEMY Lobert, Hans
UNITED STATES NAVAL ACADEMY Bender, Chief; Bentley, Jack
UNIVERSITY OF ALABAMA Pratt, Del
UNIVERSITY OF ARKANSAS Ellison, Bert
UNIVERSITY OF CALIFORNIA-LOS ANGELES (UCLA) Fournier, Jack
UNIVERSITY OF CHICAGO Baumgartner, Stan; DesJardien, Shorty
UNIVERSITY OF CINCINNATI Huggins, Miller
UNIVERSITY OF DELAWARE Baumgartner, Stan
UNIVERSITY OF ILLINOIS Beebe, Fred; Bradley, Jack; Brainard, Fred; Gunkel, Red; O'Connor, Bucky; Smykal, Frank
UNIVERSITY OF KENTUCKY Park, Jim
UNIVERSITY OF MAINE Driscoll, Mike; Lawry, Otis; McHale, Marty; Rowe, Harland
UNIVERSITY OF MARYLAND Anderson, Fred; Danforth, Dave; Herzog, Buck
UNIVERSITY OF MASSACHUSETTS King, Lee
UNIVERSITY OF MICHIGAN Altenburg, Jesse; Fisher, Ray; Killefer, Red; Lavan, Doc; Sisler, George
UNIVERSITY OF MISSISSIPPI Evans, Joe
UNIVERSITY OF OREGON Bigbee, Carson
UNIVERSITY OF PENNSYLVANIA Yerkes, Steve
UNIVERSITY OF PITTSBURGH Healy, Tom; Hoblitzell, Dick; Mitterling, Ralph
UNIVERSITY OF SOUTH CAROLINA Von Kolnitz, Fritz
UNIVERSITY OF TENNESSEE DeBerry, Hank
UNIVERSITY OF VERMONT Engle, Clyde; Gardner, Larry; Reulbach, Ed
UNIVERSITY OF VIRGINIA Dalton, Jack; Rixey, Eppa
UNIVERSITY OF WASHINGTON Mullen, Charlie
URSINUS COLLEGE Johnson, Jing; Mitterling, Ralph
UTICA, NY Burns, George; Coumbe, Fritz

VANCE, DAZZY Deberry, Hank

VANCOUVER, BRITISH COLUMBIA Costello, Dan
VANDERBILT UNIVERSITY Cook, Doc
VAUGHN, HIPPO Toney, Fred
VENICE, CA Borton, Babe; Smith, Popboy
VERMONT Fisher, Ray; Gardner, Larry; Stafford, Heinie
VERNON, CA Agnew, Sam; Borton, Babe; Corhan, Roy; James, Bill; Menosky, Mike; Schneider, Pete; Spencer, Tubby; Thomas, Claude; Wilhoit, Joe
VICTORIA, BRITISH COLUMBIA Kantlehner, Erving; McKenry, Limb
VILLANOVA COLLEGE Doolan, Mickey; Murphy, Eddie; Murphy, Mike
VIRGINIA Ayers, Doc; Boehling, Joe; Collins, Zip; Craft, Molly; Cullop, Nick; Fischer, Bill; Goodwin, Marv; Morrissette, Bill; Pick, Charlie; Robertson, Dave

WACO, TX Beck, Zinn; Dugey, Oscar; Spencer, Tubby; Walters, Roxy
WAGNER, BUTTS Wagner, Honus
WAKE FOREST COLLEGE Robertson, Dave
WALES Austin, Jimmy
WALKER, TILLY Young, Ralph
WALSH, ED, JR. Walsh, Ed
WAMBSGANSS, BILL Bagby, Jim; Mitchell, Clarence
WASHINGTON Burns, George; Davis, Harry; Donovan, Bill; Fournier, Jack; Gregg, Vean; Grover, Roy; Mullen, Charlie; Sawyer, Carl
WASHINGTON AND JEFFERSON COLLEGE Neale, Greasy
WASHINGTON AND LEE UNIVERSITY Bailey, Fred
WASHINGTON COLLEGE (MD) Walker, Tilly; Young, Ralph
WASHINGTON SENATORS Acosta, Merito; Agnew, Sam; Ainsmith, Eddie; Ayers, Doc; Barber, Turner; Bentley, Jack; Boehling, Joe; Brottem, Tony; Bush, Donie; Coveleski, Stan; Craft, Molly; Crane, Sam; Cravath, Gavvy; Dumont, George; Erickson, Eric; Evans, Joe; Foster, Eddie; Gallia, Bert; Gandil, Chick; Gedeon, Joe; Gharrity,

Pat; Goodwin, Marv; Gregg, Vean; Groom, Bob; Grover, Roy; Harper, Harry; Henry, John; Jamieson, Charlie; Janvrin, Hal; Johnson, Walter; Judge, Joe; Killefer, Red; Lavan, Doc; Lee, Billy; Leibold, Nemo; Leonard, Joe; Lewis, Duffy; Long, Tommy; Love, Slim; McBride, George; McNally, Mike; Menosky, Mike; Milan, Clyde; Moeller, Danny; Mogridge, George; Morgan, Ray; Palmero, Emilio; Peckinpaugh, Roger; Picinich, Val; Pick, Charlie; Rice, Sam; Rondeau, Henri; Russell, Allan; Sawyer, Carl; Schaefer, Germany; Schulte, Wildfire; Scott, Deacon; Severeid, Hank; Shanks, Howard; Shaw, Jim; Shotten, Burt; Smith, Earl; Smith, Elmer; Smith, Paul; Stewart, Stuffy; Thomas, Claude; Twombly, George; Vaughn, Hippo; Veach, Bobby; Walker, Tilly; Warmoth, Cy; Williams, Buff

WASHINGTON UNIVERSITY (MO) Carroll, Doc; Evans, Joe

WATERBURY, CT Donovan, Bill; Morton, Guy; Smith, Elmer; Wagner, Heinie

WATSON, JOHN Watson, Milt

WEAVER, BUCK Leibold, Nemo

WEAVER COLLEGE Fortune, Gary

WESLEYAN UNIVERSITY Lanning, Les

WEST VIRGINIA Bailey, Fred; Baumgardner, George; Cooper, Wilbur; Fisher, Wilbur; Gainer, Del; Hoblitzell, Dick; King, Lee; Louden, Baldy; Madden, Gene; Neale, Greasy

WEST VIRGINIA WESLEYAN COLLEGE Neale, Greasy

WESTERN DENTAL COLLEGE Stengel, Casey

WESTERN ILLINOIS STATE NORMAL COLLEGE Haley, Pat

WESTERN STATE NORMAL SCHOOL (WESTERN MICHIGAN) Koob, Ernie

WHEELING, WV Altenburg, Jesse; Hoblitzell, Dick; King, Lee; Neale, Greasy; Shotton, Burt

WHITE GIANTS, CHICAGO, IL Wright, Cy

WHITTAKER, WALT Carroll, Doc

WICHITA, KS Compton, Pete; Scott, Jim; Wilhoit, Joe

WICHITA FALLS, TX O'Brien, Ray

WILKES-BARRE, PA Cadore, Leon; Fischer, Bill; Maisel, George; McNally, Mike; Warner, Hooks; Zimmerman, Heinie

WILLIAMS, KEN Tobin, Jack

WILLIAMS, LEFTY James, Bill

WILLIAMS, TED Penner, Ken

WILLIAMSPORT, PA McNally, Mike; Ness, Jack; Sallee, Slim

WILSON, NC Anderson, Fred; Yerkes, Steve

WINCHESTER, KY Toney, Fred

WINGO, AL Wingo, Ivy

WINGO, IVY Rariden, Bill

WINNIPEG, MANITOBA Miller, Hack

WINSTON-SALEM, NC Ray, Carl

WISCONSIN Allison, Milo; Bancroft, Dave; Barney, Ed; Dyer, Ben; Felsch, Happy; Gharrity, Pat; Grimes, Burleigh; Konetchy, Ed; Luderus, Fred; McBride, George; Miller, Elmer; Mollwitz, Fritz; O'Mara, Ollie; Pechous, Charles; Roth, Bragg; Smyth, Red; Steele, Bob; Williams, Cy; Wyckoff, Weldon

WITTENBERG COLLEGE Bescher, Bob

WOOD, JOE Leonard, Dutch; Tesreau, Jeff

WORCESTER, MA Shay, Marty; Yerkes, Steve

WORCESTER POLYTECHNIC INSTITUTE Carroll, Doc

WORLD SERIES 1905 Ames, Red

WORLD SERIES 1906 Sullivan, Billy

WORLD SERIES 1907 Donovan, Bill

WORLD SERIES 1909 Adams, Babe; Bush, Donie; Byrne, Bobby; Gibson, George; Moriarty, George

WORLD SERIES 1910 Strunk, Amos

WORLD SERIES 1911 Barry, Jack; Crandall, Doc; Meyers, Chief

WORLD SERIES 1912 Hall, Charley; Henriksen, Olaf; Herzog, Buck; Hooper, Harry; Marquard, Rube; Tesreau, Jeff; Wagner, Heinie; Yerkes, Steve

WORLD SERIES 1913 Barry, Jack; Bush, Bullet Joe; Cooper, Claude; Demaree, Al; Lavan, Doc; Murphy, Mike; Plank, Eddie

WORLD SERIES 1914 Gowdy, Hank; Maranville, Rabbit; Murphy, Mike; Rudolph, Dick; Smith, Red; Wyckoff, Weldon

WORLD SERIES 1915 Burns, Ed; Byrne, Bobby; Cady, Hick; Chalmers, George; Foster, Rube; Leonard, Dutch; Mayer, Erskine; Paskert, Dode; Shore, Ernie; Stock, Milt

WORLD SERIES 1916 Cheney, Larry; Dede, Arte; Dell, Wheezer; Getz, Gus; Leonard, Dutch; Shore, Ernie; Shorten, Chick; Smith, Sherry; Rucker, Nap

WORLD SERIES 1917 Benton, Rube; Cicotte, Eddie; Faber, Red; Felsch, Happy; Hasbrook, Ziggy; Holke, Walter; Lynn, Byrd; Perritt, Pol; Rariden, Bill; Robertson, Dave; Schupp, Ferdie; Wilhoit, Joe

WORLD SERIES 1918 Agnew, Sam; Pick, Charlie

WORLD SERIES 1919 Benton, Rube; Cicotte, Eddie; Dubuc, Jean; Felsch, Happy; Fisher, Ray; Gedeon, Joe; Jackson, Joe; James, Bill; Kopf, Larry; Lowdermilk, Grover; Lynn, Byrd; Magee, Sherry; Maharg, Billy; McMullin, Fred; Williams, Lefty; Wingo, Ivy

WORLD SERIES 1920 Bagby, Jim; Caldwell, Ray; Coveleski, Stan; Griffith, Tommy; Johnston, Doc; Mails, Duster; Mamaux, Al; Mitchell, Clarence; Morton, Guy; O'Neill, Steve; Smith, Elmer; Smith, Sherry

WORLD SERIES 1921 Barnes, Jesse; Burns, George; Nehf, Art; Snyder, Frank

WORLD SERIES 1922 Groh, Heinie; King, Lee; Scott, Jack

WORLD SERIES 1923 Bentley, Jack

WORLD SERIES 1924 Bentley, Jack; Leibold, Nemo; Mogridge, George; Peckinpaugh, Roger

WORLD SERIES 1925 Adams, Babe; Bigbee, Carson; Carey, Max; Leibold, Nemo; Meadows, Lee; Rice, Sam

WORLD SERIES 1926 Alexander, Pete; Hornsby, Rogers; O'Farrell, Bob; Severeid, Hank; Shocker, Urban
WORLD SERIES 1927 Meadows, Lee
WORLD SERIES 1928 Maranville, Rabbit
WORLD SERIES 1929 Ehmke, Howie; Gonzales, Mike; Grimm, Charlie
WORLD SERIES 1931 Grimes, Burleigh
WORLD SERIES 1932 Grimm, Charlie
WORLD WAR I (ESSENTIAL WORK) Baird, Doug; Coleman, Bob; Gharrity, Pat; Rondeau, Henri; Saier, Vic
WORLD WAR I (MILITARY SERVICE) Alexander, Pete; Allen, Nick; Altenburg, Jesse; Anderson, Fred; Appleton Ed; Bailey, Fred; Baker, Del; Barbare, Walter; Barnes, Jesse; Barney, Ed; Barry, Jack; Batsch, Bill; Baumgardner, George; Bentley, Jack; Bergman, Al; Boehling, Joe; Borton, Babe; Brainerd, Fred; Bressler, Rube; Cadore, Leon; Cantwell, Mike; Carpenter, Paul; Chappell, Larry; Clemens, Count; Clemons, Verne; Cobb, Ty; Cooper, Claude; Crowell, Cap; Cullop, Nick; Currie, Murphy; Deberry, Hank; Des Jardien, Shorty; Donovan, Bill; Driscoll, Mike; Elliott, Rowdy; Ellison, Bert; Erickson, Eric; Evans, Bill; Evans, Joe; Faber, Red; Fabrique, Bunny; Fincher, Bill; Fisher, Ray; Fuller, Frank; Gainer, Del; Gleason, Bill; Goodwin, Marv; Gowdy, Hank; Guisto, Lou; Gunkel, Red; Haley, Pat; Halliday, Newt; Healy, Tom; Hesselbacher, George; Hill, Carmen; Hobbs, Bill; Hoblitzell, Dick; Janvrin, Hal; Johnson, Bill; Johnson, Jing; Jourdan, Ted; Kelleher, Duke; Kelleher, John; Kelly, George; Kennedy, Ray; King, Lee; Klepfer, Ed; Koob, Ernie; Lambeth, Otis; Lavan, Doc; Lawry, Otis; Leonard, Joe; Lewis, Duffy; Lindstrom, Axel; Maisel, George; Malone, Lew; Mamaux, Al; Maranville, Rabbit; Markle, Cliff; Mathewson, Christy; McElwee, Lee; McHale, Marty; Menosky, Mike; Mitchell, Clarence; Mitchell, Willie; Mitterling, Ralph; Moseley, Earl; Mullen, Charlie; Myers, Elmer; Nabors, Jack; Pennock, Herb; Rice, Sam; Richardson, Jack; Rico, Art; Ritter, Hank; Rixey, Eppa; Rowe, Harland; Scott, Jim; Seibold, Socks; Shawkey, Bob; Shay, Marty; Sheehan, Tom; Shore, Ernie; Shorten, Chick; Sicking, Eddie; Siglin, Paddy; Smith, Jack; Smith, Paul; Smykal, Frank; Smyth, Red; Terry, Zeb; Thomas, Claude; Tragesser, Walt; Twining, Twink; Twombly, George; Von Kolnitz, Fritz; Walsh, Jimmy; Warner, Hooks; Weaver, Harry; Welf, Ollie; Williams, Marsh; Witt, Whitey; Wright, Cy
WORLD WAR II (ESSENTIAL WORK) Adams, Babe; Collins, Zip; Harper, George; Holke, Walter; Jacobson, Merwyn; Konetchy, Ed; Love, Slim; Mann, Les; Murphy, Eddie; Picinich, Val; Smith, Earl; Thomas, Claude; Whitted, Possum
WORLD WAR II (MILITARY SERVICE) Altenburg, Jesse; Cantwell, Mike; Gowdy, Hank; Johnson, Jing; Lavan, Doc; O'Connor, Bucky; Von Kolnitz, Fritz
WRIGLEY, PHIL Nehf, Art

YALE UNIVERSITY Engle, Clyde; Yerkes, Steve
YAZOO CITY, MS Hendryx, Tim
YORK, PA Shaw, Jim
YOUNGSTOWN, OH Moseley, Earl; Shanks, Howard

ZIMMERMAN, HEINIE Dubuc, Jean

www.ingramcontent.com/pod-product-compliance
Lightning Source LLC
Chambersburg PA
CBHW081557300426
44116CB00015B/2911